Elroy McKendree Avery

Elements of Chemistry

A Text Book for Schools

Elroy McKendree Avery

Elements of Chemistry
A Text Book for Schools

ISBN/EAN: 9783337275778

Printed in Europe, USA, Canada, Australia, Japan

Cover: Foto ©Paul-Georg Meister /pixelio.de

More available books at **www.hansebooks.com**

OF

CHEMISTRY.

A TEXT-BOOK FOR SCHOOLS.

BY

ELROY M. AVERY, Ph.D.,
AUTHOR OF ELEMENTS OF NATURAL PHILOSOPHY, ETC.

ILLUSTRATED BY NEARLY 200 WOOD ENGRAVINGS.

NEW YORK
SHELDON & COMPANY,
No. 8 MURRAY STREET.
1881.

Dr. Avery's Physical Science Series.

THE ELEMENTS OF NATURAL PHILOSOPHY.

2d.

TEACHER'S HAND BOOK.

To accompany Avery's Natural Philosophy; containing Solutions to Problems, Additional Experiments, Practical Suggestions, etc.

3d.

THE ELEMENTS OF CHEMISTRY.

4th.

THE HIGH SCHOOL CHEMISTRY.

Containing the Elements of Chemistry, with additional chapters on *Hydrocarbons in Series*, or Organic Chemistry. It can be used in the same class with the Elements. (*In preparation.*)

5th.

TEACHER'S HAND BOOK.

To accompany Avery's Chemistries.

Copyright, 1881, by Sheldon & Co.

Electrotyped by Smith & McDougal, 82 Beekman Street, New York.

TO TEACHERS.

HAVE a room set apart, if possible, expressly for chemical operations. It is generally convenient to have this laboratory on the ground floor, for convenience in supplying water and draining off the waste. This room *must be well ventilated.* Secure a ventilating chamber (App. 22) for the laboratory, and a ventilating hood connected with the chimney flue or ventilating shaft for each pupil, if you can. If you can not do this, keep an open fire burning, so that offensive gases and vapors may be removed from the room as well as possible in that manner. Around the walls of the room, provide working benches or tables, about 75 *cm.* (2½ feet) wide. Each pupil should be allotted about a meter of working space at these tables, and *held responsible for its condition.* If the building is provided with gas and water, run pipes around the walls, and provide each pupil with a gas cock and a water cock, to which he may attach flexible tubing. Over the benches place narrow shelves, to hold the chemical reagents; beneath the benches place shelves or drawers, for holding pieces of apparatus, etc. If the building is not connected with a regular water supply, see that plenty of water is always at hand in a tank, barrel, or in pails. A small cook stove will be a great convenience.

If a room can not be set aside as a laboratory, flat tables may be laid upon the desks, and the reagents, apparatus, etc., kept in a cabinet or cupboard.

Of course, a regularly fitted laboratory, with further and better means than those above suggested, is desirable, and *should be provided*, when means can be secured for the purpose. See Frick's *Physical Technics*, Chap. I.

The chief significance of the foregoing is that, as far as possible, the experiments are to be performed by the pupil rather than for him. Make careful examination of the pupil's notes, seeking to lead him to accurate observation, intelligent discrimination between essential and merely incidental conditions and results of an experiment, as well as to precision and conciseness of statement.

Have your pupils habitually pronounce the full name of substances symbolized in this book. For example, "H_2O is composed of H and O," should be read: "Water is composed of hydrogen and oxygen."

The author would be glad to receive suggestions from teachers using this book, or to answer any inquiries they may make.

To the Pupil.

HAVE a place for everything, and keep everything in its place, when you are not using it. Clean every utensil or piece of apparatus when you have used it; never put away anything dirty. Cleanliness is a necessity in the chemical laboratory. Acquire the habit of labeling every chemical that you put away or leave for a time, writing the name or the chemical symbol in easily legible characters.

Before beginning an experiment, look over all of your preparations, be sure that everything is ready and within easy reach, or you may suddenly discover a need for another hand. Be sure that all corks and connections are well fitted. Place your materials and apparatus at your left hand and lay them down at your right, when you have used them, keeping the middle of your bench clear for operating.

Do not waste even inexpensive material. Be sure that you know *why* you do a thing before you do it. Always use the simplest form of apparatus. Do not think that you must have everything just as described by the author. If a Florence flask is called for by the text-book, and you have not one, you may be able to get along with a bottle. A hammer is not wholly necessary for the driving of a nail, although it may be desirable.

Make careful notes on all experiments *as they proceed.* "The scrap of paper well stained with acid is of much greater value than the half worked out, though clean, notes written down after the experiment has passed away." These rough notes should subsequently be neatly copied into a book, the mere copying of the observations being of great help in remembering them.

Ever keep in mind the fact that an experiment is *intended to teach something*, and that it can not serve its purpose unless it is accompanied by careful observation of the effects produced, and equally careful study of the relations borne by these effects to the conditions of the experiment.

Take an early opportunity for a careful reading of the Appendix to this book, so that you may be able to refer to it subsequently, when you need help that it may give.

In the following pages, the specific gravity of all gases is referred to hydrogen as the standard. All temperatures are recorded in Centigrade degrees.

	PAGE
TO THE TEACHER......................................	iii
TO THE PUPIL........................,....................	v

CHAPTER I.
THE DOMAIN OF CHEMISTRY.......... 1

CHAPTER II.
WATER AND ITS CONSTITUENTS.

SECTION I.—ANALYSIS OF WATER.......................	10
" II.—HYDROGEN......................................	14
" III.—OXYGEN	27
" IV.—COMPOUNDS OF HYDROGEN AND OXYGEN. ...	38

CHAPTER III.
AIR AND ITS CONSTITUENTS.

SECTION I.—AIR	45
" II.—NITROGEN..................................	50

CHAPTER IV.
SYMBOLS, NOMENCLATURE, MOLECULAR AND ATOMIC WEIGHTS...................... 53

CHAPTER V.

COMPOUNDS OF HYDROGEN, OXYGEN AND NITROGEN.

	PAGE
Section I.—Ammonia	59
" II.—Nitric Acid	65
" III.—Nitrogen Oxides	68

CHAPTER VI.

QUANTIVALENCE, RATIONAL SYMBOLS, RADICALS.... 74

CHAPTER VII.

THE HALOGEN GROUP.

Section I.—Chlorine	79
" II.—Hydrochloric Acid	87
" III.—Other Chlorine Compounds	93
" IV.—Bromine, Iodine, Fluorine	97

CHAPTER VIII.

STOICHIOMETRY........ 104

CHAPTER IX.

THE SULPHUR GROUP.

Section I.—Sulphur	110
" II.—Hydrogen Sulphide	117
" III.—Sulphur Oxides and Acids	124
" IV.—Selenium and Tellurium	137

CHAPTER X.

ACIDS, BASES, SALTS, Etc............ 140

CHAPTER XI.

BORON................. 147

CHAPTER XII.
VOLUMETRIC CONSIDERATIONS............ 151

CHAPTER XIII.
THE CARBON GROUP.

SECTION I.—CARBON...................................... 155
" II.—SOME CARBON COMPOUNDS................... 166
" III.—SOME HYDROCARBONS 177
" IV.—ILLUMINATING GAS........................ 188
" V.—SOME ORGANIC COMPOUNDS 194
" VI.—SILICON 201

CHAPTER XIV.
THE NITROGEN GROUP.

SECTION I.—PHOSPHORUS................................ 205
" II.—PHOSPHORUS COMPOUNDS.................. 211
" III.—ARSENIC AND ITS COMPOUNDS............... 217
" IV.—ANTIMONY, BISMUTH, ETC.................... 222

CHAPTER XV.
METALS OF THE ALKALIES.

SECTION 1.—SODIUM.................................... 229
" II.—POTASSIUM, ETC............................ 237

CHAPTER XVI.
METALS OF THE ALKALINE EARTHS.......... 246

CHAPTER XVII.
METALS OF THE MAGNESIUM GROUP......... 252

CHAPTER XVIII.
METALS OF THE LEAD GROUP............ 258

CHAPTER XIX.

METALS OF THE COPPER GROUP.

	PAGE
Section I.—Copper	263
" II.—Silver	267
" III.—Mercury	271

CHAPTER XX.

METALS OF THE ALUMINUM AND CERIUM GROUPS.. 275

CHAPTER XXI.

METALS OF THE IRON GROUP.

Section I.—Iron	279
" II.—Steel	290
" III.—Manganese, Cobalt and Nickel	295

CHAPTER XXII.

METALS OF THE CHROMIUM GROUP........ 299

CHAPTER XXIII.

METALS OF THE TIN GROUP............. 302

CHAPTER XXIV.

METALS OF THE GOLD GROUP............ 306

APPENDIX.. 315
INDEX... 343

CHAPTER I.

THE DOMAIN OF CHEMISTRY.

1. What is Matter?—*Matter is anything that occupies space or "takes up room."*

Everything discernible by any of our senses is matter. Everything that has weight is matter; all matter has weight.

2. Divisions of Matter.—*Matter may be considered as existing in masses, molecules, and atoms.*

Note.— The word molecule is from the diminutive of *moles*, a Latin word meaning a *mass*. Etymologically, molecule means a little mass. The word atom is from the Greek, and signifies, etymologically, a thing that can not be cut or divided.

3. What is a Mass?—*A mass is any quantity of matter that contains more than a single molecule.*

Any quantity of matter that can be appreciated by the senses, even with the aid of modern apparatus, is a mass, while many masses are too minute to be thus appreciable.

4. What is a Molecule?—*A molecule is the smallest particle of matter that can exist by itself, separate from other particles of matter;* or it is the smallest quantity of matter into which a mass can be divided by any process that does not destroy its identity or change its chemical nature. Molecules are exceedingly small, far beyond the reach of vision even when aided by a powerful microscope.

(*a.*) According to one of the best authorities, a cubic centimeter (Appendix 2) of gas, at the ordinary atmospheric pressure, contains about 1,000,000,000,000,000,000,000,000 ($=10^{24}$) molecules.

(*b.*) Natural Philosophy teaches us that heat is one kind of energy resulting from motion (Ph. § 473). But this motion of a hot body, constituting the heat of the body, is wholly invisible. The motion pertains to "parts of the body too minute to be seen separately and within limits so narrow that we cannot detect the absence of any part from its original place. We are to have the conception of a body consisting of a great many small parts, each of which is in motion. We shall call any one of these parts a molecule of the substance. A molecule may, therefore, be defined as a small mass of matter, the parts of which do not part company during the excursions which the molecule makes when the body to which it belongs is hot."

(*c.*) The molecules of any given substance are held to be exactly alike, but different from the molecules of any other substance. For example, one copper molecule is exactly like every other copper molecule, but different from every molecule of any substance that is not copper. The nature of the substance, therefore, depends upon the nature of its molecule.

5. What is an Atom ?—*An atom is the smallest particle of matter that can exist even in combination.*

(*a.*) Nearly every molecule is composed of two or more atoms. As we shall see, some molecules are very complex. The common sugar molecule contains forty-five atoms.

(*b.*) An atom may also be defined as the smallest quantity of an element that exists in any molecule.

6. Elementary and Compound Substances.—All substances are classified as being either elementary or compound. *Any substance that can not be separated, by any known means, into two or more essentially different kinds of matter, is called an* element. *Any substance that can be thus separated is called a compound.* Compounds consist of two or more elements in chemical combination. The atoms of any given element are of the same kind; those of a compound are of two or more kinds. There are as many kinds of atoms as there are elements. Sixty-six elements have been already recognized (see Appendix 1). Some of these are very abundant and widely distributed; others have been found only in such minute quantities that even their properties have not yet been satisfactorily determined. Other elements will doubtless be discovered and it is possible that some substances now considered elementary will be found to be compound. In fact, nearly every improvement in our methods of examination (see Ph., § 638, *b*) leads to the detection of elements previously unknown. Silver and gold are elements; wood and water are compounds.

7. Organic and Inorganic Substances. — *Substances that have been formed by animal or vegetable life are called organic substances; those that have not been thus formed are called inorganic.* Flesh and bone, oak and cotton are organic substances; metals, air, water, etc., are inorganic.

(*a*.) This distinction is less important than formerly. Of late years, chemists have succeeded in producing several "organic" substances from "inorganic" materials. The old barrier between organic and inorganic chemistry is being broken down, and many chemists now look forward, not hopelessly, to a future when even food may be made in the chemical laboratory as well as in the fields and pastures.

8. Forms of Attraction.—Each of the three divisions of matter has its peculiar form of attraction. The attractions of masses and molecules pertain more particularly to natural philosophy; the attraction existing between atoms pertains chiefly to chemistry. *Atomic attraction is called chemism or chemical affinity.*

Experiment 1.—Pulverize separately a teaspoonful each of loaf-sugar and potassium chlorate (chlorate of potash) and mix them together upon a porcelain plate. Dip a glass rod (Appendix 4, *a*) into strong sulphuric acid and hold the rod in a horizontal position over the mixture and close to it but so as not to touch it. Notice that there is no peculiar action visible. Now hold the rod in a vertical position, so that a drop of acid will fall upon the mixture. The mixture is immediately ignited.

Experiment 2.—Into a mortar, put a bit of potassium chlorate the size of a grain of wheat, and cover it with powdered sulphur. Notice that there is no peculiar action visible. Now rub them together vigorously with the pestle. A sharp explosion or a succession of minute explosions will take place.

☞ See the *Caution* following Experiment 36.

Experiment 3.—Cover a bit of phosphorus, the size of a pin head, with pulverized potassium chlorate and wrap the materials in a bit of soft paper, so as to form a minute torpedo. The phosphorus and the particles of potassium chlorate lie close together, but no action takes place. Now place the torpedo on a small anvil or other smooth, hard surface and *force the phosphorus and potassium chlorate closer together* by a blow with a hammer. A violent explosion takes place.

9. Peculiarities of Chemical Affinity.—The foregoing experiments illustrate the fact that *atomic attraction is effective at insensible distances only*. In only a few cases is it possible by mechanical means to bring solid particles sufficiently near each other for the desired chemical action. The necessary freedom of molecular motion (Ph., §§ 54, 55, 57), is generally secured by solution, fusion or vaporization of one or more of the materials used. Hence solvents and heat are important agents in the chemical laboratory. Another peculiarity is that *atomic attraction is most energetic between dissimilar substances.*

(*a.*) A body is dissolved or "in solution" when it is so finely divided and its particles are so completely dispersed through the water or other solvent that they can neither be seen nor separated from the liquid by filtering.

10. Physical and Chemical Changes.

A physical change is one that does not change the composition of the molecule, and, therefore, does not change the nature of the substance acted upon. A chemical change is one that does change the composition of the molecule and, therefore, does change the nature of the substance.

(*a.*) A piece of marble may be ground to powder, but each grain is marble still. Ice may change to water and water to steam, yet the nature of the substance is unchanged. Such as these are physical changes. But if the piece of marble be acted upon by sulphuric acid, a brisk effervescence takes place, caused by the escape of carbon dioxide, which was a constituent of the marble; calcium sulphate (gypsum), not marble, will remain. (Experiment 185.) The water may, by the action of electricity, be decomposed into hydrogen and oxygen. (Experiment 12.) Such as these are chemical changes.

Experiment 4.—Rub together in a mortar 4 *g.* of sodium sulphate crystals and 2 *g.* of potassium carbonate. The two solids form a liquid. Repeat the experiment with ice and salt.

Experiment 5.—Saturate 4 *cu. cm.* of water with calcium chloride (§ 291). Add slowly 0.5 *cu. cm.* of sulphuric acid. The two transparent liquids form a white, opaque solid. [Ph., § 524 (4).]

Experiment 6.—Moisten the inner surface of a beaker glass, or clear tumbler, with strong ammonia water, and place a few drops of the liquid in the glass. Cover it with a glass plate (or piece of writing paper). Moisten the inner surface of a similar clear glass vessel with hydrochloric (muriatic) acid. Invert the second vessel over the first, mouth to mouth, so that the contents of the two

FIG. 1.

vessels shall be separated only by the glass plate. Each vessel is filled with an invisible gas. Now remove the glass plate. The invisible gases diffuse into each other and form a dense cloud that slowly settles in the form of a white powder.

Experiment 7.—Dissolve five or six lumps of loaf-sugar in a beaker glass or a tea-cup with as little warm water as possible. Place the beaker glass upon a large plate and into the syrup slowly pour strong sulphuric acid, stirring the contents of the beaker glass at the same time. A black, porous solid will fill the glass, and probably overflow upon the plate.

Experiment 8.—In a conical test-glass, or a test-tube, dissolve a few crystals (0.5 g.) of silver nitrate in 10 cu. cm. of water. In a second test-glass, place a similar solution of lead nitrate; in a third, a solution of mercuric chloride (corrosive sublimate); in a fourth, 10 cu. cm. of chlorine water (Exp. 86), to which a few drops of a freshly prepared dilute solution of starch have been added. Each solution will be as clear as water. To each, add a few drops of the colorless solution of potassium iodide, and notice the colors produced, yellow, orange, scarlet and blue.

Experiment 9.—Into a glass tube 2 cm. in diameter, and 15 or 20 cm. in length, having one end closed and rounded like a test-tube, place 20 mg. of freshly burnt charcoal. Draw the upper part of the tube out to a narrow neck. Fill the tube with dry oxygen and seal the tube by fusing the neck. Weigh the tube and its contents very care-

FIG. 2.

fully. By gradually heating the rounded end of the tube, the charcoal may be ignited and, with sufficient care, entirely burned without breaking the tube. When the charcoal has disappeared, weigh the tube and its contents again. The chemical changes that led to the disappearance of the charcoal have caused no change in the weight of the materials used. See App. 4, *c* and *d*.

Experiment 10.—Put a few small pieces of zinc into a test-tube and pour some strong nitric acid upon them. Reddish fumes appear, and the tube becomes warm.

11. Characteristics of Chemical Action.—From the preceding pages we learn that atomic attraction is a very powerful agent in its own field, but that it acts only upon the minutest divisions of matter (atoms) and at distances too small to be perceptible. The resulting action leads to a general change of properties, physical and chemical, always excepting weight. This exception is the direct result of the indestructibility of matter (Ph., § 37). Every atom of matter has a certain definite weight, and as, in these changes, the atoms are merely rearranged but none destroyed or created, the sum total of the weights of these atoms must remain unchanged. Whenever these atoms rush together (synthesis, § 18) they develop heat, which is thus a frequent result of chemical action (Ph., § 568). As will be seen from the next paragraph, chemical action takes place between definite quantities of matter only.

Experiment 11.—Fine iron filings and powdered sulphur may be mixed in any proportion. From such a mixture the iron may be removed by a magnet; the sulphur may be removed by solution in carbon disulphide (§ 201), filtration and subsequent evaporation of the filtrate. The iron is still iron, the sulphur is still sulphur. In the mixture the *free* iron or sulphur particles may be detected with a microscope. Now mix thoroughly 4 *g*. of the powdered sulphur with 7 *g*. of the iron filings, and place the mixture in an ignition tube (Appendix 4, *a*) about 12 *cm*. long. By wooden nippers, hold the tube over the gas or alcohol lamp (Appendix 15), as shown in the figure. The sulphur melts and combines with the iron to form ferrous sulphide (sulphide or sulphuret of iron). There is no longer anything to be attracted by a magnet, or to be dissolved by carbon disulphide. The microscope reveals no particle of either constituent of the mixture. The ferrous sulphide, which contains the iron and the sulphur, differs from both in appearance and properties. It always consists of 7 parts of iron to 4 parts of sulphur by weight (or 56 : 32), however or wherever obtained. Instead of using the ignition-tube represented in Fig. 3, the mixed iron and sulphur may be placed in a small Hessian crucible (Appendix 21), covered with a similar inverted crucible and heated in a coal fire.

FIG. 3.

12. Mixtures and Compounds. — Mixtures of two or more substances may be formed by mingling them in all conceivable proportions, but a compound formed by chemical action consists of certain invariable proportions of its constituents. Thus, oxygen and hydrogen may be mixed in any desired proportion, but they will unite to form water only in the ratio of eight parts to one by weight, or one part to two by volume. When iron rusts, the oxygen of the air combines with the metal at the rate of 3 grams or ounces of oxygen to 7 grams or ounces of iron. No chemist can make 3 grams of oxygen unite with 6 grams of iron. *In a mixture, the constituents are said to be free; in a compound, they are said to be combined or in combination.*

(*a.*) Gunpowder is composed of charcoal, sulphur and potassium nitrate (nitre or saltpeter) *mechanically mixed*. The potassium nitrate may be washed out by water and, by evaporating the water, may be secured in the solid form. The sulphur may then be removed from the mixture, as in Experiment 11. The charcoal will be left alone. The constituents of gunpowder could not be thus separated if they were in chemical union. When gunpowder is ignited, the constituents *combine* to form enormous volumes of gaseous products.

13. Chemistry Defined. — *Chemistry is the branch of science that examines the elements and their compounds experimentally, and investigates the laws that regulate their combination.*

(*a.*) The experimental examination above mentioned has to do with the properties and composition of substances and the known or possible chemical changes they may undergo.

(*b.*) Such changes as we have seen in the foregoing experiments can not be foretold ; they can be ascertained only by experiment ; *i. e.*, by placing the substances in question under circumstances that the chemist can control and vary. Hence, chemistry is called an *experimental science.*

CHAPTER II.

WATER AND ITS CONSTITUENTS.

SECTION I.

ANALYSIS OF WATER.

14. The First Question.—One of the most familiar substances in nature is water. Its appearance, uses, occurrence, and many of its valuable properties are matters of common observation and every day application. We know that it furnishes the units of weight (Ph., § 36), of specific gravity (Ph., § 242), and of specific heat (Ph., § 532). We know that it may assume the solid, liquid and gaseous forms in succession. While these and many others are well-known facts, the healthy mind still asks, "Of what is it made?" This very question, *"Of what is it made?"* which thus confronts the young chemist at the threshold of the science, will force itself upon his attention at every step of his progress. It, therefore, deserves careful consideration. Working together, we shall find an answer.

Experiment 12.—The apparatus represented in Fig. 4 consists of a vessel containing water (to which a little acid has been added to increase its conductivity) in which are immersed two platinum strips which constitute the two electrodes of a galvanic battery. Glass tubes containing acidulated water are inverted over the platinum electrodes. A battery of three or four Grove cells will answer very well for our present purpose (Ph., § 384). When the

FIG. 4.

circuit is closed and the current passed through the water between the electrodes, bubbles will be noticed rising in the glass tubes and gradually displacing the water therefrom. Gas will accumulate about twice as rapidly in the tube covering the negative electrode (Ph., § 377) as in the other.

15. Another Question.—By the time the water has been displaced from one of the tubes, we shall, perhaps, be wondering what is in the tube. This question, "*What is it?*" is also continually recurring to the chemist. Lift the tube carefully, holding it mouth downward, and gently cover its mouth with the thumb. It *looks* like air; *is* it air? To obtain our answer, we must, as usual, try an experiment.

Experiment 13.—Light a taper or dry splinter of wood, and thrust it into the tube, as shown in Fig. 5. The taper flame will be extinguished and the gas will burn at the mouth of the tube. Notice the appearance of the flame. The taper may be withdrawn and relighted at the mouth of the tube and the experiment repeated. *Was it air in the tube?*

FIG. 5.

We have now interrogated Nature, conversing with her in her own language. The question being properly put, she answered that it was not air. The answer was intelligible and satisfactory. As a matter of present convenience, *we shall call this gas hydrogen.*

16. What is in the other Tube?—By this time the other tube is probably full of gas, generated at the positive electrode. If so, break the circuit (Ph., § 376) and remove the tube, closing its mouth as before. Is *it* air? Is it hydrogen?

Experiment 14.—To put these questions in proper form, light the taper and let it burn until a spark will remain upon the wick when the flame is blown out. Thrust the glowing taper (or a glowing splinter) into the tube. The taper is rekindled and burns with *unusual* vigor and brilliancy.

The answer is as prompt and unmistakable as before. It was not air; it was not hydrogen. For purposes of present convenience, *we shall call this gas oxygen.*

17. The Synthesis of Water.—So far, we have seen that water is composed of oxygen and hydrogen, there being twice as great a volume of the latter as of the former. We have also learned that these gases look like common air, but that, in their action upon burning substances, they are very different from air and from each other. If we wish to know whether water has any other constituent, or suspect that these gases came from the small quantity of acid used to increase the water's conductivity for the electric current, it would be natural to try to unite these gases and see what the product is. For such an experiment we are not quite ready. By the analysis of *something* we have secured separated oxygen and hydrogen; for their synthesis, it is desirable that we know more about them (Exps. 28 and 53).

18. Analysis, Synthesis, and Metathesis.— By chemical analysis, we mean the breaking up of a compound into its constituent parts (Exp. 12); by chemical synthesis, we mean the union of two or more substances to form one, different from any of its constituents (Exp. 27). Synthesis is chiefly used to prove the results of analysis. Metathesis consists in the interchange of dissimilar atoms or groups of atoms between two sets of molecules, and implies that the structure of these molecules is not otherwise altered (§ 74 *a*). It may almost be regarded as a concurrence of analysis and synthesis.

Section II.

HYDROGEN.

☞ *Symbol*, H; *specific gravity, 1; atomic weight, 1 m. c.* (§ 62); *molecular weight, 2 m. c.; quantivalence, 1* (§ 92).

19. Occurrence.—It was long thought that hydrogen did not occur free in nature, but it has been found uncombined in meteors, volcanic gases, and the solar and stellar atmospheres. In combination, it is almost everywhere, being found in water, in petroleum, and in all animal and vegetable substances.

Note.—The word hydrogen is derived from the Greek *hudor* (= water) and *gennao* (= I produce).

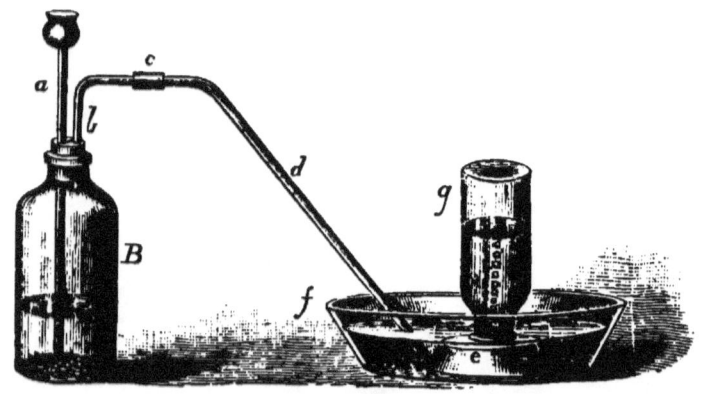

Fig. 6.

20. The Apparatus.—Provide a good bottle, about 20 *cm.* (8 in.) high, and having a mouth about 2.5 *cm.* (1 in.) in diameter. See that the edges of the bottle are smooth, so that they will not cut the cork. Get a caoutchouc stopper or fine grained cork (App. 9) that will fit the mouth of the bottle snugly, and furnish it with a funnel tube, *a*, and a delivery tube, *b*, (App. 4, *b*) as shown in Fig. 6. The funnel tube should be of such a length that, when the cork is in its place, the tube will reach within 1 *cm*. (⅜ in.) of the bottom of the bottle. To the delivery tube, *b*, connect a piece of glass tubing, *d*, bent near each end. The connection may be made by a short piece of snugly fitting rubber tubing, *c*. If desirable, *c* and *d* may be replaced by a piece of rubber tubing of suitable length. The lower end of *d* terminates beneath the inverted saucer or tin plate, *e*, placed in the pan, *f*. The saucer has a notch in its edge for the admission of *d*, and a hole in the middle of its bottom; this hole should be a little larger than the delivery tube. Into the pan, pour enough water to cover the saucer. Fill a bottle, *g*, with water and invert it over the hole in the bottom of *e*. Atmospheric pressure will keep the water in *g*. (Ph., § 275.)

21. The Preparation.—Granulate some zinc by melting about 250 *g*. (½ lb.) in a Hessian crucible or iron ladle, and slowly pouring it, while very hot, into a pail or tub of water, from as great a height as you can conveniently reach. Put about 25 *g*. (1 oz.) of this granulated zinc (clippings of ordinary sheet zinc will answer, but not so well) into the gas bottle, *B*, pour in water until the bottle is about a quarter full and replace the cork. *Be sure that all of the joints about the mouth of the bottle are tight.* To test this, place the delivery tube between the lips and force air into the bottle until water rises in the funnel tube and nearly fills the funnel. Place the end of the tongue against the end of the delivery tube to prevent the escape of air from the bottle. If the water retains its elevation in *a*, the joints are tight. If the water falls in *a* to the level of that in *B*, the apparatus leaks and *must be put into satisfactory condition before going on*. Pour sulphuric or hydrochloric acid through the funnel tube, *a*, in small quantities, not more than a thimble full at a time. Gas will be generated with lively effervescence in *B* and bubble up in *g*, displacing the water therefrom. This method of collecting a gas, by the displacement of water, is called "collecting over water." It will be thus briefly indicated hereafter.

22. The Collection.—The gas first delivered will be mixed with the air that was in the apparatus at the beginning of the experiment. This should be thrown away, as *it is dangerously explosive*. When a quantity of gas about equal to the contents of the gas bottle has thus been allowed to escape, fill a test tube or small *wide-mouthed* bottle with the gas, remove it from the water pan, being careful to hold it mouth downward, and bring a lighted match, or other flame, to the mouth. If the gas burns with a puff, or slight explosion, it is not yet free from air. In this way continue to test the gas, as it is delivered, until it burns quietly at the mouth of the tube and within it. Keep the end of the delivery tube, *d*, under water until you are sure that the hydrogen is unmixed with air. Do not, at any time, bring a flame into contact with any considerable quantity of hydrogen until you have established its non-explosive character by testing a small quantity as just described. For such tests, bottles are not so good as test tubes or cylinders (App. 7), as they confine the gas more and thus increase the danger in case of an explosion. Add acid through the funnel tube from time to time, as may be necessary to keep up a brisk effervescence in the gas bottle. Fill several bottles with the unmixed gas, slipping the mouth of each, as it is filled, into a saucer containing enough water to seal the mouth of the bottle and prevent the escape of the hydrogen. If you have used the pneumatic trough (App. 12) instead of the water pan, the bottles may be left upon the shelf of the trough, which should be a little below the surface of the water. At your earliest convenience, fill one of the gas holders (App. 13) with hydrogen.

Note.—There are several other ways of preparing hydrogen. Some of them will be considered subsequently.

23. The Reaction.—The hydrogen just prepared resulted from the action of the zinc upon the acid, water being used to dissolve the solid compound thus formed. Resulting from this action we have the hydrogen gas and a chemical compound called zinc chloride if hydrochloric acid was used, or zinc sulphate if sulphuric acid was used. This compound remains dissolved in the water of the gas bottle. The zinc chloride or sulphate may be obtained separate by filtering and evaporating the solution. We may represent hydrogen by the symbol H, and zinc by the symbol Zn. Hydrochloric acid is composed of hydrogen and chlorine (an element which we shall soon study § 104) and may be represented by HCl. The zinc chloride is composed of zinc and chlorine and may be represented by $ZnCl_2$. In fact, chemists of all nations represent these substances by these convenient abbreviations and other substances by similar symbols, as will be explained soon (§ 56). The chemical changes that took place in the gas bottle may be represented by the following equation (§ 127):

$$Zn + 2HCl = ZnCl_2 + H_2.$$

The free zinc united with the chlorine of the acid to form the zinc chloride, thus setting free the hydrogen of the acid. As hydrogen is a gas, it bubbled through the water causing the effervescence. As zinc chloride is a soluble solid, it was dissolved by the water. From the clashing together of atoms in this reaction, much heat was developed (Ph., §§ 674, 676). At the close of the experiment, small black particles are sometimes to be seen floating in the solution in the gas bottle. These are bits of carbon that were present, as impurities, in the zinc.

FIG. 7.

Experiment 15. — Instead of "collecting over water," collect the gas by "upward displacement," as follows: Bring the delivery tube, d, of the gas bottle (Fig. 6) or gas holder into a vertical position. Hold over it a test tube, or small bottle, as shown in Fig. 7, and cause the H to flow rapidly through the tube, d. In a few moments the air will be driven from the test tube and replaced with H. That this gas is not mixed with air (after allowing the H to flow a sufficient length of time) may be shown by testing it in the manner described in § 22. *What does this experiment teach?*

Experiment 16.—Refill the bottle with H, cover the mouth, turn the bottle right side up, remove the cover and quickly apply a flame. How does the H flame differ from those previously seen? Why?

Experiment 17.—Take two cylinders or large test tubes of equal size. Fill one of them, a, with H. Bring the mouth of a to that of b, gradually turn a from its inverted position, as shown in Fig. 8, until it is upright below b. Place a upon a table and in half a minute test the two tubes with a flame. If the experiment has been neatly performed, it will be found that b, which had air, now has H.

FIG. 8.

and that *a*, which had H, now has air. The H was *poured upward* from *a* to *b*. This is called "upward decantation," and is possible because of the extreme levity of this gas as compared with the surrounding air.

Experiment 18.—Equipoise two beaker glasses, as shown in Fig. 9. Fill the inverted beaker with H, by upward decantation. The equilibrium will be destroyed, and the glass containing H will rise.

FIG. 9.

Experiment 19.—To the flexible rubber delivery tube of a gas holder containing H, attach the stem of an ordinary clay pipe, or a small glass funnel. With the gas flowing slowly (the flow being controlled by the stop-cock), dip the pipe into a saucer of soap suds, and, when a film is formed over the mouth of the pipe, turn its mouth upward and open the stop-cock wider. The bubble soon breaks away from the pipe and rises like a balloon.

Note.—The last experiment will be more satisfactory if the soap solution be prepared by making a strong solution of white castile soap in warm soft water that has been recently boiled, and adding half its volume of glycerin. Shake the mixture thoroughly, and it is ready for use.

Experiment 20.—Over a vertical tube delivering H, hold a

sheet of gold leaf or unglazed paper. The gas will pass through the gold or paper, and may be lighted on the upper side of the sheet.

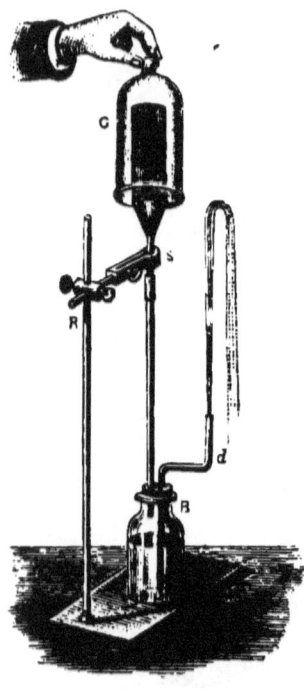

FIG. 10.

Experiment 21.— The remarkably rapid diffusion of H may be shown as follows: Cement with sealing-wax the porous cup of a Grove cell to a glass funnel, mouth to mouth. Prolong the stem of the funnel, *s*, with a glass tube passing snugly through the cork of the bottle *B*. The funnel may be supported by the retort stand, *R*, and connected to the glass tube by a piece of rubber tubing. The bottle is to be half full of water and provided with a delivery tube, *d*, drawn out to a jet above and dipping into the water below. When a bell glass, *G*, containing H is placed over the porous cell, the H diffuses inward so much more rapidly than the air can diffuse outward that an increased pressure is exerted on the surface of the water in *B*. If all of the joints are tight, water will be thrown from the jet, as shown in Fig. 10. The experiment may be simplified by allowing the tube, *s*, to dip into water in an open vessel. Bubbles will rise through the water.

Experiment 22.—The diffusion of H may be shown more easily but less prettily by closing one end of a glass tube 3 or 4 *cm.* (1¼ in.) in diameter and about 30 *cm.* (12 in.) long, with a plug of plaster of Paris 1 or 2 *cm.* thick, filling it with H by upward displacement and placing the mouth of the tube in a tumbler of water. The outward diffusion of the gas through the porous septum reduces the pressure on the water in the tube, which is then forced upward by atmospheric pressure. An argand lamp chimney answers well for the experiment. The plug may be inserted by spreading a stiff paste of the plaster and water in a layer of the desired thickness upon a piece of writing-paper and pressing one end of the chimney down into it. In an hour or two the plaster will have set. The paper may then be easily removed and the plaster outside the tube broken off. Allow it to dry over night before using. In filling the tube with gas, hold it so that the septum will be covered with the fleshy part of the hand to prevent premature diffusion. The water may be colored with cochineal or indigo or ink.

Experiment 23.—To show the effect of H upon sounds produced in it, fill a large bell glass with the gas, suspend it mouth downward, and strike a bell in it, as shown in Fig. 11. Instead of the bell, one of the small squeaking toys well-known to children may be sounded in the H. When the gas has been purified (§ 26), the pupil may with safety inhale it *once or twice* and try to speak or to sing bass with his lungs filled with it (Ph., § 424).

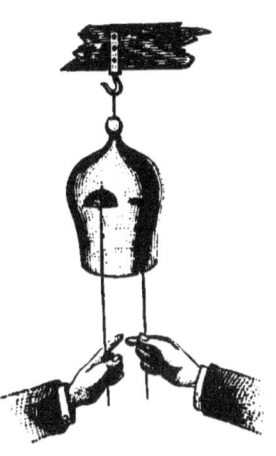

FIG. 11.

24. Physical Properties.—

Hydrogen is a transparent, colorless, tasteless, odorless gas, as may be seen by direct inspection. It is the lightest known substance. One liter of it weighs 0.0896 grams, *which weight is called a crith;* 100 cu. in. weighs 2.14 grains. It refracts light much more powerfully than air (Ph., § 612), and is often taken as the standard of specific gravity for aëriform bodies. It has recently been liquefied by subjecting it to a very great pressure (Ph., §§ 58, 59, 277), at a very low temperature. Because of its extreme lightness, it diffuses more rapidly than any other known substance, and has a peculiar effect upon sounds produced in it (Ph., § 426). It is only sparingly soluble in water, 100 volumes of the liquid absorbing only one or two of the gas.

(*a.*) H is about $14\frac{1}{2}$ times as light as air, 11,000 times as light as water, 150,000 times as light as mercury, and 240,000 times as light as platinum.

(*b.*) That H is not very soluble in water is shown by the fact that it may be collected over water. But the metal palladium absorbs or "occludes" several hundred times its volume of H, forming what seems to be a true alloy. For this and other reasons it is thought by some that H is the vapor of a highly volatile metal.

(c.) We have many metallic solids and one metallic liquid (§ 334) which may be solidified by cold. Why may we not, it is asked, have a metallic gas? H *has been* liquefied; it *may be* solidified. In fact, it is claimed that H has been solidified.

Mercury vapor is present in the " vacuum " of every thermometer and barometer. As we know a metal that is liquid under ordinary circumstances and solid or gaseous under peculiar conditions, it is not difficult to conceive a metal that is gaseous under ordinary circumstances and liquid or solid under peculiar conditions. The metallic nature of H has not yet been generally admitted.

(d.) Palladium, at a red heat, occludes 935 times its volume of H and 376 times its volume at the ordinary temperature. After absorbing the gas, the tenacity, specific gravity, thermal and electric conductivity of the metal are diminished. Platinum, at a red heat, absorbs 3.8 times its volume of H.

Experiment 24.—Repeat Exp. 13, and describe the phenomena fully. What two *chemical* properties of H does this experiment illustrate?

Experiment 25.—Repeat Exp. 19, and while the bubble is in the air, touch it quickly with a lighted taper. Be sure to see all that the experiment shows, and then tell what you see.

FIG. 12.

Experiment 26.—Replace the bent delivery tube of the gas bottle with a straight one having the upper part drawn out to form a jet. After the H has been escaping for some time, test small quantities of it until you are sure that it is unmixed with air. Then, *and not until then*, apply flame to the jet. This is the " Philosopher's candle." Hold a small coil of fine wire in the upper part of the flame. Describe *fully* the flame of the " Philosopher's candle " (Fig. 13).

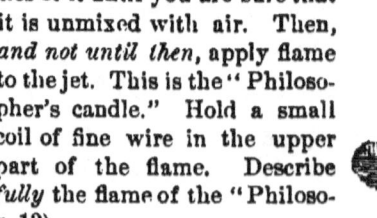

FIG. 13.

Experiment 27.—Over the flame of the "Philosopher's candle," hold a clear, dry, cold tumbler. In a few moments the clear glass will become dimmed with a sort of dew, evidently caused by the condensation of *some vapor formed by the burning of* H *in air.*

Experiment 28. — Pass a stream of H from the gas holder through a U-tube, a, (Fig. 14), containing calcium chloride, *which will retain any aqueous vapor* that may be mixed with the gas. To the further end of this drying tube attach a piece of glass tubing, b, drawn out to form a jet. Over the jet, place the bulb of a thistle or funnel-tube, c, which is bent and connected by a perforated cork to one leg of the U-tube, d. In the other leg of this U-tube, place a loosely fitting test tube, e, nearly filled with ice-water. The hydrogen flame should be 13 or 14 mm. ($\frac{1}{2}$ in.) long. The size of the flame may be largely controlled by regulating the pressure at the gas holder. In four or five minutes, an appreciable quantity of liquid will be found in the bend of d; by keeping the flame steadily burning for half an hour, a considerable quantity of the liquid will be secured. *This liquid is water.* Why was the gas passed through the drying tube? Why was the test tube of cold water placed in the leg of d?

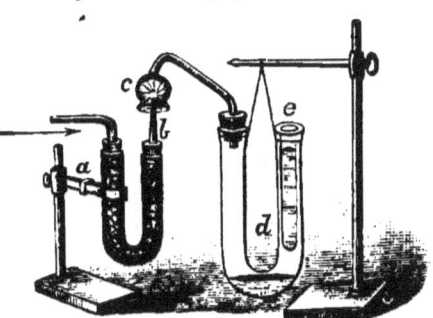

Fig. 14.

Note.—The leg of d that contains e would better be connected by rubber tubing with an aspirator (App. 13), and the flow of steam and air through c and d thus increased.

Experiment 29.—Over the flame of the "Philosopher's candle," hold a glass tube, t, 30 or 40 cm. (12 or 15 in.) long, as shown in Fig. 15. By moving the tube up and down, a position will be found in which the apparatus gives forth a musical tone. If the experiment does not work at first, vary the size of the flame or change the tube, t, for a larger or smaller one. The current of air drawn upward into t (Ph., § 541) gives rise to a series of minute explosions which follow in such rapid succession that a continuous sound is produced (Ph., §§ 429, 469, a.). See Fig. 15.

Note. — The two-necked bottle, w, shown in Fig. 15 (p. 24), is called a Woulffe bottle. Such bottles are also made with three necks. As the mouths are smaller than that of the gas bottle previously described, tight joints are more easily secured. Woulffe bottles are very convenient for many purposes. See App. 6.

Experiment 30.—If you have a piece of platinum sponge, the size of a pea, make for it a support by winding a fine wire spirally into the form of a little cup. Heat the sponge to redness in the lamp, and when cold, hold it 2 or 3 *cm.* above a small jet of dry H. The cold gas soon heats the cold sponge to redness; the sponge in turn ignites the gas. In repeating the experiment, the preliminary heating of the sponge, probably, will not be necessary. (§ 398, *b.*)

FIG. 15.

Note.—The heating of the sponge drives off traces of certain absorbable gases, such as ammonia, which interfere with the inflaming power of the platinum. This property of platinum has been explained by saying that the metal condenses or even liquefies a film of H and one of oxygen on its surface, and that the two condensed elements when brought together, under circumstances of such intimate contact, chemically unite at the ordinary temperature, the heat of such union exciting the combination of the rest of the gases.

25. Chemical Properties.—Hydrogen is an element, combustible at about 500° C. (App. 3), *i. e.*, it combines chemically with the oxygen of the air at that temperature. Its flame is pale (almost non-luminous under ordinary atmospheric pressure) but intensely hot. The burning of a given weight of it, as 1 *g.*, yields more than 34,000 heat units (Ph., § 569), it having thus the greatest heating power of any known substance. Whenever burned, either in the free state or in combination with other elements (*e. g.*, alcohol or petroleum), the product of its combustion is water. It does not support ordinary combustion or respiration. When immersed in it, a lighted taper is extinguished and an animal is suffocated, in both cases because of the absence of oxygen. It forms an explosive mixture with air or oxygen. It is the standard of atomic weight (§ 64) and of quantivalence (§ 92).

Experiment 31.—Pass the delivery tube from the gas holder to the bottom of a drying bottle, a, nearly filled with pieces of pumice-stone saturated with concentrated sulphuric acid. As the gas rises through the drying bottle it comes into contact with a large surface of acid, which eagerly robs it of any watery vapor with which it may be loaded. Into the bulb of the tube, c, put about 15 g. ($\frac{1}{2}$ oz.) of the black oxide of copper. Weigh the tube and its contents very carefully, make a note of the weight and connect c with the delivery tube of a. Fill the U-tube, d, with calcium chloride, weigh this tube and its contents very carefully, make a note of the weight and con-

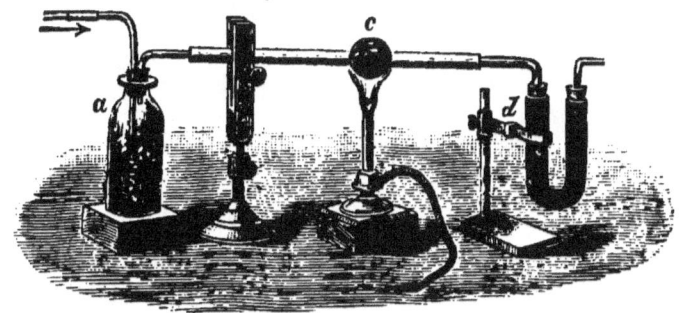

Fig. 16.

nect d with c, as shown in Fig. 16. The connections with c may be made with perforated corks. In all of the weighings, remove the corks and connecting tubes. Pass H from the gas holder through the apparatus until it is delivered from d unmixed with air. Then bring a small flame under the bulb of c. Notice that the copper oxide, when heated in H, changes in color from black to red, and that, near the end of c, is formed a dew which subsequently disappears. Continue the operation until the contents of the bulb remain red when the lamp is removed and the flow of gas checked by the stop-cock of the gas holder. When the apparatus has cooled, disconnect the parts, carefully weigh c with its contents, and d with its contents, and note the weights. We shall find that the contents of c have lost in weight and that those of d have gained, the gain at d being about $\frac{1}{8}$ greater than the loss at c. In the meantime, the copper oxide has been changed to metallic copper. In technical phrase, the copper oxide was "reduced" by the H.

26. Purification.—The materials used in the generation of hydrogen are seldom free from impurities. In consequence, the hydrogen is frequently mixed with carbon dioxide (CO_2) and hydrogen sulphide (H_2S), as well as watery vapor. These impurities may be removed by passing the gas through a series of bottles, as shown in Fig. 17, in which a contains lime-water or a solution of

Fig. 17.

caustic soda (§ 270); b, a weak solution of silver nitrate; c, lumps of charcoal (§ 188); and d, strong sulphuric acid, calcium chloride, or other drying material. If the gas is to be collected over water, the last bottle is of no use.

27. Uses.—On account of its lightness, hydrogen has been used for the inflation of balloons. On account of the intense heat produced by its combustion, it is used for melting platinum (§ 397) and other refractory substances and in producing the calcium light (Exp. 49). As we have seen, it is useful in reducing metallic oxides, the metals thus formed being remarkably free from impurities.

28. Tests.—Hydrogen is easily identified by its physical properties, especially its lightness, its ready inflammability and the extinction of a taper flame placed in it.

Section III.

OXYGEN.

☞ *Symbol*, O; *specific gravity, 16; atomic weight, 16 m. c.; molecular weight, 32 m. c.; quantivalence, 2.*

29. Occurrence.—Of all the elements, oxygen is the most abundant and the most widely diffused. One-fifth of the air, by weight, is free oxygen, and eight-ninths of water, by weight, is combined oxygen. It has been estimated that three-fourths of the animal world, four-fifths of the vegetable world, one-half of the mineral world, and fully two-thirds of the whole world is oxygen.

Note.—The word oxygen is derived from the Greek *oxus* (=acid) and *gennao* (=I produce). The name arose from the erroneous belief that oxygen is a necessary constituent of an acid. The element studied in the last section has a better claim to the title of "acid-former," but there is little probability that either of the names will ever be changed.

30. Preparation.—Oxygen is generally prepared by the decomposition of potassium chlorate by heat. Pulverize 5 $g.$ of clean potassium chlorate ($KClO_3$) and mix it thoroughly with an equal weight of black oxide of manganese (MnO_2) that has been previously heated to redness and allowed to cool. Place the mixture in an ignition tube (App. 4, *a*) of such size that the tube will be not more than a third full. Close the tube with a perforated cork, carrying a delivery tube. Support the ignition tube in a slanting position and apply heat, as shown in Fig. 18 (p. 28). The upper part of the mixture should be heated first and the heat so regulated that the evolution of gas shall be nearly uniform. Collect the gas over water in bottles of about 250 *cu. cm.* (½ pt.) capacity. The first

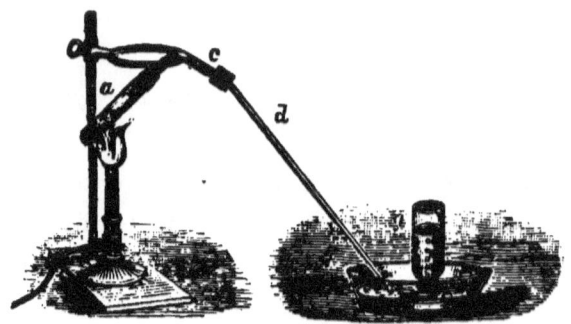

FIG. 18.

half bottle full of the gas may well be rejected. *Why?* Remove the end of the delivery tube from the water, or, better still, break the connection at *c* before removing the lamp. *Why?*

As soon as it is convenient, fill one of the larger gas holders with oxygen. For this purpose it will be better to use larger quantities of the materials, and heat them in a flask. This flask may be of glass, but a retort of copper or iron, expressly constructed for the purpose, is desirable in every laboratory. (See App. 22.)

Caution.—Commercial MnO_2 is sometimes adulterated with carbon. When such a mixture is heated with $KClO_3$, it gives rise to dangerous explosions. Hence, a new or doubtful sample may well be tested on a small scale by heating it with $KClO_3$ in a test-tube.

31. The Reaction.—At the close of the process just described, the ignition-tube will contain manganese dioxide, (MnO_2, black oxide of manganese) and potassium chloride (KCl). The KCl is easily soluble in water; the MnO_2 is not. After the tube has cooled, by agitating its contents with water and filtering, the MnO_2 *may all be recovered unchanged*. It suffered no chemical change and was used only because, in some way still obscure, it caused the $KClO_3$ to decompose more quietly and at a lower temperature. Powdered glass or fine sand might be used with similar results. This effect, produced by what seems to be the mere presence of a substance, has been called *catalysis*.

$$2KClO_3 + 2MnO_2 = 2KCl + 2MnO_2 + 3O_2,$$
or............ $2KClO_3 = 2KCl + 3O_2.$

(*a*.) Pure $KClO_3$ needs to be heated to 350° C. to decompose it; when mixed with MnO_2, the $KClO_3$ decomposes at 200° C. It has been suggested that the MnO_2 is capable of a higher degree of oxidation, and that the higher oxide easily parts with some of its O, forming again the lower oxide. In this way the MnO_2 would act as a *carrier of* O, taking it from the $KClO_3$ and then setting it free. (Compare § 149, *d*.) But this is mere hypothesis.

32. Physical Properties.

—Oxygen is a transparent, colorless, tasteless, odorless gas, not to be distinguished by its appearance from hydrogen or ordinary air. It refracts light less powerfully than air. One liter of it (under ordinary conditions of temperature and atmospheric pressure) weighs 16 criths or 1.43 *g*. As it is about one-tenth heavier than air, it may be collected by downward displacement, but it is more satisfactorily collected over water. It is only sparingly soluble in water, 100 volumes of the liquid absorbing about three of the gas. Like hydrogen, it has recently been liquefied by subjecting it to high pressure and low temperature.

Note.—The bottles containing the O for the experiments immediately following should be prepared by grinding their lips flat with emery powder, as described in App. 4, *h*. Have ready several greased glass plates with which to close the mouths of the bottles thus prepared. During the combustions, it will be well to keep the mouths of the bottles covered loosely, as with cardboard.

Experiment 32.—Repeat Experiment 14, holding the bottle right side up, and allow the taper to burn until the flame dies out. Remove the taper and cover the mouth of the bottle. Label the bottle "No. 1."

FIG. 19.   *Experiment 33.*—Into a second bottle of the gas, thrust a splinter of dry wood, having a glowing spark at its end. When aflame, withdraw it, blow out the flame and repeat until the gas fails to rekindle the splinter. Cover the mouth of the bottle. Label this bottle "No. 2."

Experiment 34.—Place a lighted candle on a stand between two boys, A and B. Let B fill his mouth with O from the gas holder. A may blow out the flame, leaving a glowing wick; B may then puff O upon the wick and relight it. Repeat the experiment until the mouthful of O is exhausted. B need not inhale the O, but if a little does get into his lungs it will do no harm.

Note.—If convenient, perform the next six experiments in a darkened room.

Experiment 35.—Secure a piece of charcoal made from oak or other bark, if you can; otherwise use charcoal made from wood. Around the charcoal, wind one end of a fine wire, to form a handle. Have ready a bottle containing a liter *or more* of O. Ignite the charcoal at the lamp and thrust it into the bottle. Brilliant combustion will take place and continue until all of the charcoal, or all of the O, is consumed. Cover the bottle as before, and label it "No. 3."

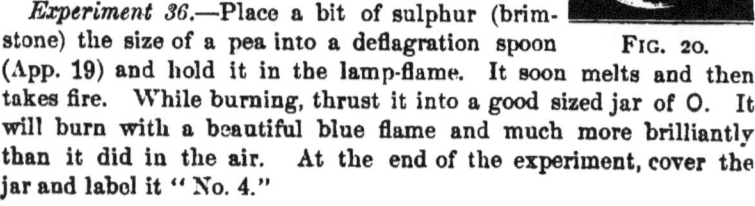

Experiment 36.—Place a bit of sulphur (brimstone) the size of a pea into a deflagration spoon   FIG. 20. (App. 19) and hold it in the lamp-flame. It soon melts and then takes fire. While burning, thrust it into a good sized jar of O. It will burn with a beautiful blue flame and much more brilliantly than it did in the air. At the end of the experiment, cover the jar and label it "No. 4."

§ 32 OXYGEN. 31

Caution.—Phosphorus should not be handled with naked, dry fingers. It ignites easily by friction or slight elevation of temperature. Phosphorus burns are serious. Under water, it may be handled and even cut with safety. When taken directly in the fingers, the fingers should be wet.

Experiment 37.—A larger glass vessel is desirable for this experiment. A good-sized bell glass, such as is used in air pump experiments, or a globe,

FIG. 21.

such as is used for keeping gold-fish, will answer well. In the middle of a large plate or tray containing water 4 or 5 *cm.* deep, place a metal support rising several *cm.* above the surface of the water. From a stick of phosphorus, cut, *under water*, a piece the size of a large pea, dry it thoroughly between pieces of blotting or filter paper, place it upon the support in the tray, ignite it with a hot wire and quickly invert over it the bell glass or globe of O. The combustion is exceedingly energetic and indescribably brilliant. The metal support for the phosphorus may be protected from combustion by coating its upper surface with lime, chalk, or plaster of Paris. The experiment has been called the "Phosphoric Sun." At first, part of the gas may bubble out at the mouth of the globe, but as the dense fumes formed by the burning of the phosphorus are absorbed, water will rise within the vessel. Then pour more water into the tray, if necessary, and label the globe "No. 5."

Experiment 38.—Heat an iron rod, as thick as an ordinary lead pencil, to bright redness. Bring it quickly in front of a jet of O from the gas holder. It will burn with beautiful effects, throwing off sparks and dropping globules of iron oxide.

Experiment 39. — Form a spiral of *fine* iron wire (piano-forte wire is preferable) by winding the wire upon a lead pencil or piece of glass tubing; wind some waxed thread upon the lower end of the wire, or dip the end of the wire into melted sulphur so that a small sulphur bead shall adhere to the wire. At the bottom of a vessel containing 2 or 3 liters of O place a layer of water or sand. Ignite the thread or sulphur and quickly place the wire in the O. The burning wax, or sulphur, heats the end of the wire to redness. The wire then burns with beautiful scintillations. The experiment may be made more brilliant by using a coiled watch spring instead of the iron wire. The watch spring, which may be had gratis of almost any jeweler, is to be softened by heating it to redness and allowing it to cool slowly; it may then easily be coiled. Wind the lower end of the spring with twine and dip it into melted sulphur, to prepare the kindling material. The kindling matter should be no larger in quantity than is necessary to heat the wire or spring to the necessary temperature; any excess interferes with the success of the experiment, by consuming the free O and forming undesirable compounds in the jar. The melted metal globules sometimes fuse their way into or through the glass bottom of the jar, when the water or sand is not provided to prevent such a result.

Fig. 22.

Experiment 40.—Blow a jet of O into the flame of an alcohol lamp. In the flame thus produced hold a piece of watch spring or steel wire. It will burn with brilliant scintillations.

Experiment 41.—Into bottle No. 1, put a piece of moistened blue litmus paper; it will be reddened. Now pour in a little clear lime water (slacked lime dissolved in water), cover the mouth of the bottle tightly with the palm of the hand and shake the bottle vigorously; a partial vacuum will be formed (Exp. 190) and the clear lime water will become turbid and soon yield a white precipitate. *The reddening of the blue litmus paper shows the presence of an acid.* The colorless gas formed by the burning of the taper in O has united with the water to form an acid. What is this colorless gas? The turbidity of the lime water and the precipitate (§ 200) show that it is carbon dioxide (CO_2), sometimes called carbonic anhydride, but, more frequently, carbonic acid gas. The carbon (symbol = C) of the taper united with the O (synthesis):

$$C + O_2 = CO_2.$$

Experiment 42.—Try the contents of jars Nos. 2 and 3 with a lighted taper. The flame is extinguished as promptly as it would be by water. Numerous gases act in this way. We have seen that H_2 extinguishes flame; but this gas is not kindled as we know that H would be. Try the contents with moistened blue litmus paper. The paper is reddened. Have you *any idea* of what the gas is? Try the gas with clear lime water. We have the turbidity, *etc.*, as before. What do you now think the gas is? The dry wood burned in No. 2 was largely carbon, and the charcoal burned in No. 3 was nearly pure carbon. In either case,

$$C + O_2 = CO_2.$$

Experiment 43.—Test the contents of jar No. 4 with a lighted taper. The flame is promptly extinguished as before. Test with the moistened blue litmus paper. The paper is reddened as before. What does this reddening show? Does the jar contain H? Does it contain O? Do you *think* that it contains carbon dioxide? Why? Test with clear lime water. *Does* it contain carbon dioxide? How was this gas formed? Was any carbon used in its production? The gas is sulphur dioxide (SO_2) sometimes called sulphurous anhydride or sulphurous acid gas (§ 144). Write the reaction for its formation. The symbol for sulphur is S.

Note.—If a very little of the SO_2 be inhaled, it will be quickly recognized as the irritating gas familiar to all from the use of sulphur matches. If we turn to jar No. 5 we shall find that the phosphoric oxide (P_2O_5) formed by the combustion of the phosphorus was dissolved in the water. If this water be tested with blue litmus paper it will be found to have acid properties. We have thus formed oxides of carbon, of sulphur and of phosphorus, and seen that these oxides unite with water to form acids (§ 163). If the litmus paper used in testing these gases had been *dry* instead of *wet* it would not have been reddened. The oxide of iron (Fe_3O_4) formed in experiments 38 and 39, are solid and insoluble in water.

33. Chemical Properties.—Oxygen is chiefly marked by its great chemical activity. It enters into combination with all the elements except fluorine (§ 120). In the ordinary use of the term, combustion is chemical union with oxygen with the resulting phenomena of heat and light.

34. Uses.—Oxygen is used in countless ways in the laboratories of Nature and of man. It is essential to the processes of animal respiration, ordinary combustion, fermentation and decay. It is used in the arts to increase the intensity of combustion for purposes of heat and light, and in medicine as an anæsthetic.

Fig. 23.

Experiment 44. — Fill the lungs with air. Slowly exhale the air through a tube so that the air shall bubble up through clear lime water in a clear glass bottle. The lime-water quickly becomes turbid, as in Exp. 41, showing that CO_2 is one of the products of respiration.

35. Relation to Animal Life.—All animal creatures are adapted to the absorption of free oxygen, either that of the air or that held in solution by water. The oxygen, when inhaled, enters into chemical combination with various parts of the animal structure, and is then exhaled as CO_2. We thus see that oxygen is necessary to animal life, for which reason it was formerly called *vital air*. The chemical changes occurring in the animal are the same as those exhibited in Experiments 32 and 33, excepting so far as rapidity of combustion or vigor of chemical activity is concerned. The heat thus evolved (Ph., § 674, *e*) keeps the temperature of the body above that of surrounding inanimate objects; when this chemical action ceases (death), the temperature of the body falls to that of its surroundings. When, by any means, the supply of oxygen is cut off, this chemical action is arrested and the victim dies. This effect may follow from choking, drowning, or the inhalation of even non-poisonous gases that contain no free oxygen, as hydrogen or nitrogen. These do not poison; they suffocate. Every part of every animal is being continually burned up by oxygen. Unless the loss be made good by proper food, emaciation and final death must follow. As we shall soon see, common air is diluted oxygen. An animal breathing pure oxygen can not live long, because it lives so fast; there are undue excitement, over action, fever and speedy death.

Experiment 45.—Into a large test tube filled, over water, with nitric oxide (NO, § 83) pass a small quantity of O. The two colorless gases combine eagerly, forming dense red fumes, which are rapidly dissolved in the water.

Experiment 46.—Dissolve a piece of potassium hydrate (caustic potash, KHO) the size of a pea, in 10 *cu. cm.* of water and pour the solution into a long test tube filled with O. Add a few flakes of pyrogallic acid. Close the mouth of the tube with the thumb and shake the contents. The liquid will be blackened. Place the mouth of the tube under water and remove the thumb. Water will rise in the tube to fill the partial vacuum formed by the absorption of the O in the tube by the liquid mixture.

36. Tests.—Free oxygen, not much diluted with other gases, is most easily tested by plunging into it a glowing splinter, as in Exp. 33. The only other gas that will thus rekindle the splinter is nitrous oxide (laughing gas, N_2O ; § 79). This test, though generally enough, is not conclusive. The properties of oxygen, illustrated in the last two experiments, *i. e.*, that of forming red fumes with nitric oxide and of blackening a mixture of dissolved potassium hydrate and pyrogallic acid and of being rapidly absorbed thereby, constitute unmistakable tests for the presence of free oxygen.

37. Ozone.—In addition to the ordinary form of oxygen, which contains two atoms in each molecule, a remarkable variety is known in which there are three atoms to each molecule. *This condensed and more active form of oxygen is called ozone.* In changing oxygen to ozone there is a volumetric condensation of one-third. It is formed at the + electrode in the electrolysis of water; by the discharge from an electric machine through air or oxygen; or by the slow oxidation of phosphorus in moist air, etc. It is best prepared by electric apparatus devised for that purpose, but the phosphorus or ether method is more convenient.

Experiment 47.—Prepare a cylinder of phosphorus 3 or 4 *cm.* long, by scraping its surface clean under water. (Remember the *caution* preceding Experiment 37.) Place the cylinder in a clean bottle of 1 or 2 liters capacity, and pour in enough water to half cover the cylinder. Close the mouth of the bottle with a plate of glass or a loose stopper, and set the bottle in a warm place (20° C. or 30° C.). In 10 or 15 min., notice the fog above the phosphorus. Allow the bottle to remain for several hours. The feeble, chlorine-like odor of ozone will be discernible. A still more convenient method is to place a few drops of ether in a tall beaker glass, and stir the quickly formed vapor with a hot glass rod.

Experiment 48.—Prepare two slips of white paper by dipping them into a solution of starch and potassium iodide (Exp. 99). Thrust one of these into a bottle of O; no change will be noticed. Thrust the other test paper into the bottle or beaker glass containing ozone; the white paper will be promptly colored blue. The energetic ozone displaces the iodine.

$$2 KI + O_3 = K_2O + O_2 + I_2.$$

The free iodine colors the starch blue. (Exp. 122.)

38. Properties of Ozone.—Ozone has been prepared only in small quantities, but it manifests its presence by its peculiarly energetic action. It is one of the most powerful oxidizing agents known. It is unquestionably present in pure country and sea air, and noticeably absent in the atmosphere of large cities, where its oxidizing influence upon organic and other deleterious matter results in partial disinfection and its own transformation into oxygen and oxygen compounds. In its oxidizing action, its volume is supposed to undergo no change, the third atom of the ozone molecule (O_3) entering into combination and leaving the two atoms of the ordinary oxygen molecule (O_2). It is changed by heat into ordinary oxygen with increase of volume, the change being instantaneous at 237° C.

(*a.*) It was formerly thought that ozone had its counterpart in a form of oxygen, having one atom to the molecule, and called *antozone*. "Further experiments have, however, proved that antozone is nothing more than hydrogen dioxide." (§ 44.)

39. Allotropism.—We have seen that ozone manifests characteristics decidedly different from those of ordinary oxygen. Still, its fundamental, chemical identity with oxygen is unquestionable. For example, the potassium oxide (K_2O) that it formed by displacing the iodine of the potassium iodide, in Experiment 48, is identical with the potassium oxide formed in any other way. *This capability of existing in different forms with chemical identity undestroyed is called allotropism.* Ozone is an allotropic modification of oxygen.

Section IV.

COMPOUNDS OF HYDROGEN AND OXYGEN.

40. Combustion of Hydrogen.—When hydrogen is heated to the temperature of about 500° C., in the presence of free oxygen, the two elements enter into chemical union, forming water (H_2O). This was shown in a general way in Experiment 28. *Whatever the conditions under which hydrogen is burned in oxygen or in air, the sole product is water.* This is true, even in the combustion of a compound containing hydrogen, as has been previously stated (§ 25). The clashing together of the hydrogen and oxygen atoms involved in the combustion (§ 11) develops an extraordinary amount of heat (Ph., § 472), *viz.*, 34,462 heat units; *i. e.*, the combustion of a given weight of hydrogen in oxygen develops enough heat to warm 34,462 times that weight of water from 0° C. to 1° C., or more than 62,000 times that weight of water from 32° F. to 33° F. The experiments in this section are intended to set forth the principal features of the direct synthesis of hydrogen and oxygen.

41. The Compound Blowpipe.—The compound or oxyhydrogen blowpipe consists of a double tube, one inside the other, as shown in Fig. 24. The interior tube

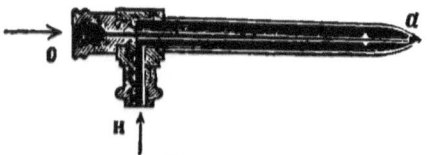

Fig. 24.

is connected by rubber tubing with the oxygen gas holder; the outer tube, with the hydrogen gas holder. Hydrogen is first turned on and ignited at *a*. Oxygen is then turned on until the flame is reduced to a fine pencil. The pressure at the gas holders should be steady, the amount thereof being easily determined by trial.

Experiment 49.—Hold bits of iron and copper wire, watch springs, strips of zinc, *etc.*, in the flame of the compound blowpipe. They will be readily dissipated with characteristic luminous effects. A fine wire of platinum, an exceedingly refractory metal, is readily melted, and silver can be thus distilled. A piece of lime or chalk, freshly scraped to a point and held in the flame, is heated to such a high degree of incandescence that it produces a light of remarkable intensity. This is essentially the Drummond or calcium light. The temperature of the oxyhydrogen flame has been estimated to be above 2800° C.

Experiment 50. — Over the jet, *a*, of the compound blowpipe, slip a piece of rubber tubing. Allow both gases to flow through the apparatus, and dip the tubing into a metallic dish full of soap-suds until a mass of foam has formed, as shown in Fig. 25.

FIG. 25.

Close the stop-cocks at the gas holders or the blowpipe, remove the tubing from the soap-suds, and then touch the foam with a flame carried at the end of a stick about a meter in length. A violent explosion will take place. (See § 22 and the *Note* following Exp. 19.)

Note.—If you have no compound blowpipe, introduce one volume of O and two of H into a gas bag or small gas holder (App. 13). The gases will soon become thoroughly mixed by diffusion, when they may be passed into the soap-suds through the rubber tubing. Remember that this mixture is *dangerously explosive; be sure that there is no possibility of flame coming into contact with the contents of the gas bag or the connected tubing.* The explosion just described was free from danger, because the restraining wall of the explosive mixture was only a thin film of H_2O, the flying fragments of which could do no harm. If the contents of your gas holder should explode, the flying fragments would probably do serious damage. It is advisable to throw away the mixed gases that may remain at the close of the experiments with them. Any attempt to burn these gases *previously* mixed, even as they issue from the jet of the compound blowpipe, will result in an explosion.

Experiment 51.—Repeat Experiment 19, using the mixed gases instead of H and guarding carefully against an accidental explosion. The bubble, or a mass of bubbles, dipped from the dish shown in Fig. 25, may be safely exploded while resting in the palm of the hand.

Note.—A hydrogen pistol may be made of a tin tube 3 or 4 *cm.* in diameter and 15 or 20 *cm.* in length, closed at one end. The open end is to be fitted with a cork, and the closed end provided with a small opening the size of a pin hole. By placing the thumb over the pin hole, the pistol may be filled over water with the mixed gases, the cork put into place, and the pin hole presented to a candle or lamp flame. The cork is the bullet of this pistol. The pistol may be *partly* filled with H by upward displacement, thus providing a mixture of H and air, that is less violently explosive because of the dilution of the O of the atmosphere.

Experiment 52.—A tall tin cup filled with a detonating mixture of H and O may be inverted over a piece of platinum sponge. The sponge may be supported a few inches above the table by the wire used in Exp. 30. In a few moments the mixed gases will be exploded.

§ 42. The Eudiometer.—The eudiometer is an instrument for determining the proportions in which gases unite. It consists of a strong glass tube with two platinum wires fused into the sides, near the closed end. The wires nearly touch within the tube. One of the most common forms, devised by Ure, consists of a U-tube with the closed arm, *b*, graduated to cubic centimeters. It is represented in Fig. 26.

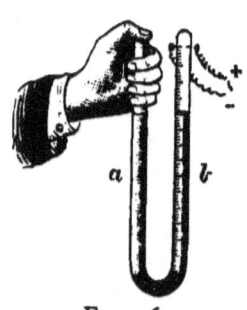

FIG. 26.

Experiment 53.—Fill the eudiometer with water and hold it with the open arm, *a*, horizontal, under water and under the closed arm, *b*. By means of a rubber tube carrying a short piece of glass tubing drawn out to a fine jet, pass about 20 *cu. cm.* of pure O from the gas holder into *b*. Be sure that the air had been previously driven out of the delivery tube; make the measurement with the eudiometer erect and the water standing at the same level in both tubes. Water may be removed from *a*, if necessary to this end, by means of a pipette (App. 5.) Now introduce about 50 *cu. cm.* of pure H into *b*, and note the exact amount of gas therein as before. It may prove difficult to introduce *exactly* 20 and 50 *cu. cm.* A little variation matters not, *provided* that you measure accurately the amounts actually introduced, and that the volume of the H is more than twice that of the O. Suppose that the first measurement shows 21 *cu. cm.* of O, and that the second shows 75 *cu. cm.* of mixed gases. Then you have introduced 54 *cu. cm.* of H. Close the open end firmly with the thumb, leaving a cushion of air between it and the surface of the water, as shown in Fig. 26. Produce an electric spark between the ends of the platinum wires in the mixed gases. [Ph., § 371 (21), (33), (35), § 411.] The spark produces combination between the O and part of the H. On removing the thumb and bringing the liquid surfaces to the same level, it will be found that there are only 12 *cu. cm.* of gas in *b*. By filling *a* with water and closing it with the thumb, the gas may be easily passed from *b* into *a*, and thence, under water, to a convenient vessel for testing. It will be found to be pure H. The 21 *cu. cm.* of O has united with 42 *cu. cm.* of H to form a minute quantity of H_2O, leaving the 12 *cu. cm.* of H because there was no O with which it could unite. See § 12. If the eudiometer had been kept at a temperature above 100° C., or 212° F., and the gases confined by mercury instead of water, *b* would have contained 42 *cu. cm.* of steam and 12 *cu. cm.* of H. The volume of steam would be the same as that of the H that entered into its composition. The combination was accompanied by a diminution of volume equal to that of the O entering into chemical union. In other words, three volumes shrink to two volumes in the process of combination. Representing equal volumes of the gases by equal squares, the volumetric composition of H_2O and the condensation just mentioned may be represented to the eye as follows:

$$\boxed{H} + \boxed{H} + \boxed{O} = \boxed{H_2O}$$

As O is 16 times as heavy as H [Ph., § 253 (3)], the one volume of O weighs 8 times as much as the two volumes of H. Hence, we see that the gravimetric composition of water is 8 parts of O to 1 of H, as previously stated.

Experiment 54.—Support a wide tube of clear glass in a vertical position. A bottomless bottle, the neck of a broken retort, or a lamp-chimney will answer well. Through the perforated cork that closes the upper end, pass a stream of H from the gas holder. When the air has been driven out of the bottle, apply a flame at the lower end and regulate the flow so that the gas burns slowly at the opening. From another gas holder, pass a current of O through a piece of glass tubing drawn out to form a small jet. As the jet passes through the burning gas, the O takes fire and burns in an atmosphere of H.

FIG. 27.

43. Combustibles and Supporters of Combustion.—Since all ordinary combustion takes place in the air, which furnishes the necessary supply of oxygen, it is customary to speak of oxygen as a supporter of combustion, and the hydrogen or other substance that thus unites with the oxygen as a combustible. The experiment just given shows that this distinction has no reason for its continued existence except custom and convenience. When oxygen and hydrogen atoms clash together in chemical union, we have combustion, and it makes no difference whether the hydrogen emerges into an atmosphere of oxygen, or the oxygen emerges into an atmosphere of hydrogen. We shall, however, continue to speak of burning hydrogen and carbon instead of burning oxygen.

44. Hydrogen Dioxide.—While water, H_2O, is the only compound of H and O found in nature, another (H_2O_2), containing twice as much O, may be produced by chemical means. It is a sirupy, colorless liquid, and at 100° C. separates into H_2O and O with almost explosive violence. It has no "practical" value, but is of considerable theoretical importance. It may be considered as composed of two groups of HO; thus, (HO)—(HO). This group is called hydroxyl. Hydrogen dioxide, or peroxide, $(HO)_2$, is sometimes called free hydroxyl. (§ 97.)

Exercises.

1. What is the difference between a chemical and a physical change? Make your answer as explicit as you can, and illustrate.

2. (*a.*) Describe briefly the common method for the preparation of O, omitting no essential. (*b.*) Tell what you can of H and its preparation.

3. (*a.*) Give the symbol, atomic weight and chemical properties of O. (*b.*) What is meant by oxidation?

4. (*a.*) What is an element? (*b.*) How many are known? (*c.*) What gases enter into the composition of water? (*d.*) Prove your answer in two ways, one method being the reverse of the other. (*e.*) What name do you give to each method?

5. When a current of steam is passed through an iron tube nearly filled with bright iron turnings or filings, the tube being placed across a furnace and its middle portion heated to redness, large quantities of a combustible gas that may be collected over water are delivered from the tube. (*a.*) What do you suppose the gas to be? Why? (*b.*) Will the iron turnings in the tube weigh more or less at the end of the experiment than they did at the beginning? Why?

6. (*a.*) How many hydrogen oxides are known? Name them. Define chemistry. (*b.*) What is the difference between chemistry and physics?

7. (*a.*) What is the distinction between organic and inorganic compounds? (*b.*) Between a mixture and a compound?

8. (*a.*) If 240 *cu. cm.* of H and 120 *cu. cm.* of O be made to combine, what will be the name of the product? (*b.*) If the experiment be performed in a vessel having a temperature above that of boiling water, what will be the name and volume of the product?

9. If 300 *cu. cm.* of steam be condensed to water and the water decomposed (Exp. 12), what will be the volume and composition of the product?

10. (*a.*) What weight of H is there in 8,064 *g.* of H_2O? (*b.*) What volume of H? (*c.*) What is a crith?

11. Give a possible explanation for the fact that recently heated but cool platinum sponge will explode a mixture of H and O.

12. What is meant by the *reduction* of copper oxide?

13. How could you tell O from H?

14. State the principal difference between ordinary O and its allotropic modification.

15. (*a*.) If a mixture of 50 *cu. cm.* of H and 50 *cu. cm.* of O be exploded in an eudiometer, what will be the name and volume of the remaining gas? (*b.*) What precaution must be taken in measuring the gases?

Chapter III.

AIR AND ITS CONSTITUENTS.

Section I.

AIR.

45. Occurrence.—The earth is surrounded by an atmosphere of air extending to a height variously estimated at from 50 to 200 miles.

Experiment 55.—Repeat Experiments 45 and 46, using common air instead of O. These *tests* show the presence of free O in the air.

Experiment 56.—When mercury (Hg) is heated in air it is gradually changed into red oxide of mercury (red precipitate). The mercury oxide weighs more than the mercury used, showing that, though it

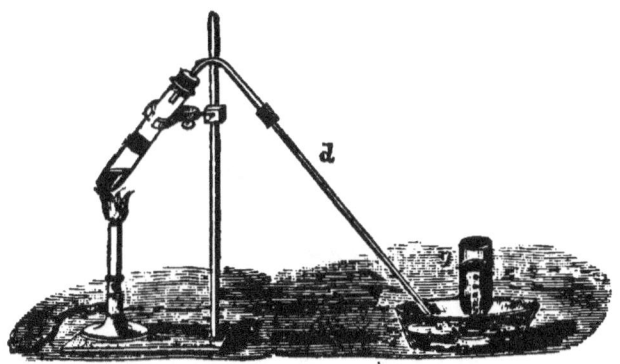

Fig. 28.

may have lost something in the process, it has more than made good any such imaginary loss by the gain of something from the air. The process is slow and you would better buy the oxide. Put about 10 g.

of this red mercury oxide into an ignition-tube 20 *cm.* long, provided with a perforated cork and delivery-tube. Close the tube and support it over the lamp-flame in some such way as that shown in Fig. 28. The ignition-tube should be in an oblique position so as to expose at least 3 or 4 *cm.* of its length to the flame. As the mercury oxide becomes heated, gas will be delivered and may be collected over water in small bottles. The first bottle-full collected should be thrown away, as it contains the air that was in the apparatus at the beginning of the experiment. When the gas is no longer delivered freely, remove the delivery-tube from the water, wipe the adhering liquid from it, and *then* remove the lamp. By testing the gas on hand you will see that it is O. The O came from the mercury oxide, to form which it was given up by the air. At the close of the experiment, minute globules of metallic mercury will be found upon the sides of the upper part of the ignition-tube. With proper apparatus, the experiment might be continued until all of the mercury oxide disappeared, leaving behind only metallic mercury. The *synthesis* of Hg and O gave us the oxide; the *analysis* of the oxide gave us back the identical atoms of Hg and O.

Experiment 57.—At one end of the beam of a balance, suspend a long vertical tube, *a*, containing a taper, and a bent tube, *c*, containing potassium hydrate (caustic potash, KHO). The taper may

FIG. 29

be supported on a cork, perforated so as to admit air freely to a, which should be about 4 cm. in diameter. Connect the two tubes by a piece of rubber tubing and equipoise them and their contents by weights at w. Instead of equipoising the tubes, they may be weighed carefully, before and after the experiment, as in Exp. 31. Connect the tube, c, with a gas holder, g, filled with H_2O, which on being allowed to escape at i produces a current of air through the tubes, and thus maintains the combustion of the taper, which should now be lighted. The head of H_2O in the aspirator, g, and the size of the connecting tubes should be such as to produce a strong current through the apparatus. In addition to lumps of KHO in c, it is well to fill the bend of c with an aqueous solution of KHO, through which the gases will bubble. The H_2O and CO_2 (§ 196), formed by the combustion of the H and C of the taper, are absorbed by the KHO. After the taper has burned for a few minutes, the tubes, a and c, are disconnected from the gas holder and allowed to hang freely from the beam. They will be found to be heavier than before the burning of the taper, the added weight being that of the O of the air that has entered into combination with the H and the C of the taper.

Experiment 58.—Provide a cork about 5 cm. in diameter and 2 cm.

FIG. 30.

in thickness. Cover one side with a thin layer of plaster of Paris mixed with H_2O. The paste may be raised near the edge of the cork so as to produce a concave surface. Dry the cork thoroughly and you have a convenient capsule for floating upon H_2O. For a single experiment, the cork may be covered with dry powdered chalk or lime. Upon this capsule, place a piece of phosphorus *that has been dried* by wrapping it in blotting or filter paper. Float the capsule upon H_2O, ignite the phosphorus with a hot wire, and cover it with a bell-glass or other wide-mouthed vessel. While the phosphorus is burning, hold the bell-glass down with the hand. The phosphorus combines with the O of the air, forming dense fumes of phosphoric oxide (P_2O_5). These fumes are soon absorbed by the H_2O, which rises in the bell-glass to occupy the space vacated by the O.

Experiment 59.—When the fumes of P_2O_5 have been absorbed, slip a glass plate under the mouth of the bell-glass and place it mouth upward, without admitting any air. If the bell-glass be capped, as shown in Fig. 30, it need not be removed from the water-pan ; H_2O should be poured into the pan until the liquid outside the receiver is at the same level as that inside. Test the gaseous contents with a lighted taper. The flame is extinguished, but the gas does not burn. It is neither O nor H. It is nitrogen, an element that we shall study in the next section.

46. Composition of Air.—Air is composed chiefly of oxygen and nitrogen. Very careful determinations show its volumetric and gravimetric composition to be as follows:

	By Volume.	By Weight.
Oxygen	20.9 %	23.1 %
Nitrogen	79.1	76.9
	100.	100.

This composition of the air is nearly but not quite constant at different times and places. The air also contains small quantities of carbon dioxide (CO_2), more or less watery vapor, traces of ammonias, *etc.*

47. Physical Properties.—The air, when pure, is transparent, colorless, tasteless, and odorless. Under standard conditions (temperature, 0°C.; barometer, 760 *mm.*) a liter of it weighs 1.2932 *g.* or 14.45 criths. It is therefore 14.45 times as heavy as hydrogen. It presses upon the surface of the earth with a force of 1.033 *Kg. per sq. cm.* or 15 lb. *per* sq. in. (Ph., §§ 273, 494.)

48. Chemical Properties.—The chemical properties of air are those of its several constituents. Its oxygen supports combustion, the energy of the combustion being checked by the diluting nitrogen. Its nitrogen manifests all of the properties of nitrogen. Its watery vapor condenses when the temperature falls, just as any other watery vapor would do. Hence, we have dew and frost. When a stream of air is passed through lime-water, its carbon dioxide renders the clear liquid turbid, just as carbon dioxide always does (Exp. 44).

49. Air is a Mixture.—The first sentence in the preceding paragraph intimates that the constituents of our atmosphere are not chemically united but merely mixed; that each of them is free (§ 12). This fact is shown by the following additional considerations :

(*a*.) When the constituents are mixed in the proper proportions they form air, but there is no change of volume or manifestation of heat, light, or electricity.

(*b*.) The composition of air is slightly variable (§ 12).

(*c*.) Each gas dissolves in H_2O independently of the other. When H_2O is boiled, it loses the gases it held in solution. Collection and analysis of these gases show that they are 32% O and 68% nitrogen. The H_2O absorbed O just as if there was no nitrogen present; it absorbed nitrogen just as if no O was present. This increased richness in O is of vital importance to fishes (§ 35). If the constituent gases were chemically united, they would be absorbed by H_2O in the proportion stated in § 46.

(*d*.) The gases do not unite in any simple ratio of their atomic weight. As will be seen subsequently (§ 91), this is a very important consideration.

SECTION II.

NITROGEN.

☞ *Symbol,* N · *specific gravity,* 14; *atomic weight,* 14 m. c.; *molecular weight,* 28 m. c.; *quantivalence,* 3 (*or* 5).

50. Occurrence. — Nitrogen is widely diffused in nature. It is found free in some of the nebulæ and in the earth's atmosphere. In combination, it exists in a number of minerals, as the sodium and potassium nitrates (nitre) of Peru and India. It also forms an essential part of most animal and vegetable substances.

51. Preparation. — The usual way of preparing nitrogen is to burn out, with phosphorus, the oxygen from a portion of air confined over water, as shown in Experiment 58. Instead of the burning phosphorus, a jet of burning hydrogen may be used. The nitrogen thus prepared is not perfectly pure, but nearly enough so for ordinary purposes.

(*a.*) Any method of getting the O of the air to enter into combination and form a compound that is easily removed from the residual N will answer. Thus, if a slow stream of air be passed over bright copper turnings, heated to redness in a glass tube, the O will unite with the copper, leaving the N to be collected over H_2O.

(*b.*) Pure N may be obtained by chemical processes, such as heating ammonium nitrite, which decomposes into H_2O and N, as follows:

$$(NH_4)NO_2 = 2H_2O + N_2.$$

52. Physical Properties.—Nitrogen is a transparent, colorless, tasteless, odorless gas. It is a little lighter than air or oxygen, and 14 times as heavy as hydrogen, a liter weighing 1.2544 $g.$, or 14 criths. It is very slightly soluble in water.

FIG. 31.

Experiment 60.—Fill a bell-glass with O, and a stoppered bell-glass of the same size with N. Cover their mouths with glass plates and bring them mouth to mouth, as shown in Fig. 31. Remove the stopper and the glass plates and introduce a lighted taper having a long wick (or a pine splinter). As the taper passes through the N, the flame is extinguished; if the wick be still glowing, it will be rekindled in the O. By moving the taper up and down from one gas to the other, it may be rekindled repeatedly before the gases become mixed by diffusion.

53. Chemical Properties.—The leading characteristic of nitrogen is its inertness. Its properties are chiefly negative. It enters into *direct* combination with but few elements. It is neither a combustible nor a supporter of combustion. It is not poisonous; we are continually breathing large quantities of it. It kills by suffocation, by cutting off the necessary supply of oxygen, just as hydrogen or water does. Its compounds are generally unstable and energetic. Some of them are decomposed by being lightly brushed with a feather or by a heavy step on the floor (§ 113).

54. Uses.—The chief use of nitrogen is to dilute the oxygen of the air and thus prevent disastrous chemical activity, especially in the processes of respiration and combustion.

55. Tests.—Nitrogen may be recognized by its physical properties and its refusal to give any reaction with any known chemical test.

Exercises.

1. What is meant by allotropism? Analysis? Synthesis?
2. What is the difference between an elementary and a compound molecule?
3. Why does the burning of alcohol yield steam?
4. Why does the gas bottle become heated in the preparation of H?
5. What is a crith?
6. Is H poisonous? Can you live long in an atmosphere of H? Why?
7. Is O poisonous? Can you live long in an atmosphere of O? Why?
8. Why is the word "oxygen" a misnomer?
9. Is the ordinary method of preparing O analytic or synthetic?
10. What is the chief characteristic of O?
11. Why is the inner rather than the outer tube of the compound blowpipe used for O?
12. Name five constituents of ordinary air.
13. State five reasons for holding that the air is a mixture.
14. What is the weight of 1 $cu. m.$ of N? Of O?
15. How many criths are there in a gram?

CHAPTER IV.

SYMBOLS, NOMENCLATURE, MOLECULAR AND ATOMIC WEIGHTS.

56. Atomic Symbols. — Chemists have a shorthand way of writing the names of the substances with which they deal. In chemical notation, each element is represented by the initial letter of its Latin name. When the names of two or more elements begin with the same letter, the initial letter is followed by the first distinctive letter of the name. Thus, C stands for carbon, Ca for calcium, and Cl for chlorine. This use of Latin initials secures uniformity among chemists of all countries. In only a few cases do the Latin and English initials differ. The symbols of all the elements will be found in Appendix 1. These symbols of the elements are frequently used to represent their respective substances in general. Thus, we speak of a liter of O, but in the symbols of compound bodies and in equations representing chemical reactions (§ 127), the symbol of an element represents a single atom. To represent several atoms, we use figures placed at the right of the symbol and a little below it. Thus, H_2 means two atoms of hydrogen. (See § 165, a.)

57. Molecular Symbols. — The symbol of a molecule is formed by writing together the symbols of its constituent atoms indicating the number of each kind, as just stated. A molecule of water consists of three atoms, two of hydrogen and oxygen; hence, its symbol is H_2O. Like the atomic symbols of the elements, these symbols of the molecules of compound substances are used to represent their respective substances in the mass. Thus, we speak of a liter of H_2O, but in the equations representing reactions, each of these symbols represents a single molecule. To represent several molecules, we place the proper figure before the symbol. Thus, $3H_2O$ represents three molecules of water, or six atoms of hydrogen and three of oxygen.

Note.—The symbol of a molecule is sometimes spoken of as its formula. Chemical notation is the written language of the science.

58. Nomenclature of the Elements. — The nomenclature of chemistry is an attempt to represent the composition of a substance by its name. The names of the elements were generally chosen arbitrarily, although some of them allude to some prominent property, as chlorine from the Greek *chloros*, signifying green, and as has been already stated in the cases of hydrogen and oxygen. Chemical nomenclature is the spoken language of the science.

59. Nomenclature of Binary Compounds.— The names of binary compounds (those containing only two elements), have the characteristic termination -*ide*. Compounds of single elements with oxygen are called *oxides;* similar compounds with chlorine are called *chlorides;* those with sulphur are called *sulphides, etc., etc.* Thus, we have lead oxide, silver chloride and hydrogen sulphide. When any two elements unite in more than one proportion, one or both of the words constituting the name are modified, as in hydrogen peroxide, carbon disulphide, mercurous chloride and mercuric chloride.

60. Nomenclature of Ternary Compounds.

—The most important compounds containing three or more elements are the acids. The most important of these consist of hydrogen and oxygen united to some third element, which is the characteristic one and gives its name to the acid. The terminations *-ic* and *-ous* are used with the name of the characteristic element to indicate a greater or less amount of oxygen in the acid. Thus we have:

Nitr*ic* acid ....HNO_3 | Sulphur*ic* acid.....H_2SO_4
Nitr*ous* acid........HNO_2 | Sulphur*ous* acid....H_2SO_3

The hydrogen of any acid may be replaced with different metallic elements, giving us the large and important class of compounds called *salts*. The generic name of the salt is formed by changing the *-ic* termination of the name of the acid to *-ate*, or by similarly changing *-ous* to *-ite*. Thus, phosphor*ic* acid furnishes phosph*ates*, while phosphor*ous* acid furnishes phosph*ites*. The specific name of the salt is derived from that of the element used to replace the hydrogen of the acid. Thus we have:

Nitr*ic* acid..........HNO_3 | Potassium nitr*ate*....KNO_3
Nitr*ous* acid........HNO_2 | Potassium nitr*ite*.....KNO_2

Sulphur*ic* acid.....H_2SO_4 | Potassium sulph*ate*.K_2SO_4
Sulphur*ous* acid....H_2SO_3 | Potassium sulph*ite*..K_2SO_3

(*a*.) Some chemists prefer to modify the name of the replacing element making it an adjective, *e. g.*, potassic nitrate. In the case of English words that can not be adapted to such adjective forms, the Latin word is used; *e. g.*, plumbic nitrate for lead nitrate. In some cases old forms are still frequently used; *e. g.*, chlorate of potash for potassium chlorate, or protosulphate of iron for ferrous sulphate. In some cases, a strict adherence to systematic chemical nomenclature would lead to the use of inconvenient names, as potassium aluminum sulphate for common alum. In the so-called organic compounds this inconvenience would frequently be very marked.

61. Ampère's Law.—The corner-stone of modern chemistry, as distinguished from the chemistry of the last generation, is a proposition known as Ampère's or Avogadro's law, the evidence in support of which can not be satisfactorily presented in this place. It may be stated as follows: *Equal volumes of all substances in the gaseous condition, the temperature and pressure being the same, contain the same number of molecules.*

62. The Microcrith.—A liter of hydrogen weighs .0896 $g.$, or one crith. It has been *estimated* that a liter of hydrogen, or of any other gas, contains 10^{24} molecules. Then each molecule of hydrogen weighs $\frac{1}{10^{24}}$ criths, and each hydrogen half-molecule weighs $\frac{1}{2 \times 10^{24}}$ criths. The weight of the hydrogen half-molecule has been called a microcrith ($m.\ c.$), and the term is so convenient that we shall use it. It must be remembered that the *absolute* value of a $m.\ c.$ is, as yet, unknown, because the number 10^{24}, used above, is only an "estimate." When physicists determine accurately the number of molecules in a given volume of a gas, the chemist will know the absolute value of a $m.\ c.$ It will answer all of our present purposes to remember that *a microcrith is the weight of one atom of hydrogen, and that it is a real unit, measuring a definite quantity of matter,* for, as we shall soon see, the hydrogen half-molecule is a hydrogen atom (§ 174).

63. Molecular Weights.—The hydrogen molecule weighs 2 $m.\ c.$ Knowing that oxygen is sixteen times as heavy as hydrogen and remembering Ampère's law, it is evident that the oxygen molecule must weigh 32 $m.\ c.$ Similarly, we see that the nitrogen molecule weighs 28 $m.\ c.$, *etc.* In brief, *the molecular weight (in microcriths)* *of a substance is twice the specific gravity (hydrogen standard) of the substance in the aeriform condition.* Dry steam being nine times as heavy as hydrogen, its molecular weight is 18 *m. c.* At the same time, the molecular weight must equal the sum of the weights of the atoms in the molecule. The combining weight of a chemical compound is its molecular weight.

(*a.*) The only known method for determining the molecular weight of a compound with certainty is the determination of its vapor density. The molecular weight of a compound that is not volatile, or volatile only at a temperature so high as to prevent the determination of its vapor density, or that is not volatile without decomposition, must be considered as unknown or, at least, doubtful.

64. Atomic Weights. — The chemist is able to analyze any known compound, and to determine the exact proportion of the elements constituting it. We have already seen how he determines the molecular weights. One method of determining the atomic weights will be best understood from an example.

(*a*). Suppose the chemist wishes to determine the atomic weight of O. He begins with steam and finds, from its specific gravity, that its molecular weight is 18 *m. c.*, and, by analysis, that $\frac{8}{9}$ of this is O. He proceeds in this way with all of the gaseous or volatile compounds of O, and tabulates some of the results, as follows:

Substances.		Weight of Molecule.	Weight of O in Molecule.	
Water..................	H_2O	18 *m. c.*	16 *m. c.*	16 *m. c.* × 1.
Carbon monoxide.....	CO	28 "	16 "	"
Nitric oxide...........	NO	30 "	16 "	"
Alcohol................	C_2H_6O	46 "	16 "	"
Ether	$(C_2H_5)_2O$	74 "	16 "	"
Carbon dioxide........	CO_2	44 "	32 "	16 *m. c.* × 2.
Nitrogen peroxide.....	NO_2	46 "	32 "	"
Sulphur dioxide.......	SO_2	64 "	32 "	"
Acetic acid............	$C_2H_4O_2$	60 "	32 "	"
Sulphur trioxide......	SO_3	80 "	48 "	16 *m. c.* × 3.
Methyl borate........	$(CH_3)_3BO_3$	104 "	48 "	"
Ethyl borate..........	$(C_2H_5)_3BO_3$	146 "	48 "	"
Ethyl silicate	$(C_2H_5)_4SiO_4$	208 "	64 "	16 *m. c.* × 4.
Osmium oxide........	OsO_4	263 "	64 "	"
Etc., etc.				
Oxygen	O_2	32 "	32 "	16 *m. c.* × 2.

He notices that the smallest weight of O in any of these compounds is 16 $m.c.$, and that all the others are simple multiples of this. *He cannot believe that this is mere chance,* especially as he finds similar results in determining other atomic weights. The only explanation possible is that this 16 $m.c.$ is the weight of a definite quantity of O, and that it represents the least quantity of O that can enter into combination (§ 5). Hence, 16 $m.c.$ is the atomic weight of O, and the substances analyzed contain respectively one, two, three and four atoms of O to the molecule. Of course, the symbols in the second column of the table above can not be determined until after the determination of the atomic weights of the elements involved. The table also shows that the O molecule consists of two atoms. The combining weight of an element is its atomic weight.

65. Composition of Elementary Molecules.

—Chemists have ascertained that hydrogen, oxygen, nitrogen, chlorine, bromine, iodine, sulphur, selenium, tellurium and potassium have two atoms to the molecule; that cadmium and mercury have one, and that phosphorus and arsenic have four. Nothing is yet known concerning the composition of the other elementary molecules. When the specific gravity of the vapor of any of the other elements is *accurately determined,* the molecular weight of that element becomes a matter of knowledge (§ 63). Then, knowing both the molecular and the atomic weight, the composition of the molecule is at once removed from the region of hypothesis to that of fact.

Exercises.

1. Which will, under similar conditions, occupy the more space, 100 molecules of H or 100 molecules of N?

2. (*a.*) From what acid may we consider that sodium sulphate is formed? (*b.*) Sodium sulphite?

3. (*a.*) Write the symbol for hydrogen monoxide. (*b.*) For hydrogen dioxide.

4. What is the molecular weight of a vapor that is 23 times as heavy as H?

5. How many microcriths are there in a gram?

Chapter V.

COMPOUNDS OF HYDROGEN, OXYGEN AND NITROGEN.

Section I.

AMMONIA.

66. Occurrence.—Ammonia (NH_3) exists in small quantities in the air, whence it is brought down to the earth by rain and dew. It is formed by the putrefaction of animal and vegetable matter. The ammonia of commerce is chiefly obtained from ammoniacal salts incidentally produced in the manufacture of coal gas. Ammonia is familiar to many under the name of hartshorn.

67. Preparation.—The preparation of ammonia is sufficiently illustrated by the next three experiments.

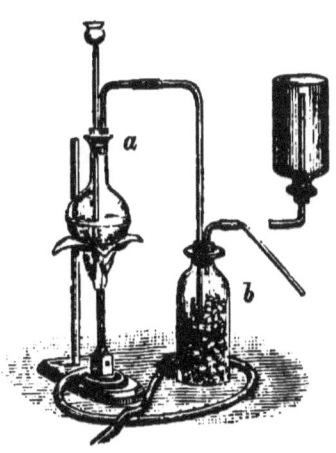

Fig. 32.

Experiment 61.—Into a half liter flask, pour about 200 *cu. cm.* of strong ammonia water (NH_4HO). Close the flask, *a*, with a cork carrying a funnel tube and a delivery tube, as shown in Fig. 32. The delivery tube should pass to the bottom of a tall drying bottle, *b*, containing about a liter of quicklime broken into small pieces. Gently heat the liquid in *a*, and NH_3 (which is a gas) will be given off. After passing through b it may be collected by upward displacement or over mercury. If collected over mercury, the funnel tube in a must have a considerable length.

Experiment 62.—In a mortar, or the palm of the hand, rub together equal weights of pulverized ammonium chloride (sal-ammoniac, NH_4Cl) and quicklime (CaO). Notice the smell before and after rubbing.

$$2NH_4Cl + CaO = CaCl_2 + H_2O + 2NH_3.$$

Experiment 63.—Mix 25 or 30 $g.$ of pulverized ammonium chloride with 50 to 60 $g.$ of freshly slaked lime ($CaO + H_2O = CaH_2O_2$), that has been allowed to cool. Place the mixture in a half liter flask and add enough H_2O to cause it to aggregate in lumps when stirred with a rod. When the mixture is gently heated, NH_3 is produced in accordance with the reaction,

$$2NH_4Cl + CaH_2O_2 = CaCl_2 + 2H_2O + 2NH_3.$$

The gas, after being dried, may be collected in bottles by upward displacement and the bottles corked. This is the most common way of preparing NH_3 in the laboratory.

FIG. 33.

Experiment 64.—Fill a liter bottle, a, with NH_3 by upward displacement. By holding at the mouth of the inverted bottle a moistened strip of turmeric paper or red litmus paper, the experimenter will be able to tell when the bottle is filled; the turmeric will turn brown or the litmus blue. Close the bottle with a cork (a rubber stopper is preferable) through which passes a small glass tube. Place the end of this tube in H_2O, colored with red litmus solution (App. 24). The H_2O will, in a moment, rush into the bottle with violence, changing from red to blue as it enters (see Exp. 106).

Experiment 65.—From the flask of Experiment 63, pass the gas through a series of Woulffe bottles, partly filled with H_2O, as shown in Fig. 34. The delivery tube of one bottle terminates under H_2O in the next. A safety tube, s, (open at both ends) passes through the cork in the middle neck of each bottle. The delivery tube of the generating flask should *not* dip into the H_2O of the first bottle. This precaution prevents the possibility of H_2O being forced back into the heated

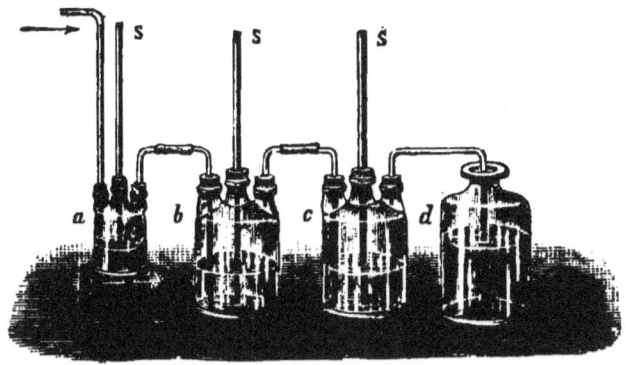

Fig. 34.

flask and breaking it. It is well to keep the Woulffe bottles in vessels containing cold H_2O, as heat is evolved in the condensation of the NH_3. At the end of the experiment, put the ammonia water just prepared into convenient bottles, cork tightly, and save for future use.

68. Physical Properties.—Ammonia is a colorless, irrespirable gas and has a pungent odor. It is much lighter than air, its specific gravity being $8\frac{1}{2}$, i. e., a liter of it weighs 8.5 criths (.7616 g.). It liquefies under a pressure of $6\frac{1}{4}$ atmospheres at 10°C., $4\frac{1}{2}$ atmospheres at 0°C., or 1 atmosphere at −40°C. The liquid solidifies at −75°C. Under ordinary conditions, the liquid rapidly evaporates, producing intense cold (Ph., § 526). It is remarkably soluble in water, one volume of which absorbs 803 volumes of the gas at 14°C., or 1148 at 0°C. This saturated solution (aqua ammonia) has a specific gravity of .85.

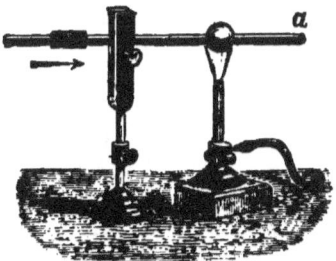

Fig. 35.

Experiment 66. — From a gas holder containing five volumes of H and two volumes of nitric oxide (NO, § 83), pass a stream of the mixed gases through a bulb tube containing platinized asbestos, as indicated in Fig. 35. The gases escaping at a will redden moistened blue litmus paper. Heat the bulb; the H and N combine, NH_3 is formed, and, as it escapes at a, turns the reddened paper blue again.

Experiment 67. — From the drying-bottle of Experiment 61, lead the delivery tube, d, through a narrow glass cylinder to its upper end, as shown in Fig. 36. As the NH_3 issues at a, try to light it; it will refuse to burn. Through the flexible tube, b, pass a current of O into the cylinder. The jet of NH_3 being now surrounded by an atmosphere of O, may be lighted; it will burn with a yellowish flame.

Experiment 68. — Pass a stream of O from the gas holder through a strong aqueous solution of NH_3 in a flask. Heat the flask and bring a flame into contact with the mixed gases as they issue from the neck of the flask. They will burn with a large yellow flame.

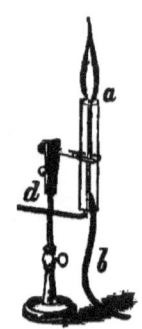

FIG. 36.

Experiment 69. — Upon a piece of broadcloth or dark colored calico, let fall a few drops of dilute sulphuric acid. The acid will produce red spots. Apply ammonia water to the spots and they will disappear. This is a familiar experiment in most laboratories.

69. Chemical Properties. — Ammonia and its aqueous solution have strong alkaline properties (§ 168), neutralizing acids and restoring vegetable colors changed by acids. The gas is combustible only when mixed with oxygen.

70. Composition. — Analysis of ammonia shows that it is composed of fourteen weights of nitrogen to three weights of hydrogen, or of one volume of nitrogen to three of hydrogen, the four volumes of the constituents being condensed to two volumes of the compound. This may be represented to the eye as follows:

$$\boxed{\begin{array}{c}H\\1\ m.c.\end{array}} + \boxed{\begin{array}{c}H\\1\ m.c.\end{array}} + \boxed{\begin{array}{c}H\\1\ m.c.\end{array}} + \boxed{\begin{array}{c}N\\14\ m.c.\end{array}} = \boxed{NH_3,\ 17\ m.c.}$$

In other words, when ammonia gas is decomposed, it doubles its volume, yielding half its volume of nitrogen, and one and a half times its volume of hydrogen.

(*a.*) Suppose 100 *cu. cm.* of NH_3 to be confined over mercury in a eudiometer. By producing electric sparks in it, the gas is decomposed and increases its volume to 200 *cu. cm.* Add, say 100 *cu. cm.* of O and produce a spark in the mixed gases. There is a shrinkage of 225 *cu. cm.*, the gases now measuring 75 *cu. cm.* The shrinkage was due, of course, to the formation of H_2O. Hence, two-thirds of the 225 *cu. cm.*, or 150 *cu. cm.*, was H, and the other 75 *cu. cm.* was O. But, as we introduced 100 *cu. cm.* of O, and only 75 *cu. cm.* of it has combined, the other 25 *cu. cm.* must be in the eudiometer as part of the residual 75 *cu. cm.* Consequently, we have left 50 *cu. cm.* of N, and 25 *cu. cm.* of O. The 50 *cu. cm.* of N and the 150 *cu. cm.* of H came from the 100 *cu. cm.* of NH_3.

71. Uses. — Ammonia water is largely used in the laboratory and as a detergent. It is also largely used in the preparation of sodium carbonate, in the production of aniline colors and in the manufacture of indigo. Liquid ammonia is used in the freezing of artificial ice.

Experiment 70.—Prepare 100 *cu. cm.* of the "Nessler re-agent," as follows: into 80 *cu. cm.* of H_2O put 3.5 *g.* of potassium iodide, and 1.3 *g.* of mercuric chloride (corrosive sublimate, $HgCl_2$, *a deadly poison*). Heat to the boiling point and stir until the solids are dissolved. Add a saturated solution of $HgCl_2$ in H_2O, drop by drop, until the color of the red mercuric iodide is just perceptibly permanent. Then add 16 *g.* of potassium hydrate (caustic potash), or 12 *g.* of sodium hydrate (caustic soda), and add H_2O until the solution measures 100 *cu. cm.* The reagent should be of a slightly yellowish tint. If it be colorless, add a little more of the $HgCl_2$ solution, until the permanent tint is just perceptible. Place the liquid in a well-stoppered bottle.

Drop about 2 *cu. cm.* of the Nessler reagent into 50 *cu. cm.* of a very weak solution of NH_3 and stir the mixture, which will be changed to a brown color; the more NH_3 in the solution, the deeper the brown. Save the rest of the reagent in carefully stoppered bottles.

AMMONIA.

72. Tests.—The tests for ammonia are its pungent odor, its turning moistened red litmus paper blue, the fumes of ammonium chloride it produces with hydrochloric acid (Exp. 6), and the test with the Nessler reagent. The ammonia of ammoniacal compounds may be generally set free by heating the compound with potassium hydrate and then detected by the above means. Ammonia tests play an important part in the analysis of potable waters—the development of ammonia indicating contamination by organic matter.

EXERCISES.

1. (*a.*) What weight of H is contained in $17\,g.$ of NH_3? (*b.*) What volume of H?

2. (*a.*) What volume of H can be produced by the decomposition of $2\,l.$ of NH_3? (*b.*) What weight of H?

3. (*a.*) What weight of H can be united with $28\,g.$ of N to form ammonia? (*b.*) What volume of H?

4. (*a.*) What weight of N can be united with $9\,g.$ of H to form NH_3? (*b.*) What will be the weight of the product?

5. (*a.*) If $100\,cu.\,cm.$ of NH_3 be decomposed in a eudiometer, $100\,cu.\,cm.$ of O added, and an electric spark passed through the mixed gases, what gases will remain? (*b.*) What will be the volume of each?

6. Why were the safety tubes used in Exp. 65?

Section II.

NITRIC ACID.

73. Sources. — The chief sources of nitric acid, (*aqua fortis*, HNO_3,) are potassium nitrate (saltpetre or nitre,) which is obtained in abundance in India, and sodium nitrate (Chili saltpetre or soda nitre), which is found as an efflorescence on the soil of a sterile region in Chili and Peru, and exported in large quantities from those countries.

74. Preparation. — Nitric acid is always prepared from a nitrate by distillation with sulphuric acid (H_2SO_4).

(*a.*) Into a quarter liter retort, *a*, having a glass stopper, put 50 *g.* of pulverized potassium nitrate (KNO_3,) or 40 *g.* of pulverized sodium nitrate ($NaNO_3$,) and 35 *cu. cm.* of strong H_2SO_4. The materials should be introduced through the tubulure, *s*, and care taken that none falls into the neck of the retort. It is well to use a paper funnel for the nitrate and a funnel tube for the acid. Replace the stopper and place the retort upon sand in a shallow sheet iron or pressed tin pan, supported by a ring of the retort stand over the lamp, or upon wire gauze, as shown in the figure. The use of the "sand bath" or gauze lessens the danger of breaking the retort. Place the neck of the retort loosely in the mouth of a Florence flask, *r*, or other convenient receiver, kept cool by H_2O. It is well to cover the receiver with cloth or bibulous paper; the H_2O may be brought by a rubber tube siphon (Ph., § 298) from a pail of H_2O sufficiently elevated.

Fig. 37.

As the retort is heated, the nitrate

liquefies, reddish fumes appear, and HNO_3 condenses in the neck of the retort and in the receiver. The fumes in the retort will soon disappear; continue the distillation until they reappear.

$$KNO_3 + H_2SO_4 = HKSO_4 + HNO_3.$$

Transfer the HNO_3 to a glass stoppered bottle and save it for future use. After the retort has become thoroughly cool, the solid residue, acid potassium sulphate, should be dissolved by heating with H_2O, and then removed.

(*b.*) In the arts, the retort is made of cast iron and the distillate is condensed in earthenware receivers. A higher temperature and frequently only half as much H_2SO_4 are used.

$$2KNO_3 + H_2SO_4 = K_2SO_4 + 2HNO_3,$$
$$2NaNO_3 + H_2SO_4 = Na_2SO_4 + 2HNO_3.$$

75. Physical Properties.—Nitric acid is a fuming liquid, colorless when pure, but generally slightly tinted with the fumes seen in the retort during its preparation. It has a specific gravity of 1.52, freezes at -55°C., and boils with partial decomposition at 86°C. It may be mixed with water in all proportions, the aqua fortis of commerce containing from 40 to 60 *per cent.* of nitric acid.

Experiment 71.—Pulverize a few grams of charcoal and heat it. Upon the heated charcoal, pour a little strong HNO_3. The charcoal is rapidly oxidized to combustion.

Experiment 72.—From the end of a meter stick, drop a thin slice of phosphorus into strong HNO_3. The phosphorus is oxydized to violent combustion.

Experiment 73.—Into dilute HNO_3, dip a skein of white sewing silk. In a few minutes, remove and wash it thoroughly with H_2O. The silk will be permanently colored yellow.

Experiment 74.—Put a sheet of "Dutch leaf," which may be obtained of a sign painter, into a test tube and pour upon it a small quantity of HNO_3. The metal is instantly dissolved.

76. Chemical Properties.—Nitric acid is a powerful oxidizing agent, and one of the most corrosive known substances. It colors nitrogenous animal substances (*e. g.*, silk, skin and parchment) yellow, and converts many non-nitrogenous substances (*e. g.*, cotton and glycerine) into violently explosive compounds. It dissolves all of the common metals except gold and platinum, forming nitrates.

Experiment 75.—Cover a smooth piece of brass or copper with a film of beeswax. With a sharp instrument, write your name upon the metal, being sure to cut through the wax. Cover the writing with strong HNO_3, In a few moments, the name will appear in a tracery of minute bubbles. A few moments later, wash the acid away with H_2O and remove the wax. The autograph will be etched upon the metal.

77. Uses.—Nitric acid is largely used in the laboratory and in the arts, in the manufacture of gun cotton, nitroglycerin, *etc.*, and in the preparation of aqua regia (§ 114). Engravers use it for etching on copper and steel.

Experiment 76.—Into a test tube, put a few bits of copper and cover them with HNO_3. The red fumes of nitric oxide appear, and the liquid is colored blue by the copper nitrate formed.

Experiment 77.—Into a test tube, put a few *cu. cm.* of a dilute solution of indigo. Add HNO_3 until the blue solution is bleached.

78. Tests.—In testing for nitric acid, first try blue litmus paper. If this test paper be not reddened when dipped into the liquid in question, the liquid is not an acid. If it be reddened, the liquid is *some* acid. As the nitrates are all easily soluble, tests for nitric acid yield no precipitates. Free nitric acid may be detected by its bleaching an indigo solution, or by its forming red fumes when added to copper bits or filings. Nitrates show the same effects when heated with sulphuric acid, because of the nitric acid thus set free. The nitrates also deflagrate when thrown upon burning charcoal.

Section III.

NITROGEN OXIDES.

Experiment 78.—In a small evaporating dish (App. 21), place a few cu. cm. of HNO_3 and add an equal bulk of H_2O. In another vessel, place a small quantity of NH_4HO similarly diluted. Into the first liquid, dip a strip of blue litmus paper. The change of color shows an acid. Dip this litmus paper (now red) into the other liquid. The restoration of the blue color shows the presence of an alkali. To the first liquid, add the second, in small quantities at first, and finally drop by drop. Stir the mixture continually with a glass rod, and test with blue litmus paper after each addition of NH_4HO. At last, it will be found that the mixture will neither redden blue litmus paper nor restore red litmus paper to its original blue. It has neither an acid nor an alkaline reaction. The acid has been "neutralized" by the alkali, and we have a solution of a *neutral salt*. Without boiling the liquid, evaporate it until, when the glass rod is removed, the adhering liquid becomes almost solid upon cooling. Crystals will now form upon the cooling of the liquid; these crystals are to be carefully drained and dried. They are ammonium nitrate (NH_4NO_3).

79. Nitrogen Monoxide. — Nitrogen monoxide (nitrogen protoxide, nitrous oxide, laughing gas, N_2O,) is prepared by decomposing ammonium nitrate by heat.

(*a.*) Into a small Florence flask, *f,* place a tablespoonful of NH_4NO_3. Heat gently and carefully over the sand bath or a piece of wire gauze, and collect the gas over warm H_2O.

$$NH_4NO_3 = N_2O + 2H_2O.$$

To show that H_2O is produced, interpose, between the Florence flask and the water pan, a condensing bottle placed in ice water, as shown at *c*, in Fig. 38. Test the liquid that collects in this bottle by dropping a small piece of potassium into it. The

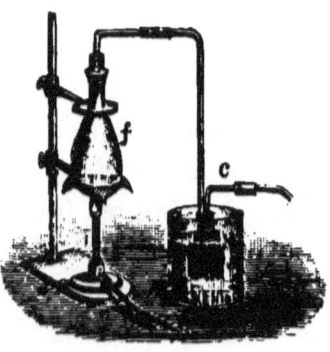

FIG. 38.

flask would break before *all* of the NH_4NO_3 was decomposed, but by heating a small quantity of the nitrate upon platinum foil, it will be seen that no residue is left.

Experiment 79.—Repeat Exps. 33, 36, and 37, using N_2O instead of O. (These are simply combustions in O, the N_2O being decomposed into its elements.)

80. Properties.—Nitrogen monoxide is a colorless, sweet tasting gas, and a good supporter of combustion. One liter of it weighs 22 criths. It may be liquefied and solidified by cold and pressure. When the liquid is mixed with carbon disulphide and evaporated in a vacuum, it produces the remarkably low temperature of —140° C. (Ph., § 526). It is largely soluble in alcohol or water, but less so in warm water. When pure and mixed with one-fourth its volume of oxygen, it may be safely inhaled, producing the effects that have secured for it the name of *laughing gas*. If its inhalation is continued, it acts as an anæsthetic.

81. Composition.— The composition of nitrogen monoxide is strictly analogous to that of steam (Exp. 53), two volumes of nitrogen uniting with one of oxygen to form two of this compound.

| N. 14 m.c. | + | N 14 m.c. | + | O 16 m.c. | = | N_2O 44 m.c. |

When decomposed by electric sparks, it yields 1½ times its own volume of mixed gases, as represented by the typical squares above.

82. Hyponitrous Acid.—This acid (HNO) has not yet been prepared, but the corresponding salt, potassium hyponitrite (KNO), is known. We may *imagine* this reaction : $N_2O + H_2O = 2HNO$.

83. Nitric Oxide.—Nitric oxide (nitrosyl, NO,) is prepared by the action of dilute nitric acid upon copper clippings, turnings or filings. The gas may be collected over water. The apparatus is arranged as shown in Fig. 6. The generating bottle is, at first, filled with red fumes (§ 87) but the gas collected over water is colorless. Save the blue solution of copper nitrate [$Cu(NO_3)_2$].

$$3Cu + 8HNO_3 = 2NO + 3Cu(NO_3)_2 + 4H_2O.$$

Experiment 80.—Into a bottle of NO, lower a burning splinter, a burning candle, or sulphur burning in a deflagrating spoon (App. 19). It will not burn in the gas.

Experiment 81.—Into a bottle of NO, lower a deflagrating spoon containing a bit of vigorously burning phosphorus, the size of a pea. It will continue to burn with great brilliancy.

Experiment 82.—In a jar of NO, place a few drops of carbon disulphide. Close the bottle for a few minutes to allow the liquid to evaporate and its vapor to mix with the NO. In a dark room, bring a lighted taper to the open mouth of the jar, as shown in Fig. 39. The mixture burns with a vivid light rich in actinic rays (Ph., § 651).

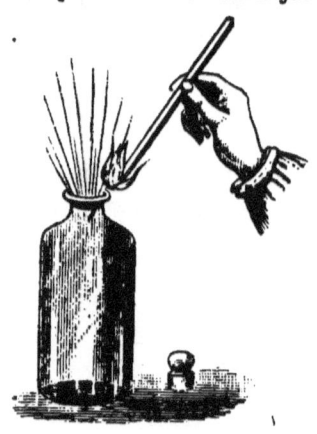

FIG. 39.

Experiment 83.—Into a jar of NO, standing in the water pan, pass a stream of O from the gas holder. After the red fumes, that are promptly formed have been dissolved by the H_2O, repeat the experiment several times, noticing the phenomena carefully.

Experiment 84.—Fill a large bell glass with NO at the water bath. Cover the mouth under H_2O with a glass plate, invert the bell glass and remove the plate (Fig. 40). The NO absorbs O from the air and forms a cloud of the now familiar red fumes (Exp. 45).

84. Properties.—The leading property of nitric oxide is its strong attraction for oxygen. Its relation to combustion is peculiar. Ordinary combustibles will not burn in it at all; phosphorus may be melted in the gas without kindling, but when once well aflame it burns with great energy. The gas is colorless and slightly soluble in water. One liter of it weighs 15 criths.

85. Composition. — This is the first compound that we have studied, the gaseous constituents of which unite without condensation. One volume of oxygen unites with one volume of nitrogen to form two volumes of nitric oxide.

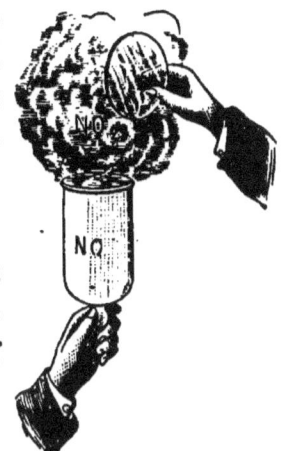

Fig. 40.

N		O		NO
14 m.c.	+	16 m.c.	=	30 m. c.

86. Nitrogen Trioxide. — This gas (nitrous anhydride, N_2O_3,) is an obscure compound that unites with water to form nitrous acid (HNO_2).

$$N_2O_3 + H_2O = 2HNO_2.$$

87. Nitrogen Peroxide. — Nitrogen peroxide (nitryl, NO_2,) is the brownish red gas with which we have so frequently met in our experiments with nitric acid and the nitrogen oxides. It is best prepared by bringing together two volumes of nitric oxide and one volume of oxygen, both constituents being perfectly dry. It is an energetic oxidizing agent (§ 152, d). It may be liquefied and solidified. In the presence of water it forms acid compounds, probably a mixture of nitric and nitrous acids.

Experiment 85. — Pass 250 cu. cm. of O into a bottle filled with H_2O, colored with blue litmus. Then pass in 250 cu. cm. of NO.

Red fumes of NO_2 are produced but soon absorbed by the H_2O. Pass in another 250 *cu. cm.* of NO. If the O and NO are pure, the O will be wholly used to form NO_2, all of which will be absorbed by the H_2O. The acids thus produced turn the colored water from blue to red.

Fig. 41.

88. Composition.— The composition of nitrogen peroxide, by volume and by weight, may be represented as follows:

$$\boxed{\begin{array}{c}N\\14\ m.c.\end{array}} + \boxed{\begin{array}{c}O\\16\ m.c.\end{array}} + \boxed{\begin{array}{c}O\\16\ m.c.\end{array}} = \boxed{\begin{array}{c}NO_2\\46\ m.c.\end{array}}$$

89. Nitrogen Pentoxide. — Nitrogen pentoxide (nitric anhydride, N_2O_5) is a crystalline white compound, so unstable that it spontaneously decomposes in a sealed tube into oxygen and nitrogen peroxide. It is particularly interesting on account of its relation to nitric acid.

$$N_2O_5 + H_2O = 2HNO_3.$$

90. Law of Definite Proportions.—The truth stated in § 12 has been verified by numberless analyses and may be formulated as follows: *Any given chemical compound always contains the same elements in the same proportions.*

91. Law of Multiple Proportions. — *If two substances combine to form more than one compound, the weight of one substance being considered as constant, the weights of the other vary according to a simple ratio.*

§ 91   NITROGEN OXIDES.   73

(*a.*) This important principle is best illustrated by the nitrogen oxides just studied.

NAMES.	SYMBOLS.	BY GRAVIMETRIC ANALYSIS.				BY VOLUMETRIC ANALYSIS.			
		ACTUAL		RATIO		ACTUAL		RATIO	
		Weight of N.	Weight of O.	Weight of N.	Weight of O.	Volumes of N.	Volumes of O.	Volumes of N.	Volumes of O.
Nitrogen monoxide	N_2O	28	16	$1\frac{3}{4}$	1	2	1	2	1
Nitric oxide.......	NO	14	16	$1\frac{3}{4}$	2	1	1	2	2
Nitrogen trioxide..	N_2O_3	28	48	$1\frac{3}{4}$	3	2	3	2	3
Nitrogen peroxide.	NO_2	14	32	$1\frac{3}{4}$	4	1	2	2	4
Nitrogen pentoxide	N_2O_5	28	80	$1\frac{3}{4}$	5	2	5	2	5

Attention is called to the consecutive numbers, 1, 2, 3, 4, and 5, in the columns headed "Ratio."

(*b.*) This law necessarily results from the definition of an atom (§ 5). Since the atoms can not be divided, the elements can combine only atom by atom and, consequently, either in the ratio of their atomic weights or some simple multiple of that ratio.

EXERCISES.

1. Is the air a mixture or a compound? Why?
2. State the points of resemblance and difference between O and N.
3. (*a.*) Is the process of preparing O analytic or synthetic? (*b.*) Of preparing NO_2? (*c.*) N_2O?
4. How could you prove the presence of O in air?
5. If two liters of N and one of O be combined, what will be the name and volume of the product?
6. (*a.*) How is ammonia water prepared? (*b.*) How is liquid ammonia prepared? (*c.*) What will result from the decomposition of a liter of laughing gas into its constituent elements? (*d.*) Write the reaction for the preparation of NH_3.
7. When N_2O is mixed with H and the mixture exploded, N and a compound vapor are formed. Write the reaction.

CHAPTER VI.

QUANTIVALENCE, RATIONAL SYMBOLS, RADICALS.

92. Quantivalence.—In hydrochloric acid (HCl), one atom of chlorine unites with one of hydrogen. In water, one atom of oxygen unites with two of hydrogen. In ammonia, one atom of nitrogen unites with three of hydrogen. In marsh gas (CH_4), one atom of carbon unites with four of hydrogen. One atom of potassium may replace one atom of hydrogen in nitric acid (HNO_3) yielding potassium nitrate (KNO_3), while one atom of copper replaces two atoms of hydrogen in sulphuric acid (H_2SO_4) forming copper sulphate ($CuSO_4$). One atom of potassium can replace one atom of hydrogen, but no more; one atom of copper can replace two atoms of hydrogen, but no less. *The quantivalence of an atom or group of atoms (§ 97) expresses the number of hydrogen atoms with which it can combine or for which it may be exchanged;* e. g., the quantivalence of potassium is one, that of oxygen is two.

(*a.*) Atoms are classified according to their quantivalence as monads, dyads, triads, tetrads, pentads, hexads and heptads, from the Greek numerals. They are similarly described by the adjectives univalent, bivalent, trivalent, quadrivalent, quinquivalent, sexivalent, and septivalent, from the Latin numerals. Thus, oxygen is a dyad, or it is bivalent; carbon is a tetrad, or it is quadrivalent.

(*b.*) The quantivalence of an element may be *absolute* or *apparent*. Absolute (or true) quantivalence is conceived to be a property of atoms, invariable for any one atom under like conditions. It is a power that may or may not be exerted to its full extent. With our present limited knowledge, it is impossible to determine the absolute quantivalence of an element with certainty. Apparent quantivalence is the combining power that an atom exhibits in any given compound. It may or may not be the same as its absolute quantivalence. The quantivalence of N *apparent* in NH_3 is three; *i. e.*, N there appears to be a triad. Its quantivalence apparent in NH_4Cl is five; it there appears as a pentad. When atoms of the same element act with different quantivalences, they frequently form compounds as dissimilar as atoms of different kinds would do. A change in the apparent quantivalence of an atom implies a change in all of its chemical relations. N_2O is as different from N_2O_5 as H_2O is.

(*c.*) The quantivalence of an atom is indicated by Roman numerals placed above, or minute marks placed above and at the right of the symbol, as $\overset{IV}{C}$ or N'''. They should not be confounded with the figures below and at the right of the symbol.

(*d.*) Sometimes the words "valence," "equivalence" and "atomicity" are used in the sense in which we have used the word quantivalence. The word "atomicity" more properly refers to the number of atoms in a molecule.

(*e.*) The quantivalence of many common elements is not yet satisfactorily determined. Quantivalence should not be confounded with chemism or affinity. H and Cl have a very great affinity for each other, but each is univalent.

93. Graphic Symbols of Atoms.—The graphic symbol of an atom represents its quantivalence by lines or *bonds* radiating from the symbol, as follows:

Monad,	*Dyad*,	*Triad*,	*Tetrad*,	*Pentad*,	*Hexad*.
H—	O=	N≡	C≣	=P≡	≡S≡

The *number* of bonds is significant; their *direction* is not. Thus, the graphic symbol of an atom of oxygen may be written –O–, O=, Ȯ–, –Ǫ, O<, *etc., etc.*

94. Empirical and Rational Symbols.—
Molecular symbols are of two classes, empirical and rational. An empirical symbol is based upon analysis, expresses the

kind and number of atoms in a molecule, and represents all that we *know* about the constitution of the molecule. H_2O, HNO_3, *etc.*, are empirical symbols. A rational symbol attempts to represent, in addition to this, the possible modes of formation and decomposition of substances and are sometimes necessary to enable us to distinguish between substances having the same empirical symbol but endowed with different properties (§ 216). Graphic and typical symbols are included under this head.

95. Graphic Symbols. — A constitutional or graphic symbol is one that indicates the constitution of a molecule; not, indeed, by showing the arrangement of the atoms in space, for we know nothing at all about that, but by showing which atoms are united with each other in the molecule. It is composed of the graphic symbols of the constituent atoms:

(*a.*) The graphic symbol of H_2O may be written H–O–H; that of H_3N, H–N(H)–H; that of CO_2, O=C=O; that of HNO_3, H–O–N(=O)=O and that of $\overset{vi}{S}O_3$, O=S(=O)=O. It will be noticed that each atom has the number of bonds that represents its quantivalence.

96. Typical Symbols. — Chemical symbols are sometimes written in accordance with one of several types, *e. g.*, free hydrogen or hydrochloric acid, water, ammonia and marsh gas.

The underlying idea is that the chemical constitution of all known substances is modelled upon a limited number of types. By replacing atomic symbols in the type by others of the same quantivalence, we can obtain the symbol for any other member of the class.

(a.) Examples of typical symbols are given below:

Free Hydrogen.
$\left.\begin{array}{l}H\\H\end{array}\right\}$

Water.
$\left.\begin{array}{l}H\\H\end{array}\right\}O$

Ammonia.
$\left.\begin{array}{l}H\\H\\H\end{array}\right\}N$

Marsh Gas.
$\left.\begin{array}{l}H\\H\\H\\H\end{array}\right\}C.$

Hydrochloric Acid.
$\left.\begin{array}{l}H\\Cl\end{array}\right\}$

Sodium Hydrate.
$\left.\begin{array}{l}Na\\H\end{array}\right\}O$

Methyl-amine.
$\left.\begin{array}{l}(CH_3)'\\H\\H\end{array}\right\}N$

Methyl Silicide.
$\left.\begin{array}{l}CH_3\\CH_3\\CH_3\\CH_3\end{array}\right\}Si.$

Methyl Hydride.
$\left.\begin{array}{l}CH_3\\H\end{array}\right\}$

Sulphuric Acid.
$\left.\begin{array}{l}(SO_2)''\\H_2\end{array}\right\}O_2$

Trimethyl-amine.
$\left.\begin{array}{l}CH_3\\CH_3\\CH_3\end{array}\right\}N$

Lead Methyl.
$\left.\begin{array}{l}CH_3\\CH_3\\CH_3\\CH_3\end{array}\right\}Pb.$

(b.) These typical symbols are not to be considered as suggesting similar properties in the substances referred to any one type. They simply suggest similarity in the supposed grouping of the atoms in the molecule.

(c.) It will be noticed, from the examples above, that a compound radical (§ 97) may take its proper place in a typical symbol, replacing an atom or more of H according to its quantivalence and that a substance (e. g., H_2SO_4) may be represented as built upon the type of the double molecule of the typical compound. A triple molecule may be thus used, e. g., glycerin = $\left.\begin{array}{l}(C_3H_5)'''\\H_3\end{array}\right\}O_3$.

(d.) Typical symbols are of great assistance in classification, especially in the case of the carbon compounds.

97. Simple and Compound Radicals.

— An atom or group of atoms that seems to determine the character of a molecule is called a radical. Such an atom is called a simple radical; such a group of atoms is called a compound radical. In the graphic symbols given above, it will be noticed that, in each case but one (SO_2), every atom has its quantivalence fully satisfied; *i. e.*, each bond of each atom is engaged. Such atomic groups are said to be saturated. But the group, $O{=}\underset{\|}{S}{=}O$, has two free bonds.

Such an unsaturated group of atoms is called a compound radical. It may enter into combination like a simple atom, always acting with a quantivalence equal to the number of unsatisfied bonds.

(*a.*) The names of compound radicals generally terminate in *-yl*, as nitrosyl (NO) and nitryl (NO_2). Two of these atomic groups may unite, like two atoms, to form a saturated molecule. If, from H–O–H, we remove one atom of H, we have the compound radical H–O–, called hydroxyl. Two of these univalent groups may unite to form H_2O_2 (§ 44), as follows: (HO)–(HO) or H–O–O–H.

Exercises.

1. Considering Cl to be a monad, write the graphic symbols for Cl_2O, Cl_2O_3, HClO and $HClO_3$.

2. What quantivalence for Cl is indicated by the symbol—
$$H-O-Cl \underset{\|}{=} O\ ?$$
$$O$$

3. Write three graphic symbols for SO_2, two of which shall represent it as a compound radical (sulphuryl) and all of which shall represent S as a dyad.

4. Write two graphic symbols for SO_3, one of them representing S as a dyad, the other representing S as a hexad.

5. Name the substances, symbolized as follows, indicating the symbols for compound radicals:

$$N\underset{O}{\overset{=}{=}}N\ ;\quad -N=O\ ;\quad -O-N=O\ ;\quad \begin{array}{c}O=N\\O=N\end{array}\!\!\!\!\!>O\ ;$$

$$NO_2-N\!\!<\!\!\begin{array}{c}O\\O\end{array};\quad H-O-N\!\!<\!\!\begin{array}{c}O\\O\end{array};\quad \begin{array}{c}O\\\|\\H-O-N=O\end{array}$$

State the difference between the indications given by the last two symbols.

CHAPTER VII.

THE HALOGEN GROUP.

SECTION I.

CHLORINE.

☞ *Symbol*, Cl ; *specific gravity, 35.5 ; atomic weight, 35.5 m. c. ; molecular weight, 71 m. c. ; quantivalence, 1, (3, 5, or 7).*

98. Occurrence.—Chlorine does not occur free in nature, but it is very abundant and widely diffused, being a constituent of common salt (sodium chloride, NaCl), and of potassium chloride (KCl). Every liter of sea-water may be made to yield about five times its volume of chlorine.

Note.—The name comes from the Greek *chloros*, meaning green. The elementary character of chlorine is seriously questioned, but the gas has not yet been shown to be compound.

99. Preparation.—Chlorine is generally prepared, directly or indirectly, from common salt (NaCl).

(*a.*) Melt a small quantity of NaCl in a Hessian crucible over a coal fire, and pour the fused salt upon a stone slab or brick floor. When the NaCl is cool, put about 30 g. of it into a liter Florence flask, add 30 g. of manganese dioxide (MnO_2) and 35 $cu. cm.$ of strong sulphuric acid (H_2SO_4), previously diluted with an equal bulk of H_2O. The stopper of the flask should have a delivery tube passing to the bottom of a tall, dry, glass cylinder. It is well to provide a safety tube (App. 12) for the flask. Shake the flask to mix the materials, place it upon a sand bath and heat *gently*. Cl is evolved and is collected in the cylinder by downward displacement. When the cylinder is full, close the mouth with a greased glass plate. The yellowish green color of the gas enables the experimenter to see when the cylinder is full. Be careful not to inhale the gas. Perform all experiments with Cl in a draught of air or in a ventilating closet (App. 23) if you have one.

$$2NaCl + MnO_2 + 3H_2SO_4 = MnSO_4 + 2H\bar{N}aSO_4 + 2H_2O + Cl_2.$$

(b.) Another way of preparing Cl is to use 12 g. of MnO_2 and 25 cu. cm. of hydrochloric (muriatic) acid instead of the NaCl, MnO_2 and H_2SO_4. The gas may be collected, although with loss, over hot water or strong brine.

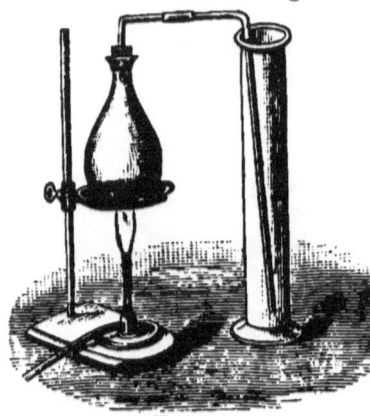

FIG. 42.

$$4HCl + MnO_2 = MnCl_2 + 2H_2O + Cl_2.$$

(c.) The easiest way of preparing Cl is to put a small bottle of chloride of lime, bleaching powder ($CaOCl_2$), say 15 or 20 g., into the bottom of a glass vessel of several liters capacity, and then, by means of a funnel tube passing through the pasteboard cover of the large jar, to pour dilute H_2SO_4 upon the $CaOCl_2$.

Experiment 86.—Prepare some chlorine water by passing a current of Cl through H_2O, in a series of Woulffe bottles, arranged as in Exp. 65, except that the tubes should not dip so far under the surface of the H_2O. The solution formed is heavier than H_2O. The chlorine water may be preserved for a considerable time by placing it in bottles wrapped in opaque paper and closed with greased stoppers. If we wish to absorb the whole of a small quantity of Cl, we may pass it into an inverted retort filled with H_2O, as shown in Fig. 43.

FIG. 43.

§ 100   CHLORINE.   81

Experiment 87.—Into a jar filled with Cl, pour H_2O until the jar is a third full of the liquid. Close the mouth of the bottle with the hand and shake the bottle. The gas will be absorbed, a vacuum formed and the bottle held against the hand by atmospheric pressure (Fig. 44).

FIG. 44.

100. Physical Properties.—

Chlorine is a yellowish green, irrespirable gas with a suffocating odor and astringent taste. Even a very small quantity of it in the air produces violent coughing and irritation of the air passages, when it is inhaled. Any attempt to breathe it undiluted would doubtless prove fatal. It is about $2\frac{1}{2}$ times as heavy as air, one liter weighing 35.5 criths. It may be liquefied by pressure or cold. It is largely soluble in water, one volume of which, at 10°C., dissolves $2\frac{1}{2}$ volumes of the gas. The solution has most of the properties of the gas, and, when saturated, gives off the gas freely on exposure to the air.

Experiment 88.—Fill a tall bottle or cylinder holding 500 *cu. cm.* or more with Cl. The gas may well be dried by passing it over calcium chloride, as in Exp. 28, or by passing it over fragments of pumice saturated with sulphuric acid (H_2SO_4), as in Exp. 31, or by allowing the gas to bubble through H_2SO_4. Slowly sift freshly prepared filings of metallic antimony into the bottle. The two elements will combine with the evolution of heat and light. Filings of metallic arsenic or bismuth give similar effects.

Experiment 89.—Place a thin slice of dry phosphorus in a deflagrating spoon and place it in a jar of Cl. The gas and the solid combine directly with a pale flame.

Experiment 90.—Burn a jet of H, or illuminating gas, in an atmosphere of Cl, as represented in Fig. 45. Reverse the conditions and burn a jet of Cl in H (see Fig. 27). Try to burn a jet of Cl in O, and a jet of O in Cl.

FIG. 45.

Experiment 91.—Pour chlorine water into a solution of hydrogen sulphide (H_2S, § 137). The Cl robs the H_2S of its H to form HCl, while the S is precipitated.

FIG. 46.

Experiment 92.—In a darkened room, mix equal volumes of H and Cl, previously prepared in the light. With the mixture, fill three stout soda bottles. Wrap one of the bottles with a towel, remove the cork and apply a flame to the mouth of the bottle. The mixed gases combine with an explosion. The towel will protect the experimenter if the explosion break the bottle. Wrap the second bottle with a towel to which a string, two or three meters long, has been attached. Carry the covered bottle into a sunny place and, by means of the string, re-

§ 100   CHLORINE.   83

move the towel. The sun's direct rays cause the mixed gases to explode.

This experiment succeeds best with a thin glass bulb filled with a gaseous mixture obtained by the electrolysis of hydrochloric acid. On exposing one of these bulbs to bright day light, or to the electric

FIG. 47.

or magnesium (Fig. 47) light, a sharp explosion occurs, produced by the synthesis of the gases prepared by electrolytic analysis.

Place the third bottle in *diffused* sun light. The two gases will unite gradually and quietly. Allow the bottle to remain for future use.

Experiment 93.—Fill five wide mouthed bottles with dry Cl and close their mouths with greased glass plates. Heat some oil of turpentine ($C_{10}H_{16}$) over the water bath (App. 10). Fasten a tuft of shredded tissue paper or of cotton to a wire or splinter, dip it into the hot turpentine, and *quickly* plunge it into the first bottle of Cl. The paper or cotton will generally take fire and burn with a very dense smoke (Fig. 48). Into the second bottle, thrust a burning dry wood splinter; into the third,

FIG. 48.

FIG. 49.

thrust a burning piece of paper; into the fourth, a burning wax or tallow taper (Fig. 49); into the fifth, a deflagrating spoon containing burning petroleum. Note the effect in each case.

Note.—The combustibles used in the last experiment contain H and carbon (C). This H combines with the Cl and sets the C free, as smoke.

Experiment 94.—Fill a tall tube with Cl and invert it over a cup of H_2O. Place the tube in a sunny place. After a few days, test the gaseous contents of the tube for O, and the water for an acid. Seek for the odor of Cl.

Note.—If two volumes of olefiant gas (C_2H_4) be mixed with four volumes of Cl, the C will be set free, as dense smoke; $C_2H_4 + 2Cl_2 = 4HCl + C_2$. If the air be exhausted from a flask containing a few leaves of "Dutch metal" (very thin copper) and Cl admitted into the vacuum, the copper leaf will burn, forming yellow fumes of copper chloride. If sodium be melted in a spoon and placed in a jar of *moist* Cl, the synthesis will yield common salt: $Na + Cl = NaCl$. Potassium is similarly attacked by either moist or dry Cl.

101. Chemical Properties. — Chlorine is a very energetic chemical agent. It unites directly with all of the elements except oxygen, nitrogen and carbon, its attraction for hydrogen being very remarkable. It is even able to decompose water, combining with the hydrogen and liberating the oxygen.

Experiment 95.—Pass a current of *dry* Cl through a bulb or U-tube containing a bit of dry calico print. After a few moments, attach a second tube containing a bit of similar calico that has been moistened. Notice that the Cl now passes the dry calico without bleaching it, but that it quickly bleaches the moist calico with which it subsequently comes into contact.

Note.—Pink or blue paper cambric is desirable for the above experiment.

Experiment 96.—Nearly fill seven test tubes with chlorine water. Into the first, pour a few drops of indigo solution; into the second, litmus solution; into the third, cochineal solution; into the fourth and fifth, aniline dyes of different colors; into the sixth, the colored petal of a flower, and into the seventh put a strip of colored calico or paper cambric. The colors will quickly disappear.

Experiment 97.—Upon a piece of printed paper, write your name in ink, Dip the paper into chlorine water. The written characters will be bleached out; the printed characters will remain.

Experiment 98.—Repeat Exp. 91, noticing the odor of H_2S before the addition of the chlorine water and its absence after such addition.

102. Uses.—Chlorine is of great use in the arts as a bleaching and disinfecting agent, its action depending very largely upon its attraction for hydrogen. The non-mineral coloring matters are largely composed of oxygen, hydrogen, nitrogen and carbon. When such coloring matter is brought into contact with chlorine in the presence of moisture, the chlorine attacks the hydrogen of both, the nascent oxygen thus liberated from the water greatly aiding the chlorine in the decomposition of the coloring substance. Colorless compounds are formed by a process of chlorination and oxidation. Chlorine has little effect upon mineral or carbon colors.

Experiment 99.—Prepare a quantity of thin starch paste by boiling 20 *cu. cm.* of H_2O and stirring into it 0.5 *g.* of starch previously reduced to the consistency of cream by thoroughly mixing with a few drops of H_2O. In this paste, dissolve a piece of potassium iodide, half the size of a pea. Into a test tube, put 10 *cu. cm.* of H_2O and 5 or 6 drops of this mixture of starch and potassium iodide. Shake the tube vigorously for a few seconds and let a few drops of chlorine water fall into it. Notice the blue color thus formed.

Experiment 100.—Into the solution of starch and potassium iodide, dip two or three strips of white paper. Hold one of these strips of *test* paper in a current of Cl. The white paper is turned to blue. Remove the stopper from the bottle containing chloride of lime (bleaching powder) and hold another strip of the test paper in the atmosphere of Cl that fills the upper part of the bottle. The paper is instantly colored blue.

Note.—The Cl decomposes the potassium iodide; the free iodine colors the starch (see Exp. 121).

Experiment 101.—Place a strip of gold leaf in saturated chlorine water. The gold will be dissolved.

Experiment 102. — Dissolve a few crystals of silver nitrate ($AgNO_3$) in H_2O. Add a few drops of a solution of common salt ($NaCl$). A white curdy precipitate of silver chloride ($AgCl$) is formed.

Experiment 103.—Wash the AgCl obtained in the last experiment and try to dissolve it in HNO_3. It will prove to be insoluble in that liquid.

Experiment 104.—Wash the AgCl of the last experiment and try to dissolve it in strong ammonia water. It will dissolve.

103. Tests. — Free chlorine is easily distinguished by its odor; pure chlorine, by its color. Chlorine is also easily detected by its bleaching action upon organic coloring matters, or by its forming a blue color with a mixture of starch and potassium iodide. This last mentioned reaction is very delicate, but an excess of chlorine removes the color and the same effect is produced by bromine, ozone and a few other actively oxidizing substances. Many of its compounds yield, with solutions of silver salts, precipitates of silver chloride, insoluble in nitric acid.

(*a.*) By adding a solution of silver nitrate to that of a soluble chloride (*e. g.*, $KCl + AgNO_3$), one part of Cl in a million parts of H_2O may be detected, a faint opalescence appearing.

EXERCISES.

1. When chlorine water is exposed to sunlight, HCl is formed and O is set free. (*a.*) Write the reaction. (*b.*) What volume of Cl is necessary thus to set free 20 *cu. cm.* of O?

2. Cl unites with the metals acting as a monad. (*a.*) Symbolize the binary compounds of Cl with the following: Na'; K'; Cu''; Au'''; Ag'; Fe''; Zn''; $(Fe_2)^{vi}$. (*b.*) Symbolize the nitrates formed by replacing the H in HNO_3 by the several metals just mentioned.

SECTION II.

HYDROCHLORIC ACID.

104. Source.—Hydrochloric acid (hydrogen chloride, chlorhydric acid, muriatic acid, HCl) is the only known compound of hydrogen and chlorine. The hydrogen is generally furnished by sulphuric acid (H_2SO_4) and the chlorine by common salt (sodium chloride, NaCl), the cheapest and most abundant source of chlorine. The pure acid is a gas, the aqueous solution of which constitutes the muriatic acid of commerce.

(*a.*) HCl is found in the exhalations of active volcanoes, especially Vesuvius and Hecla, and in the waters of several South American rivers that have their rise in volcanic regions.

105. Preparation.—Hydrochloric acid is almost always prepared from common salt by distillation with sulphuric acid.

(*a.*) Into a liter Florence flask, put 30 *g.* of fused NaCl and 30 *cu. cm.* of H_2SO_4. Heat the flask gently over the sand bath and collect by downward displacement in dry jars, as in the preparation of Cl. By holding a piece of moistened blue litmus paper at the mouth of the jar, the experimenter may easily tell when the jar is full. Compare this paragraph carefully with § 74.

$NaCl + H_2SO_4 = HCl + HNaSO_4$.

(*b.*) At a higher temperature,

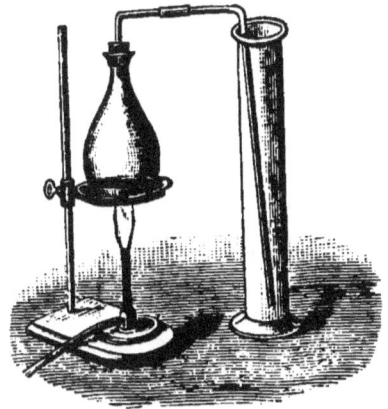

Fig. 50.

the same quantity of H_2SO_4 would combine with twice as much NaCl, yield twice as much HCl, and leave sodium sulphate (Na_2SO_4) instead of hydrogen sodium sulphate ($HNaSO_4$), according to this equation:

$$2NaCl + H_2SO_4 = 2HCl + Na_2SO_4.$$

The greater heat necessary for this latter reaction would be severe upon the apparatus. At the end of the experiment, the $HNaSO_4$ remaining in the flask may be easily removed with warm H_2O.

(c.) HCl may be prepared by the direct union of equal volumes of its constituents (see Exp. 92).

(d.) In the arts, the retort used is an iron cylinder and the gaseous acid is dissolved in H_2O, contained in a series of earthenware Woulffe bottles. In this apparatus, either of the reactions above mentioned may take place. Very large quantities (thousands of tons weekly) of the acid liquid are made as an incidental product of the manufacture of sodium carbonate (§ 268).

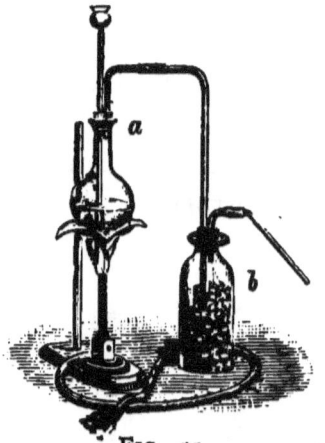

FIG. 51.

(e.) Dry, gaseous HCl may be obtained by heating the acid liquid and passing the gas given off through a drying tube or bottle. See Exp. 61.

Experiment 105.—Fill a long test tube with dry HCl and invert it over mercury. Thrust a bit of ice into the mouth of the tube.

FIG. 52.

The ice and gas will quickly disappear, the mercury rising in the tube. *Explain.*

Experiment 106.—Fill a bottle with dry HCl. Close the bottle with a cork carrying a glass tube and invert it over H_2O, colored with blue litmus (Fig. 52). The H_2O will soon enter with violence, and its color will be changed from blue to red. Instead of passing the tube from *a* into colored water in an open vessel, as shown in the figure, it may be passed through the cork of a closed bottle into the liquid. If this bottle be provided with a bent tube, air may be forced into the bottle and thus enough H_2O forced into a to begin the absorption without waiting for the HCl to diffuse downward through the tube. Compare Exp. 64.

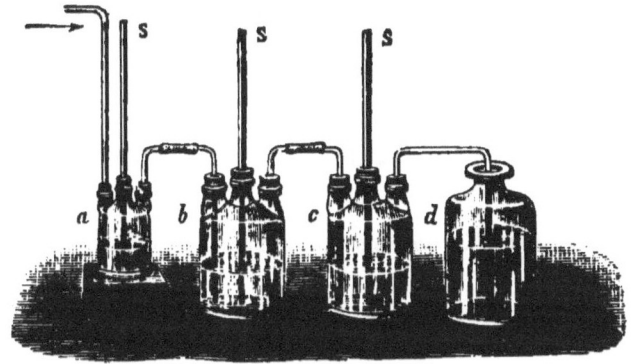

FIG. 53.

Experiment 107.—Pass HCl from the generating flask through a series of Woulffe bottles arranged as in Exp. 65, except that the delivery tube from each bottle should barely dip into the H_2O of the next bottle. It is well to place the Woulffe bottles in H_2O to keep them cool. When the gas ceases to flow, test the contents of each bottle with blue litmus paper. Bottle the liquid and save for future use.

106. Physical Properties.—Hydrochloric acid is a colorless gas having an acid taste and pungent odor. It is irrespirable and neither combustible nor a supporter of combustion. It is a little heavier than air, its specific gravity being 18.25, *i. e.*, a liter of it weighs $18\frac{1}{4}$ criths (1.6352 $g.$). It liquefies under a pressure of 40 atmospheres, this liquid having a specific gravity of 1.27. The gas is remarkably soluble in water, one volume of which, at the ordinary temperature, absorbs about 450 volumes of the gas, or more than 500 volumes at 0°C. This saturated solution, the muriatic acid of commerce, fumes strongly in the air, has a specific gravity of 1.21 and readily gives up the acid gas when heated. If pure, it freezes at temperatures below —40°C. to a butter-like mass having the composition $HCl + 2H_2O$.

Experiment 108.—Nearly fill a test tube with dilute, commercial HCl and drop into it a few pieces of granulated zinc (see § 21). The zinc is quickly dissolved. What gas escapes? Write the reaction.

107. Chemical Properties.—Hydrochloric acid acts upon many metals and their oxides, forming chlorides, most of which are soluble in water.

(*a.*) The liquefied HCl does not act upon any of the metals except Al.

Experiment 109.—If the second bottle used in Exp. 92 was strong enough to stand the explosion without breaking, open it with its mouth under mercury. Notice that no mercury enters the bottle and that no gas escapes. Try it with the third bottle used in that experiment. Then test the contents of the bottles with moistened blue litmus paper. The reddening of the paper shows that we have an acid; it is HCl. We have shown that the volume of the HCl is the same as that of the gases that united to form it. *How was this shown?*

Experiment 110.—Fit a U or V shaped tube to a wooden stand by clamping it with strips of tin or cementing it with plaster of Paris. Through each of two corks pass a wire attached to a strip of platinum. Half fill the tube with HCl, insert the corks snugly, push the wires down until the platinum strips are immersed in the acid liquid and connect the wires with the poles of a galvanic battery (Ph., §§ 397,

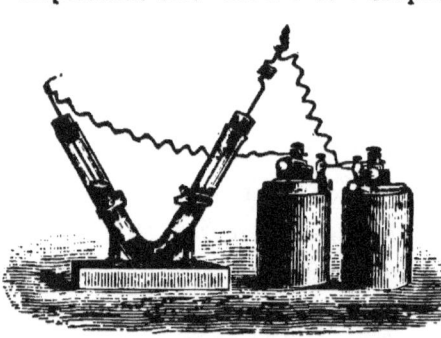

FIG. 54.

398, 401). At the end of four or five minutes, remove the cork that carries the negative electrode (Ph., § 377) and apply a lighted match. H was present, mixed with the air that was in that arm of the tube at the beginning of the experiment. Remove the other cork and thrust a bit of moistened litmus or turmeric paper into that arm of the tube. The bleaching of the paper and the peculiar odor show the presence of Cl. Of course, delivery tubes may be provided for the corks and the gases collected separately (see Fig. 4). Exact experiments of this kind are difficult on account of the solubility of Cl in H_2O, but when made they show that equal volumes of H and of Cl are liberated.

108. Composition. — The composition of hydrochloric acid has been accurately determined, both analytically and synthetically. Such determinations show that one volume of hydrogen combines with one volume of chlorine to form two volumes of hydrochloric acid gas. The composition may be graphically represented as follows:

$$\boxed{\begin{array}{c} H \\ 1\ m.c. \end{array}} + \boxed{\begin{array}{c} Cl \\ 35.5 \\ m.c. \end{array}} = \boxed{\begin{array}{c} HCl \\ 36.5\ m.c. \end{array}}$$

The chemical action effects neither volumetric nor gravimetric change. It should be noticed that hydrochloric acid differs from most of the other acids in that *it contains no oxygen* (§ 60).

109. Uses.—Hydrochloric acid is used in preparing chlorine, potassium chlorate (§ 281), chloride of lime (bleaching powder, § 292), ammonium chloride, *etc., etc.* It is of very frequent use in the chemical laboratory and has become almost indispensable in the manufacturing arts. It acts directly upon most of the metals, forming metallic chlorides, *e. g.*, zinc chloride.

Experiment 111.—Repeat Exps. 6, 102, 103 and 104, using a solution of HCl instead of the solution of NaCl, mentioned in Exp. 102.

110. Tests.—Hydrochloric acid gas may be detected by its reddening moistened blue litmus paper and its forming dense fumes of ammonium chloride (NH_4Cl) when brought into contact with ammonia gas (Exp. 6). Its aqueous solution may be detected by its reddening blue litmus paper and forming, with a solution of silver nitrate, a precipitate (AgCl) soluble in ammonia water but insoluble in nitric acid.

EXERCISES.

1. When ammonium chloride (sal ammoniac, NH_4Cl) is acted upon by H_2SO_4, we have a reaction partly represented as follows:

$$2NH_4Cl + H_2SO_4 = (NH_4)_2SO_4 + \text{\_\_\_\_}$$

Complete the equation.

2. A strip of paper moistened with a certain solution and exposed to Cl turns blue. (*a*.) What is the solution? (*b*.) Explain the reaction. (*c*.) What other gas will produce the same change of color?

3. The vapor of mercury is 100 times as heavy as H. The atomic weight of mercury is 200 *m. c.* What is the number of atoms in a mercury molecule?

4. Show that a molecule of H contains two atoms.

5. Define and illustrate quantivalence.

6. What is a chemical experiment?

SECTION III.

OTHER CHLORINE COMPOUNDS.

111. Chlorine Oxides.—Chlorine does not unite *directly* with oxygen, but it may be made to do so by indirect means. Five oxides of chlorine are recognized by chemists, of which only three have been isolated.

(a.)
1. Chlorine monoxide (hypochlorous oxide)......Cl_2O.
2. Chlorine trioxide (chlorous oxide).............Cl_2O_3.
3. Chlorine tetroxide (chloryl)..................Cl_2O_4.
4. Chlorine pentoxide (chloric oxide)............Cl_2O_5.
5. Chlorine heptoxide (perchloric oxide).........Cl_2O_7.

(b.) Cl_2O is an explosive, yellow gas, formed by passing dry Cl over mercuric oxide:

$$2Cl_2 + 2HgO = Hg_2OCl_2 + Cl_2O.$$

It liquefies at —20°C.

Cl_2O_3 is a greenish, yellow, unstable gas, prepared by the reduction of chloric acid, thus:

$$2HClO_3 + N_2O_3 = Cl_2O_3 + 2HNO_3.$$

Cl_2O_4 is an explosive gas obtained by the action of sulphuric acid (H_2SO_4) upon potassium chlorate ($KClO_3$). It is sometimes called free chloryl, the molecule being considered as composed of two compound radicals:

$$O = \underset{|}{Cl} = O \text{ or } (ClO_2)', \text{ thus:}$$

$(ClO_2) - (ClO_2)$. See §§ 94, 95. Cl_2O_5 and Cl_2O_7 have not yet been isolated, but their compounds are known.

(c.) Note the varying quantivalence of the Cl in these several oxides, and that it is represented by the series of *odd* numbers, 1, 3, 5 and 7.

Experiment 112.—Pulverize separately 1 *g.* of sugar and 1 *g.* of potassium chlorate ($KClO_3$). Mix them intimately upon a piece of paper and, from a glass rod dipped in H_2SO_4, let a drop of acid fall upon the mixture. The Cl_2O_4 thus set free causes an energetic combustion.

Experiment 113.—In a test glass, place 1 $g.$ of $KClO_3$ (not pulverized). Add a few *small* pieces of phosphorus and nearly fill the glass with H_2O. By means of a pipette (App. 5), bring H_2SO_4 into contact with the $KClO_3$. The phosphorus burns under H_2O in the Cl_2O_4 thus set free.

FIG. 55.

112. Chlorine Acids.—From four of these chlorine oxides results a corresponding list of acids and salts (see § 60). The molecular symbols for the acids may be obtained from those of the corresponding oxides.

(*a.*) The addition of H_2O to the symbol of the oxide will give *double the symbol* of the acid:

$Cl_2O + H_2O = H_2Cl_2O_2 = 2HClO$, hypochlorous acid.
$Cl_2O_3 + H_2O = H_2Cl_2O_4 = 2HClO_2$, chlorous acid.
$Cl_2O_5 + H_2O = H_2Cl_2O_6 = 2HClO_3$, chloric acid.
$Cl_2O_7 + H_2O = H_2Cl_2O_8 = 2HClO_4$, perchloric acid.

(*b.*) The most important of these acids are $HClO$, because of its relation to calcium hypochlor*ite*, and $HClO_3$, because of its relation to potassium chlor*ate*.

(*c.*) The last two paragraphs may be summarized as follows:

Oxides.	Acids.	Salts.
1. Cl_2O	$HClO$	$NaClO$, sodium hypochlorite.
2. Cl_2O_3	$HClO_2$	$NaClO_2$, sodium chlorite.
3. Cl_2O_4	?	?
4. ?	$HClO_3$	$KClO_3$, potassium chlorate.
5. ?	$HClO_4$	$KClO_4$, potassium perchlorate.

113. Nitrogen Chloride.—"Chlorine combines with nitrogen, though only indirectly, to form a very remarkable compound, the composition of which has not yet been determined. If an excess of chlorine gas be passed into a solution of ammonia, drops of an oily liquid are seen to form, which, on being touched, explode with fearful violence, so that the greatest caution must be used in manipulating even traces of this body. The explosive nature of this compound arises from the fact that its constituent elements are very loosely combined and separate with sudden violence."—*Roscoe.*

Caution.—Do not try to prepare nitrogen chloride. It is far too dangerous for a school experiment.

Experiment 114.—Put a small piece (4 or 5 *sq. cm,*) of gold leaf into a test tube and pour in strong HNO_3 until the tube is a third full. Put a similar piece of gold leaf into another test tube and pour in a like quantity of HCl. If the leaf *is gold leaf*, neither liquid will dissolve it. Pour the contents of one tube into the other. The gold leaf will quickly dissolve in the mixed acids.

114. Aqua Regia.—Gold, platinum and many metallic compounds, are insoluble in either nitric or hydrochloric acid, but are easily soluble in a mixture of these acids, especially when heated in the mixture. The acids react upon each other, chlorine is set free and, in the "nascent" condition, acts upon the metal or metallic compound more energetically than it would otherwise do.

(*a.*) The name "aqua regia" (royal water) was given by the old alchemists because the mixture was able to dissolve gold, the "king of metals." The mixture is sometimes called nitro-hydrochloric acid.

(*b.*) The expression "nascent" state or condition has appeared before. It is used to describe the condition of a chemical agent at the moment it is set free from some compound. What constitutes the essential features of the "nascent" state is not known. We can not yet tell *what the difference* between "nascent" H or Cl and ordinary H or Cl is, but we can tell what the difference in *their effects* is. The most marked effect is greatly increased chemical energy. We shall see other cases in illustration as we proceed.

(*c.*) It is probable that "nascent" Cl is in the atomic condition and ordinary Cl in the molecular condition. They might be symbolized as follows: Cl and Cl_2 or Cl— and Cl—Cl (§§ 93, 94).

Exercises.

1. What chlorine oxide has trivalent Cl?

2. (*a.*) Write the graphic symbol for chloric acid. (*b.*) What is the quantivalence of the Cl?

3. (*a.*) Write the graphic symbol for $HClO_4$. (*b.*) What is the quantivalence of the Cl?

4. Define atom; atomic weight; microcrith.

5. (*a.*) If 20 *l.* of H be exploded with O, how many liters of O will be required? (*b.*) How many liters of dry steam will be produced?

6. (*a.*) If 15 *l.* of H be mixed with 10 *l.* of O and the mixture exploded, how many liters of dry steam will be produced? (*b.*) Will any elementary gas remain free? If so, give its name and volume.

7. (*a.*) How many grams of H are there in 36 *g.* of H_2O? (*b.*) How many grams of O? (*c.*) How many liters of H? (*d.*) How many liters of O?

8. (*a.*) 24 *l.* of oxygen will yield how many liters of ozone? (*b.*) 30 *l.* of ozone is equal to how many liters of oxygen?

9. Why should Cl— or H— have greater affinity for another element than Cl—Cl or H—H?

10. (*a.*) How many kinds of atoms are known? (*b.*) How many kinds of molecules?

SECTION IV.

BROMINE, IODINE, AND FLUORINE.

☞ BROMINE ; *symbol*, Br ; *specific gravity, at 0° C., 3,187 ; atomic weight, 80 m. c. ; molecular weight, 160 m. c. ; quantivalence, 1 (5 or 7).*

115. Source.—Bromine does not occur free in nature, but is found combined with metals, especially as magnesium bromide, in sea water and in the water of certain salt wells and springs.

(*a.*) Much of the Br made in the United States comes from the salt wells of Ohio and West Virginia. The bittern that remains after the crystallization of the NaCl contains magnesium bromide in such quantities that Br is profitably extracted from it.

Note.—The name is derived from the Greek *bromos*, meaning a stench.

Experiment 115.—Into a flask of two or three liters capacity, put a few drops of Br and cover the flask loosely. In a few minutes the jar will be filled with the heavy red vapor of Br.

Experiment 116.—Into the jar of vaporized Br, introduce a strip of moistened litmus or turmeric paper. It will be bleached.

Experiment 117.—Add a few more drops of Br, and after it has vaporized, introduce a thin slice of dry phosphorus. It will ignite.

Experiment 118.—Into a tall jar filled with Br vapor, let fall a few freshly prepared filings of metallic antimony. The result is much like that of Exp. 88.

116. Properties, etc. — Bromine is a dark red liquid of disagreeable odor, very volatile at ordinary temperatures and highly poisonous. It is sparingly soluble in water and easily soluble in ether or carbon disulphide. Its vapor has a specific gravity of 80, being more than five times as heavy as air. Its chemical properties closely resemble those of chlorine, but it is less active. Its attraction for hydrogen fits it for bleaching and disinfecting uses. Some of the bromides are used in medicine and photography.

(*a.*) With the exception of mercury, Br is the only element liquid at ordinary temperatures.

(*b.*) Br forms acids as follows: hydrobromic, HBr; hypobromous, HBrO; bromic, HBrO$_3$; perbromic. HBrO$_4$. They closely resemble the corresponding Cl compounds.

(*c.*) Br, when swallowed, acts as an irritant poison; when dropped upon the skin, it produces a sore that is very difficult to heal.

(*d.*) Br has very little action upon sodium, but combines energetically with potassium, sometimes with almost explosive violence.

☞ IODINE; *symbol*, I; *specific gravity*, *4.95*; *atomic weight*, *127 m. c.*; *molecular weight*, *254 m. c.*; *quantivalence*, *1 (3, 5, or 7)*.

117. Source.—Iodine compounds exist in very minute quantities in the water of the sea and of some saline springs. From sea water, the iodide is absorbed by certain marine plants. The ashes (kelp) of these sea weeds contain sodium and magnesium iodides. Iodine is obtained by heating the kelp with sulphuric acid and manganese dioxide. Iodine is thus set free in the form of a beautiful violet colored vapor which soon condenses to a solid.

Experiment 119.—Put a small piece of I into a dry test tube. Heat the test tube in the flame and notice that the I vaporizes without visible liquefaction (Ph., § 509). Notice that the vapor is very heavy as well as very beautiful. If the upper part of the tube be cold, minute I crystals will condense there.

Experiment 120.—Place some I upon a heated brick and cover the whole with a large bell-glass. This gives a good exhibition of the beautiful vapor.

Experiment 121.—Prepare some starch paste, as in Exp. 99, and dilute 5 or 6 drops of it with 10 *cu. cm.* of H_2O. Dissolve a very small piece of I in alcohol and add a drop of the alcoholic solution to the dilute starch. The starch will be colored blue even when the alcoholic solution is very dilute. The blue color will disappear upon heating the solution and reappear upon cooling it.

Experiment 122.—Drop a few crystals of I into a large bottle. Dip a strip of white paper into the colorless starch paste and suspend it in the bottle. The paper may be held in place by the stopper of the bottle. As the I sublimes and diffuses through the bottle, it soon comes into contact with the starch and colors the paper blue.

Note.—A moment's reflection will show that in this experiment the quantity of I that actually comes into contact with the starch and changes its color is almost immeasurably small. Starch will detect the presence of one part of I in 300,000 parts of H_2O.

Experiment 123.—Add a few drops of the alcoholic solution prepared in Exp. 121 to 10 *cu. cm.* of H_2O in a test tube. Owing to the sparing solubility of I in H_2O, most of the I will be precipitated. Pour 5 *cu. cm.* of this aqueous solution into a test tube, add 8 or 10 drops of carbon disulphide (CS_2) and shake the contents of the tube. On standing for a few moments, the CS_2 will settle to the bottom, when it will be seen to be colored purple-red; the color is due to the I dissolved in the CS_2. Carbon disulphide will detect the presence of one part of I in 1,000,000 of H_2O.

Experiment 124.—Pour 10 *cu. cm.* of H_2O into each of three tall test glasses. Add a few drops of a solution of potassium iodide to each. To the first, add a few drops of a solution of lead acetate (sugar of lead). Brilliant yellow lead iodide is formed. To the second, add a few drops of a solution of mercurous nitrate. Yellowish-green mercurous iodide is formed. To the third, add a few drops of a solution of mercuric chloride (corrosive sublimate). Scarlet mercuric iodide is formed.

118. Properties, etc.—Iodine is a blue-black, crystalline solid having a metallic lustre. Its vapor has a specific gravity of 127; it is the heaviest known vapor. Iodine is very sparingly (1:5500 at 10°C.,) soluble in water but readily dissolves in alcohol, ether, chloroform, carbon disulphide or aqueous solutions of the metallic iodides.

Its chemical activity is less than that of bromine. It is used in medicine, photography and the manufacture of aniline green. The blue color it forms with starch, its beautifully colored vapor, and the purple-red color it forms with carbon disulphide form delicate tests for free iodine.

(*a.*) I forms acids as follows, hydroiodic, HI; iodic acid, HIO_3; periodic acid, H_5IO_6. They closely resemble the corresponding Cl and Br compounds.

(*b.*) I has no action upon sodium, but when it is heated with potassium an explosive combination takes place.

Experiment 125.—Upon 0.25 g. of pulverized I, placed in a porcelain capsule, pour enough strong ammonia water to cover it and allow it to stand for 15 or 20 minutes. At the end of that time, stir up the powder at the bottom of the liquid and pour a quarter of the contents of the capsule upon each of four small filters (App. 8). Wash the powder well with cold H_2O, and then remove the filters with their contents from their funnels. Pin the filters to pieces of board and allow them to dry without heating. When the powder is dry, it may be exploded by brushing it with a feather or by jarring it with a blow upon the table. The powder is nitrogen iodide.

119. Nitrogen Iodide.—Nitrogen iodide is much less explosive than nitrogen chloride (§ 113) but it should not be prepared by the pupil except in very small quantities. Nitrogen forms a similar compound with bromine.

☞ FLUORINE; *symbol*, F; *atomic weight, 19 m. c.; quantivalence, 1.*

120. Source.—Fluorine occurs in nature in fluor spar (calcium fluoride, CaF_2), and in cryolite (sodium and aluminum fluorides, $3NaF + AlF_3$). It has also been found in minute quantities in the teeth, bones and blood of animals.

Note.—Fluor spar is a mineral found somewhat abundantly in various parts of the world, especially in Derbyshire and Cornwall, England. Cryolite is found in large quantities in Greenland.

121. Properties.—Fluorine is a very remarkable element in that it is the only one that forms no compound with oxygen and that it has, so far, resisted all of the attempts made to obtain it in the free state. When set free from one compound, it attacks the substance nearest at hand to form a new compound. It surpasses chlorine in its power of combining with hydrogen and the metals, and has a remarkable tendency to combine with silicon. The difficulties in the way of its preparation and collection have prevented its satisfactory study by chemists. Consequently, but little is known concerning free fluorine. Its compounds closely resemble those of chlorine, bromine and iodine.

Note.— F has been considered subsequently to Cl, Br and I, because of the comparative lack of knowledge concerning it. There are good reasons why, in grouping them, F should precede Cl, Br and I.

Experiment 126.—Rub a heated piece of glass with beeswax. If the glass be hot enough to melt the wax, it may easily have one of its surfaces covered with a thin layer of nearly uniform thickness. Let the glass cool. With any pointed instrument, write a name or draw a design, being careful that every stroke cuts through the wax and exposes the glass below. In a small tray made of lead (platinum is better, but a saucer that you are willing to spoil will answer), mix a spoonful of powdered fluor spar or cryolite with enough H_2SO_4 to make a thin paste. Place the prepared glass (waxed side down) over the tray; heat the tray gently (not enough to melt the wax) and set it aside in a warm place for two or three hours. (*Do not inhale the acid fumes.*) Clean the glass by scraping it and rubbing with turpentine. The name or design will be seen etched upon the glass.

Experiment 127.—Upon a pane of glass that will fit the window of your chemical laboratory, or the glass front of one of your laboratory cases, etch the proper designation of the class, the date, and the *autographs* of the individual members of the class. The "class artist" may add an appropriate border and emblematic designs, *ad libitum*.

Experiment 128.—Coat the convex surface of a watch glass with wax, write a name upon it, place it upon a small lead saucer containing mixed CaF_2 and H_2SO_4, fill the watch glass with H_2O to keep the wax from melting, and hold the saucer in the lamp flame. The etching will be finished in a few minutes.

122. Hydrofluoric Acid.—This acid (HF) is distinguished from all other substances by its power of corroding glass. It evidently corresponds closely to the other hydrides of this group (*i. e.*, HCl, HBr and HI) but it is more energetic than any of them. It is readily prepared, as above, by distilling some fluoride with sulphuric acid, *e. g.*,

$$CaF_2 + H_2SO_4 = CaSO_4 + 2HF.$$

(*a.*) The reaction is closely analogous to that for the distillation of NaCl with H_2SO_4 (§ 105, *a*). The solution of HF is also used for etching glass. HF, when dry, does not act on glass, but the slightest trace of H_2O renders it capable of doing so.

123. The Halogen Group.—Fluorine, chlorine, bromine and iodine constitute one of the most clearly defined and most remarkable natural groups known to chemistry. They exhibit a marked gradation in properties and close analogies in their elementary condition and in their corresponding compounds.

(*a.*) Concerning their gradation of properties:

1. At the ordinary temperature, F is a gas; Cl is a gas; Br is a liquid and I is a solid.
2. Liquid Cl is transparent; Br is but slightly so; I is opaque.
3. Cl has a specific gravity of 35.5; Br vapor, 80; I vapor, 127.
4. F has an atomic weight of 19 *m. c.*; Cl, 35.5 *m. c*; Br, 80 *m. c.*; I, 127 *m. c.*
5. Generally speaking, their chemical activities are graded in the inverse order, being greatest in the case of F; less in Cl; still less in Br and least in I. (In the case of such natural groups the chemical activities frequently vary inversely as the atomic weights.) The atomic weight of Br is nearly the mean of those of Cl and I $\left(\frac{35.5 + 127}{2} = 81.25\right)$ and, in general chemical deportment, Br stands half way between the other two elements.

(*b.*) Concerning their analogies:

1. Their binary compounds with potassium and sodium resemble

§ 123   THE HALOGEN GROUP.   103

sea salt. Hence, these compounds are called haloid salts and their elements, halogens (Greek, *halos*, salt and *gennao*, I produce).

2. Each of them combines with H, equal volumes of the constituent gases uniting without condensation, to form the haloid acids, HF, HCl, HBr and HI.

3. These haloid acids all have a great attraction for H_2O forming aqueous solutions that have the same chemical properties as the acids themselves.

EXERCISES.

1. Give two of the most marked physical properties of H, and two of its distinctive chemical properties.

2. What is a triad? A pentad? A quadrivalent atom? A bivalent compound radical? Illustrate each.

3. By passing the vapor of I with H over platinum sponge heated to redness, a strongly acid gas is synthetically formed. What is its name, its molecular weight and its specific gravity?

4. A large jar, about a quarter full of chloride of lime had been standing for some time until the upper part contained a gas given off by the chloride. Into this gas, a moistened slip of paper was thrust. The paper was instantly colored deep blue. What was the gas and with what was the test paper moistened? Explain the phenomenon.

5. What analogies exist between members of the Halogen group?

6. Symbolize the chlorides, bromides, iodides, chlorates, bromates and iodates of the following: K', Na', Ag', Cu'', Zn'', Au''', Pt^{Iv}.

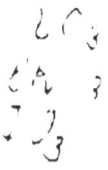

Chapter VIII.

STOICHIOMETRY.

124. Reactions and Reagents. — *Any change in the composition of a molecule is called a chemical reaction. Substances acting in such a chemical change are called reagents.*

(*a.*) Changes in molecular composition are of three kinds:
1. Changes in the kind of the constituent atoms.
2. Changes in the number of the constituent atoms.
3. Changes in the relative positions of the constituent atoms.

(*b.*) When H burns in air, the H and O *react* upon each other; they are the *reagents* used to produce a molecular change.

125. Expression of Reactions. — In any given substance of homogeneous composition, the molecules are all alike. The nature of the mass depends upon the nature of the molecule. The mass may be fittingly represented by the molecule. Any chemical change in the mass may be represented by a corresponding change in the molecule. Hence, *chemical reactions are generally expressed in molecular symbols.*

126. Factors and Products. — *The molecules that go into a reaction are called factors; the molecules that come from it are called products.*

(*a.*) In the preparation of H (§ 23), the factors were Zn and 2HCl; the products were $ZnCl_2$ and H_2.

127. Chemical Equations. — *Chemical reactions are very commonly and conveniently represented by equations, placing the sum of the factors equal to the sum of the products.*

(*a.*) The equality results from the indestructibility of matter (Ph., § 37). It indicates that the number of each kind of atoms in the products is equal to the number of the same kind of atoms in the factors. The atoms are differently arranged but not a single one is gained or lost. From this it follows that the symbols in *the two members of the equation represent the same number of microcriths.* The chemical change does not effect any change in weight. (See Exp. 9.)

(*b.*) Re-examine the equations already given, showing their agreement or disagreement with the above statements.

(*c.*) The equation also represents the relative weights of the several substances engaged in the reaction. The equation $H_2 + O = H_2O$ means, *literally*, that 2 *m. c.* of H united with 16 *m. c.* of O yields 18 *m. c.* of H_2O, but the *relation* is equally true for larger quantities of matter. Thus we may learn from it that 2 *g.* of H unites with 16 *g.* of O to form 18 *g.* of H_2O, or that 12 *Kg.* of H unites with 96 *Kg.* of O to form 108 *Kg.* of H_2O.

(*d.*) *Strictly speaking*, it is not proper to represent a fractional part of a molecule as entering into or resulting from a chemical reaction, as we do when we write $H_2 + O = H_2O$. To obviate the error of representing an *atom of free* O, we should indicate twice the quantity of each substance, as follows: $2H_2 + O_2 = 2H_2O$. But, *for the sake of convenience*, chemists generally write the equations in the simpler form, as the gravimetric relations expressed are the same.

(*e.*) The equation, written in complete molecules, also represents volumetric relations. Remembering Ampère's law (§ 61), we easily see that $2H_2 + O_2 = 2H_2O$ indicates that two (molecular or other) volumes of H unite with one of O to yield two volumes of dry steam, *e. g.*, 2 *l.* of H and 1 *l.* of O unite to form 2 *l.* of dry steam.

128. Gravimetric Computations. — Knowing the equation for any given reaction and the atomic weights of the several elements involved, we are able to solve a great many problems concerning the weight of substances appearing as factors or products. From the data now known and those given in the problem, make the following proportion:

As the number of microcriths of the given substance is to the number of microcriths of the required substance so is the actual weight of the given substance to the actual weight of the required substance.

(*a.*) The number of microcriths is to be taken, of course, from the equation. A few examples are given:

1. How much H can be obtained from HCl by using 20 $g.$ of Zn (zinc)?

Solution.—Write the reaction with the molecular weights of the several reagents.

$$\underset{65\ m.c.}{Zn} + \underset{73\ m.c.}{2HCl} \overset{2(1+35.5)}{=} \underset{136\ m.c.}{ZnCl_2} + \underset{2\ m.c.}{H_2}.$$

Form the proportion according to the above rule:

$$65\ m.c. : 2\ m.c. :: 20\ g. : x\ g.$$
$$\therefore x = 0.61538\ g.\ \text{or}\ 615.38\ mg.\ \text{of H.}—Ans.$$

2. How much HCl will be required?

$$65\ m.c. : 73\ m.c. :: 20\ g. : x\ g.$$
$$\therefore x = 22.46\ g.\ \text{of dry HCl.}—Ans.$$

3. How much $ZnCl_2$ will be produced?

$$65\ m.c. : 136\ m.c. :: 20\ g. : x\ g.$$
$$\therefore x = 41.846\ g.\ \text{of}\ ZnCl_2.—Ans.$$

4. How much Zn is necessary to prepare 1 Kl of H?

As one liter of H weighs 1 crith or .0896 $g.$, 1000 $l.$ weighs 89.6 $g.$

$$65\ m.c. : 2\ m.c. :: x\ g. : 89.6\ g.$$
$$\therefore x = 2912\ g.\ \text{or}\ 2.912\ Kg.\ \text{of Zn.}—Ans.$$

129. Volumetric Computations.—Every equation written in the molecular symbols of aeriform substances may be read by volume. For example $2H_2 + O_2 = 2H_2O$ may be read: two volumes of hydrogen unite with one volume of oxygen to form two volumes of dry steam. We give a few examples.

(*a.*) 1. How much steam is formed by the combustion of 1 *l.* of H?

Solution.—By referring to our equation, we see that the volumes of H and of H_2O are equal, because it shows an equal number of molecules for those substances, and we know, from Ampère's law, that equal numbers of gaseous molecules will occupy equal volumes. Hence, the combustion of 1 *l.* of H will give 1 *l.* of dry steam.

2. How much O is needed to burn up 500 *cu. cm.* of H?

Solution.—The equation for the combustion of H shows that the volume of O is half that of the H. Hence, it will require half of 500 *cu. cm.* or 250 *cu. cm.* of O.

3. How much H must be burned to form 4 *l.* of steam?

Solution.—The equation shows a relation of equality between the volumes of H and of H_2O (as in the first example). Consequently, 4 *l.* of steam requires 4 *l.* of H.

4. How much O can be obtained from the electrolysis of 3 *l.* of steam?

Solution.—The equation shows that the volume of O is half that of aeriform H_2O. Hence, 3 *l.* of steam will yield 1.5 *l.* or 1500 *cu. cm.* of O.

130. Percentage Composition. — The method of solving problems of this kind will be illustrated by examples, as follows:

(1.) What is the percentage composition of HNO_3?

Solution.—The molecular weight of HNO_3 is 1 *m. c.* + 14 *m. c.* + 48 *m. c.* = 63 *m. c.*

63 *m. c.* : 1 *m. c.* :: 100% : 1.59%, the proportion of H.
63 *m. c.* : 14 *m. c.* :: 100% : 22.22%, " " N.
63 *m. c.* : 48 *m. c.* :: 100% : 76.19% " " O.
                                100.00%

(2.) The vapor density of a certain compound is 14. Analysis shows that 85.7% of it is O and 14.3% is H. What is its symbol?

Solution.—If its vapor density is 14, its molecular weight is 28 *m. c.* (§ 63).

$$100\% : 85.7\% :: 28\ m.\ c. : 24\ m.\ c. = C_2.$$
$$100\% : 14.3\% :: 28\ m.\ c. : 4\ m.\ c. = H_4\ \text{or}\ 2H_2.$$

Therefore, the symbol is C_2H_4.

Note.—Gaseous volumes will vary with pressure (Ph., § 284) and temperature (Ph., § 492). In comparing such volumes, measured under different conditions, the proper correction must be made for this variation (Ph., § 494). It is common to refer gaseous volumes to a temperature of 0°C. and a pressure of 760 *mm*. The branch of chemistry that deals with the numerical relations of atoms is called stoichiometry. The gravimetric and volumetric and percentage computations above are stoichiometrical computations.

Exercises.

1. What do atomic weights express? What weight of O can be obtained by decomposing 9 *g.* of steam?

2. Give the law of multiple proportions, and illustrate it by the compounds of N and O.

3. Find the percentage composition of H_2SO_4.

4. Upon heating potassium dichromate ($K_2Cr_2O_7$) with a sufficient quantity of HCl, one may obtain $Cr_2Cl_6 + 2KCl$ and water and chlorine. Write the reaction.

5. (*a.*) How much Zn is needed to obtain 20 *g.* of H? (*b.*) How much, if the Zn contains 5 *per cent.* impurities?

6. (*a.*) How much O would be necessary to burn 500 *cu. cm.* of H? (*b.*) If the experiment were performed in an atmosphere at a temperature of 100°C., what would be the name and volume of the product? (*c.*) How much would be necessary to burn 5 *g.* of H?

7. (*a.*) What liquid is used in the preparation of HCl? (*b.*) What is the greatest amount of HCl that can be prepared by using 196 *g.* of that liquid?

8. (*a.*) What is the difference between hydrochloric acid and muriatic acid? (*b.*) What is aqua regia? (*c.*) Name and symbolize the five oxides of N.

9. (*a.*) Explain the difference between a bivalent and an univalent metal. (*b.*) What is quantivalence?

10. When HI gas is passed through a heated glass tube, it is decomposed, and a violet color appears. Account for the appearance of the color.

§ 130 PERCENTAGE COMPOSITION. 109

11. The reaction of Cl upon NH_3 is as follows:
$$8NH_3 + 3Cl_2 = N_2 + 6NH_4Cl.$$

(*a.*) What weight of Cl is necessary to the production of 12.544 *g.* of N? (*b.*) What volume of Cl?

12. Marsh gas is 8 times as heavy as H. Analysis shows that ¾ of its weight is C and the rest H. The atomic weight of C is 12 *m. c.* What is the symbol for marsh gas?

13. What is the normal volume of a quantity of O that measures 1 *l.* at a barometric reading of 756 *mm.*? (Ph., § 494.)

CHAPTER IX.

THE SULPHUR GROUP.

SECTION I.

SULPHUR.

*Symbol*, S; *specific gravity*, *1.96 to 2.07*; *atomic weight*, *32 m.c.*; *molecular weight*, *at 1000° C.*, *64 m.c.*; *quantivalence*, *2 (4 or 6)*.

131. Occurrence.—Both free and combined sulphur are found in nature. Free sulphur is found in certain volcanic regions, especially Sicily, occurring sometimes in the form of transparent yellow crystals, called "virgin sulphur," but generally mixed with earthy materials.* It is found in combination with hydrogen or with the metals, as sulphides; and with oxygen and many metals, as sulphates.

(*a.*) Among the native sulphides, we may mention hydrogen sulphide (sulphuretted hydrogen, H_2S), a gaseous constituent of the waters of "sulphur springs"; lead sulphide (galena, PbS); zinc sulphide (blende, ZnS); copper sulphide (chalcocite, CuS) and iron disulphide (pyrite, FeS_2), *etc.*

(*b.*) Among the native sulphates we may mention calcium sulphate (gypsum, $CaSO_4$); barium sulphate (barite or heavy spar, $BaSO_4$) and sodium sulphate (Glauber salt, Na_2SO_4).

(*c.*) S is found in animal and vegetable tissues.

(*d.*) Nearly all of the S of commerce comes from Sicily. Some of the native crystals here found are 5 or 7 *cm.* in diameter.

§ 132 SULPHUR. 111

132. Preparation.—Native sulphur is freed from most of its earthy impurities near the place where it is found and thus fitted for purposes of commerce. The process is one of fusion or of distillation. Sulphur is also obtained from pyrite by heat.

(*a.*) One method of obtaining crude sulphur from the native earthy

FIG. 56.

material is represented in Fig. 56. The earthy material is heated in earthenware pots, *a a*; the vaporized S passes over into the similar pots, *b b*, placed outside the furnace. The S vapor here condenses to a liquid and then runs out into wooden vessels partly filled with H_2O. It is said that this process is unknown in Sicily.

(*b.*) When the earth is very rich in S, it is sometimes heated in large kettles. The S melts and the earthy matter settles to the bottom, leaving the liquid S to be dipped out from above. Sometimes the earth is piled up in a heap and heated, the heat coming from the combustion of a part of the S or of other fuel previously added in proper quantity. The melted S flows from the heap or settles into a cavity at the bottom. In this latter process, which is largely used in Sicily, two-thirds of the S is lost by its combustion.

(*c.*) Pyrite (iron pyrites, FeS_2) is sometimes piled up with fuel, which is then ignited. The heat frees part of the S of the FeS_2 and melts it. The melted S settles into cavities provided for that purpose.

(*d.*) The crude S, provided by the foregoing processes, is then further purified by distillation. It is melted in a tank, *a*, runs

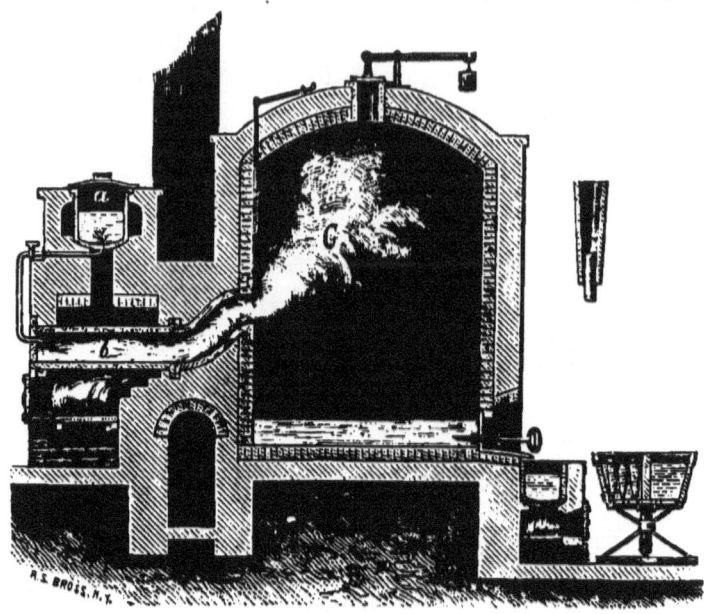

FIG. 57.

through a pipe into the iron retort, *b*, where it is vaporized. The vapor passes from *b* into the large brick chamber, *C*, where it condenses. When the walls of *C* are cold, the S condenses in the form of a light powder known as "flowers of sulphur"; when the walls of *C* are hot, the S condenses to a liquid, and collects on the floor of the chamber, whence it is drawn off and run into moulds to form "roll brimstone."

Experiment 129.—Put 80 *g.* of small pieces of S into a test tube of 80 *cu. cm.* capacity. Hold the test tube in the lamp flame. Notice that it melts, forming a *limpid* liquid of light yellow color. Heat it hotter and notice that it becomes viscid and dark colored. Heat it hotter and notice that it becomes almost black. Invert the test tube and notice that the S has become so viscid that it will not run out from the tube. Heat it hotter and notice that it again becomes fluid. Heat it until it boils and notice that it is converted into a light yellow vapor.

Experiment 130.—Pour half of the boiling S of the last experi-

§ 132　　　　　SULPHUR.　　　　　113

FIG. 58.

ment, in a fine stream, into a large vessel nearly full of cold H_2O. The S when taken from the H_2O will be found to have no crystalline structure, to be soft, nearly black *and plastic*. Allow the S remaining in the test tube to cool slowly and quietly, under close observation. Notice that it repasses through the viscid and limpid states and finally solidifies *with a crystalline structure*. The needle like crystals may be seen shooting out from the cooling walls of the tube into the liquid.

Experiment 131.—Melt 200 *g*. of S in a Hessian crucible. Allow it to cool until a crust forms over the top. Through a hole pierced in this crust, pour out the remaining liquid S. When the crucible is cool, break it open. It will be found lined with needle shaped crystals.

FIG. 59.

Note.—The crucible may be spared by pouring all of the melted S into a pasteboard box or other convenient receptacle and securing the formation of the crystals there.

Experiment 132.—Dissolve a piece of S in carbon disulphide (CS_2). The CS_2 will quickly evaporate, leaving behind crystals of S, that resemble the native crystals.

Note.—The many forms of crystals have been classified into six systems of crystallization:

1. Isometric—axes equal.
2. Tetragonal ⎫
3. Hexagonal ⎬ lateral axes equal.
4. Orthorhombic ⎫
5. Monoclinic ⎬ axes unequal.
6. Triclinic ⎭

The crystals of S formed by fusion (Exp. 131) are monoclinic; the native crystals and those formed by solution and evaporation are orthorhombic. Substances which, like S, crystallize under two systems are called *dimorphous* (two formed). Sulphur is not only thus dimorphus, but the plastic variety (Exp. 130) is *amorphous* (without crystalline form). Other substances, like titanium dioxide, crystallize in three distinct forms and are said to be *trimorphous*. A variation in crystalline form is accompanied by differences in other physical properties, as specific gravity, hardness, refractive power, *etc*. Different substances that crystallize in the same form are said to be *isomorphous*. Substances that exhibit a double isomorphism are said to be *isodimorphous*. The trioxides of arsenic and antimony are isodimorphous.

133. Physical Properties. — Sulphur manifests remarkable changes when heated. It melts at 115°C.; becomes dark colored and viscid at 230°C.; regains its fluidity at above 250°C., and boils at 450°C. On cooling, these changes occur in inverse order. The specific gravity of its vapor at 500°C. is 96, but at 1000°C. it is 32. This seems to indicate that at 500°C. the molecule is composed of six atoms, which are disassociated at a higher temperature, so that, at 1000°C., the molecule is composed of only two atoms. It exists in three distinct forms, orthorhombic, monoclinic and amorphous.

(*a.*) The orthorhombic or natural form of S is brittle and soluble in carbon disulphide, petroleum or turpentine. Its specific gravity is 2.05.

(*b.*) The monoclinic form is brittle and unstable. After exposure to the air for several days, each transparent, needle shaped crystal is converted into a large number of the orthorhombic or permanent crystals, thus becoming opaque. Its specific gravity is 1.96. It is formed as shown in Exp. 131.

(*c.*) The amorphous form is plastic and insoluble in CS_2. Exposed to the air, it gradually assumes the ordinary brittle form at ordinary temperatures; heated to 100°C., it instantly changes, and evolves enough heat to raise its temperature to 110°C. Its specific gravity is 1.96. It is formed by pouring S, heated above 250°C., into cold H_2O, as shown in Fig. 58.

FIG. 60.

Experiment 133.—Mix intimately 4 *g.* of flowers of S and 8 *g.* of copper filings. Heat the mixture in an ignition tube (see Exp. 11) until the elements unite with a vivid combustion to form copper sulphide (CuS).

Experiment 134.—Burn a small piece of S in the air and notice the peculiar blue light and the familiar odor of the suffocating gaseous product (§ 144).

134. Chemical Properties. —Sulphur unites with oxygen at the comparatively low temperature of about 250°C. It enters energetically into union with most of the elements, in many cases with the evolution of light.

135. Uses.—Sulphur is largely used in the manufacture of sulphuric acid, vulcanized india-rubber, friction matches and gunpowder and in bleaching straw and woolen goods.

136. Tests.—Free sulphur is easily recognized by its color and by its odor when burned. Combined sulphur may be detected by mixing the compound with pure sodium carbonate and fusing the mixture before the blowpipe on charcoal. The fused mass contains sodium sulphide. When it is placed on a silver coin and water added, a brown stain of silver sulphide is formed on the coin.

Note.—Sulphides were formerly called sulphurets.

Exercises.

1. Why are the ends of friction matches generally dipped in melted S?
2. When S is prepared from pyrite, Fe_2S_4 is formed. Write the reaction.
3. By bringing Br and P together in the presence of H_2O, both phosphoric (H_3PO_4) and hydrobromic acids are formed. (*a.*) What weight of Br is necessary to yield 5 *g.* of the colorless gas, HBr? (*b.*) What weight of Br is necessary to yield 10 *l.* of HBr?
4. I acts upon $KClO_3$, forming potassium iodate and setting Cl free:

$$2KClO_3 + I_2 = 2KIO_3 + Cl_2.$$

(*a.*) How much Cl by weight may thus be freed by 10 *g.* of I? (*b.*) How much by volume?
5. (*a.*) How many grams of H may be prepared by the use of 260 *g.* of Zn? (*b.*) How many liters? (*c.*) How many grams of HCl are necessary?
6. (*a.*) If 20 *g.* of H be exploded with O, how many grams of O are necessary? (*b.*) How many grams of dry steam will be produced?
7. (*a.*) 1 *cu. cm.* of H_2O will yield, by electrolysis, how many

cu. cm. of H? (*d.*) The explosion of these gases will yield how many *cu. cm.* of dry steam?

8. (*a.*) If ozone could be produced from $KClO_3$, how many grams of the former could be produced from 10 *g.* of the latter? (*b.*) How many liters of the former?

9. (*a.*) Is gunpowder manufacture a chemical or a physical process? Why? (*b.*) The combustion of gunpowder? Why?

10. Calomel and corrosive sublimate are each composed of Hg and Cl atoms. Why do the two substances differ, their atoms being of the same kind?

11. What is the difference between organic and inorganic matter?

12. State two peculiarities of chemical affinity.

13. The constituents of air are free. Is the air a compound?

SECTION II.

HYDROGEN SULPHIDE.

137. Occurrence. — Hydrogen sulphide (hydrogen monosulphide, sulphuretted hydrogen, hydrosulphuric acid, H_2S) occurs native in certain volcanic gases and is the characteristic constituent of the waters of "sulphur springs." It is generated by the putrefaction of animal matter and causes the peculiar odor of rotten eggs.

138. Preparation. — Hydrogen sulphide may be prepared by the direct union of its constituents, but it is generally prepared by the action of dilute sulphuric or hydrochloric acid upon iron sulphide (ferrous sulphide, FeS).

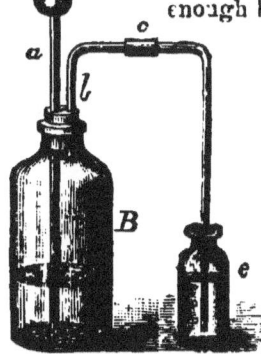

Fig. 61.

(*a.*) Into a gas bottle, arranged as for the preparation of H (§ 20), put about 10 *g.* of FeS, replace the cork snugly, add enough H_2O to seal the lower end of the funnel tube, and place the bottle out of doors, or in a good draft of air, to carry off any of the offensive H_2S that may escape. Let the delivery tube dip 5 or 6 *cm.* under cold H_2O, contained in another bottle, *e*. Add a few *cu. cm.* of H_2SO_4 or HCl. Bubbles of gas appear in *e* and are absorbed by the H_2O. Add acid in small quantities, as in the preparation of H, until the H_2O in *e* smells strongly of the gas. Remove the gas bottle and cork tightly.

$$FeS + H_2SO_4 = FeSO_4 + H_2S,$$
$$\text{or} \ldots\ldots FeS + 2HCl = FeCl_2 + H_2S.$$

(*b.*) Fig. 62 represents a convenient piece of apparatus for the preparation of H_2S. It consists of three bulbs of glass, the lower two, *b* and *c*, being in a single piece, the tubular prolongation of the upper one, *a*, being ground to fit gas tight into the neck of *b* at *l* and extending downward nearly to the bottom of *c*. Lumps of

FeS, as large as can be admitted through the tubulure at m, are introduced into b, the stricture at e, surrounding the prolongation of a, preventing them from falling into c. The tubulure at m is then closed by a cork carrying a glass stop-cock. The dilute acid (1 part H_2SO_4 + 14 parts H_2O) is poured in through the safety tube, t, passes into c and rises into b, covering the FeS. H_2S is generated in b, and escapes through the stop-cock at m. When this stop-cock is closed, the confined gas presses on the surface of the liquid in b and forces it into c and a. When the acid is no longer in contact with the FeS, the generation of H_2S ceases, and the gas in b is held, under pressure, ready for use. The acid may be removed from the apparatus by the tubulure at n, when it is necessary to renew it.

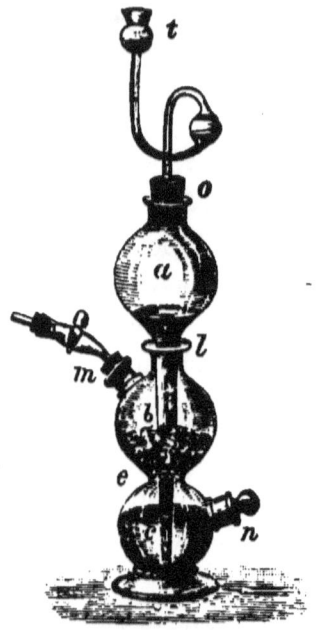

FIG. 62.

(c.) Argand lamp chimneys frequently break at the neck near the bottom. Into such a broken chimney, put a glass ball of such size that it will not pass through the stricture. Support the chimney by a perforated cork, in a vessel containing dilute acid and provide a delivery tube, as shown in Fig. 63. Place lumps of FeS in the chimney above the glass ball, replace the cork with the delivery tube, push the chimney down through the large cork into the acid; the generation of H_2S begins. When the reaction has continued as long as desired, lift the chimney out of the acid by sliding it up through the large cork. Any member of the class can make this piece of apparatus, which is very convenient when only a small quantity of H_2S is wanted at a time. Of course, it is not *necessary* that the argand lamp chimney be broken. In the figure, the open vessel is supposed to contain ammonia water, to retain the H_2S that may escape solution in the H_2O of the middle bottle.

FIG. 63.

(*d.*) If desirable, the gas may be collected over *warm* H_2O.

(*e.*) H_2S may be prepared by heating a mixture of equal parts of S and paraffin. By regulating the temperature, the evolution of H_2S may be controlled. When the mixture is allowed to cool, the evolution of the gas ceases; when the mixture is again heated, H_2S is again given off. This is a very convenient method of preparing H_2S, but, it is said, that it sometimes leads to explosions. The chemical changes involved in the process are still obscure.

139. Physical Properties. — Hydrogen sulphide is a colorless gas, having a sweetish taste and the offensive odor of rotten eggs. It may be liquefied and solidified by cold and pressure. Its specific gravity is 17, it being, thus, a little heavier than air. At ordinary temperatures, water dissolves a little more than three times its volume of the gas. The solution has the peculiar odor of the gas and a slightly acid reaction.

Experiment 135.—Bring a flame to the open mouth of a jar of H_2S. The gas will burn with a pale blue flame, forming H_2O and SO_2 and depositing a slight incrustation of S on the inside of the jar.

Experiment 136.—Fill a Volta's pistol [Ph., § 371 (85)] with a mixture composed of three volumes of O and two volumes of H_2S. Pass an electric spark from the electric machine or induction coil through the mixed gases. They will explode violently, complete combustion taking place.

Experiment 137.—Attach a drying tube, containing calcium chloride, to the delivery tube of the gas bottle. Provide the dry- ing tube with a jet made of glass tubing. When all of the air has been expelled from the apparatus, *and not till then,* hold a lighted match to the jet. (A mix- ture of H_2S and air is ex- plosive.) The gas will burn with a blue flame. Hold a dry bottle over the flame. Moisture will con- dense on the sides of the bottle. This liquid will red- den blue litmus paper.

$$2H_2S + 3O_2 = 2H_2O + 2SO_2$$

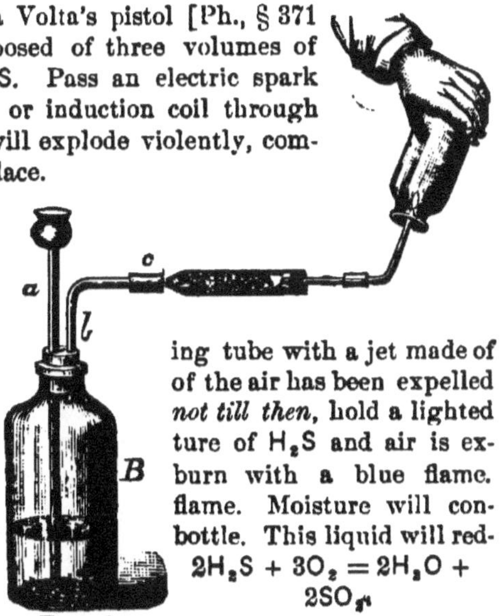

FIG. 64.

Experiment 138.—Burn a jet of H_2S, using the apparatus arranged as described in Exp. 28. Test the liquid that accumulates in the bend of d with blue litmus paper.

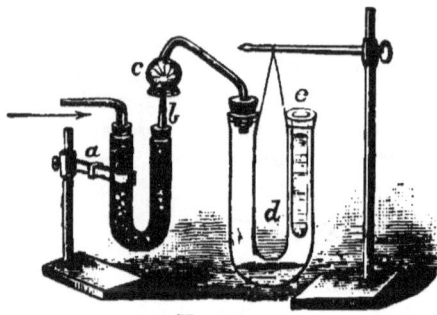

Fig. 65.

Experiment 139.— Interpose a glass tube between the drying tube and the jet (Fig. 65). Heat this tube. The H_2S will be decomposed and the S be deposited on the cold part of the tube. The product that *now* accumulates in the bend of d will not redden blue litmus paper. The analysis of H_2S is here followed by the synthesis of H_2O.

Experiment 140.—Fill a glass cylinder with H_2S and a similar one with Cl. Bring the cylinders together, mouth to mouth. HCl is formed and S deposited.

Experiment 141.—Let a few drops of fuming HNO_3 fall into a globe of H_2S. The gas will be decomposed with an explosion. Try the experiment with strong H_2SO_4 or with Nordhausen acid (§ 156).

Experiment 142.—Moisten a bright silver or copper coin and hold it in a stream of H_2S. The coin will be quickly blackened by the formation of a metallic sulphide. The same effect will follow the dipping of the bright coin into a solution of H_2S in H_2O (sulphuretted hydrogen water). See § 138, *a*.

Experiment 143.—Write your name in a colorless, aqueous solution of lead acetate (sugar of lead). Hold the autograph, before drying, in a stream of H_2S. The lead sulphide formed renders the invisible writing legible.

Experiment 144.—Make a sketch in the same colorless liquid and allow it to dry. At any convenient time, float the paper containing the invisible design upon H_2S water. The figure will "come out" promptly.

Experiment 145.— Connect five bottles, as shown in Fig. 66. Put a dilute solution of lead acetate or nitrate into a: an acid solution of arsenic into b; one of antimony into c; a dilute solution of zinc sulphate, to which a little NH_4HO has been added, into d;

NH₄HO into *e*. Pass a current of H_2S from the generator through the bottles. A black lead sulphide will be precipitated in *a*; yellow arsenic sulphide, in *b*; orange antimony sulphide, in *c*; white zinc sulphide, in *d*. The zinc sulphide is soluble in dilute acids. The NH_3 was added to the contents of *d* to destroy the acidity of the solution, to the end that the sulphide might be precipitated.

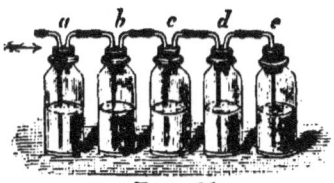

FIG. 66.

140. Chemical Properties.—Hydrogen sulphide is easily combustible, the products of its combustion being water and sulphur dioxide (§ 144). It is readily decomposed by heat and by certain metals in the presence of moisture and by many oxidizing agents. It precipitates metallic sulphides from solutions of the compounds of many metals. It may be liquefied by cold and pressure. Its solution reddens blue litmus. The gas is very poisonous when breathed, and even when much diluted its respiration is very injurious. Under such circumstances, the best antidote is the inhalation of very dilute chlorine obtained by wetting a towel with dilute acetic acid and sprinkling over it a few decigrams or grains of bleaching powder.

141. Composition.—The composition of hydrogen sulphide may be ascertained by heating metallic tin in a known volume of the gas. The gas will be decomposed, the sulphur combining with the tin as tin sulphide and the hydrogen being set free. The volume of hydrogen will be the same as that of the hydrogen sulphide decomposed. When a platinum wire spiral is heated red hot in a known volume of hydrogen sulphide by the passage of an electric current (Ph., § 387), the gas is decomposed, both of its constituents being set free. The volume of the hydrogen will again be the same as that of the hydrogen sulphide. Careful analyses have proved that the gravimetric and volumetric composition of this gas may be expressed by the following diagram:

$$\boxed{\begin{array}{c}\text{H}\\1\ m.c.\end{array}} + \boxed{\begin{array}{c}\text{H}\\1\ m.c.\end{array}} + \boxed{\begin{array}{c}\text{S}\\32\ m.c.\end{array}} = \boxed{\begin{array}{c}\text{H}_2\text{S}\\34\ m.c.\end{array}}$$

(*a.*) The *three* atoms in the molecule of H_2S occupy the same volume as the *two* atoms in the molecule H_2. In other words, molecular volumes are equal (§ 61).

142. Uses and Tests.—Hydrogen sulphide is very extensively used in the chemical laboratory as a reagent, forming sulphides that are characteristic (in color, solubility or some other easily recognized property) for certain metals or groups of metals. It is easily detected by its odor or by holding in it a strip of paper wet with an aqueous solution of lead acetate.

Note.—Hydrogen persulphide (H_2S_2) is known to chemists. It is a yellow, transparent, oily liquid.

Exercises.

1. Write the reaction for Exp. 135.
2. When metallic tin is heated in H_2S, the gas is decomposed. The S unites with the tin. (*a.*) Name the solid and gaseous products. (*b.*) How will the volume of this gaseous product compare with that of the H_2S decomposed?
3. When a spiral of platinum wire is heated in an atmosphere of H_2S, the gas is decomposed with the deposition of solid S. What volume of H can thus be set free from a liter of H_2S?
4. The reaction resulting from passing a current of H_2S through an aqueous solution of Br is as follows:

$$H_2S + Br_2 = 2HBr + S.$$

(*a.*) What volume of H_2S is needed to yield 4 *l.* of HBr? (*b.*) What

§ 142   HYDROGEN SULPHIDE.   123

weight of Br will thus combine with 10 g. of H_2S? (c.) What weight of Br will yield 25 l. of HBr?

5. How many grams of NH_4HO will just neutralize 63 g. of HNO_3?

6. (a.) How many liters of O will unite with 20 l. of NO to form NO_2? (b.) How many each of O and NO to form 30 l. of NO_2?

7. Arsenic vapor is 150 times as heavy as H. (a.) What is the molecular weight of As? Explain. (b.) The atomic weight of As is 75 m. c. How many atoms are there in an As molecule?

8. (a.) What name would you apply to a substance that has only one kind of atoms? (b.) One that has two kinds? (c.) One that has three kinds?

9. Give Ampère's Law. Define chemistry.

10. Symbolize the sulphides of Na', K', Ag', Ca'', Cu'', C^{IV}.

11. What weight of S in 10 l. of S vapor under normal pressure at 500°C.? (b.) At 1050°C.?

12. Calculate the percentage composition of cryolite.

SECTION III.

SULPHUR OXIDES AND ACIDS.

143. Sulphur Oxides.—Sulphur and oxygen unite to form two acid-forming oxides (or anhydrides) symbolized as SO_2 and SO_3. These unite with water to form the acids symbolized as H_2SO_3 and H_2SO_4.

(*a.*) In addition to these, we are acquainted with sulphur sesquioxide (S_2O_3), which has no corresponding known acid; with hyposulphurous acid (H_2SO_2), which has no corresponding known oxide; with sulphur peroxide (S_2O_7), and with the thionic acids (§ 158). The compound, S_2O_3, is called a sesquioxide because the number of its O atoms is $1\frac{1}{2}$ times the number of its S atoms, the Latin prefix, *sesqui*, meaning one and a half.

144. Sulphur Dioxide.—This oxide of sulphur (sulphurous oxide, sulphurous anhydride, sulphurous acid gas, sulphuryl, SO_2) is the sole product of the combustion of sulphur in the air or in oxygen. It is the only compound of sulphur and oxygen that can be formed by direct synthesis (Exps. 36 and 43).

145. Preparation.—As ordinarily prepared by burning sulphur in the air, the sulphur dioxide is mixed with nitrogen from the air. When the pure anhydride is wanted, it is generally prepared from strong sulphuric acid by heating it with copper, silver or mercury.

(*a.*) Put 20 or 30 *g.* of small bits of copper and 60 *cu. cm.* of strong H_2SO_4 into a flask and apply heat. The gas that is evolved may be purified by passing through H_2O in the wash bottle, *b* (Fig. 67), and then collected by downward displacement or over mercury or absorbed in H_2O, as shown at *c*. A solution of copper sulphate, (blue vitriol, $CuSO_4$), remains in the flask.

$$2H_2SO_4 + Cu = CuSO_4 + 2H_2O + SO_2.$$

§ 145   SULPHUR OXIDES AND ACIDS.   125

(*b.*) A solution of SO_2 in H_2O is often wanted in the laboratory. It may be formed by reducing H_2SO_4 with charcoal.

$$2H_2SO_4 + C = 2SO_2 + 2H_2O + CO_2.$$

The mixed gases may be passed through H_2O in a series of Woulffe bottles (Fig. 34); very little of the CO_2 will be absorbed.

(*c.*) It is well to save bits of copper, such as pieces of wire, shells of metallic cartridges, fragments of sheet copper, *etc.*, for they will be of frequent use in the study of chemistry.

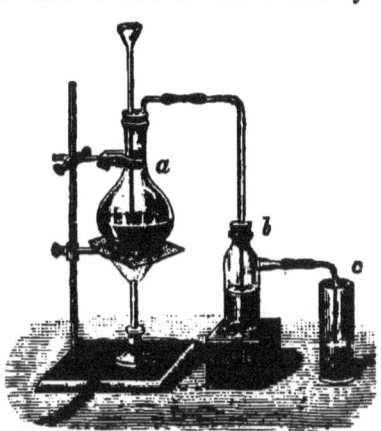

FIG. 67.

FIG. 68.

Experiment 146.—From the generating flask, *a* (Fig. 67), pass the SO_2 through a bottle or tube packed in ice; then dry the cool gas with H_2SO_4 (Exp. 31) or $CaCl_2$ (Exp. 28); then pass the dry gas through a U-tube packed in salt and pounded ice (Ph. § 521). The SO_2 will condense to a liquid at the low temperature thus produced. If the U-tube has good glass stop cocks, as shown in the figure, the liquid SO_2 may be sealed and preserved. Or the two arms of a common U-tube may have been previously drawn out to make a narrow neck upon each; after the condensation of the SO_2, these necks may be fused with the blowpipe flame and the liquid thus sealed for preservation.

Caution.—The following experiment is hardly safe for performance by the teacher in the class or by the pupil. Such a pressure on the *inside* of a glass tube of *uncertain qualities*, as glass tubes generally are, is not to be trifled with. Although less satisfactory, it may be safer to rest the case upon the assertion of the author.

Experiment 147.—To show the liquefaction of SO_2 by pressure, draw out one end of a strong glass tube (2 *cm.* in diameter) to a point. Fill the tube with dry SO_2 by displacement. Into the open end, thrust a snugly fitting, greased, caoutchouc stopper. With a stout rod, force the stopper into the tube until the SO_2 occupies about a fifth of its original volume. Liquid SO_2 will collect at the pointed end of the tube.

Experiment 148.—Pour some of the liquid SO_2 upon the surface of mercury contained in a capsule, and blow a current of air over it by means of a bellows. The mercury will be frozen.

Experiment 149.—If you have a thick, platinum crucible, heat it red hot and pour some of the liquid SO_2 into it. The SO_2 will assume the "spheroidal state," like that of the globules of H_2O sometimes seen upon the top of a hot stove, the temperature of the liquid being below its boiling point. If, now, a little H_2O be poured in, the SO_2 will be instantly vaporized by the heat taken from the H_2O (Ph. § 526), which therefore at once becomes ice. By some dexterity, *the lump of ice may be thrown out of the red-hot crucible.*

Experiment 150.—Wrap the bulb of an alcohol thermometer in cotton wool and pour some of the liquid SO_2 upon it. The change of sensible into latent heat effected by the vaporization of the SO_2 produces a diminution of temperature and the thermometer falls, perhaps as low as —60°C.

Experiment 151.—Pour a quantity of the liquid SO_2 into nearly ice cold H_2O; a part will evaporate at once, another part will dissolve in the H_2O, and a third part of the heavy, oily liquid will sink to the bottom of the vessel. If the part which has thus subsided be stirred with a glass rod, it will boil at once, and the temperature of the H_2O will be so much reduced that some of it will be frozen.

Experiment 152.—Add a few drops of the aqueous solution of SO_2 to a weak solution of potassium permanganate. The red color will disappear, owing to reduction by SO_2.

Experiment 153.—Burn some S under a bell glass within which are some moist, bright colored flowers. The flowers will be bleached. The color may be partly restored by dipping some of the flowers into dilute H_2SO_4 and others into NH_4HO.

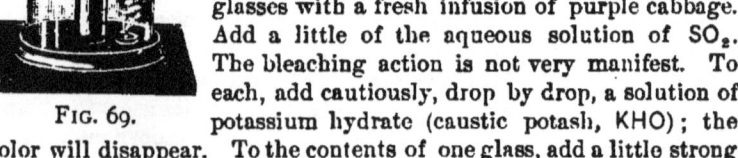

FIG. 69.

Experiment 154.—Partly fill each of two glasses with a fresh infusion of purple cabbage. Add a little of the aqueous solution of SO_2. The bleaching action is not very manifest. To each, add cautiously, drop by drop, a solution of potassium hydrate (caustic potash, KHO); the color will disappear. To the contents of one glass, add a little strong H_2SO_4; a red color appears. To the other add more of the solution of KHO; a green color appears.

Experiment 155.—Suspend a small lighted taper in a lamp chimney placed so that a current of air can enter from below. At the lower end of the chimney, place a small capsule containing burning S. Place a piece of window glass over the top of the chimney so as to confine the SO_2 within the chimney. The taper quickly ceases to burn.

146. Properties.—Sulphur dioxide is a transparent, colorless, irrespirable, suffocating gas. It has a specific gravity of 32, being nearly $2\frac{1}{4}$ times as heavy as air. It condenses to a liquid at $-10°C.$, and solidifies when cooled below $-76°C.$ The liquid has a specific gravity of 1.49, and vaporizes rapidly in the air at the ordinary temperature, producing great cold. It has a great affinity for oxygen. Under the influence of sunlight, it unites directly with chlorine, acting as a dyad compound radical and forming sulphuryl chloride, $(SO_2)''Cl_2$. It bleaches many colors, not by destroying the coloring matter, as chlorine does, but by uniting with it to form unstable, colorless compounds. When, by the action of chemical agents, the sulphur dioxide is set free from the colorless compounds thus formed, the color reappears. It is neither combustible nor a supporter of ordinary combustion.

147. Composition.—The composition of sulphurous anhydride is represented by the following diagram:

$$\boxed{\begin{array}{c}O\\16\ m.c.\end{array}} + \boxed{\begin{array}{c}O\\16\ m.c.\end{array}} + \boxed{\begin{array}{c}S\\32\ m.c.\end{array}} = \boxed{SO_2, 64\ m.c.}$$

148. Uses and Tests.—Sulphur dioxide is largely used in the manufacture of sulphuric acid and for bleaching straw, silk and woollen goods. It is also used as an antichlor for the purpose of removing the excess of chlorine present in the bleached rags from which paper is made, and as an antiseptic. When free, it is easily detected by its odor, familiar as that of burning matches, and by its blackening a paper wet with a solution of mercurous nitrate.

149. Sulphurous Acid.—Sulphur dioxide is freely soluble in water, forming sulphurous acid (hydrogen sulphite, H_2SO_3). When this liquid is boiled, it decomposes into water and sulphur dioxide; when it is cooled below 5°C., it yields a crystalline hydrate of sulphurous acid with a composition of $H_2SO_3 + 14H_2O$. On standing, it absorbs oxygen from the air and changes to sulphuric acid (H_2SO_4). As one or both of the hydrogen atoms in its molecule may be replaced by a metal, it gives rise to two series of compounds, called sulphites (§ 170). The term "sulphurous acid" is frequently applied to sulphur dioxide, but such use of the term is seriously confusing and objectionable.

150. Sulphur Trioxide.—When dry oxygen and dry sulphurous anhydride are mixed and passed over heated platinum sponge or platinized asbestos, they combine, forming dense fumes of sulphur trioxide (sulphuric oxide, sulphuric anhydride, SO_3). When these fumes are condensed in a dry, cool receiver, they form white, silky, fiber-like crystals resembling asbestos. Sulphur trioxide may be prepared more easily by gently heating Nordhausen acid (§ 156) and condensing the vapor given off, as in the method above described. When perfectly dry, it does not exhibit any acid properties and may be moulded with the fingers without injury to the skin. It has so great an attraction for water that it can be preserved only in vessels hermetically sealed. It unites with water with a hissing sound and the evolution of much heat, forming sulphuric acid.

$$SO_3 + H_2O = H_2SO_4.$$

151. Sulphuric Acid.—Sulphuric acid (hydrogen sulphate, oil of vitriol, H_2SO_4), occurs free in the waters of certain rivers and mineral springs. It has been estimated that one river, the Rio Vinagre, in South America, carries more than 38,000 $Kg.$ of this acid to the sea daily. Sulphuric acid is to the chemical arts what iron is to the mechanical arts, as it enters, directly or indirectly, into the preparation of nearly every substance with which the chemist deals. It has been said that the commercial prosperity of any country may be well measured by the quantity of sulphuric acid that it uses.

152. Preparation.—Sulphuric acid is formed by the addition of water to sulphur trioxide. The water may be added at the time of the formation of the anhydride or subsequently. For this purpose, the sulphuric anhydride is formed by the oxidation of sulphurous anhydride by means of the nitrogen oxides or acids. The direct method of oxidation described in § 150 being too expensive, the indirect method soon to be described is employed.

(*a.*) In a bottle having a capacity of 1 $l.$ or more, burn a bit of S. In the atmosphere of SO_2 thus formed, place a stick (or a glass rod carrying a tuft of gun cotton) dipped in strong HNO_3. Red fumes of NO_2 will appear The red fumes show that the HNO_3 has been robbed of part of its O.

$$2HNO_3 + SO_2 = H_2SO_4 + 2NO_2.$$

In the presence of moisture, SO_2 is able to reduce (take O from) HNO_2, HNO_3, N_2O_3 or NO_2. In the process just described, the SO_2 *reduced* the HNO_3; the HNO_3 *oxidized* the SO_2.

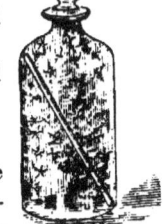

Fig. 70.

(b.) The manufacture of H_2SO_4 may be prettily represented by the following lecture table process: A large glass globe or flask is filled with air or oxygen and provided with five tubes, as shown in Fig. 71. One tube connects it with a flask which furnishes a current of SO_2 (§ 145, a.); another connects it with a second flask or bottle, which furnishes a current of NO (§ 83); the third connects it with a

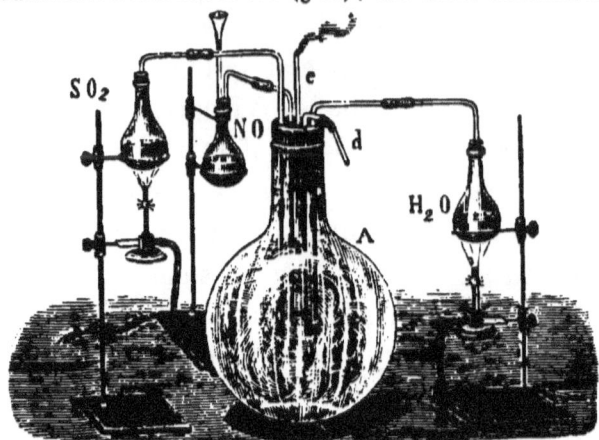

FIG. 71.

flask which furnishes a current of steam; by the tube, d, a supply of air or O is admitted, from time to time, into the globe. The fifth tube, e, allows the escape of the waste products of the reaction; it may be connected with an aspirator.

(1.) NO enters the globe and takes O from the air. The ruddy fumes of NO_2 are seen.

(2.) On admitting a current of SO_2, the red fumes of NO_2 disappear and white "leaden-chamber crystals" form on the walls of the globe. The NO_2 has been reduced and the SO_2 oxidized.

(3.) On admitting steam, the crystals disappear, and dilute H_2SO_4 collects at the bottom of the globe.

(4.) If air be admitted, red fumes again appear and the process may be repeated.

(c.) In the manufacture of H_2SO_4, the SO_2 is formed by burning crude S or pyrite (FeS_2) in kilns provided for that purpose. The pyrite, in moderately sized lumps, is placed on the grates of the kilns, about 250 Kg. (500 or 600 lb.) at a time. When the burning is once started, it is kept up by placing a new charge on top of the one nearly burned out. The quantity of air admitted is carefully regulated by a door placed below the pyrite kilns. The SO_2 and other gases are drawn through all of the apparatus by the draft of a large chimney. The nitrogen oxides are furnished, sometimes by a continued supply of liquid HNO_3 in the chambers, but more often by the reaction of sodium nitrate and H_2SO_4 heated by the burning pyrite. The air, SO_2 and nitrogen oxides are carried into a series of three or more huge leaden chambers where they come into contact with a constant supply of steam. These lead chambers are sometimes 30 $m.$ long, 6 to 7 $m.$ wide and about 5 $m.$ high, having thus a capacity of 900 to 1000 $cu. m.$ or about 38,000 $cu. ft.$ They are supported by a wooden framework, placed on pillars of brick or iron.

FIG. 72.

The general appearance is shown in Fig. 72. The H_2SO_4 formed in the chambers accumulates on the floor. The process is conducted so that this "chamber acid" has a specific gravity of 1.55, as a stronger acid absorbs the nitrogen oxides. After leaving the lead chambers, the nitrogen oxides, which are supplied in excess, are absorbed by concentrated H_2SO_4 in what is called a "Gay-Lussac tower," while the nitrogen escapes. The "chamber acid," which contains 64 *per cent.* of H_2SO_4, is then concentrated in the "denitrating" or "Glover tower," where it is mixed with the "nitrated acid" from the Gay-Lussac tower and exposed to the evaporating influence of the hot gases as they pass from the kilns into the chambers, or by evaporation in leaden pans, until it has a specific gravity of 1.7 and contains 78 *per cent.* of H_2SO_4. If concentrated beyond this point, the hot acid attacks the lead of the pans. In this form, the acid is technically called brown oil of vitriol as it is slightly colored by organic impurities. It is largely sold for a great variety of purposes. Further concentration and purification are carried on in glass retorts of from 75 to 150 $l.$ capacity or in large platinum stills (some of which cost as much as £6,000), until the liquid contains 98 *per cent.* of H_2SO_4 and has a specific gravity of upwards of 1.8.

(*d.*) Although we have no reason to think that some of the reactions in the manufacture of H_2SO_4 are not simultaneous, we may, with propriety, trace them as if they were really consecutive; *e. g.*,

(1.) $S + O_2 = SO_2.$
(2.) $2HNO_3 + SO_2 = H_2SO_4 + 2NO_2.$
(3.) $SO_2 + NO_2 = SO_3 + NO.$
(4.) $SO_3 + H_2O = H_2SO_4.$
(5.) $NO + O = NO_2.$

In reality, most of the O used for the oxidation of the SO_2 comes from the air, admitted to the chambers through the kiln. The part taken in the process by the nitrogen oxide is very interesting, it acting as a carrier of O from the air to the SO_2. Theoretically, but not practically, a single molecule of HNO_3 or of NO would be sufficient for the manufacture of an unlimited amount of H_2SO_4, as may be seen by repeating the equations above (omitting the second) in a series continued to any extent desired. But, since air is used instead of pure O, the N thus introduced into the chambers has to be removed, and, in its passage out, sweeps away much of the nitrogen oxides, which then have to be supplied anew.

Experiment 156.—Place 27 *cu. cm.* of H_2O in a graduated tube. Slowly add 73 *cu. cm.* of H_2SO_4. When the mixture has cooled, notice that its volume is about 92 *cu. cm.* instead of 100 *cu. cm.*

Caution.—In mixing H_2O and H_2SO_4, pour the H_2SO_4 into the H_2O, not the H_2O into the H_2SO_4. If the lighter liquid be poured on top of the heavier, it will float there and great heat will be developed at the level where they come into contact. This heat might form steam of sufficient tension to burst through the heavier liquid above and do damage by scattering the H_2SO_4. When the above directions are followed, the H_2SO_4 mixes with the H_2O as it falls through it.

Experiment 157.—Place 30 *cu.cm.* of H_2O in a beaker glass of about 250 *cu. cm.* capacity. Into this, pour 70 *cu. cm.* of concentrated H_2SO_4 in a fine stream. Stir the mixture with a test tube containing alcohol or ether, colored with cochineal or other coloring matter. The liquid in the test tube will boil. Holding the test tube in a pair of nippers, ignite the vapor escaping from the test tube. The test tube may be closed with a cork carrying a delivery tube and the jet ignited. It will give a voluminous flame. With a chemical thermometer (App. 3), take the temperature of the liquids before and after mixture. If the test tube stirrer contain H_2O instead of the more volatile liquids mentioned, the H_2O will boil.

Experiment 158.—Dip a splinter of wood into H_2SO_4. It will be charred as if by fire.

Experiment 159.—Dissolve 50 $g.$ of crystallized sugar in 20 $cu.$ $cm.$ of hot H_2O. To this syrup, when cool, add a little H_2SO_4 and stir the two together. The mixture will become hot and form a voluminous, black porous mass.

153. Properties.—The sulphuric acid of commerce is largely known as oil of vitriol. It has a specific gravity of about 1.82. It generally contains, as impurities, lead sulphate from the chambers and evaporating pans, and arsenic from the pyrite. For most purposes, however, it answers as well as the "H_2SO_4, C.P.," or chemically pure acid. The pure acid is a colorless, oily, very corrosive liquid with a specific gravity of 1.842 at the ordinary temperature (1.854 at 0°C. and 1.834 at 24°C.). It has a very remarkable attraction for water, the combination being marked by a condensation of volume and the evolution of much heat. It may be mixed with water in all proportions. When exposed to the air at ordinary temperatures, it does not vaporize but absorbs water from the atmosphere, thus increasing both its weight and volume. On account of this hygroscopic action, it should be kept in well stoppered bottles.

Sulphuric acid removes water from many organic substances, completely charring some, like sugar and woody fiber, and breaking others, as alcohol and oxalic acid, into new compounds (see §§ 213 and 193). It is one of the most energetic acids known. Diluted with 1,000 times its bulk of water, it still reddens blue litmus. It liberates most of the other acids from their salts.

154. Uses.—Sulphuric acid is used as a drying agent for gases, in the preparation of most of the other acids, in the manufacture of soda, phosphorus and alum, in the preparation of artificial fertilizers, in the refining of petroleum, in the processes of bleaching, dyeing, *etc.* In fact, there is scarcely an art or trade in which, in some form or other, it is not used, it being employed directly or indirectly in nearly all important chemical processes. It is the most important chemical reagent we have and is made in immense quantities, upwards of 850,000 tons being produced yearly in Great Britain alone.

155. Tests.—The most convenient test for free sulphuric acid is the charring of organic substances. A paper moistened with a natural water containing the free acid, and then dried at 100°C. will be completely charred. The acid or solutions of its salts give a white insoluble precipitate with barium chloride or calcium chloride.

156. Nordhausen Acid.—Nordhausen acid (disulphuric acid, fuming sulphuric acid, $H_2S_2O_7$), is prepared by the distillation of dried iron sulphate (green vitriol, $FeSO_4$), in earthen retorts. It is a heavy, oily liquid with a specific gravity of 1.89. It fumes strongly in the air and hisses like a hot iron when dropped into water. It is used chiefly for dissolving indigo.

(*a.*) The name, Nordhausen acid, is due to the fact that it was formerly prepared in Nordhausen, Saxony. At the present time, the acid comes almost wholly from Bohemia. The propriety of the term, disulphuric acid, is shown by the equation, $2H_2SO_4 - H_2O = H_2S_2O_7$. It may be considered as SO_3 dissolved in H_2SO_4, for, when heated, it separates into those substances, $H_2S_2O_7 = SO_3 + H_2SO_4$.

157. Sulphur Sesquioxide and Hyposulphurous Acids.—Sulphur sesquioxide (S_2O_3) is a rare, bluish green compound, resembling malachite in appearance. It easily decomposes into sulphur dioxide and sulphur. Hyposulphurous acid (H_2SO_2) is a very unstable, yellow liquid with powerful reducing properties. Its salt, hydrogen sodium hyposulphite ($HNaSO_2$), is used for the reduction of indigo in dyeing and calico printing.

158. Thionic Acids.—Besides the foregoing, there is a well defined series of sulphur acids, but they are of much less importance. Their corresponding oxides are unknown.

(*a*.) Thiosulphuric acid .... $H_2S_2O_3$
  Dithionic acid .... $H_2S_2O_6$
  Trithionic acid .... $H_2S_3O_6$
  Tetrathionic acid .... $H_2S_4O_6$
  Pentathionic acid .... $H_2S_5O_6$.

(*b*.) The thiosulphuric acid is better known by the misnomer of "hyposulphurous" acid, which properly designates the compound symbolized by H_2SO_2. In similar manner, the thiosulphates (*e. g.*, sodium thiosulphate, $Na_2S_2O_3$), are commonly, but improperly, spoken of as "hyposulphites."

Note.—The word, *thionic*, comes from the Greek name for S.

159. Sulphur Oxides and Oxyacids.—The known sulphur oxides and oxyacids are symbolized in tabular form below for purposes of convenient study:

Oxides	S_2O_3	SO_2	SO_3				
Acids	H_2SO_2	....	H_2SO_3	H_2SO_4	$H_2S_2O_3$	$H_2S_2O_6$	$H_2S_3O_6$	$H_2S_4O_6$	$H_2S_5O_6$

EXERCISES.

1. (*a.*) What is the molecular weight of SO_2? (*b.*) The specific gravity of the gas? (*c.*) Its percentage composition?

2. H_2S and SO_2 are often found in volcanic gases. When they come into contact, they decompose each other. Write an equation explaining the occurrence of native S in volcanic regions.

3. Why can not H_2SO_4 be used for drying H_2S (Exp. 141).

4. (*a.*) How much HNO_3 can be formed from 306 *g.* of KNO_3? (*b.*) How much H_2SO_4 will be required? (*c.*) What will be the yield of $HNaSO_4$? (*d.*) If the product be Na_2SO_4, what will be the amount thereof?

5. Write the graphic symbol for H_2SO_4 : (*a,*) Representing S as a dyad. (*b.*) As a hexad.

6. Write the graphic symbol for $H_2S_2O_7$, introducing SO_2 twice as a bivalent radical. ($H_2S_2O_7$ = anhydrosulphuric acid.)

7. The symbol for potassium sulphate is K_2SO_4; that for lead sulphate is $PbSO_4$. (*a.*) What is the quantivalence of potassium? (*b.*) Of lead? (See § 60.)

8. How would you write the symbol of a binary compound containing a dyad and a triad?

9. How much HNO_3 will just neutralize 1200 *g.* of ammonium hydrate?

10. (*a.*) How much NH_3 may be formed from 42.8 *g.* of NH_4Cl? (*b.*) How much CaH_2O_2 must be used?

11. (*a.*) What volume of Cl may be obtained from 1 *l.* of dry HCl? (*b.*) What weight?

12. When aeriform H_2O and Cl are passed through a porcelain tube heated to redness, HCl and O are formed. (*a.*) Write the reaction in molecular symbols. (*b.*) What volume of O may be thus obtained from 2 *l.* of steam? (*c.*) How will the volume of HCl formed compare with that of the O? (*d.*) In what simple way may the O be freed from mixture with HCl?

13. (*a.*) From 100 *g.* of $KClO_3$, how many grams of O may be obtained? (*b.*) How many liters?

14. H_2O and N are among the products formed when NH_4Cl and $NaNO_2$ are heated together in a flask. Write the reaction.

15. (*a.*) I mix H and Cl, and expose the mixture to sunlight. What happens? (*b.*) I add NH_3 to the product just formed. What is the name of this second product?

16. What is the more common name for oxygen dioxide?

SECTION IV.

SELENIUM AND TELLURIUM.

☞ SELENIUM ; *Symbol*, Se; *specific gravity, 4.3 to 4.8 ; atomic weight, 79 m. c. ; molecular weight, 158 m. c.*

160. Selenium.—This element is a rare substance, of little industrial importance, but of considerable interest to the chemist. It is occasionally found free, but generally in combination as a selenide. Like sulphur, it exists in several allotropic forms. The native form melts at about 217°C. and boils with a deep yellow vapor below a red heat. In its leading properties and chemical behavior, it resembles sulphur, as will appear in § 162. It burns with an odor resembling that of decaying cabbages. It offers a very great resistance to the passage of the electric current, the resistance being wonderfully diminished by the action of light. The property last mentioned, has recently been utilized in the construction of the photophone and the element thus endowed with added interest and importance.

☞ TELLURIUM ; *Symbol*, Te ; *specific gravity, 6.25 ; atomic weight, 128 m. c. ; molecular weight, 256 m. c.*

161. Tellurium.—This element is even more rare than selenium. It has a metallic lustre and in some of its physical properties, such as the conduction of heat and electricity, it resembles the metals. It melts at about 500°C. and volatilizes at a white heat in a current of hydrogen. Its chemical behavior, however, allies it to sulphur and selenium. With hydrogen, it forms hydrogen telluride (H_2Te), which can not be distinguished by its smell from hydrogen sulphide.

Note.—The name, *selenium*, is from the Greek word meaning *the moon*, and the name, *tellurium*, from the Greek word meaning *the earth*.

162. The Sulphur Group. — Oxygen, sulphur, selenium and tellurium form a natural group. The resemblances between the last three members of the group are as well marked as those of the chlorine group. As the atomic weight increases, the chemical activity diminishes, selenium being about midway between sulphur and tellurium. Their specific gravities, melting and boiling points, show a similar gradation.

(*a.*) Some of the chemical resemblances of the members of this group are easily visible in the following table:

Hydrogen oxide. H_2O	Hydrogen sulphide. H_2S	Hydrogen selenide. H_2Se	Hydrogen telluride. H_2Te
Iron oxide. FeO	Iron sulphide. FeS	Iron selenide. FeSe	Iron telluride. FeTe
....	Sulphur dioxide. SO_2	Selenium dioxide. SeO_2	Tellurium dioxide. TeO_2
....	Sulphur trioxide. SO_3	Selenium trioxide. SeO_3 (?)	Tellurium trioxide. TeO_3
....	Sulphurous acid. H_2SO_3	Selenous acid. H_2SeO_3	Tellurous acid. H_2TeO_3
....	Sulphuric acid. H_2SO_4	Selenic acid. H_2SeO_4	Telluric acid. H_2TeO_4
Ethyl oxide (ether). $(C_2H_5)_2O$	Ethyl sulphide. $(C_2H_5)_2S$	Ethyl selenide. $(C_2H_5)_2Se$	Ethyl telluride. $(C_2H_5)_2Te$
Ethyl hydrate (alcohol). $(C_2H_5)HO$	Ethyl hydrogen sulphide. $(C_2H_5)HS$	Ethyl hydrogen selenide. $(C_2H_5)HSe$	Ethyl hydrogen telluride. $(C_2H_5)HTe$

§ 162 THE SULPHUR GROUP. 139

EXERCISES.

1. (a.) Give the physical and chemical properties of H. (b.) Explain the structure of an oxy-hydrogen blowpipe.

2. What chemical process is illustrated when you prepare H?

3. (a.) State two ways in which the analysis of H_2O may be effected. (b.) Give the composition of H_2O by volume and by weight. (c.) What weight of each constituent in a $Kg.$ of H_2O?

4. A chemist wishes 50 $Kg.$ of H. What substances shall he use in making it, and how much of each?

5. (a.) H_2SO_4 is poured upon nitre; name the two substances that you obtain. (b.) Write the reaction.

6. (a.) What is the least amount of H_2SO_4 that will completely react with 4 $lb.$ of KNO_3? (b.) How much will the liquid product weigh?

7. (a.) From 8 $Kg.$ of KNO_3, how much HNO_3 can be liberated? (b.) How much H_2SO_4 is the least that would be required?

8. (a.) Give the names and symbols for the oxides of N. (b.) Give the law of multiple proportion.

9. (a.) What is the difference between air and water, chemically considered? (b.) Give one chemical and one physical property of O and of NH_3.

10. Write the reactions for the preparation of Cl, HF, SO_2, H_2S, and state at least one leading property of each.

11. When a hot metallic wire is plunged into a certain binary acid gas, violet fumes are seen. What is the gas?

12. (a.) How is Cl obtained? (b.) Explain the reaction. (c.) Give the most remarkable chemical properties of the substance.

13. (a.) What is the most common compound of Cl? (b.) Find its percentage composition.

14. (a.) Give the atomic weight of each of the elements that you have studied. (b.) What is meant by atomic weight?

CHAPTER X.

ACIDS, BASES, SALTS, ETC.

163. Acids.—The word acid is difficult of satisfactory definition. The term signifies a class of compounds that generally have a sour taste, a peculiar action upon vegetable colors (*e. g.*, the reddening of blue litmus), and that unite with other compounds (bases) of an opposite quality to form a third class of compounds (salts) possessing the characteristics of neither of the first two classes. *The only constituent common to all acids is hydrogen which is replaceable with an electro-positive or metallic element.*

(*a.*) The term, *acid*, is sometimes used to designate certain compounds that contain no H, as SO_3, CO_2, *etc.* Such use of the term is incorrect and seriously confusing.

(*b.*) The binary acids consist, almost exclusively, of H combined with some member of the halogen group (§123). Their names all have the termination -*ic*.

(*c.*) We may suppose the ternary acids to be formed of hydroxyl (HO, § 44), and a negative radical, as:

HNO_3; (HO)–(NO_2); H–O–(NO_2); $H-O-N\begin{smallmatrix}O\\ \\O\end{smallmatrix}$.

H_2SO_4; $(HO)_2=(SO_2)$; H–O–(SO_2)–O–H; $H-O-\underset{\underset{O}{\parallel}}{\overset{\overset{O}{\parallel}}{S}}-O-H$.

H_3PO_4; $(HO)_3\equiv(PO)$; H–O–(PO)–O–H; $H-O-\underset{\underset{H}{\overset{|}{O}}}{\overset{\overset{O}{\parallel}}{P}}-O-H$.
Phosphoric acid.

The atom of "saturating" O shown in each case in the fourth column becomes a part of the negative radical as shown in the second and third columns. Similarly, the "linking" oxygen becomes a part of the hydroxyl.

(*d.*) Acids take their names from their non-metallic or negative radicals. If only two ternary acids of a non-metallic element are known, the one in which the molecule contains the greater number of O atoms takes the termination -*ic* ; the other takes the termination -*ous*. Sometimes the radical forms three or even four ternary acids. The acid in which the molecule contains a number of O atoms greater than that of the -*ic* acid takes the prefix *per-* ; the one in which the number is less than that of the -*ous* acid takes the prefix, *hypo-*. The use of these prefixes and suffixes will be made clear by a study of the following examples :

$HClO_4$ ....*perchloric* acid.
$HClO_3$ ....*chloric* acid.
$HClO_2$ ....*chlorous* acid.
$HClO$ ....*hypochlorous* acid.

H_2SO_4 ....*sulphuric* acid.
H_2SO_3 ......*sulphurous* acid.
H_2SO_2 ..*hyposulphurous* acid.

Unfortunately, there is a lack of uniformity among chemists in the nomenclature of acids and salts ; hence, a certain amount of confusion in the literature of the science. (See § 60.)

164. Basicity of Acids. — The hydrogen of an acid that may be replaced by a metal is called basic hydrogen. If the acid molecule has one atom of basic hydrogen, the acid is called a mono-basic acid. If it has two such atoms, the acid is called a di-basic acid. Similarly, we have tri-basic and tetra-basic acids.

(*a.*) The basicity of an acid molecule depends upon the number of its directly exchangeable H atoms and may generally be represented by the number of hydroxyl groups it contains. For example :

HNO_3 is a mono-basic acid.................(HO) — (NO$_2$)'.

H_2SO_4 is a di-basic acid........................$\genfrac{}{}{0pt}{}{(HO)}{(HO)}$(SO$_2$)''.

H_3PO_4 is a tri-basic acid......................$\genfrac{}{}{0pt}{}{(HO)}{(HO)}{(HO)}$(PO)'''.

Be it remembered, however, that the basicity of an acid molecule depends, not upon the total number of its H atoms, but upon the number of them that are endowed with this peculiar power of direct exchange from metallic atoms. H_3PO_4 is called tribasic, not because it has three H atoms but because it may form three distinct salts with one metal (§ 170).

165. Anhydrides.—An oxide of a non-metallic (or electro-negative) element, which, with the elements of water, forms an acid, is called an anhydride. Nitrogen peroxide (N_2O_5) and sulphur*ic* and sulphur*ous* oxides are anhydrides. Acid oxide is a better name.

166. Bases.—The word base indicates a very important class of ternary compounds, opposed in chemical properties to the acids. The bases restore most colors that have been reddened by an acid. Like the acids, they may be considered hydroxyl compounds; unlike the acids, their hydroxyl is united with a metallic (or electro-positive) radical. The chief characteristic of a base is its power of reacting with an acid to form water and a salt. The characteristic difference between an acid and a base is that the hydrogen of the former may be replaced by a metallic atom; that of the latter by a non-metallic atom.

(*a.*) The term, *base*, is frequently, but ill-advisedly, used to designate certain compounds that neutralize acids and form salts but that contain no H, as CaO (§ 290), *etc.* Basic oxide is a better name.

(*b.*) The H of a base that may be replaced by a non-metallic element is called acid hydrogen. We have mon-acid, di-acid, tri-acid bases, *etc.* KHO, $Ca(HO)_2$, $Al(HO)_3$ and $Ti(HO)_4$ represent bases.

(*c.*) "The hydroxyl compounds of the elements that have a markedly metallic character are bases. The hydroxyl compounds of the elements that have a markedly non-metallic character are acids. The hydroxyl compounds of the elements that are neither markedly metallic nor non-metallic sometimes act as bases and sometimes as acids. Thus, SbO(HO), antimonyl hydroxide, is a weak base or a weak acid, exhibiting one character or the other according to the nature of the compound with which it is brought into contact."

167. Hydrates.—The basic oxides unite with water to form hydrates or hydroxides. Thus, $K_2O + H_2O =$ 2KHO, potassium hydrate or caustic potash. In similar manner, we may produce Na'HO, sodium hydrate; Ca''(HO)$_2$ or Ca''H$_2$O$_2$, calcium hydrate, *etc.* The hydrates are bases.

(*a.*) A hydrate may be considered as a metallic compound of hydroxyl.

(*b.*) Some of the hydrates yield solutions that corrode the skin and convert the fats into soaps. They are called alkalies. Potassium and sodium hydrates are alkalies.

168. Basic Ammonia.— Ammonia water, in its physical relations, resembles a simple aqueous solution of a gas, while, in its chemical relations, it acts like an alkaline hydrate. On this account, its symbol is often written on the water type, thus: $\left.\begin{array}{c}(NH_4)'\\H\end{array}\right\}$ O, or (NH$_4$)HO. This symbol assumes the existence of a univalent compound radical, NH$_4$. This *purely hypothetical* radical is called ammonium, and is considered a metal. The group of frequent occurrence *in combination*. Ammonium hydrate, (NH$_4$HO) has been termed "the volatile alkali."

Experiment 160.—Repeat Exp. 78. The ammonium nitrate thus produced is the substance we used in the preparation of nitrous oxide (N$_2$O).

$$HNO_3 + (NH_4)HO = (NH_4)NO_3 + H_2O.$$

Experiment 161.— Repeat Exp. 160 using a dilute solution of potassium hydrate (caustic potash, KHO) instead of NH$_4$HO. The crystals thus produced are KNO$_3$, the substance used in preparing HNO$_3$ (§ 74, *a*).

$$HNO_3 + KHO = KNO_3 + H_2O.$$

169. Salts.—In the experiments just given, the products of the metathesis were water and a new class of compounds called salts, so named on account of their general resemblance to common salt (NaCl), a type of this class of compounds. A salt is a compound formed—

(1.) By replacing one or more of the hydrogen atoms of an acid with electro-positive (metallic) atoms or radicals. Compare HNO$_3$ and KNO$_3$.

(2.) By replacing one or more of the hydrogen atoms of a base with electro-negative (non-metallic) atoms or compound radicals. Compare KHO and K(NO$_2$)O or KNO$_3$.

(3.) By the direct union of an anhydride and a basic oxide. Thus, calcium sulphate results from the direct union of sulphuric anhydride and calcium oxide (quicklime): SO$_3$ + CaO = CaSO$_4$.

Note.—Of these three views of the formation of a salt, the first is the one most frequently taken, but occasionally the other two are convenient. An acid is sometimes called a "hydrogen salt;" *e. g.*, hydrogen nitrate (HNO$_3$).

170. Classification of Salts.—Salts may be normal (or neutral), double, acid or basic.

(*a.*) A normal salt is one that contains neither basic nor acid H. All of the basic H of the acid or acid H of the base from which it was formed has been replaced as stated in the last paragraph. K$_2$SO$_4$ and CuSO$_4$ are normal salts.

(*b.*) A double salt is one in which H of the acid from which it was formed has been replaced by metallic (or positive) atoms of different kinds. For example, common alum, Al$_2'''$K$_2'$(SO$_4$)$_4$, is a double salt.

(*c.*) An acid or hydrogen salt is one that contains basic H. Only part of the H of the acid from which it was formed has been replaced, on account of which, in most cases, it still acts like an acid, reddening blue litmus. The hydrogen potassium sulphate, HKSO$_4$, mentioned in § 74 (*a.*) is an acid or hydrogen salt.

(*d.*) A basic salt is one that contains acid H. Only part of the H of the base from which it was formed has been replaced, on account of which, in many cases, it still acts like a base, turning reddened litmus to blue. For example, lead hydrate is a base with the symbol, Pb''H$_2$O$_2$ or H$_2$PbO$_2$. Replacing half of this H with the acid radical, NO$_2$, we have H(NO$_2$)PbO$_2$, the symbol for lead hydronitrate, a basic salt.

(*e.*) A binary acid will yield a binary salt when its H is replaced. Thus, HCl yields NaCl.

171. Sulphur Salts.—In the ternary compounds (acids, bases, and salts) so far studied, the molecules have been bound or linked together by bivalent oxygen. But there is another distinct class of ternary molecules in which the constituent atoms are linked together by bivalent sulphur. In these molecules, the sulphur may be "linking," "saturating," or both. The compounds are named and symbolized in the same way as the corresponding oxygen compounds. Thus:

The type H — O — H has its analogue in H — S — H or H_2S.
KHO or K — O — H " " K — S — H.
K_2CO_3 or $K_2 = O_2 = (CO)$ " " $K_2 = S_2 = (CS)$ or K_2CS_2.

In nomenclature, these "sulphur salts," (in which term, acids and bases are included) are distinguished from the corresponding "oxygen salts" by prefixing *sulpho-*. Thus, the analogue of potassium hydrate is called potassium sulphohydrate; that of potassium carbonate is called potassium sulphocarbonate. The "sulphur salts" are not so numerous or so well known as the "oxygen salts,"

EXERCISES.

1. (*a.*) What is the difference between an atom and a molecule? (*b.*) Between a physical and a chemical property? (*c.*) Define and illustrate base, acid, salt. (*d.*) State the differences between an -*ic*, an -*ous*, and an -*ate* compound.

2. (*a.*) Why is sulphurous acid said to be dibasic? (*b.*) What is the difference between an acid sulphite and a normal sulphite? (*c.*) Between an acid sulphite and a hydrogen sulphite?

3. (*a.*) Write the empirical symbol for the hydrate of the monad radical, nitryl. (*b.*) For the hydrate of $(SO_2)''$.

4. Why are there no acid nitrates?

5. (*a.*) Write the symbols of the most common oxygen and hydrogen compounds with elements of the chlorine group. (*b.*) Give the quantivalence of each element. (*c.*) State the gradation of physical and chemical properties among these elements. (*d.*) Give easy tests for Cl and I.

6. (*a.*) Give the usual mode of liberating Cl, and write out the reaction. (*b.*) Find what *per cent.* the Cl is of the substance that furnishes it.

7. Write the reactions expressing the preparation of at least $5H_2SO_4$, using not more than two molecules of HNO_3.

8. When mercuric oxide (HgO) is heated, it decomposes. Write the reaction. (Owing to the high price of HgO, this reaction is seldom employed.)

9. State the composition of water, both volumetric and gravimetric.

10. When O is prepared from MnO_2, Mn_3O_4 is formed. Write the reaction.

11. When a current of H_2S is passed through a solution of a certain salt, copper sulphide ($Cu''S$) is precipitated with the formation of H_2SO_4. Write the reaction.

12. You are given NaCl and H_2SO_4 and required to fill a jar with HCl. Describe the process and sketch the apparatus you would use.

13. Complete the following equation with the symbol for a single molecule: $BaO_2 + 2HCl = BaCl_2 + $

CHAPTER XI.

BORON.

☞ *Symbol, B; specific gravity, 2.68; atomic weight, 11 m. e.; quantivalence, 3.*

172. Boron.—This element may be obtained in the crystalline form with a specific gravity as given above. These crystals are nearly as hard, lustrous and highly refractive as the diamond. It may also be obtained in the amorphous form as a soft brown powder, or in scales with a graphite-like lustre. It is not found free in nature. It has one oxide (boron trioxide, boric or boracic anhydride, B_2O_3). Its most important compound is borax (sodium pyroborate, $Na_2B_4O_7$), large quantities of which are found in California. Boron is the only non-metallic element that forms no compound with hydrogen. It is remarkable for its direct union (§ 53) with nitrogen, the union being attended by the evolution of light and the product having the composition, BN.

(*a.*) It forms BCl_3, BF_3, *etc.*

Experiment 162.—Heat some boric acid crystals (§ 173) in a clean iron spoon. The heated crystals first melt and then become viscous as the H_2O is driven off. Touch this mass with a glass rod and draw out the adhering mass into long threads. This viscous substance is B_2O_3.

$$2H_3BO_3 = B_2O_3 + 3H_2O.$$

Experiment 163.—Dissolve 6 *g.* of powdered $Na_2B_4O_7$ in 15 or 20 *cu. cm.* of boiling H_2O. Add 3 or 4 *cu. cm.* of HCl or 2 *cu. cm.* of H_2SO_4; stir and allow to cool. Crystals of boric acid (H_3BO_3) will be formed.

Experiment 164.—Dissolve a few crystals of H_3BO_3 in alcohol. Upon igniting the alcohol and stirring the solution, the flame will be of a beautiful green color; or add a little C_2H_6O and H_2SO_4 to a solution of $Na_2B_4O_7$. Heat the materials and ignite the vapor; the flame will be tipped with green.

173. Boric Acid.—Boric acid (orthoboric acid, boracic acid, H_3BO_3) may be freed from any borate by the action of almost any other acid, in consequence of which it is considered a very feeble acid. It may be formed by the union of the oxide with water:

$$B_2O_3 + 3H_2O = 2H_3BO_3.$$

(*a.*) Upon heating H_3BO_3 to 100°C. it is changed to metaboric acid: $H_3BO_3 - H_2O = HBO_2$.

(*b.*) Upon further heating at 140°C. for a long time, this is changed to pyroboric acid: $4HBO_2 - H_2O = H_2B_4O_7$,

or, $4H_3BO_3 - 5H_2O = H_2B_4O_7$.

(*c.*) The characteristic green color which the acid gives to the alcohol flame affords a convenient test for its presence.

(*d.*) Native H_3BO_3 is found free in the volcanic regions of Tuscany whence nearly all that is brought into commerce is obtained. Volcanic jets of steam, charged with H_3BO_3 issue into natural or artificial ponds or lagoons, the water of which condenses the steam and becomes charged with the acid. (Fig. 73.) Upon evaporation, these waters yield pearly crystals of H_3BO_3.

These steam jets are called *suffioni*. Deep borings into the earth have been made, constituting successful artificial *suffioni*. Basins of masonry are built at different levels on a hill side, each of which surrounds two or three *suffioni*. Water from a spring or lagoon is conducted into the upper basin and is charged by the *suffioni* for twenty-four hours. This water is then conducted by a wooden pipe to a second basin, where it is further charged, and so on through six or eight basins, when the H_2O contains two or three *per cent.* of H_3BO_3. From the last basin, a thin sheet of the liquid is run over a corrugated sheet of lead, 125 *m.* long and 2 *m.* wide. This lead sheet is heated by the *suffioni* below it; the liquid is thus economically concentrated by evaporation. The liquid is further concentrated by evaporation in lead pans until the acid begins to crystallize. These lagoons produce about 1,500 *Kg.* of H_3BO_3 daily.

Exercises.

1. What is the molecular weight of boron trioxide?

2. What *per cent.* of B in orthoboric acid?

3. Write the symbol of calcium (Ca″) pyroborate.

4. (*a.*) What is the basicity of H_3BO_3? (*b.*) Is $Mg_3(BO_3)_2$ an acid or a double salt?

5. (*a.*) What results from heating H_2SO_4 with Cu, NaCl and MnO_2 respectively? (*b.*) If the latter two are acted upon together, what results?

6. How much Zn must be used to generate sufficient H to raise in the air, by its buoyancy, a balloon weighing 1,270.5 *g.*?

7. By strongly heating MnO_2, it is reduced to a lower oxide, thus:

$$3MnO_2 = Mn_3O_4 + O_2.$$

(*a.*) What weight and (*b.*) what volume of O can be thus prepared from 50 *g.* of MnO_2?

8. State the method of preparing HNO_3 and the amount of each substance needed for 10 *lb.* of the acid.

9. Write a graphic symbol for $HP‴O_3$; for HPO_3.

(10.) (*a.*) What is a salt? How is it formed? (*b.*) How does a chloride differ from a chlorate? Illustrate by potassium compounds.

11. (*a.*) What is the weight

Fig. 73.

of the Cl in 5 *lb.* of common salt? (*b.*) What *per cent.* of O is there in potassium chlorate?

12. Give the economic properties of chlorine, and show on what they depend.

13. Give two of the most useful compounds of HNO_3 with some use of each.

14. Sulphur trioxide may be obtained by heating concentrated H_2SO_4 with P_2O_5. Write the reaction.

CHAPTER XII.

VOLUMETRIC.

174. A Deduction. Let us imagine such a fractional part (about $\frac{1}{10^{21}}$, see § 62) of a liter of hydrogen, that it shall contain 1,000 hydrogen molecules. By Ampère's law, the same volume of chlorine will contain 1,000 chlorine molecules. By the direct union of these (§ 108), we shall have formed two such volumes (about $\frac{2}{10^{21}}$ l.) of hydrochloric acid gas, which, according to Ampère's law, must contain 2,000 molecules.

$$1000\ H_2 + 1000\ Cl_2 = 2000\ HCl.$$

But each molecule of hydrochloric acid (HCl) contains one hydrogen atom and one chlorine atom. Consequently, the 2,000 acid molecules will contain 2,000 hydrogen atoms and 2,000 chlorine atoms. Since these 2,000 hydrogen *atoms* of the product are identical with the 1,000 hydrogen *molecules* of the factor, it follows that each hydrogen molecule contains two atoms or that *the hydrogen molecule is diatomic*. In the same way we see that the chlorine molecule is diatomic.

175. The Unit Volume. — As the weight of the hydrogen atom is taken as the standard of atomic weight and called a microcrith, so the volume of the hydrogen atom is taken as the standard of atomic volume and called the unit volume. At present, the *absolute* value of the unit volume is as unknown as the absolute value of the microcrith. The accurate determination of the one will carry with it the determination of the other (§ 62). *The unit volume is the volume of one atom of hydrogen; it is a real unit measuring a definite quantity of matter.* The (gaseous) molecular volume is always two unit volumes.

(*a.*) The symbols of the diatomic elements (§ 65) represent one unit volume and the respective atomic weights of the several substances; *e. g.*, $O = \left\{ \begin{array}{l} 16\ m.\ c.,\ \text{or,} \\ 1\ \text{unit volume} \end{array} \right\}$ of oxygen. The symbols of the monatomic elements represent two unit volumes and the respective atomic weights of those substances; *e. g.*, $Hg = \left\{ \begin{array}{l} 200\ m.\ c.,\ \text{or,} \\ 2\ \text{unit volumes} \end{array} \right\}$ of mercury. The symbols of the tetratomic elements represent one-half unit volume and the respective atomic weights of these substances; *e. g.*, $P = \left\{ \begin{array}{l} 31\ m.\ c.,\ \text{or,} \\ \frac{1}{2}\ \text{unit volume} \end{array} \right\}$ of phosphorus. See § 240, *e*.

176. Law of Gay-Lussac.—*The ratio in which gases combine by volume is always a simple one; the volume of the resulting gaseous product bears a simple ratio to the volumes of its constituents* (see § 91).

(*a.*) The following modes of volumetric combination illustrate the truth and meaning of the law.

(1.) 1 unit volume + 1 unit volume = 2 unit volumes.
  E. g., HCl; HBr; HI; NO.
  Condensation = 0.

(2.) 2 unit volumes + 1 unit volume = 2 unit volumes.
  E. g., H_2O; H_2S; N_2O; NO_2.
  Condensation = $\frac{1}{3}$.

(3.) 3 unit volumes + 1 unit volume = 2 unit volumes.
  E. g., H_3N; SO_3.
  Condensation = $\frac{1}{2}$.

EXERCISES.

1. (*a.*) What is a unit volume? (*b.*) A microcrith? (*c.*) What is the relation of specific gravity to combining weight? (*d.*) Give the specific gravity of $HCl, NH_3, Cl,$ and CO_2.

2. How could you prove from a molecule of steam that the molecules of O and H have each two atoms?

3. (*a.*) How is O prepared in large quantities? (*b.*) Give the reaction.

4. (*a.*) Name three physical properties of O. (*b.*) Two chemical properties. (*c.*) How can these chemical properties be shown? (*d.*) Mention one use of O in the arts. (*e.*) One use in the natural world. (*f.*) Mention three of its most important compounds.

5. (*a.*) Explain what is meant by the atomic weights of H and O. (*b.*) Explain the terms atom and molecule as applied to H_2O.

6. (*a.*) If 180 *cu. cm.* of NH_3 be decomposed by electric sparks into its elements, what will be the volume of each of these elements? (*b.*) If then 130 *cu. cm.* of O be introduced and another electric spark produced in the containing vessel, the temperature being $16°C.$, what will be the volume of the remaining gaseous contents of the vessel?

7. (*a.*) Name two chemical properties of H that are the reverse of two of O.

8. (*a.*) How is HNO_3 prepared on a large scale? (*b.*) How can you show that an acid is an acid? (*c.*) What are alkalies? (*d.*) What is "laughing gas"? (*e.*) Name three oxides of N.

9. (*a.*) What are bases? (*b.*) What class of elements forms acids? (*c.*) What class of elements forms bases? (*d.*) What is a salt?

10. (*a.*) What is the combining weight of a chemical compound? (*b.*) $HNO_3 + KHO = KNO_3 + H_2O.$ What is the relative amount of the substances used?

11. Give the most remarkable chemical properties of Cl and I and their industrial applications.

12. (*a.*) Where is S found? (*b.*) How is H_2S made, and what are its properties? (*c.*) What is meant by oxidizing agents and what by reducing agents?

13. When a thin stream of H_2SO_4 flows into a retort filled with broken bricks heated to redness, the following reaction takes place:

$$H_2SO_4 = SO_2 + H_2O + O.$$

(*a.*) What weight and (*b.*) what volume of O can be thus prepared from 50 *g.* of H_2SO_4, *C. P.*? (*C. P.* = chemically pure.)

14. MnO_2 and HCl are heated together. Give the properties of the gas evolved.

154 VOLUMETRIC. § 176

— 15. Write the symbol for the hydrate of sulphuryl.

16. (*a.*) A small quantity of H_2SO_4 is poured upon Zn in a flask. Give the chemical reaction. (*b.*) Substitute HCl for the H_2SO_4; indicate the resultant change, if any. (*c.*) If iron be substituted for Zn, what change?

17. How many liters of Cl may be prepared from 87.6 *g.* of HCl?

18. What weight of each substance must be used to prepare 120 *l.* of H_2S?

19. How much H_2SO_4 will dissolve 120 *g.* of Zn?

20. Describe the preparation of HCl, NH_3, and N_2O. Give the reaction in each case. Name a chemical property of each.

21. (*a.*) What is the difference between chemical and physical properties? (*b.*) What is an element? (*c.*) What is a chemical compound?

22. (*a.*) What is the composition of air? (*b.*) Is the air a chemical compound?

CHAPTER XIII.

THE CARBON GROUP.

SECTION I.

CARBON.

☞ *Symbol, C; atomic weight, 12 m. c.; quantivalence, 4.*

177. Occurrence.—Two allotropic modifications of carbon, the diamond and graphite, are found free in nature. Carbon is also found free in an impure form, as mineral coal. Combined with hydrogen, it occurs in petroleum, bitumen, *etc.* Combined with oxygen, it forms a constituent of the atmosphere upon which all vegetable life is directly dependent. United with oxygen and calcium, it is found as limestone, chalk and marble. All organic bodies contain carbon and when any of these is heated out of contact with oxygen there remains a third allotropic variety, amorphous carbon or charcoal. Certainly, carbon is a very abundant and important element.

(*a.*) The chemical identity of these several allotropic forms is shown by the fact that, when highly heated with O, they all form the same compound, CO_2, 12 parts of any variety of C uniting with 32 parts of O to form 44 parts of the oxide.

Experiment 165.—Arrange the apparatus as shown in Fig. 74. Two thick copper wires pass through a caoutchouc stopper that closes the mouth of a cylinder filled with O. The enclosed ends of the copper wire are joined by a spiral of fine platinum wire. Place

FIG. 74.

a small diamond, if you have one to spare, in the spiral at a, and pass the electric current from a battery of eight Grove's cells through the wires. The platinum is heated to whiteness and the diamond takes fire. On breaking the circuit, you will see a brilliant combustion resulting in the complete disappearance of your diamond. If a small quantity of clear lime water has been previously placed in the cylinder, it will remain clear until the diamond has burned. Upon agitating the lime water, at the close of the combustion, it will be rendered milky in appearance, thus showing the formation of CO_2. See Exp. 44.

178. The Diamond. — Diamond is a crystalline solid, brilliant, transparent and generally colorless. Diamonds are most frequently found in the form of rounded pebbles and cut into the desirable forms by pressing the surface of the stone against a revolving metal wheel covered with a mixture of diamond dust and oil, diamond being the only substance hard enough to cut the gem. Thus, we see that it is the hardest known substance. It does not conduct heat or electricity and, when polished, has a magnificent lustre and high refractive power upon light (Ph., § 613, a.). These properties, together with its permanence and rarity, make it the most precious of gems. Its specific gravity is 3.5. One of the long standing problems of chemistry has recently been solved by the production of artificial diamonds.

(a.) The diamond undergoes no change at the ordinary temperature, but, when heated between the carbon electrodes of a strong electric current, it softens, swells up and is changed to a black mass resembling coke. When heated in O, it burns to CO_2, as explained in Exp. 165. In hydrogen or any atmosphere that has no chemical action upon it, the diamond may be heated to the highest furnace temperature without change. "The Regent" diamond is valued at £125,000.

179. Graphite.—Graphite or plumbago is familiarly known as the "black-lead" of the common "lead pencil." It is found abundantly in nature in the crystalline and amorphous forms, the crystals being wholly unlike those of the diamond. It is opaque, nearly black, and has a semi-metallic lustre. It is very friable and has an unctuous feel. It is a good conductor of heat and electricity. It is unalterable in the air at ordinary temperatures. Its specific gravity varies from 2 to 2.5. It is used in making pencils, lubricating machinery, in making crucibles especially for the manufacture of steel, as a stove polish and in electrotyping (Ph., § 400).

(*a.*) For many years, graphite was supposed to contain lead; whence the names plumbago and black-lead. The name, graphite, is from the Greek word, *grapho*, (= I write).

180. Intermediate Forms.—Intermediate between graphite and charcoal are the forms of carbon known as mineral coal, coke and gas carbon.

181. Mineral Coal.— Mineral coal consists of the remains of the vegetation of the carboniferous era in the earth's geologic history. The woody fibre has undergone a wonderful transformation through the means of heat and pressure. When a considerable part of the hydrogen, oxygen and nitrogen of the original woody material remains in this product, the coal is called soft or bituminous. These elements may be largely removed from bituminous coal by distillation. Soft coal generally contains sulphur impurities and cakes in burning. When the coal has been subjected to a sort of natural distillation, so that it has been deprived of nearly all of its hydrogen, oxygen and nitrogen, it is called hard coal or anthracite. There is a somewhat complete gradation of coals from anthracite down to lignite and peat, in which the wood is but little changed.

Experiment 166.—Half fill a good sized ignition tube (one about 15 *cm.* long will answer well) with coarsely powdered bituminous coal. Close its mouth with a cork carrying a delivery tube made of

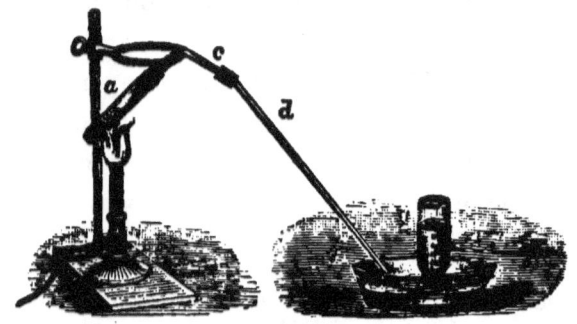

FIG. 75.

good sized glass tubing that terminates in a water bath. Support the ignition tube in a sloping position and heat the coal. Collect the gas in small bottles as it is delivered in the water bath. The gas will burn as if it were ordinary illuminating gas. When the ignition tube has cooled, break it and examine the *coke* that it contains.

182. Coke.—When bituminous coal is distilled, it yields a variety of volatile hydrogen-carbon compounds (hydrocarbons) and a solid, porous residue called coke. The latter is an incidental product of the manufacture of illuminating gas but is also made on a large scale for use in iron smelting, the volatile constituents of the coal being allowed to escape. (§ 221, *b*.)

183. Gas Carbon.—Gas carbon is a very hard, compact substance that is formed as a crust on the inner sur-

§ 184 CARBON. 159

face of the retorts at gas works. It is a good conductor of heat and electricity and is largely used in the manufacture of galvanic batteries (Ph., §§ 383, 385) and of the carbon electrodes of electric lamps (Ph., § 389.).

Experiment 167.—Repeat Exp. 166, using splinters or shavings of wood instead of soft coal. When the gas is no longer evolved, remove the end of the delivery tube from the water pan and imbed it in a thick paste of plaster of Paris to prevent the entrance of air to the ignition tube. When the apparatus has cooled, the *charcoal* may be removed without breaking the tube.

Experiment 168.—Heat a piece of charcoal upon platinum foil and notice that it burns with a simple glow, *i. e.*, without any flame.

184. Charcoal.—Charcoal is generally prepared by the distillation or incomplete combustion of wood. In England, where wood is scarce, small wood and saw-dust are distilled in cast iron retorts, the volatile products being collected. In this country, where wood is yet abundant, the process is more primitive, the volatile products generally going to waste.

(*a.*) The common method of burning charcoal is to pile up sticks of wood in a large heap around a central flue, covering it with turf

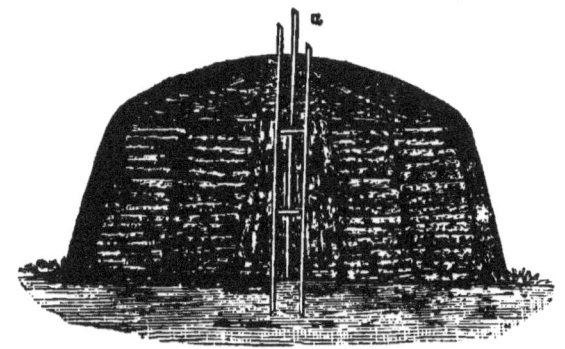

Fig. 76.

and earth, leaving holes at the bottom for the admission of air and a hole at the top of the central flue. The fire is kindled at the bottom of the central flue, and the rate of combustion controlled by regulating the supply of air, the process often requiring several weeks. At the proper time, all of the openings are closed and the fire thus suffocated. The method depends upon the fact that the volatile constituents of the wood are more easily combustible than the C and thus unite with the limited supply of O. In some parts of the country, charcoal is burned in permanent kilns, instead of turf covered heaps.

(*b.*) The charcoal retains the form of the wood from which it was made, the shape of the knots and even the concentric rings being plainly visible. Its volume is about 65 or 70 *per cent.* and its weight about 25 *per cent.* of the wood from which it was formed.

Experiment 169.—Set fire to a lump of rosin and hold a cold plate over the flame. Soot will be deposited upon the plate.

Experiment 170.—Press a spoon or plate down upon a candle flame so as nearly to extinguish the flame. Soot will be deposited upon the spoon.

Experiment 171.—Partly fill a spirit lamp with turpentine, light the wick and cover the lamp with a bell glass or wide mouthed jar. Thrust a pencil or chalk crayon under one edge of the bell glass so as to raise it from the table and admit a small supply of air to the flame. Soot will collect upon the sides of the bell glass.

FIG. 77.

185. Lampblack.—When a hydrocarbon, like rosin, turpentine, wax, petroleum, *etc.*, is burned, the hydrogen is first oxidized. If the supply of oxygen be insufficient for the complete combustion, the carbon set free by the decomposition of the compound will be left in a finely divided, amorphous state, as soot or lamp-black. The same effect will appear if the temperature of the flame be reduced below that at which carbon burns, as was the case in Exp. 169. Lampblack is manufactured on the large scale by burning tar, rosin, turpentine, petroleum, or the natural gases of petroleum (gas wells) in a supply of air insufficient for complete combustion and leading the smoky products into large chambers, where they are deposited. It is largely used as a pigment and in the manufacture of india and printer's inks.

186. Bone-black.—Bone-black, which is the most important variety of "animal charcoal," is prepared by charring powdered bones in iron retorts. The calcium phosphate of the bone remains and forms about 90 *per cent.* of the black porous mass. The charcoal is consequently left in a very finely divided or porous condition, spread over the particles of the phosphate or distributed among them. For this reason, it has greater absorptive and decolorizing power than vegetable charcoal (Exp. 180).

Experiment 172.—Mix 2.5 g. of black copper oxide (CuO) with 0.25 g. of powdered charcoal. With some of the mixture, partly fill a small ignition tube and heat it strongly. Metallic copper will remain in the tube while the C will unite with the O of the CuO and escape as a gas. The C has *reduced* the CuO and the CuO has *oxidized* the C.

187. Charcoal as a Reducing Agent.—Owing to the energetic union of carbon and oxygen at high temperatures, charcoal is largely used as a reducing agent. Anthracite and coke are also used for the same purpose. The preparation of metals from their ores (metallurgy) depends in a very large degree upon this property of carbon.

Experiment 173.—Break a piece of charcoal into two. Attach a sinker to one of the fragments and immerse it in H_2O. Notice the bubbles rise as the H_2O enters the pores of the charcoal and forces out the air previously absorbed. The experiment may be improved by placing the beaker glass containing the H_2O and the C under the receiver of an air pump and exhausting the air.

Experiment 174.—Place the other fragment of the charcoal on the fire, and when it has been heated to full redness for some time, plunge it quickly into H_2O. Notice that it needs no sinker to keep it under H_2O and that very few bubbles escape from it through the liquid.

Experiment 175.—Fill a long glass tube with dry NH_3 at the mercury bath (Exp. 61). Heat a piece of charcoal to redness to remove the air from its pores and plunge it into mercury. When the charcoal is cool, thrust it into the mouth of the cylinder. The gas will be absorbed by the charcoal and mercury will rise in the tube (Ph., § 275).

FIG. 78.

Experiment 176.—Repeat the last experiment, using dry HCl instead of NH_3.

188. Charcoal as an Absorbent.

—The porous nature of charcoal gives it a remarkable power of absorbing gases. Beech wood charcoal has been known to absorb 170 times its own volume of dry ammonia. Other gases, liquefiable with comparative readiness (*e. g.*, HCl, SO_2, H_2S, N_2O, CO_2) are absorbed in large but variable proportions, while gases that are coercible only with difficulty (*e. g.*, O, H and N) are absorbed much more sparingly.

This power depends upon the fact that all gases *condense* in greater or less degree upon the surface of solid bodies with which they come into contact. It is said that 1 *cu. cm.* of compact (boxwood) charcoal exposes a surface of 0.5 *sq. m.* The more easily the gas is liquefied the more largely is it absorbed by charcoal, which, at least, points toward the conclusion that in such absorption it is, at least, partly liquefied.

Experiment 177.—Into a bottle of H_2S put some powdered charcoal. Shake the bottle for a moment. The offensive odor of the H_2S will have disappeared.

Experiment 178.—Into the neck of a funnel, thrust a bit of cotton wool and cover it to the depth of 2 or 3 *cm.* with powdered charcoal. Through this solution, pass a quantity of H_2O charged with H_2S (§ 138, *a.*). The filtered liquid will be free from offensive odor.

Experiment 179.—Place a small crucible filled with freshly ignited and nearly cold powdered charcoal into a jar kept supplied with H_2S. When the charcoal is saturated with the gas, quickly transfer it to a jar of O. The charcoal will burst into vivid combustion.

189. Charcoal as a Disinfectant.—By condensing offensive and injurious gases and bringing them into intimate contact with condensed oxygen, charcoal acts as an energetic disinfectant. The fetid products of animal and vegetable decay are not only gathered in but actually burned up. This property is retained by the charcoal for a long time and, when lost, may be restored by ignition. A dead animal may be buried under a thin covering of charcoal and waste away without giving off any offensive odor. This oxidizing power of charcoal fits it for use as a disinfectant in hospitals, dissecting rooms and elsewhere, and forms the foundation of much of the utility of charcoal filters for water for drinking purposes.

Fig. 79.

Experiment 180.—Place a dilute solution of the blue compound of iodine and starch (Exp. 121), of indigo dissolved in $H_2S_2O_7$ (§ 156), of cochineal and of potassium permanganate in each of four flasks To each, add recently ignited bone-black. Cork the flasks, shake their contents vigorously, and pour each liquid upon a separate filter. The several filtrates will be colorless. If the first part of any filtrate be colored, pour it back upon the filter for refiltration.

190. Charcoal as a Decolorizer.—As illustrated in the above experiment, charcoal, and especially animal charcoal or bone-black, is able to remove the color as well as odor from many solutions. This power seems to depend more upon the *adhesion* between the carbon and the particles of coloring matter than upon oxidation. Brown sugar is purified, by filtering its colored solution through layers of bone-black. If ale or beer be thus treated, it loses both its color and bitter taste. Thus we see that charcoal can remove other substances than coloring matter from solutions. Sulphate of quinine and strychnine may be thus removed. This property of charcoal (and bone-black) is utilized in the preparation or purification of many chemical or pharmaceutical compounds.

191. Other Properties of Carbon.—Carbon, in all of its forms, is practically infusible and non-volatile, but it may be slightly fusible and volatile at the high temperature of the voltaic arc. Although it has great chemical activity at high temperatures, it seems to be unalterable at the ordinary temperature of the air. The lower ends of stakes and fence posts are often charred before embedding them in the earth to render them more durable. Charred piles driven in the River Thames by the ancient Britons in their resistance to the invasion of their country by Julius Cæsar, about 54 B.C., are still well preserved. Wheat, charred at the destruction of Herculaneum and Pompeii, in 79 A.D., still appears as fresh as if recently prepared. Perfectly legible manuscripts, written in ink made of lamp-black, have been exhumed *with Egyptian mummies*. Carbon is unique, in that it forms a very large number of volatile hydrogen compounds. These compounds are called hydrocarbons.

Note.—Binary compounds of carbon were formerly called carburets.

EXERCISES.

1. Is charcoal lighter or heavier than H_2O?
2. (*a.*) I burn a piece of wood in the open air; what becomes of it? (*b.*) What volume of steam will result from burning 100 *g.* of H?
3. (*a.*) State the useful properties of charcoal. (*b.*) How much O is needed to burn 500 *g.* of charcoal? (*c.*) How many liters of CO_2 will be produced?
4. Give the characteristics of three allotropic modifications of carbon, and give a leading property of each.
5. How would you prepare a solution of HCl?
6. Write the symbol for sulphuryl oxide.
7. Write the typical and empirical symbols for nitrosyl hydrate and nitryl hydrate.
8. Write the reaction for the combustion of turpentine in Exp. 93.
9. Give proof of the fact that diamond is carbon.
10. In what way does the disinfecting power of C differ from that of Cl?
11. Is C a bleaching agent? Why?
12. Would it not be a great improvement in quinine to filter it through charcoal and thus remove its intensely bitter taste? Why?
13. Symbolize compounds of $\overset{\text{iv}}{C}$ with L', M'', Q''', $\overset{\text{iv}}{R}$ and $\overset{\text{iv}}{X}$, these last letters symbolizing hypothetical elements.
14. Write graphic symbols for $H_2\overset{\text{iv}}{S}O_2$ and $H_2\overset{\text{iv}}{S}O_3$.

##

SOME CARBON COMPOUNDS.

192. Carbon Oxides.—There are two oxides of carbon, having the molecular symbols CO and CO_2. The first may be considered the product of incomplete combustion of carbon; the second, that of complete combustion. Both of them are gaseous.

193. Carbon Monoxide.—Carbon monoxide (carbon protoxide, carbonic oxide, carbonous oxide, carbonyl, CO) yields, when burned, the characteristic blue flame often seen playing over a freshly fed coke or anthracite fire. It may be prepared in many ways, only two of which will be given here.

Experiment 181.—Pulverize 5 *g.* of potassium ferrocyanide and place it in a quarter liter Florence flask. Add 25 *cu. cm.* of strong H_2SO_4 and heat gently, removing the lamp as soon as the gas begins to come off rapidly. The gas may be passed through a solution of potassium hydrate (KHO) and collected over H_2O.

Experiment 182.—Place a small quantity of oxalic acid $(H_2C_2O_4)$ in a small Florence flask, add enough strong H_2SO_4 to cover it, place upon a sand bath and heat gently. The H_2SO_4 removes H_2O from the $H_2C_2O_4$ and leaves a mixture of CO and CO_2. The CO_2 may be removed by passing the mixed gases through a solution of KHO, as in the last experiment, or by collecting over H_2O rendered alkaline by such a solution.

194. Properties.—Carbon monoxide is a colorless, odorless, poisonous gas. It is a little lighter than air, having a specific gravity of 14 (*sp. gr.* = .967, air standard). It is scarcely soluble in water, but is wholly absorbed by an acid or ammoniacal solution of cuprous chloride (Cu_2Cl_2). It is liquefiable only with extreme difficulty. Like hydrogen, it does not support combustion but is combustible. It burns with a pale blue flame and yields carbon dioxide (CO_2) as the sole product of its combustion. It is an *active poison* and doubly dangerous on account of its lack of odor. One *per cent.* of it in the air is fatal to life, which it destroys, not merely by excluding oxygen (suffocation), as hydrogen, nitrogen, *etc.*, do, but by *direct action as a true poison*. As this gas is formed in charcoal and anthracite fires, and as it secures an easy passage through faulty joints and *even through cast iron plates heated to redness*, it is the frequent cause of oppression, headache and danger in stove or furnace-heated and ill-ventilated rooms. Carbon monoxide is rightly chargeable with many of the ill effects usually attributed to the less dangerous carbon dioxide.

(*a.*) CO is readily oxidized to CO_2 and CO_2 is easily reduced to CO. Thus, when air enters at the bottom of an anthracite fire, the O unites with the C to form CO_2. As the CO_2 rises through the glowing coals above, it is reduced to CO. $CO_2 + C = 2CO$. When this heated CO comes into contact with the air above the coals, it burns with its characteristic blue flame and forms CO_2.

(*b.*) Under the influence of sunlight, two volumes of CO unite directly with two volumes of Cl, forming two volumes of carbonyl chloride or phosgene gas ($COCl_2$). It will be noticed that here, CO acts as a dyad compound radical.

195. Uses.—Carbon monoxide is an important agent in many metallurgical operations, on account of its power to reduce metallic oxides. It may be used instead of hydrogen in Exp. 31. In the reverberatory furnace, the air supply is regulated so that the fuel burns to carbon monoxide, which, in a highly heated condition, plays over the metallic oxides on the hearth and, by abstracting oxygen from them for its own combustion to carbon dioxide, reduces them to the metallic condition.

196. Carbon Dioxide.—Carbon dioxide (carbonic anhydride, CO_2, often improperly called carbonic acid or carbonic acid gas) is always formed when carbon or any carbon compound is burned under conditions that afford an abundant supply of oxygen. It may be easily obtained by the decomposition of carbonates, such as marble, chalk, or limestone. It is a product of animal respiration, of fermentation and of the decay and putrefaction of all animal and vegetable matter. It is produced in large quantities in burning limestone to quicklime.

$$CaCO_3 = CaO + CO_2.$$

Experiment 183.—Repeat Exps. 42 and 44. The white precipitate that causes the turbidity is calcium carbonate ($CaCO_3$).

$$CaH_2O_2 + CO_2 = CaCO_3 + H_2O.$$

Experiment 184.—Mix 11 $g.$ of red oxide of mercury and 0.3 $g.$ of powdered charcoal. Heat the mixture and collect over H_2O the gas that is given off. Test the gas with lime water. The O that

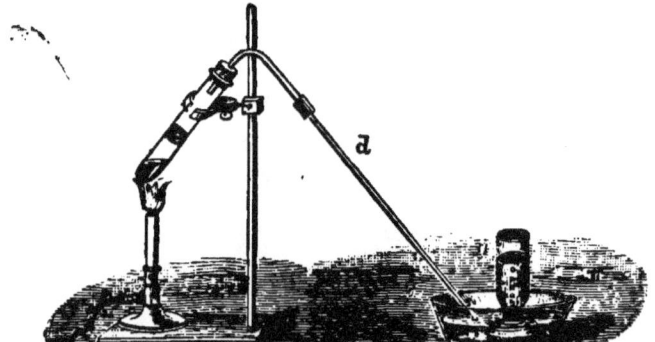

FIG. 80.

united with the C came from the mercury oxide. $2HgO + C = CO_2 + 2Hg$. Examine the ignition tube carefully for traces of metallic mercury. In similar manner, many solid, liquid and gaseous bodies that are rich in O give it up readily to unite with C and form CO_2. In other words, such bodies are "reduced" by the C.

§ 196 SOME CARBON COMPOUNDS. 169

Experiment 185.—Into a bottle, arranged as described in § 20, put a handful of small lumps of marble or chalk ($CaCO_3$). *Prepared crayons will not answer.* Cover the lumps with H_2O and add small quantities of HCl from time to time as may be needed to secure a continued evolution of gas. Collect several bottles of the gas over

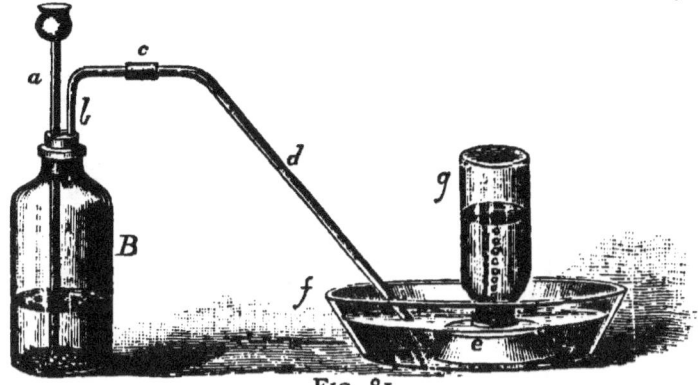

Fig. 81.

H_2O. Replace the tube *d* by one bent downward at right angles near *c*. Insert the vertical part of this tube in a bottle. As this gas is heavier than air, it may be collected thus by "downward displacement."

$$CaCO_3 + 2HCl = CaCl_2 + H_2O + CO_2.$$

Note.—HCl is better than H_2SO_4 in preparing CO_2 from $CaCO_3$ because $CaCl_2$ is more easily soluble than $CaSO_4$. Old mortar, powdered oyster shells, coral or limestone will answer instead of marble or chalk, but marble is preferable as there is less frothing.

Experiment 186.—Arrange two flasks containing lime water, as shown in Fig. 82. Apply the lips to the tube and inhale and exhale air through the apparatus. In a few moments, the lime water in *C*, through which the air passes *from* the lungs, will become milky, while that in *B*, through which the air passes *to* the lungs, remains clear. See Exp. 44. Unrespired air forced through lime water by means of a small bellows or other means will not produce such turbidity.

Experiment 187.—Dissolve 50

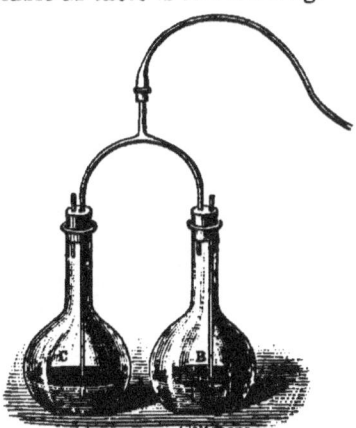

Fig. 82.

cu. cm. of molasses in about 400 *cu. cm.* of H_2O and place the liquid in a half liter flask. Add a few spoonfuls of yeast, cork the flask and connect its delivery tube with a small bottle, *b, filled* with H_2O. A delivery tube should extend from the bottom of *b* into a cup, *c*. Put the apparatus into a warm place and fermentation will soon begin. As the liquid in *F* ferments, bubbles of gas will rise through it and pass over into *b*, forcing a corresponding quantity of H_2O into *c*. When *b* is nearly full of this gas, remove its stopper and test its contents with a flame and with lime water. The gas is CO_2 (§ 200). Let the liquid in *F* remain in a warm place for two or three days. Cork and save for future use.

Fig. 83.

The sugar ($C_6H_{12}O_6$) of the molasses was decomposed into alcohol (C_2H_6O) and CO_2. The C_2H_6O remains dissolved in the liquid in F.

Fig. 84.

Experiment 188.—Suspend a light glass or paper jar from one end of a scale beam and counterpoise it with weights placed in the scale pan at the opposite end. Pour CO_2 into the jar and it will descend.

Experiment 189.—Partly fill a wide mouthed jar with CO_2. Throw an ordinary soap bubble into the jar. It will float on the surface of the heavy gas.

Experiment 190.—Fill a long necked Florence flask with CO_2. Pour in a little H_2O, close the mouth with cork or finger, shake the bottle and then open the mouth under water. Part of the CO_2 will have been dissolved in the H_2O, and more H_2O will enter the flask to fill the partial vacuum. Close the mouth, shake again, and once more open the mouth under water. More H_2O will enter. In this way, all of the CO_2 may be dissolved in H_2O. After agitating CO_2 and H_2O in a test tube closed by the thumb or palm of the hand, the tube and contents may be held hanging from the hand, supported by atmospheric pressure. (Ph., § 293.)

197. Physical Properties.—Carbon dioxide is a colorless gas, so heavy that it may easily be poured from one vessel to another. Its specific gravity is 22, it being $1\frac{1}{2}$ times as heavy as air. In consequence of its high specific gravity, it diffuses but slowly and often accumulates in wells, mines and caverns (see article, "Grotto del Cane," in any encyclopædia). Under a pressure of 50 atmospheres at the ordinary temperature, it condenses to a liquid whose specific gravity is 0.83. The rapid expansion of this liquid, when released from pressure, produces a temperature low enough to freeze part of itself to a white, snow-like mass. This solid carbon dioxide, when mixed with ether, produces a degree of cold that quickly freezes mercury, and in a vacuum, yields a temperature of $-110°C$. The gas is soluble in water, volume for volume at ordinary temperatures and pressures; more largely, at lower temperatures or higher pressures.

Experiment 191.—From a large vessel filled with CO_2, dip a tum-

Fig. 85.

blerful of the gas and pour it, as if it were H_2O, upon the flame of a taper burning at the bottom of another tumbler. The flame will be extinguished.

Experiment 192.—Fasten a tuft of "cotton wool" to the end of a wire or glass rod, dip it into alcohol, ignite and quickly thrust the large flame into a bottle of CO_2. The flame will be instantly extinguished.

Experiment 193.— Fasten a piece of magnesium ribbon, 15 or 20 cm. (6 or 8 in.) long to a wire, ignite the ribbon and quickly plunge it into a jar of CO_2. It will continue to burn, leaving white flakes of magnesium oxide (MgO) mixed with small particles of black C. Rinse the jar with a little distilled H_2O, pour the H_2O into an evaporating dish, add a few drops of HCl and heat. The MgO will dissolve, leaving the black particles floating in the clear liquid.

198. Chemical Properties.

Carbon dioxide, being the product of complete combustion, is incombustible. It is a non-supporter of ordinary combustion. Its solution in water is often considered true carbonic acid (H_2CO_3). The gas may be completely absorbed by a solution of potassium hydrate (KHO).

Experiment 194.— Pass a stream of CO_2 through lime water. Notice that the formation of $CaCO_3$ soon renders the water turbid but that, the current being continued, the turbidity soon disappears. When the water has thus lost its milky appearance, boil it. The excess of CO_2 will escape in bubbles; the liquid will become turbid again and deposit a precipitate of $CaCO_3$.

199. Uses, etc.

Carbon dioxide has been successfully used for extinguishing fires in coal mines, even when the fires had raged for years and defied all other attempts at putting them out. The efficiency of the common, portable "fire extinguishers" depends upon this same property of carbon dioxide. Water charged with large quantities of the gas is sold under the meaningless name of "soda water." While we thus see that it is not poisonous when taken into the stomach, it is injurious when breathed into the lungs. When largely diluted with air, it has a narcotic effect and its presence to the extent of nine or ten *per cent.* of the atmosphere is sufficient to cause suffocation and death. When we remember that the processes of respiration and combustion (*e. g.*, the combustion of illuminants) are robbing the atmosphere of occupied rooms of the invigorating oxygen and yielding immense quantities of injurious carbon dioxide, we see that it is not easy to overestimate the importance of systematic school and household ventilation, even ignoring the many other causes for its necessity. While thus destructive of animal life it is essential to vegetable existence.

Water containing carbon dioxide in solution is capable of dissolving calcium carbonate and other substances that are insoluble in pure water. In this way, many rocks are disintegrated, stalagmites and stalactites formed, or the soil fitted for the needs of plants. It is also used in "corroding" lead for use as a paint (lead carbonate) and in the preparation of sodium and other carbonates.

200. Test.—The precipitation of calcium carbonate when carbon dioxide is passed through lime water or shaken with it, is the most common test for the gas. Its power of extinguishing flame is often a convenient but not a definite means of detecting its presence.

201. Carbon Disulphide. — Carbon disulphide (CS_2) is prepared synthetically on a large scale by passing sulphur vapor over glowing coke or charcoal.

$$C_2 + 2S_2 = 2CS_2.$$

Caution.—In performing experiments with CS_2, see that there is no flame near.

Experiment 195.—Put a few drops of CS_2 into each of four small test tubes. Into the first tube put a little powdered S; into the second, a few crystals of I; into the third, a very small piece of P; into the fourth, a little H_2O. Notice the solubility of the S, I and P in CS_2 and the insolubility of CS_2 in H_2O.

Experiment 196.—Wet a block of wood and place a watch crystal upon it. A film of H_2O may be seen under the central part of the glass. Half fill the crystal with CS_2 and rapidly evaporate it by blowing over its surface a stream of air from the lungs or a small bellows. So much heat is rendered latent in the vaporization that the watch crystal is firmly frozen to the wooden block. (Ph., §§ 526, 527.)

Experiment 197.—Into a glass cylinder, pour a few drops of CS_2. In a few moments the cylinder will be filled with the heavy vapor of CS_2. Thrust the end of a glass rod, heated not quite to redness, into the cylinder. The vapor will be ignited. See Exp. 82.

$$3O_2 + CS_2 = CO_2 + 2SO_2.$$

FIG. 86.

202. Properties.—Ordinary carbon disulphide is a liquid of light yellow color and offensive odor. Its vapor is injurious to animal and vegetable life and exceedingly inflammable. As it is heavier than water and insoluble therein, it is easily preserved under water. It is diathermanous, has a highly refractive effect upon light (Ph., §§ 552, 553, 613), evaporates rapidly at ordinary temperatures and boils at about 46°C., yielding a heavy vapor that ignites at about 150° C., and that forms an explosive mixture with air.

(*a.*) When pure, CS_2 is colorless and has an agreeable odor resembling that of chloroform.

203. Uses.—Carbon disulphide is used as a solvent for phosphorus, iodine, sulphur, and many resins and oils.

It is used largely in the extraction of fats and oils and in the cold process of vulcanizing caoutchouc.

204. Cyanogen. — This compound of carbon and nitrogen (CN or Cy) is a univalent radical ($-C\equiv N$). It was the first compound radical isolated. It will be noticed that it has two symbols, the first of which indicates its chemical composition. It is generally prepared by heating the cyanide of gold, silver or mercury, and collecting over mercury.

$$Hg''Cy_2 = Hg + Cy_2 \text{ or } Hg''(CN)_2 = Hg + (CN)_2.$$

Cyanogen is a colorless, poisonous, inflammable gas. It acts like a monad element, forming compounds corresponding to the chlorides, *e. g.*:—

Free chlorine................Cl_2	Free cyanogen......Cy_2 or C_2N_2
Potassium chloride..........KCl	Potassium cyanide....KCy or KCN
Hydrochloric acid...........HCl	Hydrocyanic acid... HCy or HCN

Some of the cyanides will be subsequently noticed.

205. Hydrocyanic Acid.—Hydrocyanic acid (cyanhydric acid, HCN or HCy) may be prepared by passing hydrogen sulphide over mercury cyanide heated to about 36°C. $HgCy_2 + H_2S = 2HCy + HgS$. It is a volatile, inflammable, intensely poisonous liquid. Its aqueous solution is well known as prussic acid.

Caution.—Potassium cyanide is intensely poisonous, not only when taken internally, but also when brought into contact with an abrasion of the skin, a cut or scratch.

Experiment 193.—Place a small quantity of powdered potassium cyanide in a test tube and add a few drops of strong H_2SO_4. The escaping HCy produces effervescence and may be detected by its peculiar odor, like that of bitter almonds. The reaction is similar to that between NaCl and H_2SO_4 in the preparation of HCl.

EXERCISES.

1. In Exp. 181, the potassium ferrocyanide ($K_4FeC_6N_6$) contains $3H_2O$ as "water of crystallization." Additional H_2O is furnished by the commercial H_2SO_4. Among the products are to be found potassium sulphate (K_2SO_4), iron sulphate ($FeSO_4$) and ammonium sulphate [$(NH_4)_2SO_4$]. Write the reaction for that experiment.

2. Write the graphic symbols and the names of H_2CO_3, Na_2CO_3 and $HNaCO_3$.

3. Write an equation showing what becomes of the CO_2 removed from the CO in Exp. 182.

4. Write the reaction for Exp. 182.

5. When free cyanogen is mixed with an excess of O and an electric spark passed through the mixture, an explosion occurs. On cooling, the residual gases, one of which is N, have the same volume as the original mixed gases. Write the reaction.

6. What is the weight of a liter of cyanogen gas?

7. How would you prove the solubility of HCl, NH_3 and CO_2?

8. (a.) What weight of CO_2 would be produced by burning 5 g. of C? (b.) What volume?

9. (a.) What weight of CO_2 may be obtained from 100 g. of $CaCO_3$ by the action of HCl? (b.) What volume?

10. What is the weight of 10 l. of CO_2?

11. (a.) If 20 cu. cm. of CO and 10 cu. cm. of O be mixed in an eudiometer and an electric spark passed through, what will be the name and volume of the product? (b.) Write the reaction. (c.) If this product be agitated with a solution of KHO, what will be the effect upon the gaseous volume?

12. Write the empirical symbols for nitrosyl chloride and sulphuryl chloride.

13. Give the laboratory mode of liberating CO_2, with the reaction, and the per centage composition of the source of the CO_2.

14. (a.) How many liters of CO_2 can be obtained from 200 g. of $CaCO_3$? (b.) How many, if the carbonate contains 8 per cent. of silica?

15. If sulphuryl chloride be poured into H_2O, we have the following reaction: $SO_2Cl_2 + 2H_2O = H_2SO_4 + 2HCl$. How much dry HCl may be thus prepared from 135 g. of SO_2Cl_2?

16. Describe a method of preparing O, and express, by symbols, the changes that take place.

17. How is HNO_3 prepared? Express, by symbols, the changes.

18. Explain and illustrate what you understand by quantivalence.

19. Give the specific gravity of CO_2, NH_3, HCl, and H_2, with the principle by which it is easily determined.

SECTION III.

SOME HYDROCARBONS.

206. Hydrocarbons.—The compounds of hydrogen and carbon are called hydrocarbons. They are so very numerous that any attempt at even naming them would carry us beyond the proper limits of an elementary text book. They are capable of classification into series, each one differing but little in composition and properties from its neighbors in its series. (See § 220.)

207. Marsh Gas.—Marsh gas (methyl hydride, hydrogen monocarbide, methane, CH_4) occurs free in nature, being a product of the decay of vegetable matter confined under water. In warm summer weather, bubbles often rise to the surface of stagnant pools. If the vegetable matter at the bottom of the pond be stirred, the gas bubbles will rise rapidly. The gas may be collected by filling a bottle with water, tying a funnel to its mouth, as shown in Fig. 87, and inverting it over the ascending bubbles. Of this gas, about 75 *per cent.* is marsh gas; the rest is chiefly carbon dioxide with some nitrogen. The carbon dioxide may be removed by agitating the mixed gases with lime-water. Marsh gas also escapes from seams in some coal mines and forms the dreaded "fire damp" of the miner. It also escapes in

FIG. 87.

large quantities from "gas wells" in petroleum producing regions. It is the first of a homologous hydrocarbon series known as "The Marsh Gas Series."

Experiment 199.—Into a gas pipe retort (App. 22) 15 or 20 *cm.* long, put an intimate mixture of 3 *g.* sodium acetate, 3 *g.* sodium hydrate, (caustic soda, NaHO) and 6 *g.* quicklime. Place the retort in a stove, heat to redness and collect the gas over H_2O.

FIG. 88.

Experiment 200.—The levity and inflammability of CH_4 may be shown as in the case of H, by introducing a lighted taper into an inverted jar of it. The gas will burn at the mouth of the jar, and the candle flame, as it passes up into it, will be extinguished.

Experiment 201.—Fill a tall bottle of at least one liter capacity with warm H_2O, invert it over the water pan, and pass CH_4 into it, until a little more than one-third of the H_2O is displaced; cover the bottle with a towel, to exclude the light, and then fill the rest of the bottle with Cl. Cork the bottle tightly, and shake it vigorously, to mix the gases together, keeping the bottle covered with the towel. Then open the bottle and apply a flame to the mixture. HCl will be produced, and the sides and mouth of the bottle become coated with solid C in the form of lampblack. Test for HCl with moistened blue litmus paper and with a rod wet with NH_4HO.

208. Properties.—Marsh gas is a colorless, odorless, tasteless gas, but slightly soluble in water. With the exception of hydrogen, it is the lightest known substance. It is combustible, burning with a feebly luminous, bluish-yellow flame. Its calorific power is very great (Ph., § 569). It forms an explosive mixture with air or oxygen and has been the cause of many terribly fatal explosions in ill-ventilated coal mines. When decomposed by electric sparks, it yields twice its volume of hydrogen. It may be considered a hydride of the univalent compound radical, methyl (CH_3).

(*a.*) A mixture of CH_4 with twice its volume of O is more violently explosive than a similar mixture of H and O.

209. Chloroform.—When chlorine is allowed to act on methyl hydride, the hydrogen of the latter is gradually replaced, forming successively CH_3Cl, CH_2Cl_2, $CHCl_3$ and CCl_4. Chloroform ($CHCl_3$) may be considered as marsh gas in which three hydrogen atoms have been replaced by three chlorine atoms. It is a colorless, volatile liquid, much used as an anæsthetic in surgical operations. It is manufactured by distilling dilute alcohol with chloride of lime.

Marsh Gas.
$$\begin{array}{c} H \\ | \\ H-C-H \\ | \\ H \end{array}$$

Chloroform.
$$\begin{array}{c} H \\ | \\ Cl-C-Cl \\ | \\ Cl \end{array}$$

210. Alcohol.—When the juices of plants and fruits that contain sugar, *e. g.*, the juice of the grape or apple, stand for some time in a warm place, they begin to ferment. The fermentation may be aided by the action of yeast. The fermented liquid has lost the sweet taste of the sugar because the sugar ($C_6H_{12}O_6$) has been decomposed into carbon dioxide and alcohol (C_2H_6O). See Exp. 187. The preparation of alcohol is illustrated by Exp. 202.

(*a.*) The chief peculiarity of the hydrocarbons arises from the facility with which the C atoms unite themselves one to another and thus constitute the framework of the various molecules. For example, we have the methane molecule, $H-\overset{\overset{\displaystyle H}{|}}{\underset{\underset{\displaystyle H}{|}}{C}}-H$. By replacing one atom of H with the univalent radical methyl (CH_3), we have $H-\underset{\underset{H}{|}}{\overset{\overset{H}{|}}{C}}-\underset{\underset{H}{|}}{\overset{\overset{H}{|}}{C}}-H$,

or ethane (ethyl hydride). By substituting the univalent radical, HO, for one atom of the H in ethane, we have $(HO)-\underset{\underset{H}{|}}{\overset{\overset{H}{|}}{C}}-\underset{\underset{H}{|}}{\overset{\overset{H}{|}}{C}}-H$, or ordinary alcohol (ethyl hydrate). By successive substitutions of $(CH_3)'$ for H, we may pass from CH_4 to C_2H_6, C_3H_8, C_4H_{10} or $H-\underset{\underset{H}{|}}{\overset{\overset{H}{|}}{C}}-\underset{\underset{H}{|}}{\overset{\overset{H}{|}}{C}}-\underset{\underset{H}{|}}{\overset{\overset{H}{|}}{C}}-\underset{\underset{H}{|}}{\overset{\overset{H}{|}}{C}}-H$, etc.

Experiment 202.—Pour half of the fermented liquid of Exp. 187 into a flask, F, placed on the ring of a retort stand. Connect F with an empty flask or bottle, b, having a capacity of about 100 *cu. cm.*, and placed in a water bath. Connect b with a flask or bottle, c, im-

FIG. 89.

mersed in cold H_2O, as shown in Fig. 89. Boil the liquid in F; the vapors of C_2H_6O and of H_2O pass into b, the temperature of which is *a little below* the boiling point of H_2O (100°C.) because its water bath is kept barely boiling [Ph., §§ 502 (2), 513.] Here, most of the steam is condensed while the vapor of C_2H_6O passes on to c, and is there condensed. The distillate condensed in c is dilute alcohol. If it is not strong enough to burn when a flame is brought into contact with it, it may be distilled again, or a second bottle and water bath, b', may be interposed between b and c. The experiment should not be continued after a quarter of the liquid in F has been vaporized.

Instead of condensing the C_2H_6O in the flask, c, the Liebig condenser (Ph., § 512, a.), shown in Fig. 90, may be used. Some H_2O will remain in the C_2H_6O even after re-distillation. This may be removed by quicklime.

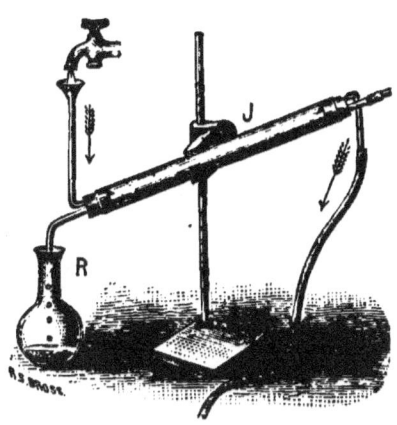

FIG. 90.

211. Properties.—Alcohol is a colorless, volatile, inflammable liquid. Its specific gravity is 0.8 and its boiling point 78°C. It absorbs moisture from the atmosphere and is capable of mixing with water in all proportions. Alcohol that contains no water is called *absolute alcohol*. Alcohol that is "90 *per cent.* proof" is considered to be of good quality. As marsh gas is considered to be a *hydride* of methyl, so ordinary alcohol is considered to be a *hydrate* (§ 167) of the univalent compound radical, ethyl (C_2H_5).

212. Uses.—Alcohol is largely used in the chemical laboratory, in pharmacy and in the arts. It affords a smokeless fuel and is an indispensable solvent for many substances (such as resins and oils) that are insoluble in water. It is the fundamental principle of all fermented and distilled liquors.

213. Ether.—Ether ["sulphuric ether," ethyl ether, ethyl oxide, $(C_2H_5)_2O$] is prepared by distilling a mixture of strong sulphuric acid and alcohol. The distillate, which is a mixture of ether and water, is condensed in a cold receiver and separates into two layers, water below and ether above. The ether is drawn off and wholly freed from water by standing over quicklime and redistillation.

(a.) The chemical reaction may be represented as follows:

Alcohol. Hydrogen Ethyl Sulphate
$(C_2H_5)HO + H_2SO_4 = H_2O + H(C_2H_5)SO_4.$

$H(C_2H_5)SO_4 + (C_2H_5)HO = (C_2H_5)_2O + H_2SO_4.$

It will be noticed that the full amount of H_2SO_4 engaged *remains at the end* of the reaction. C_2H_6O is supplied in an uninterrupted stream, and thus the distillation goes on continuously.

Caution.—Owing to the danger arising from the extreme volatility and inflammability of $(C_2H_5)_2O$, the pupil should deal with only minute quantities of this compound.

Experiment 203.—Put 10 or 12 drops of C_2H_6O and an equal quantity of H_2SO_4 into a test tube and heat gently. The peculiar odor of $(C_2H_5)_2O$ may be recognized.

Experiment 204.—Pour a small quantity of $(C_2H_5)_2O$ into the palm of the hand and notice its rapid evaporation and absorption of sensible heat (Ph., § 517).

Experiment 205.—Put a few drops of $(C_2H_5)_2O$ into a tumbler, cover loosely and, after the lapse of a minute, bring a flame to the edge of the tumbler. The heavy vapor of $(C_2H_5)_2O$ will ignite with a sudden flash.

214. Properties.—Ether is a colorless, volatile, inflammable liquid, having a specific gravity of 0.72. It is almost insoluble in water and has a strong and peculiar odor. It is largely used as an anæsthetic (§§ 80, 269) in surgical operations. Its common name, "sulphuric ether," is a misnomer as ether contains no sulphur. Ether may be considered as ethyl oxide.

Note.—The relations of C_2H_6O and $(C_2H_5)_2O$ to each other and to their compound radical, ethyl, may be made more evident by the following typical symbols (§ 96):

Water Type. Alcohol. Ether.
$\left.\begin{array}{c}H\\H\end{array}\right\}O$ $\left.\begin{array}{c}(C_2H_5)'\\H\end{array}\right\}O$ $\left.\begin{array}{c}(C_2H_5)'\\(C_2H_5)'\end{array}\right\}O$

215. Acetic Acid.—If the half of the fermented liquid of Exp. 187 remaining after Exp. 202 be tasted, after standing for a few days, it will be found to be sour. If allowed to stand long enough, it will be changed to vinegar. By a process of oxidation, the alcohol is changed to acetic acid ("pyroligneous acid," $C_2H_4O_2$,) and water. Vinegar is a dilute solution of acetic acid with coloring matter and other impurities from the juice of the fruit from which it is generally made.

(*a.*) If two atoms of H in the compound radical C_2H_5 be replaced by O we shall have the oxygenated radical C_2H_3O, called acetyl. This radical has not yet been isolated. It is, consequently, a "hypothetical, oxygenated, compound radical." Acetyl *hydride* (C_2H_3O,H), a volatile, unstable and easily oxidizable compound, is called aldehyde; acetyl *hydrate* (C_2H_3O,HO) is called acetic acid. This acid is monobasic.

(*b.*) The conversion of C_2H_6O to $C_2H_4O_2$ is represented by the following equations:

Alcohol. *Aldehyde.*
$$(C_2H_5)HO + O = H_2O + (C_2H_3O)H.$$

Acetic acid.
$$(C_2H_3O)H + O = (C_2H_3O)HO = C_2H_4O_2.$$

(*c.*) Pure $C_2H_4O_2$ is prepared by distilling a mixture of H_2SO_4 and some acetate, such as sodium acetate. Lead acetate is commonly called by the *dangerous* name, "sugar of lead;" copper acetate is called "verdigris."

(*d.*) We have already noticed the relation between ethyl, alcohol and ether. The relations of acetic acid to these may be shown as follows:

Ethyl (C_2H_5), when oxygenated, becomes acetyl (C_2H_3O).
Acetyl (C_2H_3O) with hydroxyl becomes acetic acid or acetyl hydrate ($C_2H_4O_2$).

216. Isomerism.—Acetic acid and methyl formate are two distinct substances, having different properties, but represented by the same molecular symbol, $C_2H_4O_2$. *Different substances having the same percentage composition are said to be isomeric; the substances are* called *isomers*; the peculiar phenomenon is called *isomerism*. Isomers that have the same molecular symbol, like acetic acid and methyl formate, are said to be *metameric*. Isomers that have different molecular symbols are said to be *polymeric*. Acetylene (C_2H_2) and benzene (C_6H_6) are polymers.

(*a.*) There are at least seven distinct substances having the symbol $C_{10}H_6Cl_2$, differing from each other in solubility, fusibility and chemical behavior. We can only imagine that the difference between metameric substances is due to a *difference in the arrangement* of the atoms in the molecule.

(*b.*) Isomeric substances bring clearly to view the value of rational symbols (§ 94). Formic acid (CH_2O_2) is a hydrate of the univalent radical, formyl: $\left.\begin{array}{c}CHO\\H\end{array}\right\}O$. Replacing the H in this typical symbol for formic acid by methyl (CH_3)′, we have $\left.\begin{array}{c}CHO\\CH_3\end{array}\right\}O$ as the typical symbol for methyl formate. Acetic acid is a hydrate of the univalent radical, acetyl: $\left.\begin{array}{c}C_2H_3O\\H\end{array}\right\}O$. While, therefore, the empirical symbol, $C_2H_4O_2$ affords no means of distinguishing between acetic acid and methyl formate, the typical symbols, $\left.\begin{array}{c}C_2H_3O\\H\end{array}\right\}O$ and $\left.\begin{array}{c}CHO\\CH_3\end{array}\right\}O$ represent clearly, to eye and mind, two distinct substances. Similarly, C_2H_6O represents common alcohol or methyl ether. The former is ethyl hydrate, $\left.\begin{array}{c}C_2H_5\\H\end{array}\right\}O$; the latter is methyl oxide, $\left.\begin{array}{c}CH_3\\CH_3\end{array}\right\}O$.

(*c.*) Isomerism is a peculiarity of the hydrocarbons. The several members of the olefiant gas series (§ 220) are polymers.

217. Olefiant Gas.—Olefiant gas (ethene, ethylene, hydrogen dicarbide, C_2H_4) is prepared by removing the elements of water from alcohol. It is the first of a homologous hydrocarbon series, known as "The Olefiant Gas Series."

Experiment 206.—In a large beaker glass, mix 120 *cu. cm.* of H_2SO_4 and 30 *cu. cm.* of C_2H_6O, with caution and constant stirring. Half fill a liter flask with coarse sand and pour the mixed liquids upon the sand. Close the flask with cork and delivery tube, and heat it gently upon the sand bath. The gas will be delivered mixed with aeriform C_2H_6O, $(C_2H_5)_2O$, CO_2 and SO_2, and may be collected over water. If pure C_2H_4 be desired, two wash bottles, one containing strong H_2SO_4 and the other, a solution of NaHO may be interposed between the flask and the water bath. The purpose of using the sand is to lessen the frothing in the flask.

$$C_2H_6O - H_2O = C_2H_4.$$

Experiment 207.—Apply a flame to the mouth of a bottle of C_2H_4 and force out the gas by pouring in H_2O. The C_2H_4 burns with a brilliant white flame.

$$C_2H_4 + 3O_2 = 2CO_2 + 2H_2O.$$

Experiment 208.—Fill a soda water bottle with one volume of C_2H_4 and three volumes of O. Wrap a towel about the bottle and apply a flame to the mouth of the bottle. A violent explosion will take place.

Experiment 209.—Half fill a liter flask over the water bath with C_2H_4. Then introduce, under H_2O, half a liter of Cl

FIG. 91.

into the flask, and place a small cup under the mouth of the flask. The 1,000 *cu. cm.* of mixed gases will rapidly decrease in volume, H_2O will rise in the flask and oily drops will be formed and fall through the H_2O into the cup beneath. There has been a direct synthesis of the two gases to form ethylene chloride, ("Dutch liquid," or "oil of the Dutch chemists," $C_2H_4Cl_2$). Hence the name, "olefiant gas." By agitating the $C_2H_4Cl_2$ with a solution of sodium carbonate, the former may be purified and its agreeable odor obtained. (See *Note* following Exp. 94.)

218. Properties. — Olefiant gas is colorless, combustible and irrespirable. It is slightly soluble in water, and forms an explosive mixture with three times its volume of oxygen. It may be decomposed by electric sparks, giving twice its volume of hydrogen.

219. Acetylene. — Acetylene (ethine, C_2H_2) is a

transparent, colorless gas, that burns with a strongly luminous, smoky flame. It acts as a poison when it comes into contact with the blood. It may be formed by direct synthesis of its constituents at very high temperatures. It is one of the ingredients of illuminating gas.

(a.) Carbon electrodes may be fitted to pass through apertures in a globular glass flask, through which a slow current of pure H is flowing. By passing a powerful electric current through the carbons and then separating them, the electric arc is produced in an atmosphere of H. This process results in the synthesis of C_2H_2.

220. Homologous Series.—Methane, ethene and ethine represent each a series of hydrocarbons. In each series, the addition of CH_2 to the symbol of one member, gives the symbol of the next member. *Hydrocarbons that differ thus from one another are said to belong to homologous series.*

(a.) Each series has its general formula or symbol :

Series.	General Formula.	Symbols of Members.
Marsh gas	C_nH_{2n+2}	CH_4 ; C_2H_6 ; C_3H_8 ; C_4H_{10} ; C_5H_{12}
Olefiant gas	C_nH_{2n}	C_2H_4 ; C_3H_6 ; C_4H_8 ; C_5H_{10}
Acetylene	C_nH_{2n-2}	C_2H_2 ; C_3H_4 ; C_4H_6 ; C_5H_8

Exercises.

1. (a.) What is the specific gravity of marsh gas, on the hydrogen standard? (b.) On the air standard? (c.) What will a molecule of it weigh? (d.) What will a liter of it weigh?

2. (a.) What are the products of the combustion of methyl hydride? (b.) When a liter of it is burned, what is the weight of the dioxide produced? (c.) Of the monoxide produced?

3. (a.) What volume of O is necessary to the complete combustion of a liter of CH_4? (b.) What weight of O?

4. Find the percentage composition of alcohol.

5. (a.) What is the weight of a molecule of ethyl oxide? (b.) Of a liter of ether vapor? (c.) Of a liter of liquid $(C_2H_5)_2O$?

6. (*a.*) What volume of H may be obtained by the decomposition of 500 *cu. cm.* of olefiant gas ? (*b.*) By the decomposition of 10.5 criths of ethylene?

7. Which is the heavier, C_2H_4 or N_2?

8. (*a.*) Give a short statement of the process for making sulphuric acid. (*b.*) Which is the most interesting action in the process ? (*c.*) What is the specific gravity of the acid and how is this specific gravity secured?

9. When a mixture of H and CO is exposed to the action of a series of electric sparks the following reaction takes place :

$$3H_2 + CO = CH_4 + H_2O.$$

What volume of methane can thus be produced from 12.544 *g.* of carbon monoxide ?

10. (*a.*) Show that the specific gravity of a compound gas is one half its combining weight. (*b.*) How many atoms are there in a molecule of P?

11. The composition of a compound gas is $85\frac{5}{7}$ per cent. of C and $14\frac{2}{7}$ of H; its density is 14; what is its symbol?

12. Account for the fact that 23 *g.* of C_2H_6O will, without any addition of material by the manufacturer, yield about 30 *g.* of $C_2H_4O_2$.

13. Find the symbol of a substance whose vapor density is 23 and whose analysis shows the following percentage composition :

C, 52.2 ; H, 13 ; O, 34.8.

14. Write the empirical and graphic symbols for ethyl.

15. What word more fully descriptive than isomeric may be applied to substances that have the same percentage composition and molecular weight ?

16. Symbolize the acetates of Na', K', Ca'' and $(NH_4)'$.

Section IV.

ILLUMINATING GAS.

Experiment 210.—Into a gas pipe retort, put some fragments of bituminous (soft) coal. To the delivery tube, attach a piece of glass tubing drawn out to a jet. Place the retort in a hot fire and, as the illuminating gas is delivered, ignite it at the jet.

221. Illuminating Gas.—Illuminating gas is prepared by distilling substances consisting in whole or in part of hydrogen and carbon. For this purpose, wood, resin, or petroleum is sometimes used but, far more commonly, a mixture of cannel and caking bituminous coals furnishes the desired products. A sectional view of the apparatus used is shown in Fig. 93. The coal is placed in ◠ shaped retorts, six or seven feet long, made of fire clay. The charge is about 200 *lb.* of coal to each retort. The retorts, *C*, are arranged in groups or "benches" of from three to seven, as shown in Fig. 92. All the retorts of a bench are heated to a temperature of about 1200°C. or 2200°F. by a single coke fire. After charging the retorts, their mouths are quickly closed by heavy iron plates.

Fig. 92.

Fig. 93.

(*a.*) The products of the distillation, when cooled to the ordinary temperature, are solid, liquid and gaseous. The liquid products are volatile at the high temperature of the retort.

(*b.*) The solid products are coke and gas carbon. The coke is coal from which the volatile constituents have been removed by intense heat. It is largely used as a fuel for domestic, metallurgical and other purposes. The gas carbon is an incrustation that gradually forms on the inside of the retorts. It is used for making plates for galvanic batteries and "carbons" or "candles" for electric lamps (Ph., §§ 383, 385, 389).

(*c.*) The liquid portion of the distillate is chiefly an aqueous solution of ammonium compounds, certain hydrocarbons like benzol and toluol, and a viscous coal tar which is complex in its composition.

(*d.*) The gases of the distillate are very numerous. One writer mentions nineteen light producing constituents, including benzol and toluol vapors, C_2H_2 and C_2H_4; three diluents, *viz.*, H, CO and CH_4; and fourteen impurities, including N, O, H_2O, H_2S, CO_2, SO_2 and CS_2.

(*e.*) When the volatile products leave the retort, they pass up through the ascension pipes, *i*, down the dip pipes and bubble through the seal of tar and water already collected in the long, horizontal iron tube, *mm*, called the hydraulic main. From this point forward, cooling ensues, accompanied by the condensation of vapors "and the falling of the tar particles mechanically carried along in the hot rush of the gas from the retorts." The gas is loaded with impurities from which it must be freed before it is in a salable condition.

(*f.*) From the hydraulic main, where it left much of its tar and H_2O, the gas passes through the vertical cooling pipes, *D*, called the condensers. Here it is cooled to 20°C. or 25°C. and largely freed from its tar, oils and ammonium compounds. The gas now assumes a condition less thickened and turbid and more favorable to chemical treatment. In large gas works, there are many sets of these condensers. In the Cleveland works, each set measures 840 linear feet. Every particle of gas has to pass the whole length of one of these sets of condensers.

(*g.*) In large works, an "exhauster" is placed between the hydraulic main and the condensers. By this means, the gas is pumped from the retorts and forced through the condensers, thus reducing the pressure in the retorts.

(*h.*) Chief among the impurities still remaining, are ammonium compounds, CO_2 and H_2S. These ammonium compounds are easily soluble in H_2O. Therefore, the gas is next washed in the tower or "scrubber," O. Here the gas, in a finely divided state, rises through a shower of minute particles of H_2O and, thus, has its easily soluble impurities washed out by the spray. To prevent the ascent of the gas in large bubbles, of which only the surfaces would come into contact with the H_2O, the scrubber is filled with coke, brush, or lattice work for "breaking up" both gas and H_2O into minute particles. This scrubbing also cools the gas still more and removes some of the CO_2 and H_2S. The tower is generally three or four feet in diameter and thirty or forty feet high. More than one are used in some works.

(*i.*) The gas next passes through the purifiers, M, the object of which is to remove the remaining CO_2 and H_2S. The purifier consists of boxes containing trays with perforated bottoms. These trays contain the material which removes the impurities as the gas filters through. Some works use slaked lime in the purifiers, others a mixture of copperas (iron sulphate, $FeSO_4$,) saw-dust and slaked lime. At manufacturing establishments where iron and steel articles are polished, the grindstone dust is intimately mixed with minute particles of the metal. This inexpensive mixture of grindstone dust and iron or steel is used in the purifiers of the Cleveland Gas Light and Coke Co.

(*j.*) From the purifiers, the gas is conducted to the gasholders, G. These gas holders are sometimes sixty feet high and more than 100 feet in diameter.

(*k.*) The gas, as delivered to the consumer, consists chiefly of the three diluents mentioned above, the CH_4 constituting about a third of the gas sold. These feebly luminous gases, H, CO and CH_4, serve as carriers of the six or seven *per cent.* of more highly luminous constituents, while the combustion of the former furnishes much of the heat needed for the decomposition of the latter and the raising of its carbon particles to the temperature of incandescence.

(*l.*) Other conditions being the same, and within certain limits, the higher the temperature, the greater the quantity of gas produced; the lower the temperature, the richer the quality. Similarly, the longer the time of the charge, the greater the quantity; the shorter the time, the richer the quality. A skillful mixture of grades of coal and regulation of temperature and time of charge enables the gas engineer to vary the products of the chemical processes in the retort and furnish an article that is attractive and satisfactory to the consumer, or profitable to the proprietors, or to compromise between these conflicting interests.

Experiment 211.—Heat some pieces of bituminous coal in the gas

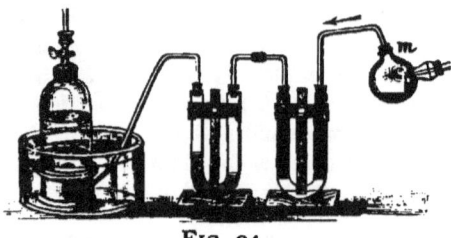

FIG. 94.

pipe or other retort and pass the gas as it is evolved through the apparatus shown in Fig. 94. The volatile liquid products will condense in the receiver. m, or "hydraulic main." Thence, the gas passes through the first arm of the U-tube and changes the color of a moistened strip of red litmus paper to blue, thus showing the presence of NH_3. In the second arm, it is tested for H_2S (§ 142). In the bend of the second tube, is placed lime water, which becomes milky, thus showing the presence of CO_2. The gas is then collected over H_2O. By lowering the capped receiver into the H_2O or by pouring more H_2O into the water bath and opening the stop-cock, the gas may be forced out and burned as it issues.

EXERCISES.

1. See App. 1. Read the following symbols, thus: N_2 represents one molecule of nitrogen consisting of two atoms: O, O_2, O_3, H_2O, $2H_2O$, H_2, $2P_4$, Cl_2, NH_3, H_2SO_4, $FeSO_4$, $Al_2(SO_4)_3$, $4Al_2(SO_4)_3$, CO_2, CO.

2. Write down the weights represented by each of the following expressions: $2HgO$, $10H_2O$, $2CS_2$, $12CH_4$, $K_2Al_2(SO_4)_4$, $24H_2O$.

3. Name the compounds symbolized as follows: CaO, MgO, ZnS, KCl, $NaBr$, AgF, H_2S, HI, KCN, SSe, PH_3.

4. If two volumes of C_2H_4 and four of Cl be mixed, a black smoke and HCl are formed. Write the reaction.

5. How much NH_3 will just neutralize 10 g. of HCl?

6. How many liters of O are necessary to combine (complete combustion) with (*a.*) 12 criths of C? (*b.*) 2 g. of S? (*c*). 10 g. of C?

7. How many liters of Cl are necessary to decompose 12 l. of HI?

8. (*a.*) Distinguish between the properties of CO and those of CO_2. (*b.*) How does each destroy life? (*c.*) Give a test for each.

§ 221   ILLUMINATING GAS.   193

9. Steam and Cl are passed through a porcelain tube heated to redness. What takes place?

10. (a.) What is meant by the basicity of an acid? (b.) By the acidity of a base? (c.) How is the name of a salt derived from that of an acid?

11. Explain the significance of each of the following symbols for potassium sulphate: K_2SO_4; K_2O,SO_3;

$$\left.\begin{array}{c}KO\\KO\end{array}\right\}SO_2 \quad \text{and} \quad \begin{array}{c}K-O\\K-O\end{array}\!\!>\!\!S\!\!<\!\!\begin{array}{c}O\\O\end{array}$$

9

Section V.

SOME ORGANIC COMPOUNDS.

222. Organic Compounds. — There are known to the chemist many substances formed by the subtle processes of animal and vegetable life. These were formerly supposed to be incapable of production in any other way and their consideration formed a distinct branch of study known as *Organic Chemistry*. But within the last few years, many of these organic compounds have been produced in the chemical laboratory from "dead matter." Each of these triumphs of modern chemistry removes a stone from the wall dividing the realms of organic and inorganic chemistry. In fact, the wall, *as a wall*, is already ruined. In this section, we shall consider a few of the almost innumerable known organic compounds. The molecular structure of most of them is very complicated.

Experiment 212. — Place a teaspoonful of the white of an egg in a test tube; add 25 *cu. cm.* of C_2H_6O. Notice the coagulation.

Experiment 213. — Place the remainder of the white of the egg in a test tube; place the test tube and a thermometer in a vessel of H_2O; heat the H_2O; notice that at the temperature of about 60°C. the white of the egg coagulates.

223. Albumen. — Albumen is a substance of very complicated structure. It is typical of a group of bodies (histogenetic) that are essential to the building up of the animal organism, of which group the leading members are albumen, fibrin and casein. These differ but little, if any, in their chemical composition, but widely in their properties. They all exist in two conditions, the soluble and the insoluble.

(*a*.) The white of the eggs of birds is the most familiar instance of albumen. It is soluble in H_2O and coagulated by heat or C_2H_6O. The albumen of plants is found chiefly in the seed. The formula, $C_{72}H_{112}N_{18}SO_{22}$, has been given for albumen, but its chemical composition has not yet been satisfactorily determined.

(*b*.) Soluble fibrin is found in the blood. It hardens on exposure to the air and, entangling the corpuscles of the blood, forms the clot. By washing the clot with H_2O, fibrin is left as a white, stringy mass. Insoluble fibrin constitutes muscular fibre.

(*c*.) Casein is found in the milk of animals. It is not coagulated by heat but is coagulable by rennet, the inner membrane of the stomach of the calf. This property is utilized in cheese making.

(*d*.) All of the albuminoids "are amorphous, and may be kept, when dry, for any length of time, but, when moist, they rapidly putrefy and produce a sickening odor."

Experiment 214.—Dilute a quantity of HCl with about six times its volume of H_2O. Place a clean bone (*e. g.*, the femur of a chicken) in the dilute acid and allow it to remain for three or four days. The mineral part of the bone will gradually dissolve, and there will be left a flexible substance which preserves the shape of the bone, and which, when dry, has a translucent, horny appearance.

Experiment 215.—Place the flexible substance left from the last experiment in H_2O and boil it for three or four hours. It will dissolve and, when the liquid cools, will assume a jelly-like condition.

224. Gelatin. — The bones and skins of animals contain a substance called ossein. The product of Exp. 214 was ossein. When this substance is boiled in water, gelatin is produced. The product of Exp. 215 was gelatin. Glue is an inferior quality of gelatin. Isinglass is nearly pure gelatin; it is made from the swimming bladder of the sturgeon. The thin plates of mica used in stoves are sometimes, *with gross impropriety*, called isinglass.

225. Sugar. — There are several varieties of sugar, among which the most important are sucrose, dextrose and levulose.

226. Sucrose. — Sucrose (cane sugar, $C_{12}H_{22}O_{11}$) is found in the juice of certain plants, as sugar cane, sugar maple and beet root. In the manufacture of cane sugar, the juice is pressed from the canes by passing them between rollers. The juice is treated with milk of lime and heated. The lime neutralizes the acids and the heat coagulates the albumen in the juice. The coagulated albumen rises and mechanically carries with it many of the impurities, some of which have combined with the lime. The scum thus formed is removed, and the liquid evaporated until it is of such a consistency that sugar crystals will form when the liquid is cooled. The crystals, when drained, are " brown " or " muscovado " sugar. The liquid remaining is molasses.

(*a.*) Brown sugar is refined by dissolving it in H_2O, filtering the solution through layers of animal charcoal and evaporating the H_2O from the filtrate. When $C_{12}H_{22}O_{11}$ is boiled, part of it is changed to a mixture of dextrose and levulose, the proportion thus changed depending upon the temperature and time of boiling. To lessen this loss *of sucrose*, the filtered solution is evaporated in large " vacuum pans " from which the air and steam are exhausted. The degree of concentration desired is thus secured more quickly and at a lower temperature (Ph., §§ 503–505,) thus lessening the loss and obviating the risk of burning. When the " mother-liquor " drains from the crystals in moulds, loaf-sugar is left; when it is driven off by a centrifugal machine, granulated sugar is left.

(*b.*) The sugar from the sap of the sugar maple or from the juice of the beet root is identical with cane sugar. As the impurities of maple sugar are agreeable to the taste of many persons, the sugar is not refined. Beet sugar is always refined, as its impurities are offensive to all.

(*c.*) When sucrose is melted and allowed to cool rapidly, *barley* sugar is formed. When it is heated to about 215°C., H_2O is expelled and *caramel* remains.

(*d.*) Lactose or milk-sugar and maltose are isomeric forms that combine with one molecule of water of crystallization ($C_{12}H_{22}O_{11} + H_2O$). The former exists in solution in the milk of mammals.

227. Dextrose and Levulose.—When a solution of sucrose is boiled or subjected to the action of yeast or an acid, it is converted into two isomeric varieties of sugar, dextrose (glucose, grape sugar, starch sugar, $C_6H_{12}O_6$) and levulose (fruit sugar, $C_6H_{12}O_6$).

$$C_{12}H_{22}O_{11} + H_2O = C_6H_{12}O_6 + C_6H_{12}O_6.$$

This mixture of dextrose and levulose is called *inverted sugar*.

(*a.*) Dextrose is found in many ripe fruits. The "candied" sugar of raisins and other dried fruits is dextrose. It crystallizes with difficulty and is generally found in a sirupy condition. It may be prepared by boiling starch in H_2O acidulated with H_2SO_4. It has less sweetening power than sucrose. Large quantities of glucose are now made from indian corn.

(*b.*) Levulose is found with dextrose in many ripe fruits, in honey, molasses, *etc*. It does not crystallize. It has less sweetening power than sucrose.

(*c.*) Dextrose and levulose may be fermented (Exp. 187); sucrose can not be fermented until after its conversion into dextrose and levulose.

(*d.*) If a beam of polarized light (Ph., § 667) be passed through a solution of dextrose, the plane of polarization will be turned toward the right (*dextra* = right hand). A solution of sucrose will turn it still more. If the beam be passed through a solution of levulose, the plane will be turned toward the left (*laeva* = left-hand).

(*e.*) Dextrose and levulose are isomeric with acetic acid, the molecule $C_6H_{12}O_6$ having three times as many of each kind of atoms as $C_2H_4O_2$. While, therefore, dextrose and levulose are said to be metameric, either one of them is polymeric with reference to $C_2H_4O_2$. See § 216.

228. Starch.—Starch ($C_6H_{10}O_5$) is a familiar substance found in grain (*e. g.*, wheat and Indian corn), in the tuber of the potato plant and in the root, stem or fruit of many other plants. It is composed of microscopic granules which swell and burst, forming a pasty mass when heated in water nearly to the boiling point. This starch paste forms a blue color with iodine (Exp. 121).

(*a.*) Tapioca, arrow-root, sago and inulin are varieties of starch.

(*b.*) When starch is heated to about 210°C., it is changed to an isomeric compound called dextrin. Unlike starch, it is soluble in H_2O, forming a mucilaginous liquid. The adhesive compound on postage stamps is largely dextrin. When starch is boiled in dilute H_2SO_4, it is converted, first into dextrin and then into glucose.

229. Bread Making.—In making bread, the water that is added to the flour forms a dough. The addition of emptyings or yeast causes fermentation to begin. As the fermentation proceeds, the carbon dioxide and alcohol vapor thus produced struggle to escape through the tenacious dough, causing the latter to "rise." In the subsequent process of kneading, the half-fermented "sponge" is evenly distributed through the loaf and the large bubbles of gas imprisoned in the dough are broken up into smaller ones and the bread thus made finer grained. After kneading, the moulded loaves are placed in the hot oven. Fermentation is stimulated by the heat, the alcohol is vaporized and, together with the carbon dioxide, expanded. As these aeriform substances escape through the loaf, they increase its size and "lightness." If the process has been satisfactorily conducted, by the time that fermentation and the escape of gas and vapor have ceased, the walls of the bread cells will be strong enough to retain their form. If the dough be allowed to stand too long before baking, the gas will escape, the still plastic walls of the bread cells will collapse and the bread "fall." If the oven be not hot enough or if the dough be too wet, a similar result will ensue and the bread will be "slack-baked." If the oven be too hot, a crust will form too quickly, the gas, being prevented from escaping, will collect at the centre and the loaf be hollow. At the surface of the loaf, a substance much like caramel is formed; this is the crust. The crust also contains dextrin. When the crust is moistened and the loaf returned to the oven, the dissolved dextrin left by evaporation gives to the crust a smooth, shining surface.

230. Cellulose.—Cellulose ($C_{18}H_{30}O_{15}$?) constitutes the outer wall of every vegetable cell and is, therefore, found in every part of every plant. It is insoluble in water or alcohol. Linen and cotton are nearly pure cellulose.

(*a.*) Cellulose has the same centesimal composition as starch ($C_6H_{10}O_5$) but is probably polymeric rather than metameric.

(*b.*) By treating cellulose with a mixture of HNO_3 and H_2SO_4, it is changed to gun cotton (nitro-cellulose, pyroxylin), an explosive substance that burns in air with a sudden flash and no smoke. Gun cotton may be considered to be cellulose with some of its H atoms replaced by the compound radical NO_2.

Experiment 216.—Dilute 25 *cu. cm.* of H_2SO_4 with 10 or 12 *cu. cm.* of H_2O. When the mixture is cold, immerse in it, for 15 or 20 seconds, a piece of filter paper. Rinse the paper in H_2O and then in dilute NH_4HO, to remove all traces of the acid. Finally, rinse the paper again in pure H_2O. The paper will have acquired greater toughness and rigidity and will resemble parchment in other respects. It has been changed to *vegetable parchment*. It may be necessary to repeat the experiment, varying the time of immersion, to get good results.

EXERCISES.

1. Why does it require more sugar to sweeten fruits when the sugar is added before cooking than it does when the sugar is added after cooking?

2. Write the symbol for dextrin.

3. Name the compounds symbolized as follows: BaO, BaO_2, Hg_2O, HgO, FeS, FeS_2, MnO, MnO_2, Mn_2O_3, FeO, Fe_2O_3, N_2O, NO, N_2O_3, N_2O_5, NO_2, P_2S_3, P_2S_5, $SnCl_2$, $SnCl_4$, $FeBr_2$.

4. How many l. of Cl are required for the complete decomposition of 10 l. of olefiant gas?

5. (a.) Give the reaction in the preparation of CO_2. (b.) How may CO_2 be distinguished from every other gas? (c.) How much of it is produced by burning 10 liters of marsh gas?

6. In the analysis of a certain compound, the following data were obtained:

Carbon... = 62.07 per cent. | Oxygen.. = 27.58 per cent.
Hydrogen., = 10.35   " | Vapor density, 4.04, on the air standard.

What is the molecular symbol of the compound?

7. (a.) Find the percentage composition of marsh gas. (b.) Of olefiant gas.

8. What weight of $KClO_3$ is necessary to the preparation of 35,000 cu. cm. of O?

9. On completely decomposing, by heat, a certain weight of $KClO_3$, I obtain 20.246 g. of KCl. (a.) What weight of $KClO_3$ did I use? (b.) What volume of O did I obtain?

10. To inflate a certain balloon properly requires 132.74 Kg. of H. What weight of Zn and of H_2SO_4 will be needed to prepare this quantity of H.

11. Write the name and a graphic symbol for $H_2S_2O_3$, introducing dyad S and hexad S.

SECTION VI.

SILICON.

☞ *Symbol*, Si ; *atomic weight,* 28 m. c. ; *quantivalence,* 4.

231. Silicon.—Although this element does not occur free in nature, it is the most abundant and widely diffused of all the elements except oxygen. Combined with oxygen alone, as silica or quartz, or with oxygen and potassium or sodium, *etc.*, as metallic silicates, it forms a large part of the earth's crust.

(*a.*) Free Si may be prepared by the action of sodium upon potassium silico-fluoride.

$$K_2SiF_6 + 2Na_2 = 2KF + 4NaF + Si.$$

(*b.*) Si exists, like C, in three allotropic forms; as a soft, brown, amorphous powder which burns easily in air or O, forming SiO_2; as hexagonal plates, corresponding to graphite in lustre and electric conductivity; as needle shaped octahedral crystals, corresponding to diamond in hardness. These octahedra are hard enough to scratch glass.

(*c.*) The only acid that attacks crystallized Si, is a mixture of HNO_3 and HF.

95.

(*d.*) There is a compound of H and Si known as hydrogen silicide (SiH_4) that is somewhat analogous to CH_4. Similar compounds are formed with members of the halogen group, as $SiCl_4$, *etc.*

232. Silicon Dioxide.—Silicon has only one oxide (silica, silicic anhydride, SiO_2). It is very abundant in nature. Its purest form is quartz or rock crystal, which is found in beautiful hexagonal prisms terminated by hexagonal pyramids. Quartz has a specific gravity of 2.6, and is hard enough to scratch glass.

(*a.*) Amethyst, cairngorm-stone and rose quartz are nearly pure crystallized SiO_2. Agate, carnelian, chalcedony, flint, jasper, onyx and opal are nearly pure amorphous SiO_2. White sand and sandstone are generally nearly pure SiO_2. Silicious sand and sand-stone are often colored yellow by an iron oxide.

(*b.*) SiO_2 is insoluble in H_2O or in any acid except HF, but it may be dissolved in a boiling solution of potassium or sodium hydrate. The potassium or sodium silicate thus formed is called "soluble glass" or "water glass." SiO_2 is dissolved in the waters of some thermal springs. The Geysers of Iceland contain dissolved SiO_2, which is deposited by the cooling waters upon objects immersed in them. SiO_2 melts in the oxyhydrogen flame to a colorless glass that remains transparent when cold.

(*c.*) SiO_2 from the soil is found in certain plants, especially grains and rushes. The outer coat of rattan contains much SiO_2, as does the leafless plant, horse tail, which is, consequently, used for polishing and scouring.

(*d.*) SiO_2 is also found in animal substances. The feathers of certain birds are said to contain 40 *per cent.* of SiO_2.

Experiment 217.—Place a few *cu. cm.* of concentrated soluble glass in a small evaporating dish and add strong HCl until the mixture shows an acid reaction. A thick jelly like mass will be formed in the liquid. Place the dish on a water bath and evaporate its contents to dryness. Heat this solid residue gently over the lamp. It will diminish in volume. Add H_2O and filter. The insoluble powder left upon the filter is precipitated SiO_2, one of the lightest known powders. This jelly like mass formed in this experiment probably is silicic acid (H_4SiO_4).

233. Natural Silicates.—Silica unites with many metallic oxides to form silicates. The natural silicates are very numerous and many of them are of a very complex composition. Thus, clay is a silicate of aluminum; feldspar is a double silicate of aluminum and potassium; mica is a triple silicate of aluminum, potassium and iron.

Experiment 218.—Add some HCl to a dilute solution of water glass. NaCl or KCl will be formed with H_4SiO_4. Pour the liquid mixture into a *dialyser*, made of parchment paper stretched over a wooden ring and floated on the surface of pure H_2O. The chloride solution passes through the membrane while the H_4SiO_4 remains dissolved in the dialyser.

Crystallizable substances, like NaCl and KCl are sometimes called *crystalloids*, and uncrystallizable substances, *colloids*. Crystalloids and colloids may be separated as in this experiment. The process is called *dialysis*.

234. Artificial Silicates.—Sodium and potassium silicates (water or soluble glass) are largely used in the arts. But by far the most important of the artificial silicates is glass, which is a mixture of a silicate of sodium or of potassium, or of both, with a silicate of one or more other metals. The composition is determined by the desired infusibility, insolubility, transparency or color of the glass.

(*a.*) Bohemian glass is a silicate of potassium and calcium. It is fusible only with difficulty and is but little acted upon by chemical reagents. It is free from color and is largely used in chemical apparatus, especially in ignition tubes.

(*b.*) Window, crown or plate glass is a silicate of sodium and calcium. It is harder than Bohemian glass, but more easily fusible and more readily acted upon by chemical reagents.

(*c.*) Bottle glass, or common green glass, is a silicate of sodium, calcium, aluminum and iron. Its color is due to the iron oxide present as an impurity in the cheap materials used. It is harder and more infusible than window glass, but more easily acted upon by acids.

(*d.*) Flint glass is a silicate of potassium and lead. It has a high specific gravity (Ph., § 253) and great refracting power (Ph., § 613, *a.*). It is the most easily fusible variety of glass and is easily acted upon by chemical reagents. "Crystal" is a pure flint glass used for optical purposes. "Strass" is a flint glass very rich in lead and having a very high refractive power. It forms the basis of the artificial gems and precious stones known as "paste."

(*e.*) Glass softens at a red heat and can then be readily worked and welded. See App. 4. At higher temperatures it becomes still softer and finally melts. On cooling, it passes from a thin, mobile liquid through all degrees of viscosity to a hard solid.

(*f.*) Glass is acted upon readily by HF (see Exp. 126). Etched glass is now much used instead of the more expensive cut glass.

(*g.*) When glass, heated almost to redness, is dipped into oil heated to 300°C. and then allowed to cool gradually, it becomes toughened. Table glass thus toughened is not readily broken by falling or being thrown, but when thrown with sufficient force to break it, it is shattered into minute pieces.

(*h.*) Glass is easily colored by the addition of the proper materials to the fused mass. Thus, a green color is produced by the addition of a ferrous or cupric oxide; blue, by a cobalt oxide; violet, by manganese dioxide; ruby, by gold, etc.

EXERCISES.

1. Give the preparation and principal properties of H_2S, CS_2, HCN, CH_4, C_2H_4 and C_2H_6O.

2. Write the symbols representing chloroform, glycerine, ether, acetic acid, cane sugar and starch.

3. (*a.*) Name the products of the combustion of CS_2 and C_2H_6O. (*b.*) Describe briefly the process of preparing illuminating gas and tell its composition.

4. Name the substances symbolized as follows: KNO_2, KNO_3, K_2SO_3, K_2SO_4, $HKSO_4$, KCl, $KClO$, $KClO_2$, $KClO_3$, $KClO_4$, $HNaSO_3$, SiH_4, SiO_2, H_4SiO_4.

5. (*a.*) Find the weight of 20 *l.* of O. (*b.*) Of 50 *l.* of Cl. (*c.*) Of 250 *l.* of NH_3.

6. What materials and what quantities would you need to prepare 50 *l.* of each of the oxides of C?

7. By heating MnO_2 with H_2SO_4 the following reaction takes place:

$$2MnO_2 + 2H_2SO_4 = 2MnSO_4 + 2H_2O + O_2.$$

(*a.*) What weight and (*b.*) what volume of O can be thus obtained from 50 *g.* of MnO_2?

8. (*a.*) Give the ordinary methods of preparing O, H and HCl. (*b.*) In what do they differ and in what do they agree? (*c.*) Find the amount of Cl, by weight and by measure, in 2 *Kg.* of HCl.

9. If 100 *l.* of CO_2 be required, by what means would you obtain it, from what materials, and what quantity of each material?

CHAPTER XIV.

THE NITROGEN GROUP.

SECTION I.

PHOSPHORUS.

☞ *Symbol,* P ; *specific gravity, 1.8 ; atomic weight, 31 m. c. ; molecular weight, 124 m. c.; quantivalence, 3 or 5.*

235. Source. — Phosphorus does not occur free in nature, but its compounds with oxygen and some metal (chiefly calcium) are found in large quantities. Calcium phosphate is found as a native mineral ; it forms, also, the greater part of the mineral constituent of animal bone.

(*a.*) The ultimate source of P is the granitic rocks, by the disintegration of which the fertile soil has been produced. All fruitful soils contain some of the phosphates, but diffused in such small quantities that their collection thence by the manufacturing chemist would be very costly. Plants collect the phosphates from the soil ; herbivorous animals obtain them by consuming the plants ; from the bones of animals, the chemist derives the phosphates from which he prepares the P that he and the manufacturer need. The process is devious and complicated but the greater part of it is inexpensive.

Note.—The name comes from two Greek words that mean a *bearer of light*, phosphorus being luminous in the dark. The alchemists used to call it "Son of Satan." Phosphides were formerly called phosphurets.

236. Preparation.—In the preparation of phosphorus, the bones are burned and powdered. This powdered bone ash is treated for about twelve hours with two-thirds its weight of strong sulphuric acid diluted with about twenty times its weight of water. This treatment yields an insoluble calcium sulphate (gypsum, $CaSO_4$) and a soluble salt called "superphosphate of lime." The insoluble sulphate is removed by filtration. The clear solution is then evaporated to a sirupy liquid, mixed with powdered charcoal, dried and finally distilled. The long neck of the earthen retort (Fig. 96) dips under water contained in b. The liberated phosphorus distils over and condenses under the water. After purification, it is melted under hot water and run into cylindrical moulds placed in cold water.

FIG. 96.

☞ See the *Caution* on page 31. Phosphorus burns are very difficult to heal.

Experiment 219.—Bury a piece of P, the size of a grain of wheat, in a teaspoonful of lamp-black or powdered bone-black, that has been freshly prepared or recently heated. The O condensed within the pores of the carbon unites with the vapor of the P, developing enough heat to melt and finally to ignite the P.

Experiment 220.—Dissolve a piece of P in CS_2. Pour some of the solution upon a piece of filter paper placed upon the ring of a retort stand. The volatile CS_2 soon evaporates, leaving the P in a finely divided state exposing a large surface to the oxidizing influence of the air. The P soon bursts into flame, which only partly consumes the paper. The burning P quickly covers the paper with a coat of incombustible and protecting varnish. If the experiment be performed in a dark room, the phosphorescence will be very marked.

Experiment 221.—Rub a piece of dry P the size of a pin head between two bits of board. The heat developed by the friction is sufficient to ignite it.

Experiment 222.—Heat a small piece of P in a dry tube with a mere trace of I. Combination promptly takes place, a small quantity of volatile phosphoric iodide is formed and the rest of the P is changed to an allotropic form known as *red phosphorus*. Try to repeat Exp. 221 with red P.

Experiment 223.—Close one end of a piece of narrow glass tubing about 30 cm. long by fusing it in a flame. In the ignition tube thus made, place a small bit of red P and heat it gently in the lamp flame. A yellow coating is quickly deposited upon the cool walls of the tube not far from the heated end. Allow the tube to cool, and cut off the end just below the yellow sublimate. Scratch this yellow deposit with a wire; it will take fire, as it is ordinary, yellow P. By heating the red P, a part of it burned, thus removing the O from the lower part of the tube. The inert N remaining there, enveloped and protected the rest of the P from combustion and thus permitted its reconversion into the ordinary variety.

Experiment 224.—Touch a slice of P with a test tube containing boiling H_2O. The P will be ignited.

Experiment 225.—Place a piece of P under H_2O warm enough to melt it. Bring a current of O from the gas-holder into contact with the melted P. The P will take fire and burn brilliantly *under* H_2O.

Experiment 226.—Repeat Exp. 3.

237. Physical Properties.

—Pure phosphorus is an almost colorless, translucent, wax-like solid. The ordinary commercial article has a feeble yellow tinge. When freshly cut, it has a garlic-like odor, often hidden by the odor of ozone, which is generally present when moist phosphorus is exposed to the air. It is insoluble in water, sparingly soluble in tur-

FIG. 97.

pentine, petroleum and other oils and easily soluble in carbon disulphide. It is soft and flexible in warm weather but brittle at low temperatures. It melts at 44°C., forming a viscid, oily liquid which boils at 290°C., yielding a colorless vapor. At 500°C. the vapor is 62 times as heavy as hydrogen. Consequently, its molecular weight is 124 *m. c.*, or four times its atomic weight. From this we conclude that the phosphorus molecule contains four atoms and that each atom occupies half the space taken up by a hydrogen atom (§ 175).

Experiment 227.—Upon a thin slice of P, place a crystal of I. The two elements promptly unite with great energy, leading to the combustion of the excess of P.

238. Chemical Properties.

Phosphorus combines readily with many of the elements, especially oxygen. It undergoes slow combustion at ordinary temperatures (forming P_2O_3) and oxidizes with great energy at a temperature not much above its melting point (forming P_2O_5). On account of this easy inflammability, phosphorus should be kept and cut under water and *never handled with dry fingers*. Owing to its slow combustion, it is feebly luminous in the dark. This phosphorescence is a familiar effect of a futile attempt at lighting an ordinary friction match in a dark room. In distillation, the oxygen in the retort must be replaced by some inert gas like hydrogen, nitrogen or carbon dioxide. Heated for several hours to about 240°C., out of contact with oxygen or any other substance capable of entering into chemical union with it, it is changed to the remarkable allotropic modification known as *red phosphorus.*

(*a.*) The difference between the ordinary yellow and the red varieties of P are shown in the following table:

1. Pale yellow,	Chocolate red.
2. Strong odor,	Odorless.
3. Specific gravity = 1.83,	Specific gravity = 2.14.
4. Phosphorescent,	Not phosphorescent.
5. Translucent,	Opaque.
6. Soluble in CS_2,	Insoluble in CS_2.
7. Subject to slow combustion,	Exempt from slow combustion.
8. Melts at 44°C.,	Melts at 255°C.
9. Changes to red variety at 240°C.,	Changes to yellow variety at 260°C.
10. Soft,	Hard.
11. Flexible,	Brittle.
12. Poisonous,	Not poisonous.

239. Uses. — Phosphorus is extensively used in the manufacture of friction matches, the match tips generally being a mixture of phosphorus, glue and potassium chlorate. "Safety-matches" are tipped with antimonous sulphide and potassium chlorate. These ignite, not by simple friction, but by rubbing on a prepared surface containing red phosphorus, manganese dioxide and sand. Ordinary phosphorus mixed with flour paste is a "rat poison" that has probably led to the burning of many houses. Phosphorus is used in medicine; many of the phosphates are important remedial agents. Phosphorus fumes produce, in the workmen in match factories, "phosphorus-necrosis, a disease in which the bones of the jaw are destroyed."

(a.) About 1200 tons are said to be made yearly, nearly all of it at two establishments, one near Birmingham, England, and the other at Lyons, France. The manufacture is dangerous, on account of the easy inflammability of the product.

EXERCISES.

1. (*a.*) Symbolize two molecules of pentad phosphorus. Three molecules of quadrivalent sulphur. (*b.*) What do $\overset{vi}{S}_2$ and $6O''_2$ represent?

2. (*a.*) What is a binary molecule? (*b.*) A ternary molecule? (*c.*) How are binary molecules named? Illustrate.

3. How much P is contained in 120 Kg. of bone ash, of which 88.5 % is $Ca_3(PO_4)_2$ and the rest $CaCO_3$?

4. (*a.*) Find the percentage composition of carbon monoxide. (*b.*) Find the symbol of a gas having the composition 27.27% C; 72.73% O, and weighing 1.9712 g. to the liter.

5. Red oxide of copper contains 88.8 parts of Cu and 11.2 parts of O, by weight. Black oxide of copper contains 79.87 of Cu and 20.13 of O. The symbol for the black oxide is CuO; what is the symbol for the red oxide?

6. What is the meaning of the following:

If from $\begin{matrix}(HO)-(NO_2)\\(HO)-(NO_2)\end{matrix}\}$ we take H_2O, $O{<}{(NO_2)\atop(NO_2)}$ will remain.

7. Can S_2 and S_4 exist at the same temperature? Explain.

8. Write the name and full graphic symbol for
$(HO)-(SO_2)-(SO_2)-(HO)$.

Section II.

PHOSPHORUS COMPOUNDS.

240. Hydrogen Phosphide. — This colorless, poisonous, ill-smelling gas, (phosphuretted hydrogen, phosphine, PH_3,) is generally prepared by heating phosphorus in a strong alkaline solution.

(*a.*) Dissolve 40 *g.* of potassium hydrate (caustic potash) or 60 *g.* of freshly slaked lime in 110 *cu. cm.* of H_2O. Place it in a flask of not more than 200 *cu. cm.* capacity; add 1 *g.* of P in thin slices, and 5 or 6 drops of $(C_2H_5)_2O$; close the flask with a cork carrying a long glass delivery tube that terminates beneath H_2O as shown in Fig 98. The volatile $(C_2H_5)_2O$ is added that its heavy vapor may force the O of the air from the flask. When the contents of the flask are boiled, gas escapes from the delivery tube and bubbles up through the H_2O. As each bubble of gas comes into contact with the air, it bursts into flame with a bright light. If the air of the room be still, beautiful expanding rings of white smoke (P_2O_5) will rise, with vortex motion, to the ceiling.

Fig. 98.

$$3KHO + P_4 + 3H_2O = 3KP(HO)_2 + PH_3.$$

(*b.*) PH_3 is easily formed by placing calcium phosphide in H_2O.

(*c.*) Two other compounds of H and P are known, of which one is liquid and the other solid at the ordinary temperature. Their proper symbols have not yet been definitely ascertained, but the liquid is generally represented by PH_2 or P_2H_4 and the solid by P_2H or P_4H_2.

(d.) Pure PH_3 is not spontaneously combustible in the air. The combustion above noticed is due to the presence of a small quantity of P_2H_4. If the gas, as it comes from the flask (Fig. 98), be passed through a tube chilled by a freezing mixture (Ph., § 521,) the P_2H_4 will be condensed. The escaping PH_3 will not take fire as it subsequently bubbles through the H_2O and comes into contact with the air.

(e.) The composition of PH_3 may be represented by the accompanying diagram:

$$\boxed{\underset{1\ m.c.}{\overline{H}}} + \boxed{\underset{1\ m.c.}{\overline{H}}} + \boxed{\underset{1\ m.c.}{\overline{H}}} + \underset{\frac{1}{2}m.c.}{\overline{P}} = \boxed{PH_3, 34\ m.c.}$$

It may now be noticed that, in the composition of the compounds previously studied, the weight of a unit volume has been the atomic weight but that in the case of P the weight of *half a unit volume* is the atomic weight. The unit volume, being half the molecular volume, would include two P atoms. Compare the above diagram with the one given for NH_3. (§ 70.)

241. Phosphorus Oxides.

— Theoretically, there are three oxides of phosphorus, having the symbols, P_2O, P_2O_3, P_2O_5.

(a.) P_2O (hypophosphorous oxide or anhydride, phosphorus monoxide) has not yet been isolated. Its compounds are known.

(b.) P_2O_3 (phosphorous oxide or anhydride, phosphorus trioxide) is formed by the slow combustion of P in a limited current of dry air. It is a white, amorphous substance, very soluble in H_2O and burns in the air to P_2O_5.

(c.) P_2O_5 (phosphoric oxide or anhydride, phosphorus pentoxide) is formed by the rapid combustion of P in an excess of O. Place a piece of thoroughly dry P, weighing 0.5 g. to 1 g. in a small dry capsule; place the capsule upon a large, dry plate; ignite the P with a hot wire and quickly cover it with a dry bell glass or wide mouthed bottle of 2 or 3 liters capacity. The capsule, plate and bell glass should be warmed to insure their being dry. The P_2O_5 will be deposited as a white fleecy powder. It absorbs

FIG. 99.

§ 242 PHOSPHORUS COMPOUNDS. 213

H_2O with great eagerness, and is sometimes used for drying gases. If left in the air, it deliquesces completely in a few minutes; if thrown into H_2O, it hisses like a hot iron and dissolves with the evolution of much heat. It may be kept in dry tubes sealed by fusion.

In preparing large quantities of P_2O_5, the following process may

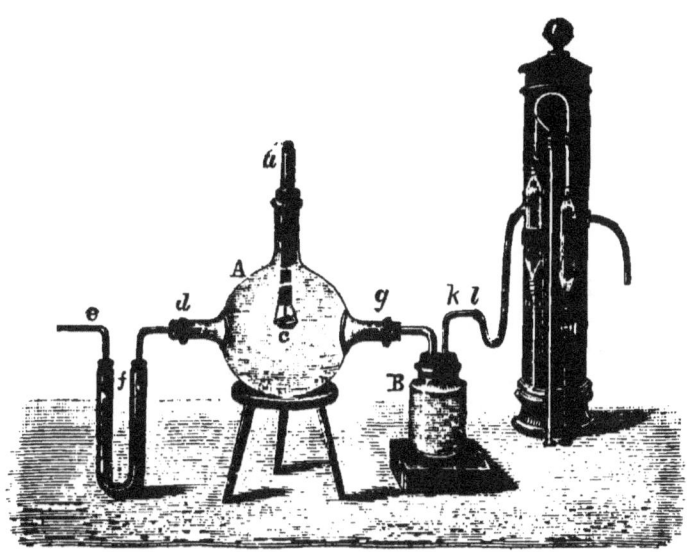

FIG. 100.

be used. *A* is a large, dry glass globe with three necks, as shown in Fig. 99. The flexible tube, *l*, being connected with an aspirator, a strong current of air is drawn through the drying tube, *f*, into the globe. A straight glass tube, closed at the upper end with a cork, passes through the neck, *a*, and carries a small crucible suspended near the centre of the globe. A piece of P is dropped through the tube into the crucible and ignited with a hot wire; the tube is then corked. The current of air being maintained, the P is soon burned to P_2O_5. Other pieces are dropped into the crucible from time to time to render the process continuous. Part of the P_2O_5 is carried over into *B*.

242. Phosphorus Acids.—Phosphorus combines with oxygen and hydrogen to form a remarkable series of acids, as follows:

$P_2O(?) + 3H_2O = 2H_3PO_2$, hypophosphorous acid.
$P_2O_3 + 3H_2O = 2H_3PO_3$, phosphorous acid.

$P_2O_5 + \begin{cases} 3H_2O = 2H_3PO_4\text{, phosphoric acid (ordinary or tribasic).} \\ 2H_2O = H_4P_2O_7\text{, pyrophosphoric acid.} \\ H_2O = 2HPO_3\text{, metaphosphoric acid.} \end{cases}$

(a.) H_3PO_2 gives a series of salts known as hypophosphites; *e. g.*, sodium hypophosphite, H_2NaPO_2. When heated, it decomposes into H_3PO_4 and PH_3. It is monobasic.

(b.) H_3PO_3 may be formed by the action of H_2O on P_2O_3, by the slow oxidation of P in moist air or by the decomposition of phosphorus trichloride by H_2O: $PCl_3 + 3H_2O = H_3PO_3 + 3HCl$. When heated, it decomposes into H_3PO_4 and H_3P. It is a tribasic acid and forms a series of salts known as phosphites; *e. g.*, normal sodium phosphite, Na_3PO_3; tri-ethyl phosphite $(C_2H_5)'_3PO_3$.

(c.) H_3PO_4 may be prepared by the direct union of P_2O_5 and boiling H_2O, but the usual process is to oxidize red P with strong HNO_3 or ordinary P with dilute HNO_3. When heated, it changes to $H_4P_2O_7$ or HPO_3, as explained below. It is tribasic, and yields normal, double and acid phosphates in great variety. This acid is sometimes, with questionable propriety, called orthophosphoric acid. It and its salts are the most important of the phosphoric series.

(d.) $H_4P_2O_7$ is formed by heating H_3PO_4 to 215°C., thus depriving it of H_2O : $2H_3PO_4 - H_2O = H_4P_2O_7$. It is tetrabasic and yields normal, double and acid pyrophosphates in great variety. The group, PO (phosphoryl) acts as a trivalent compound radical. The equation above may be written graphically as follows:

$$\text{From } (PO){<}{\begin{smallmatrix}OH\\OH\\OH\end{smallmatrix}} \quad (PO){<}{\begin{smallmatrix}OH\\OH\\OH\end{smallmatrix}} \text{ take H-O-H and } (PO){<}{\begin{smallmatrix}OH\\OH\\O\end{smallmatrix}} \quad (PO){<}{\begin{smallmatrix}OH\\OH\end{smallmatrix}} \text{ remains}$$

(e.) HPO_3 is formed by the direct union of P_2O_5 and cold H_2O, or by heating H_3PO_4 to redness, thus depriving it of H_2O: $H_3PO_4 - H_2O = HPO_3$. It is monobasic and yields only normal metaphosphates. It is sometimes called glacial phosphoric acid. If its aqueous solution be boiled, it yields H_3PO_4.

Note.—For theoretical reasons, the purely hypothetical compound, H_5PO_5, has been conceived. Such a compound would be properly called *ortho*phosphoric acid.

Exercises.

☞ *For List of Elements and their Symbols see Appendix 1.*

1. What is the apparent quantivalence of P in P_2O_5? Represent this molecule by its graphic symbol.
2. (a.) What is the name of $Ca''_3(PO_4)_2$? (b.) Why may not the symbol be written $CaPO_4$?
3. Choose between $HNa'PO_4$ and HNa_2PO_4. Give a reason for your choice.
4. Write the empirical and graphic symbols for the oxide of P'''.
5. The symbol for "microcosmic salt" is $HNa(NH_4)PO_4$. (a.) What is the systematic name of the salt? (b.) Is it a normal salt? Why? (c.) Write the symbol of the corresponding acid. (d.) What is the basicity of that acid?
6. Symbolize hydrogen disodium phosphate and dihydrogen sodium phosphate, and normal sodium pyrophosphate.
7. What is the systematic name of the sodium salt of monobasic phosphoric acid?
8. If 2 $l.$ of PH_3 were decomposed, what volume of P vapor would it yield?
9. (a.) Why is it that, while an atom of P is only 31 times as heavy as an atom of H, a liter of P vapor is 62 times as heavy as a liter of H? (b.) How many criths will a liter of P vapor weigh?
10. (a.) Is Na'_3PO_4 an acid salt? Why? (b.) Is it a double salt? Why? (c.) Is it a normal salt? Why? (d.) Is it a salt at all? Why?
11. Can you write the symbol for hydrogen sodium metaphosphate?
12. (a.) Read the equation: $2Ag'_3PO_4 + 3H_2S = 2H_3PO_4 + 3Ag_2S$.
(b.) " " $Ag_4P_2O_7 + 2H_2S = H_4P_2O_7 + 2Ag_2S$.
(c.) " " $2AgPO_3 + H_2S = 2HPO_3 + Ag_2S$.
13. Considering the silver salts symbolized in *Exercise 12* to be in aqueous solution, summarize the teaching of these three reactions with reference to the formation of phosphoric acids.
14. If one atom of O in a molecule of metaphosphoric acid be replaced by two of H, what will result?
15. What is represented by $O = P\equiv$?
16. Write the reaction for the combustion of one molecule of P, in an excess of O.
17. $Ca''_3P_2 + 6HCl = 3CaCl_2 + 2$; Complete the equation.
18. Write the reaction for the decomposition of H_3PO_3 by heat.
19. What is the difference between a phosphide and a phosphuret?
20. Read: $Pb''_3(PO_4)_2 + 3H_2SO_4 = 3PbSO_4 + 2H_3PO_4$.

21. The tube represented in Fig. 101 has a fine opening at a, burning P at c and a tube, e, connected with an aspirator so that a current of air may be drawn through the apparatus. What is the product of the combustion?

22. I have a substance insoluble in carbon disulphide but which causes HNO_3 to give off red fumes, and forms with it H_3PO_4. What is the substance? What are the red fumes?

23. (a.) If from the imaginary double molecule, $2H_5PO_5$, we take $2H_2O$, what will remain? (b.) What, if we take $3H_2O$? (c.) What, if we take $4H_2O$? (d.) What, if we take $5H_2O$?

24. (a.) If in a molecule of tribasic phosphoric acid, one of the univalent hydroxyl groups, (HO)', be replaced by an atom of H, what will result? (b.) What, if two such groups be replaced by H_2?

25. If a liter of PH_3 be decomposed by the passage of a series of electric sparks, what volume of H will it yield?

26. Write empirical and typical symbols for phosphorus trihydrate and phosphoryl trihydrate.

27. (a.) What is the apparent quantivalence of P in H_3PO_3? (b.) In H_3PO_4?

28. Give the name of the compound graphically symbolized as follows:

$$(HO)-P-O-(HO)$$
$$|$$
$$(HO)-P-O-(HO)$$

29. What does the above graphic symbol intimate concerning the quantivalence of the P?

30. Give the empirical symbol for the compound graphically symbolized as follows:

$$\begin{matrix}(HO)\\(HO)\end{matrix}\!\!>\!\!P=O$$
$$|$$
$$\begin{matrix}(HO)\\(HO)\end{matrix}\!\!>\!\!P=O$$

31. What does this last graphic symbol intimate concerning the quantivalence of the P?

32. Write the symbol for hypophosphorous acid upon the ammonia type.

33. What weight of P in 10 l. of PH_3 under normal conditions?

34. (a.) How many $cu. cm.$ of NH_3 can be obtained from 53.5 $g.$ of NH_4Cl? (b.) How many, under the conditions, 15°C. and 740 $mm.$ (Ph., § 494.)

Section III.

ARSENIC AND ITS COMPOUNDS.

☞ *Symbol*, As; *specific gravity, 5.6 to 5.9; atomic weight, 75 m.c.; molecular weight, 300 m.c.; quantivalence, 3 or 5.*

243. Occurrence and Preparation.—Arsenic is widely distributed in small quantities. It is sometimes found free in nature but more frequently combined with iron, sulphur and other elements. It is generally prepared from arsenical pyrite (mispickel, FeSAs) by sublimation or from its oxide by reduction with charcoal.

244. Properties and Uses.—Arsenic has a metallic lustre and a steel-gray color. Its vapor is 150 times as heavy as hydrogen. In its physical properties, it closely resembles a metal; in its chemical properties, it more closely resembles a non-metal. It has been called "the connecting link" between the metallic and the non-metallic elements, being closely connected with antimony and bismuth on the one hand and with phosphorus and nitrogen on the other. Like phosphorus, its molecule contains four atoms, as is shown by the specific gravity of its vapor (§ 237). It and almost all of its soluble compounds are active poisons. Heated in the air, it burns, forming the trioxide. It is used in the manufacture of shot and of fireworks.

Note.—The "arsenic" or "white arsenic" of the druggist is arsenic trioxide (As_2O_3). For the detection of As, see § 246. The arsenides were formerly called arseniurets.

245. Hydrogen Arsenide.—This very poisonous gas (arsine, arseniuretted hydrogen, AsH_3) may be formed by the action of dilute sulphuric acid upon zinc arsenide

(Zn_3As_3). The greatest care must be taken in its preparation, as a single bubble of the gas has been known to produce fatal poisoning. It is produced, in an impure state, when a solution of arsenic, or of any arsenic compound, is acted upon by *nascent* hydrogen. When burned in the air, it yields water and arsenic trioxide. Its volumetric composition is similar to that of hydrogen phosphide.

Note.—A solid compound, H_2As_2, is known to chemists.

Experiment 228.—Arrange the apparatus for the preparation of dry H, using a cold mixture of 1 part of H_2SO_4 and 3 parts of H_2O. It is well to keep the generating flask cool by placing it in a cold water bath. When the air has been expelled from the apparatus, ignite the jet. Hold a piece of cold porcelain in the flame, and notice that no colored stain is produced. (If a stain should appear, it would show that the materials used in the generating flask were impure.) *Keep the jet burning* and add, through the funnel tube, a few drops of a hot aqueous solution of As_2O_3. Notice the change in

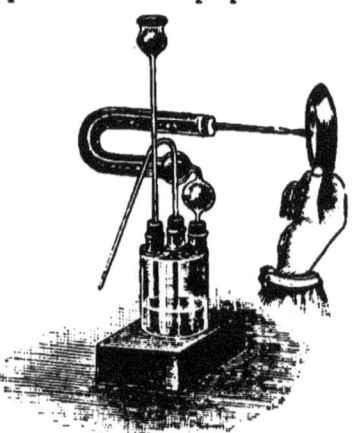

FIG. 102.

the appearance of the flame. Hold the cold porcelain in the flame. A stain having a metallic lustre will be produced. The stain is metallic As, freed from combination in AsH_3 by the heat of the flame and deposited, just as soot would be by a candle flame. Do not let the porcelain become hot enough to vaporize the As, and cause the stain to disappear. Keep the jet burning until the apparatus is placed in the ventilating closet or out of doors, to prevent the escape of AsH_3.

Experiment 229.—Clean the generating flask and repeat the experiment, using "Paris green" instead of the As_2O_3.

Experiment 230.—Boil a green paper label with HCl in a test tube. Test this solution for the presence of As, as in Exp. 228. Try the same with green wall paper or with green paint scraped from wood work.

Note.—The author has often demonstrated the presence of As in green fabrics worn as clothing in his classes.

Experiment 231.—After passing the AsH_3 through a drying tube containing potassium hydrate and calcium chloride, heat the glass tube to a red heat. The gas will be decomposed, the As being deposited as a dark band upon the cool part of the tube and the H burning with its characteristic flame at the jet. Little or no deposit will then be made on cold porcelain.

Experiment 232.—To show that the stains produced in Exps. 228-229 are As and not Sb, *which might imitate them,* touch one of the stains with a glass rod dipped into a solution of chloride of lime. If the metal dissolves, it is As and not Sb.

246. Marsh's Test. — The preceding experiments rudely illustrate Marsh's test for arsenic. The test is so delicate that 0.01 *mg.* ($\frac{1}{7000}$ grain) of the poison may be recognized with certainty. In examinations of great importance, as in trials for murder by arsenical poisoning, the purity of all materials used and the nature of the metallic deposit are carefully determined by confirmatory tests.

Experiment 233.—Place a small quantity of As_2O_3 in a tube of hard glass (Fig. 102) about 10 *cm.* long and hold the tube in a sloping position in a lamp flame until the powder is volatilized. With a magnifying lens, examine the walls of the tube where the As_2O_3 has condensed; the oxide will be seen to be brilliantly crystalline.

Experiment 234.—Make the tube used in the last experiment into an ignition tube by fusing and sealing one end of it in the lamp flame. In the bottom of the tube thus formed, place a little (a few *mg.* only) of As_2O_3 and above it, a small piece of charcoal, as shown at *c*, Fig. 102. Holding the tube horizontal, heat the charcoal splinter to redness; then gradually bring the tube into a nearly vertical position, keeping the charcoal red hot and heating the tip of the tube until the As_2O_3 is vaporized. The vapor will be reduced by the glowing charcoal and a brilliant ring of metallic As will appear at *a*.

247. Arsenic Trioxide.—Arsenic trioxide (arsenious oxide, arsenious anhydride, white arsenic, As_2O_3)

is prepared on the large scale by roasting arsenical ores with free access of air. The white smoke given off condenses to a white powder. It occurs in three varieties, the amorphous or vitreous, and two different crystalline forms, rhombic and octahedral. It is isodimorphous with antimony trioxide. It is feebly soluble in water but dissolves more readily in boiling hydrochloric acid and freely in boiling nitric acid or alkaline solutions. Heated in contact with air, it volatilizes without change. Heated in contact with carbon, it gives up its oxygen and is reduced to metallic arsenic. As a poison, it is very dangerous, because it has no warning odor and scarcely any taste and because very small quantities (0.2 g.) produce death. Its best antidote is *freshly* prepared ferric hydrate (see § 363 for its preparation), which forms with it an insoluble salt and thus prevents the poison from entering the system. When these can not be quickly obtained, the white of eggs or soap-suds should be administered promptly. Arsenic trioxide is largely used in the manufacture of pigments and of glass.

Note.—In 1873, nearly 6,000 tons of As_2O_3 were made in England alone, more than a third of which was made at a single mine. As the vapor density of this substance is 198, its molecular symbol is sometimes written, with apparent propriety, As_4O_6.

FIG. 103.

248. Arsenic Pentoxide.—Arsenic pentoxide (arsenic anhydride, As_2O_5) may be obtained by oxidizing the trioxide with nitric acid, evaporating to dryness and heating nearly to redness. It is less powerfully poisonous than the trioxide.

249. Arsenic Acids. — Arsenic forms a series of acids that presents remarkable analogies to the phosphorus acids.

$As_2O_3 + 3H_2O = 2H_3AsO_3$, arsenious acid.

$As_2O_5 + \begin{cases} 3H_2O = 2H_3AsO_4, \text{ tribasic arsenic acid.} \\ 2H_2O = H_4As_2O_7, \text{ pyroarsenic acid.} \\ H_2O = 2H\ AsO_3, \text{ metaarsenic acid.} \end{cases}$

(*a.*) When As_2O_3 is dissolved in H_2O, the solution gives a feebly acid reaction and is supposed to contain H_3AsO_3. The corresponding salts are called arsenites; *e.g.*, silver arsenite, Ag_3AsO_3.

(*b.*) H_3AsO_4 is generally prepared by treating As_2O_3 with HNO_3. The commercial form is a liquid with a specific gravity of 2, from which transparent crystals may be obtained by cooling. As it is tribasic, it yields three series of arsenates which closely resemble the corresponding phosphates in composition and crystalline form. Heated to 180°C. it loses H_2O and becomes $H_4As_2O_7$. Heated in 200°C. it loses another molecule of H_2O and becomes $HAsO_3$.

Note.—As_2O_3 is sometimes improperly called arsenious acid. Less frequently, but with equal impropriety, As_2O_5 is called arsenic acid. *Every acid contains* H.

250. Sulphides of Arsenic.

Two native sulphides of arsenic are found. The red sulphide (As_2S_2) is called realgar; it is used in making fireworks. The yellow sulphide (As_2S_3) is called orpiment; it is used as a pigment. In addition to the disulphide and the trisulphide, a pentasulphide (As_2S_5) is obtained by fusing the trisulphide with sulphur.

Exercises.

1. Write the equation representing the combustion of hydrogen arsenide.
2. What is the weight of $10As_2O_3$?
3. Name the following: H_3AsO_4; H_2NaAsO_4; HNa_2AsO_4; Na_3AsO_4; $(NH_4)Mg''AsO_4$.
4. Write a graphic symbol for $H_3P'''O_3$.
5. When AsH_3 is prepared from Zn_3As_2 and dilute H_2SO_4, $ZnSO_4$ is produced. How much AsH_3, by weight and by volume, can be prepared from 50 *g.* of Zn_3As_2?
6. (*a.*) Why is As_2O_3 said to be dimorphous? (*b.*) Why is it said to be isodimorphous with Sb_2O_3?
7. What is a dyad? A monobasic acid?
8. You are given a mixture of ordinary and red phosphorus. How will you separate the two varieties?

Section IV.

ANTIMONY, BISMUTH, ETC.

☞ ANTIMONY: *symbol*, Sb (see App. 1); *specific gravity*, 6.7; *atomic weight*, 122 m. c.; *quantivalence*, 3 or 5.

251. Source and Preparation.—The antimony of commerce is obtained from the mineral stibnite, which is an antimony trisulphide (gray antimony, antimony glance, Sb_2S_3). Antimony is, however, found native and in combination with other elements than sulphur. The stibnite is melted with about half its weight of iron ($Sb_2S_3 + Fe_3 = 3FeS + Sb_2$) or heated with coal in a reverberatory furnace.

Experiment 235.—Make two moulds by boring conical cavities in a block of plaster of Paris. See that the mould terminates below in a sharp point. Make two or three clean cut grooves in the sides of the moulds. Into one mould, pour melted lead; into the other, melted type metal. Remove the casts and notice that the lead cone is blunted at the apex while the type metal is pointed; that the ridges on the sides of the lead cone are ill defined while those on the sides of the type metal are well defined.

The lead contracts as it cools and thus shrinks from the mould. The type metal is composed of about 70 parts Pb, 10 parts Sn and 20 parts Sb. The Sn gives it toughness and the Sb hardness. The Sb tends to crystallize as it cools, thus causing the type metal to expand and force itself into every part of the mould and make a sharply defined cast (Ph., § 525).

252. Properties and Uses.—Antimony is a bluish-white metal. It is so brittle that it may be powdered in a mortar. Its crystalline tendency is so strong that, when it is cooling from the melted condition, beautiful fern-like figures are formed on the free surface of the metal. These figures may be seen on one surface of almost every cake of antimony found in commerce. It melts at 450°C.

It is not acted upon by the air at ordinary temperatures but, when melted in contact with the air, it rapidly oxidizes. At a red heat, it burns with a white flame forming antimony trioxide (Sb_2O_3). It is a constituent of tartaremetic and is largely used in the arts as a constituent of type metal, britannia metal, pewter and other valuable alloys.

(*a.*) Sb is strongly attacked by Cl (Exp. 88), forming $SbCl_3$. It is not acted upon by dilute HCl or H_2SO_4 but is easily dissolved by aqua regia. HNO_3 acts upon it, forming insoluble Sb_2O_5.

Experiment 236.—Put 30 *cu. cm.* of HCl, 10 or 12 drops of HNO_3 and 0.5 *g.* of powdered Sb into a small flask and heat the mixture gently until the metal is dissolved. Evaporate the solution to a thick syrup, the so-called "butter of antimony."

253. Antimony Compounds.—The compounds of antimony correspond closely to those of arsenic.

(*a.*) Hydrogen antimonide (stibine, antimoniuretted hydrogen, SbH_3) is formed when a soluble compound of Sb is acted upon by *nascent* H. It is analogous to AsH_3, but its metallic deposit is easily distinguished from that of the latter compound by its darker color, smoky appearance, non-volatility and other tests (Exp. 232). Its combustion yields H_2O and Sb_2O_3.

(*b.*) There are three known oxides of Sb represented by the symbols Sb_2O_3, Sb_2O_4 and Sb_2O_5. The tetroxide may be considered a mixture of the other two: $Sb_2O_3 + Sb_2O_5 = 2Sb_2O_4$. All of these oxides form acids. The trioxide is isodimorphous with arsenic trioxide.

(*c.*) There are two sulphides, Sb_2S_3 and Sb_2S_5. They unite with alkaline sulphides to form sulpho-antimonites and sulpho-antimoniates (see § 171).

(*d.*) There are two chlorides, $SbCl_3$ and $SbCl_5$. The trichloride is a soft solid, known as butter of antimony; the pentachloride is a strongly fuming liquid.

☞ BISMUTH: *symbol*, Bi; *specific gravity, 9.8; atomic weight, 210 m. c.; quantivalence, 3 or 5.*

254. Source and Preparation. — Bismuth is found in nature free, and also in combination with sulphur and other elements. Commercial bismuth was formerly prepared by heating the ore in iron tubes sloping over a furnace. As this process yields only a *part* of the *native* metal, all bismuth ores are now roasted and then smelted in a pot with iron, carbon and slag. The crude bismuth is drawn off in a melted condition from the bottom of the smelting pot after the layer of less easily fusible "cobalt-speiss" above has solidified. Most of the bismuth of commerce comes from Saxony and Bohemia.

Experiment 237.—Melt 2 or 3 $Kg.$ of Bi in a crucible. Perforate the covering crust that forms on cooling and pour out the still molten liquid within. When cool, break the crucible to obtain a view of the beautiful Bi crystals thus formed. (Compare Exp. 131.)

255. Properties and Uses.—Bismuth is a brittle, brilliant, pinkish-white metal. Of all known substances, it is the most diamagnetic (Ph., § 310). In cooling from fusion, it crystallizes more readily than any other metal. Its crystals are nearly cubical rhombohedrons, often beautifully iridescent from the film of oxide formed when the crystals were still hot. It melts at 264°C. and expands $\frac{1}{32}$ of its volume on solidifying.

In dry air at ordinary temperatures, it is unaltered, but, when strongly heated, it burns with a bluish white flame forming bismuth trioxide (Bi_2O_3). It is used in forming alloys and in the construction of thermo-electric piles (Ph., §§ 412–414).

(*a.*) Bi is acted upon readily by Cl. Cold HCl and H_2SO_4 have no action upon it. Its best solvents are HNO_3 and *aqua regia*.

(b.) There are four oxides of Bi, viz.: Bi_2O_2, Bi_2O_3, Bi_2O_4, Bi_2O_5.

Experiment 238.—Place 30 g. of Bi, 15 g. of Pb and 15 g. of Sn in boiling H_2O. Let the metals remain there until convinced that none of them can be thus melted. Then place them in an iron spoon, melt them together and pour the molten mass into cold H_2O. Immerse the alloy thus formed in boiling H_2O and notice *that it melts.* Pour the liquid alloy into a small test tube and allow it to cool. Notice that, *after several minutes,* the cooling and expanding metal bursts the glass walls that confine it.

256. Fusible Metals.—Bismuth forms, with certain other metals, alloys that melt at a temperature far below the melting point of any of their constituents. The composition and melting points of some of these are given in the following table:

	Newton's Metal.	*Rose's Metal.*	*Lichtenberg's Metal.*	*Wood's Metal.*
Bismuth................	8 parts,	2	5	4
Lead....................	5 "	1	3	2
Tin.....................	3 "	1	2	1
Cadmium................	0 "	0	0	1
Melting point..........	94°.5C.	93°.75C.	91°.6C.	60°.5C.

These melting points may be still further reduced by the addition of mercury. It will be noticed that any of these metals will melt in boiling water. If any of these melted alloys be poured into a glass vessel, the expansion in solidification will burst the glass when the metal cools. These alloys are used in obtaining casts of woodcuts, *etc.,* the cast being made when the metal has so far cooled as to be viscid. Lead, tin and bismuth are mixed in such proportions that the alloy melts at some particular temperature above 100°C. for the making of safety plugs for steam boilers (see Ph., Fig. 270, *t*). As soon as the steam reaches the pressure corresponding to the melting point of the alloy (Ph., §§ 502, 509), the plug melts and the steam escapes.

257. The Nitrogen Group.—The relations of the nitrogen group are very marked. There is an increase in specific gravity, atomic weight and metallic characteristics from nitrogen to bismuth and (in a general way) an increase in chemical activity from bismuth to nitrogen.

	N.	P.	As.	Sb.	Bi.
Specific gravity..Gas,		1.8	5.7	6.7	9.8
Atomic weight..14 $m.c.$		31 $m.c.$	75 $m.c.$	122 $m.c.$	210 $m.c.$

Each of the solids crystallizes in two forms; $i.e.$, each is dimorphous. These two crystal forms are the same for the four elements; $i.e.$, these elements are isomorphous. We may, then, say that these four elements are iso-dimorphous.

The analogies in composition and properties of the corresponding compounds of the members of this natural group are very significant. Some of them are indicated below:

Hydrides.	Trioxides.	Tetroxides.	Pentoxides.	Chlorides.	Sulphides.	Acids.
NH_3	N_2O_3	N_2O_4	N_2O_5	$NCl_3(?)$	....	HNO_3
PH_3	P_2O_3	....	P_2O_5	PCl_3	P_2S_3	HPO_3
AsH_3	As_2O_3	....	As_2O_5	$AsCl_3$	As_2S_3	$HAsO_3$
SbH_3	Sb_2O_3	Sb_2O_4	Sb_2O_5	$SbCl_3$	Sb_2S_3	$HSbO_3$
....	Bi_2O_3	Bi_2O_4	Bi_2O_5	$BiCl_3$	Bi_2S_3	....

Note.—Closely allied to the metals, antimony and bismuth, are the rarer metals, vanadium, tantalum and columbium. They especially resemble the members of the nitrogen group in that they give rise to acid-forming pentoxides.

☞ VANADIUM: *symbol*, V; *specific gravity*, 5.5; *atomic weight*, 51.2 $m.c.$

258. Vanadium.—This metal is an extremely rare element, being found only in a few scarce minerals. *Traces* of it are found to be widely distributed throughout the earth and have also been found to exist in the sun. No metal is more difficult to prepare than this, on account of the great affinity of the metal, at a red heat, for oxygen. Every trace of air or moisture must be excluded during the preparation. It is prepared as a white powder with a brilliant, crystalline, silver white appearance. It forms five oxides, analogous to the nitrogen oxides: V_2O, V_2O_2, V_2O_3, V_2O_4, V_2O_5.

☞ TANTALUM: *symbol*, Ta; *specific gravity*, 10.8 (?); *atomic weight*, 182 m. c.

259. Tantalum.—It is not certain that this metal has yet been prepared in a pure state. The name was taken from the mythological Tantalus, because the metal, "when placed in the midst of acids, is incapable of taking any of them up and saturating itself with them." Its tetroxide (Ta_2O_4) and pentoxide (Ta_2O_5) are known. Tantalic acid has the composition, $HTaO_3$.

☞ COLUMBIUM: *symbol*, Cb; *specific gravity*, 4.06. *atomic weight*, 94 m. c.

260. Columbium.—This metal is generally closely associated with tantalum. It has been obtained as a steel gray solid. It yields a dioxide (Cb_2O_2), a tetroxide (Cb_2O_4) and a pentoxide (Cb_2O_5). Columbic acid has the composition, $HCbO_3$. Columbium is sometimes called Niobium (symbol, Nb).

Exercises.

1. Write the reaction for Exp. 88.
2. What is meant by the statement that As_2O_3 and Sb_2O_3 are *isodimorphous*?
3. When a current of H_2S is passed through a solution of $SbCl_3$, Sb_2S_3 and an acid are formed. Write the reaction.
4. Write a graphic symbol for tribasic phosphoric acid, representing it (*a*.) as a compound of trivalent P. (*b*.) As a compound of pentad P.
5. Write a graphic symbol for hypophosphorous acid representing it as a compound of trivalent P. As a compound of pentad P.
6. (*a*.) How is P_2O_5 made? (*b*.) How many distinct phosphoric acids can be formed? Give their names and symbols.
7. (*a*.) How is H_2SO_4 made? (*b*.) State the difference between concentrated and fuming sulphuric acid.

8. When iodine and red phosphorus act upon each other in the presence of H_2O, the reaction may be represented thus:
$$P + 5I + 4H_2O = 5HI + H_3PO_3.$$
(a.) What weight and (b.) what volume of the binary acid gas can be obtained by using 10 g. of P?

9. Explain the reaction of sufficient quantities of common salt, MnO_2 and H_2SO_4.

10. What is a microcrith? What is quantivalence?

11. (a.) What is a chemical compound? (b.) How do you find the combining weights of compounds? Illustrate by sulphuric acid and potassium chlorate.

12. Give the symbols and names of two common compounds of S with one chemical and one physical property of each.

13. How much KNO_3 would be decomposed by 650 g. of H_2SO_4 and how much HNO_3 would be formed?

14. When anhydrous magnesium chloride, $MgCl_2$, is burned in air, a white powder and a gas are produced. The powder is magnesium oxide; the gas will color blue a strip of paper wet with a solution of KI and starch. Write the reaction.

15. When barium oxide, BaO, is gently heated to dark redness in the air it is changed to the dioxide, BaO_2. At a bright red heat this decomposes into BaO and O. How may these facts be utilized?

CHAPTER XV.

METALS OF THE ALKALIES.

SECTION I.

SODIUM.

261. Metals.—The metals, gold, silver, copper, iron, tin, lead and mercury were known to the ancients; the other metals have been discovered in comparatively recent times. The word, metal, is not capable of exact definition. At one time, when only a few metals were known, they could be easily distinguished from the non-metals by their high specific gravity and their peculiar metallic lustre. But, several of the metals now known float upon water, and several non-metallic substances have the metallic lustre. Most of the non-metals are electro-negative and form acid compounds, while the metals are generally electro-positive (Ph., § 401) and form basic compounds. The metals are generally solid at ordinary temperatures, malleable and good conductors of heat and electricity, but mercury is a liquid at ordinary temperatures.

(*a.*) The elements of the nitrogen group well exhibit the gradual transition from the distinctly non-metallic to the distinctly metallic character. N is an unquestioned non-metal; R, in some of its modifications, closely approaches the metals; As is often classed as a semi-metal; while Sb and Bi are generally classed as metals.

(*b*.) The old distinction between metals and non-metals " is not founded upon any real or essential difference of properties," but is preserved for the sake of convenience.

(*c*.) It will be well to remember that the symbols given for many metallic compounds are not necessarily true molecular symbols.' For example, the symbol for silver chloride may be AgCl but it also may be Ag_2Cl_2, or some higher multiple of AgCl. Until the vapor densities of these metallic compounds are determined, we, probably, shall not *know* the true molecular symbol of the compound or the true quantivalence of the metallic element.

☞ SODIUM: *symbol*, Na; *specific gravity*, *0.97*; *atomic weight*, *23 m. c.*; *quantivalence*, *1*.

262. Occurrence.—Free sodium is not found in nature because it unites so readily with the elements of air and water, but its compounds are very abundant and widely diffused. Its most abundant compound is sodium chloride (common salt, NaCl), from which, on account of its abundance and cheapness, nearly all of the sodium and sodium compounds of commerce and science are derived, directly or indirectly.

(*a*.) Sodium nitrate, carbonate, borate and silicate as well as cryolite (§ 120) are found in nature.

263. Preparation.—Sodium was first prepared by the electrolysis (Ph., § 397) of sodium carbonate. It is now extensively prepared by igniting a mixture of sodium carbonate and charcoal.

(*a*.) 30 *Kg.* of common soda ash (§ 268) is ground up with 13 *Kg.* of coal and 3 *Kg.* of chalk. The mixture is placed in an iron cylinder 1.2 long, which is placed in a furnace and heated to whiteness. The CO and the Na vapor escape through the delivery tube

FIG. 104.

into a receiver where the latter condenses and whence the molten metal flows into an iron vessel. The CO is burned as it escapes.

$$Na_2CO_3 + C_2 = Na_2 + 3CO.$$

Experiment 239.—Wrap a piece of Na in wire gauze and drop it into H_2O. Collect and test the gas evolved.

Experiment 240.—Fill a test tube with mercury and invert it over that liquid. Thrust a piece of Na into the mouth of the tube : it will rise to the top. Introduce a little of H_2O. Explain the resulting phenomenon and write the reaction.

Experiment 241.—Throw a piece of Na, the size of a pea, on cold H_2O. It swims about, decomposing the H_2O, freeing the H, uniting with the O and then dissolving in the H_2O. It does not evolve enough heat to ignite the H.

Experiment 242.—Throw a piece of Na upon hot H_2O, in a large, loosely stoppered bottle. The liberated H is ignited, and gives a yellow, sodium-tinted flame.

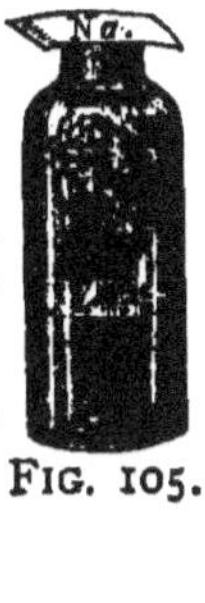

Experiment 243.—Throw a piece of Na upon thick starch paste. The liberated H burns as before, the paste preventing the rapid motion of the globule.

Experiment 244.—Melt a piece of Na cautiously under petroleum. Notice its lustre.

FIG. 105.

Experiment 245.—Ignite some C_2H_6O in a small saucer. It burns with an almost colorless flame. Sprinkle a little common salt into the burning liquid. The flame becomes yellow.

Experiment 246.—Wrap a piece of Na in cloth or filter paper and place upon a piece of moist ice. Describe and explain what follows.

264. Properties and Uses.—Sodium is a light metal having a brilliant, silver white lustre. It quickly oxidizes in moist air and decomposes water. It is a good conductor of heat and electricity, in which respect it ranks next to gold (Ph., § 539, b). It is best kept under petroleum or in a liquid or atmosphere free from oxygen. It is hard and brittle at $-20°C$.; ductile at $0°C$.; soft like wax at the ordinary temperature; semi-fluid at $50°C$. and melts at $96°C$. It is used as a reducing agent in the preparation of silicon, boron, magnesium and aluminum. Its amalgam is used in the extraction of gold from quartzose rock and as a reducing agent. Its salts impart a yellow tinge to flame.

265. Oxides.—Sodium forms two oxides, Na_2O and Na_2O_2.

266. Sodium Chloride.—Sodium chloride (common salt, NaCl) is obtained by mining rock-salt from natural deposits or by the evaporation of saline waters of certain mines, springs and lakes or of the sea. When the concentrated brine is rapidly evaporated by boiling, a

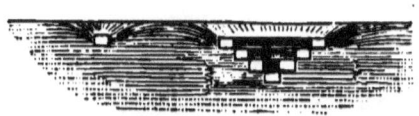 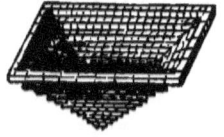

FIG. 106.

fine-grained table salt is produced; when it is evaporated slowly, a coarse salt is formed. The mother liquor from which no more sodium chloride will crystallize often contains the more soluble salts of calcium, magnesium and bromine (§ 115, a.) in paying quantities. Sodium chloride crystallizes in cubes, the edges of which are sometimes attached so as to form hopper-shaped masses. Rock salt is usually found in cubical crystals, is highly diathermanous (Ph., § 552) and of great importance in physical research. The importance and many uses of common salt are too familiar to need mention.

267. Sodium Sulphate. — Sodium sulphate (Na_2SO_4) is prepared in great quantities from salt and sulphuric acid (see § 74, b. and § 105, b.).

(a.) The NaCl and H_2SO_4 are heated in large, covered pans. The decomposition of NaCl, in the first stage of the process, is only partial.

$$2NaCl + H_2SO_4 = NaCl + HNaSO_4 + HCl.$$

The HCl is absorbed in towers filled with coke, over which H_2O is kept trickling. The pasty mass is then strongly heated.

$$NaCl + HNaSO_4 = Na_2SO_4 + HCl.$$

The HCl is absorbed as in the former stage.

(b.) The Na_2SO_4 dissolves easily in warm H_2O. When such a concentrated solution cools, ten molecules of "water of crystallization" are taken up to form Glauber's salt ($Na_2SO_4, 10H_2O$). Exposed to dry air, the Glauber's salt effloresces and is changed to Na_2SO_4 by its loss of H_2O. (Ph., § 524, 3.)

(c.) Hydrogen sodium sulphate ($HNaSO_4$) is often called sodium, di-sulphate or bisulphate of soda.

268. Sodium Carbonate.—Sodium carbonate (sal-soda, Na_2CO_3) is made in immense quantities from common salt by the Leblanc process, so called from the name of its inventor.

(a.) The first step is the preparation of Na_2SO_4 as described in the last paragraph. The Na_2SO_4 is then heated in a reverberatory furnace with an equal weight of calcium carbonate (chalk or limestone, $CaCO_3$), and about half its weight of coal. The resulting product is called "black ash," essentially a mixture of Na_2CO_3 and calcium sulphide. The soluble parts of the black ash are extracted with H_2O, evaporated to dryness and roasted in a furnace with sawdust and sold as "soda ash." This soda ash contains about 80 *per cent.* of Na_2CO_3.

(*b.*) By dissolving soda ash in hot H_2O and allowing the solution to cool and stand for several days, large transparent crystals of "washing soda" (soda crystals, $Na_2CO_3 + 10H_2O$) are formed. These crystals part with their water of crystallization by efflorescence or heating. The dry residue is Na_2CO_3 purified by the *process of crystallization,* one of the most valuable known means of purification.

(*c.*) Many salts owe their crystalline form to the presence of a definite number of molecules of H_2O, which may be driven off by heat. These aqueous molecules constitute the "water of crystallization." When soda crystals are simply exposed to the air, they part with their water of crystallization and fall to a white powder or become coated with it. The crystals are then said to "effloresce." The opaque white powder of anhydrous alum combines with 24 molecules of H_2O to form the well known crystals of common alum $[K_2Al_2(SO_4)_4 + 24H_2O]$. By heating these crystals, the water of crystallization may be driven off and the anhydrous salt left in the form of a powder.

269. Hydrogen Sodium Carbonate.—Hydrogen sodium carbonate (soda, sodium bicarbonate, $HNaCO_3$) is easily prepared by passing a stream of carbon dioxide through a solution of sodium carbonate or by exposing soda crystals to an atmosphere of carbon dioxide. It is used in medicine and in cooking.

$$Na_2CO_3 + H_2O + CO_2 = 2HNaCO_3$$
$$\text{or}\ldots\ldots\ldots Na_2CO_3, 10H_2O + CO_2 = 2HNaCO_3 + 9H_2O.$$

(*a.*) When solutions of $HNaCO_3$ and of cream of tartar are mixed, CO_2 is set free and the purgative Rochelle salt remains in solution.

(*b.*) When cake or biscuit is raised with $HNaCO_3$ and cream of tartar, the escaping CO_2 renders the dough light and Rochelle salt remains in the loaf.

270. Sodium Hydrate.—Sodium hydrate (caustic soda, sodium hydroxide, $NaHO$) is formed when sodium is thrown upon water, but in practice it is made from sodium carbonate. It is a white, opaque, brittle solid of fibrous texture. It deliquesces in the air, absorbing moisture and carbon dioxide and changing thus to the non-deliquescent carbonate, the coating of which protects the hydrate from further loss. It is a strong base, a powerful cautery and is largely used in the manufacture of hard soap. An impure variety is sometimes found in commerce under the name, "concentrated lye."

(a.) Na_2CO_3 is dissolved in boiling H_2O. Cream of lime (§ 292) is added to this hot solution until it is free from CO_2.

$$Na_2CO_3 + CaH_2O_2 = 2NaHO + CaCO_3.$$

The insoluble $CaCO_3$ is removed from the solution of NaHO and the latter evaporated until an oily liquid is obtained. This liquid solidifies on cooling and is usually cast in the form of sticks.

(b.) Caustic soda is made in large quantities as an incidental product of the manufacture of Na_2CO_3, being cheaply prepared from the liquor from which the "black ash" was deposited.

Experiment 247.—Make a strong solution of NaHO and put it into a retort or flask with some granulated Zn. Heat the flask over a sand bath or wire gauze until the liquid boils. A gas will be evolved. Collect it over H_2O and find out what it is.

271. Other Sodium Compounds.—(a.) Borax ($Na_2B_4O_7$, $10H_2O$) is sodium bi-borate or sodium pyroborate (§ 172 b). It is made by fusing or boiling boric acid with half its weight of soda-ash.

(b.) Sodium nitrate (Chili nitre, South American saltpetre, $NaNO_3$) is a deliquescent substance found in the soil of certain parts of South America.

EXERCISES.

1. Write the symbol for decahydrated sodium sulphate.
2. Write the symbol for anhydrous sodium carbonate.
3. What is the symbol for sodic chloride?
4. Write the graphic symbol for the disulphate of soda.

236   *METALS OF THE ALKALIES.*   § 271

5. The sodium obtained in practice being one-third the theoretical yield, what weight of the metal can be prepared from 159 $Kg.$ of sodium carbonate?

6. What is the percentage composition of $NaNO_3$?

7. What weight of $KClO_3$ is needed to furnish enough O to burn the H evolved by the action of 200 $g.$ of Na upon H_2O?

8. (*z.*) Find the weight of 1 *l.* of each of the following: N, CO_2, O, CH_4. (*b.*) Find the volume of 1 $g.$ of each.

9. Write the name and full graphic symbol for

$(HO) - (SO_2) - S - (SO_2) - (HO).$

SECTION II.

POTASSIUM, ETC.

☞ *Symbol*, K; *specific gravity, 0.865; atomic weight, 39.04 m. e.; molecular weight, 78.08 m. e.; quantivalence, 1, 3 and 5.*

272. Source. — Potassium compounds are found widely distributed in nature, forming an essential constituent of many rocks and of all fruitful soils. Potassium compounds are taken from the soil by the rootlets of plants, none of which can live without them. It is essential to animal life also. Free potassium is not found in nature.

273. Preparation. — Potassium is prepared by heating intensely a mixture of its carbonate with charcoal.

$$K_2CO_3 + C_2 = K_2 + 3CO.$$

(*a*.) By igniting acid potassium tartrate (crude tartar) in a covered iron crucible and quickly cooling by plunging the crucible into cold water, the desired mixture is formed as a charred, porous mass. This mixture is then heated to whiteness in a retort, when K vapor is evolved, rapidly cooled and collected under petroleum. The process is subject to the danger of serious explosions from the tendency, at the high temperature employed, of the K vapor and the CO to form an explosive compound, $K_2C_2O_2$.

(*b*.) K may be prepared on the small scale by the electrolysis of equal molecular proportions of KCl and calcium chloride. These substances are melted together over a lamp, in a small porcelain crucible into which two rods of gas carbon are dipped. These rods are made the electrodes of a battery of six or eight Bunsen cells (Ph., §§ 377, 335). The lamp is so placed that the salt around the negative electrode becomes solid while that around the positive remains liquid to allow the escape of the Cl, set free by the electrolysis. After passing the current about twenty minutes, the crucible is cooled and opened under petroleum. Pure K is found at the negative electrode (Ph., § 401).

Experiment 248.—Drop a piece of K, half the size of a pea, upon H_2O. It decomposes the H_2O, the H burns with a flame beautifully tinted with the vapor of K. If the H_2O be in an open dish, stand at a distance of a meter or more, as the combustion will terminate with a slight explosion. Test the H_2O at the end of the experiment with reddened litmus paper.

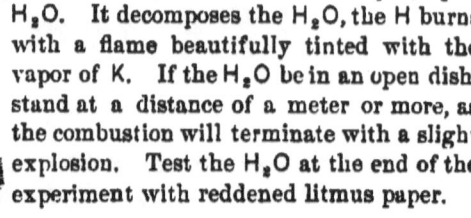

FIG. 107.

Experiment 249.—Stretch a piece of blotting paper upon a wooden tray, wet the paper with a red solution of litmus and throw upon it a small piece of Na or K. The track of the metal as it runs over the moistened paper will be written in blue lines, showing the formation of an alkaline product.

Experiment 250.—Hold a small piece of K under H_2O by means of

FIG. 108.

wire gauze or filter paper. Collect the gas evolved as shown in the figure. What is this gas?

Experiment 251.—In Fig. 109, a represents a bottle for the generation of CO_2; c, a drying tube, containing calcium chloride; e, a tube of Bohemian (hard) glass with a delivery tube, t, dipping into the bottle, i. When a lighted match thrust into i is quickly extinguished, we may know that the apparatus is filled with CO_2. Then, dry a piece of K the size of a pea by pressing it between folds of filter or blotting paper, remove t, thrust the K into e and replace t. When

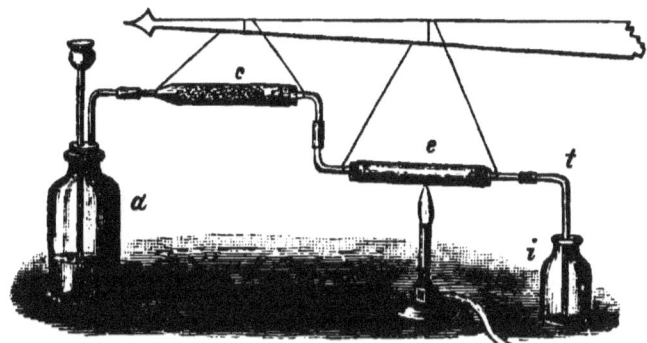

FIG. 109.

the K is heated by the lamp flame, it will burn, taking O from the CO_2 and depositing black C upon the walls of e.

$$2K_2 + 3CO_2 = 2K_2CO_3 + C.$$

The particles of black C may be made more evident by placing e in a bottle of clear H_2O, to dissolve the K_2CO_3.

Experiment 252.—Repeat Exp. 249, using a current of HCl instead of CO_2. Collect over H_2O the gas delivered through t. What is this gas? Write the reaction.

Experiment 253.—Repeat Exp. 250, using NH_3 instead of HCl. Write the reaction.

Experiment 254.—Bore a half inch hole two inches deep in a block of ice. Enlarge the *bottom* of the cavity to the size of a hickory nut. Into this cavity, drop a piece of K, the size of a pea, and notice the beautiful volcanic action. Try the experiment in a warm and darkened room.

274. Properties.—Potassium is a light metal having a brilliant bluish-white lustre. In electro-positive characteristics, it ranks third among the metals, and in lightness, second. It is brittle at 0°C.; soft like wax at 15°C., and easily welded when the surfaces are clean ; it melts at about 63°C. Its physical and chemical properties closely resemble those of sodium, but it is less used on account of its greater cost. Like sodium, it is best kept under petroleum. Its salts communicate a violet tint to flame.

275. Oxides.—Potassium forms two oxides, K_2O and K_2O_4.

276. Potassium Chloride.—Potassium chloride (KCl) is found in sea and other salt waters, and is largely prepared from the mother liquor from which the sodium chloride has crystallized, and from the Stassfurt deposit of carnallite (KCl, $MgCl_2$, $6H_2O$). It resembles sodium chloride in appearance and taste but is more easily soluble in water. It dissolves in about three times its weight of water at the ordinary temperature, producing great cold (Ph., § 521). Like sodium chloride, it crystallizes in cubes.

(*a.*) The other potassium, halogen salts, KBr, KI and KF, also crystallize in cubes, have a saline taste and easily dissolve in H_2O. KBr and KI are used in medicine and in photography.

277. Potassium Cyanide.—Potassium cyanide (KCN or KCy) is a white, fusible, deliquescent and intensely poisonous solid. As its solution dissolves silver and gold cyanides, it is largely used in electro-plating (Ph., § 399, *a*). It is a powerful reducing agent. It is isomorphous with potassium chloride. (See *Caution* preceding Exp. 198.)

278. Potassium Carbonate.—Potassium carbonate (K_2CO_3) is generally prepared in this country by leaching wood ashes to form potash-lye and evaporating the lye in large pots or kettles, whence the name of the crude article, potash. The potash, when refined, is called pearlash. A *pure* carbonate, prepared by igniting the bicarbonate, is called salt of tartar. Potassium carbonate is a deliquescent salt with a strong alkaline taste and reaction.

(a.) K_2CO_3 was formerly of more importance than now, as Leblanc's process has rendered Na_2CO_3 so much cheaper that it has largely replaced the former in commerce and the arts. As K_2CO_3 is hygroscopic and Na_2CO_3 is not, the latter is much more convenient for storing and handling.

(b.) As Na_2CO_3 is used in making hard soap, so K_2CO_3 is used in making soft soap.

(c.) The rapid extinction of American forests has greatly checked the manufacture of American potash, which industry is now not more than 20 *per cent.* of what it was 20 years ago. Similar causes have operated in Europe. Hence, other sources have been sought and large quantities are now made from the refuse material of the beet-root sugar manufacture and also from K_2SO_4 by a process similar to the Leblanc process for preparing Na_2CO_3.

279. Hydrogen Potassium Carbonate.—Hydrogen potassium carbonate (saleratus, potassium bicarbonate, $HKCO_3$) is prepared by passing a current of carbon dioxide through a strong solution of potassium carbonate.

$$K_2CO_3 + H_2O + CO_2 = 2HKCO_3.$$

280. Potassium Hydrate.—Potassium hydrate (caustic potash, potassium hydroxide, KHO) is prepared from potassium carbonate as sodium hydrate is from sodium carbonate. Its physical and chemical properties closely resemble those of sodium hydrate. It combines with fats and oils to form soft soap, and is one of the strongest bases known.

(a.) As KHO absorbs H_2O and CO_2 from the air, it is gradually changed to K_2CO_3. As this salt is deliquescent, the change goes on until all of the KHO is changed to a sirup of K_2CO_3. Consequently, it should be kept in closely stoppered bottles. It is usually cast in the form of sticks.

(b.) KHO is easily but not cheaply prepared by the action of K upon H_2O.

(c.) A solution of KHO quickly destroys both animal and vegetable substances. It is best clarified by subsidence and decantation though it may be filtered through glass, sand, asbestus or gun-cotton.

Experiment 255.—Repeat Exp. 246, using KHO instead of NaHO.

Experiment 256.—Repeat Exp. 3.

Experiment 257.—Repeat Exp. 113.

Experiment 258.—Repeat Exp. 1. The mixture may be placed in a paper or metal cylinder and the experiment tried in a dark room with good effect.

Experiment 259.—Carefully mix, with a feather, a small quantity of powdered $KClO_3$, and an equal quantity of powdered red P. The mixture will ignite when struck even a slight blow as with a glass rod.

Experiment 260.—Place a *pinch* of powdered $KClO_3$ and one of flowers of S in a mortar and rub them together with the pestle. A series of explosions will take place. A *minute* quantity of the same mixture may be exploded by a blow of a hammer.

281. Potassium Chlorate.

—Potassium chlorate (chlorate of potash, $KClO_3$) is largely used in the preparation of oxygen, and for other purposes in the laboratory. It is also used in medicine, in calico printing and in the manufacture of fire-works and friction matches. It is chiefly valuable as an oxidizing agent.

Experiment 261.—Melt some KNO_3 in an old flask. Put a basin of H_2O under the flask. Pour powdered charcoal into the melted salt and quickly remove the lamp. A brilliant combustion will take place and probably break the flask. The C is energetically oxidized forming large volumes of CO_2

282. Potassium Nitrate.

— Potassium nitrate (nitre, saltpetre, KNO_3) is found as an efflorescence on the soil in various tropical regions, especially in Bengal. It does not extend into the soil to a depth greater than that to which the air can easily penetrate. It is extracted by solution in water and evaporation. It is also found in many caverns, and is seldom wanting in a fruitful soil. It is chiefly used in the preparation of nitric acid and the manufacture of gunpowder. It is a white, inodorous solid, permanent in the air and very soluble in hot water.

(*a.*) When animal or vegetable matter decays in the presence of air and in contact with an alkaline or earthy base, the NH_3 produced is gradually oxidized to HNO_3 and "fixed" by the alkali. Thus the well-waters of most towns contain nitrates, showing that they have been contaminated by sewers, cess-pools or other causes. The artificial production of KNO_3 is regularly carried on in Sweden, Switzerland and other parts of continental Europe.

283. Lithium.—Lithium (*symbol*, Li ; *atomic weight*, 7 *m.c.*) is a rare metal and the lightest known elementary solid, its specific gravity being 0.59. It was first prepared in the metallic state in 1855. It is closely allied to sodium and potassium, but is harder and less easily oxidizable than they. It melts at about 180° C.

284. Rubidium.— Rubidium (*symbol*, Rb ; *atomic weight*, *85.2 m.c.*) is a rare metal found only in very minute quantities. Its specific gravity is 1.52. It resembles potassium so closely that it can not be distinguished from it by the ordinary wet reactions or blowpipe tests or any other means except that most delicate of all determinative processes, spectrum analysis (Ph., § 638, *b.*). It was discovered by this means in 1861. It melts at about 58° C.

285. Cæsium.—Cæsium (*symbol*, Cs ; *atomic weight, 132.5 m.c.*) was discovered by spectrum analysis in 1860, being the first element thus discovered. It closely resembles potassium and rubidium, with which it generally occurs. The only means of its detection and recognition is spectrum analysis, which, however, makes evident its minutest trace. It is the most decidedly electro-positive of all of the elements. Its specific gravity is not yet known.

286. Ammonium.—Ammonium is a name given to the compound radical, NH_4. It acts, as do the other members of this group, as an alkali, monad metal but it has not been isolated (§ 168).

(*a.*) The assuming of this hypothetical metal makes the analogies between the composition of the salts of the "volatile alkali" and the composition of those of the fixed alkalies as evident as are the analogies between their properties; e.g.

Ammonium hydrate.	Potassium hydrate.	Sodium hydrate.
$\left.\begin{array}{c}NH_4\\H\end{array}\right\}O$	$\left.\begin{array}{c}K\\H\end{array}\right\}O$	$\left.\begin{array}{c}Na\\H\end{array}\right\}O.$

287. Ammonium Chloride.—Ammonium chloride (salammoniac, NH_4Cl) is found native in certain volcanic regions and is artificially prepared in large quantities from the ammoniacal liquors of gas works. It occurs in commerce as tough, fibrous masses. It is used in medicine, in soldering to dissolve the metallic oxides, in dyeing, and in the laboratory as a convenient source of ammonia and for other purposes.

(*a*.) The ammoniacal liquor of gas works is heated with lime and the gaseous NH_3 thus evolved is passed through dilute HCl until it is saturated. The solution is evaporated and the NH_4Cl purified by recrystallization from hot H_2O or by sublimation.

Experiment 262.—Dissolve 6 *g.* of $(NH_4)NO_3$ in 10 *cu. cm.* of ice cold H_2O. Stir the mixture with a thermometer and notice the resulting temperature.

288. Ammonium Nitrate.—Ammonium nitrate (NH_4NO_3) is prepared by neutralizing dilute nitric acid with dilute ammonia water or a solution of ammonium carbonate and evaporating the solution. It decomposes by heat into water and nitrogen monoxide (§ 79). It has a saline taste, dissolves easily in half its weight of water with the production of cold (Ph., § 520).

Note.—Ammonium salts are very numerous, most of them being prepared directly or indirectly from the ammoniacal liquors of gas works. They are generally soluble in water.

EXERCISES.

1. The practical yield being half the theoretical, how much potassium may be prepared from 138 $Kg.$ of potassium carbonate?
2. What is the percentage composition of $KClO_3$?
3. What is the radical of potash?
4. Give at least one reason in favor of each of the following symbols for salammoniac: NH_3HCl and NH_4Cl.
5. Complete the following equations:
    (a.) $HNO_3 + NH_3 =$
    (b.) $H_2SO_4 + KHO =$
    (c.) $HNO_3 + PbO =$
6. What is the molecular weight of caustic potash?
7. I explode a mixture of 4 $l.$ of H and 5 $l.$ of Cl. (a.) What volume of HCl is produced? (b.) Which gas, and how much of it remains uncombined?
8. (a.) What volume of N_2O may be formed by heating 30 $g.$ of NH_4NO_3? (b.) What will the volume be at 15°C. and 740 $mm.$
9. Assuming that H_2O will absorb half its weight of NH_3, calculate the amount of NH_4Cl necessary to the production of 3 $Kg.$ of NH_4HO.
10. What substances do the following symbols represent: CH_4; C_2H_5Cl; $CHCl_3$; ${C_2H_5 \atop C_2H_5}$ O; $H-O-O-H$?
11. (a.) Write the empirical symbols and the systematic names for the following: ${C_2H_5 \atop H}$ O and ${CH_3 \atop CH_3}$ O. (b.) What is the common name for the former?
12. What is the object of having the room "warm" for Exp. 254?
13. Give the names and graphic symbols for PCl_3 and PCl_5.

CHAPTER XVI.

METALS OF THE ALKALINE EARTHS.

☞ CALCIUM : *symbol,* Ca ; *specific gravity, 1.58 ; atomic weight, 39.9 m. c. ; quantivalence 2 and 4.*

289. Calcium.—Calcium compounds occur largely diffused in nature, especially the carbonate in the forms of calcite, chalk, marble, limestone, coral, *etc.* They are found in all animal and vegetable bodies. The metal was first obtained by Davy in 1808, by the electrolysis of its chloride. Calcium is a light yellow, ductile, malleable metal about as hard as gold. It is scarcely oxidizable in dry air, easily oxidizable in moist air, burns vividly with a very bright yellow light when heated to redness in the air and decomposes water with evolution of hydrogen.

FIG. 110.

Note.—The name, calcium, is from *calx,* the Latin name for lime.

290. Calcium Oxides.—Calcium monoxide (lime, quicklime, CaO) is prepared by igniting calcium carbonate. On the large scale, lime is " burned " from limestone placed in a kiln of rude masonry often built in the side of a hill, the process requiring several days. Lime is a white, amorphous substance about three times as heavy as water. It is infusible in even the oxy-hydrogen flame (§ 397) but when so heated emits an intense light, known as the lime or calcium light (Exp. 49). It is largely used in making mortars and cements and, in the laboratory, for drying gases and liquids and for other purposes.

(*a.*) In the lime-kiln, a limestone arch is built above the fire and the remaining limestone placed upon this arch from above. When the CaO has been burned, the kiln is allowed to cool, the CaO is removed and a new charge introduced. Improved kilns also are used in which the process is continuous, the charge being introduced from above and the CaO withdrawn from below.

(*b.*) Pure CaO may be prepared by igniting crystallized calcite in a crucible with a perforated bottom, so that the CO_2 may be swept away as it is evolved.

(*c.*) When CaO is exposed to the air, it absorbs H_2O and CO_2 and falls to a powder known as air slaked lime.

(*d.*) Calcium dioxide (CaO_2) has been prepared by precipitation from lime water with H_2O_2.

291. Calcium Chloride. — Calcium chloride ($CaCl_2$) is easily prepared by the action of hydrochloric acid upon marble, and evaporation of the solution. It has a strong attraction for water, is deliquescent and is used for drying gases.

(*a.*) $CaCl_2$ may be crystallized from a saturated solution. These crystals ($CaCl_2, 6H_2O$), when mixed with snow, produce a temperature of $-48°C$. (Ph., § 521).

Experiment 263.—Add a few drops of H_2O to a small quantity of slaked CaO and rub it to a paste between the fingers. Its action can be felt as it actually dissolves or destroys a little of the skin.

Experiment 264.—Put 30 *g.* of recently burned CaO upon a saucer, hold the saucer in the palm of the hand and pour 20 *cu. cm.* of H_2O

upon it. Notice the increase of bulk and the rise of temperature. Thrust a friction match into the crumbling mass. It will be heated to the point of ignition. Sprinkle a little gunpowder upon the slaking lime; perhaps it will take fire.

Experiment 265.—Dip a piece of colored cambric or calico into a half liter of H_2O into which 15 $g.$ of chloride of lime have been stirred. Notice the effect upon the color of the cloth. Then dip the cloth into very dilute HCl or H_2SO_4. Notice the effect on the color of the cloth. Wash the cloth thoroughly in H_2O.

292. Calcium Hydrate.—When fresh, well burned lime is treated with one-third its weight of water, the direct synthesis yields calcium hydrate [calcium hydroxide, caustic lime, slaked lime, $Ca(HO)_2$, CaH_2O_2] with the evolution of great heat (Ph., § 524, 5). Calcium hydrate is a white, alkaline, caustic powder. It dissolves more easily in cold than in hot water, yielding an alkaline, feebly caustic liquid called lime water. Lime water readily absorbs carbon dioxide. Lime water containing solid particles of calcium hydrate in suspension is called milk of lime or cream of lime according to the consistency of the mixture.

(*a.*) The power of absorbing CO_2 and H_2S leads to the use of CaH_2O_2 in the purifiers of gas works. Its caustic action leads to its use (as milk of lime) in removing the hair from hides for tanning. Its alkaline properties fit it for use in making an insoluble "lime soap" for stearine candle manufacture. Mixed with sand and H_2O, it forms mortar, which absorbs CO_2 from the air and becomes a mixture of calcium hydrate and carbonate and sand that firmly binds together the bricks or stones between which it has been placed.

(*b.*) When CaH_2O_2 is exposed to the action of Cl, it forms "bleaching powder" or "chloride of lime" which is made in immense quantities. This substance may be considered a mixture of calcium chloride and calcium hypochlorite ($CaCl_2 + CaCl_2O_2$) or a double salt, $CaOCl_2$, at once a chloride and a hypochlorite of calcium, $\begin{matrix} Cl \\ ClO \end{matrix} \Big\}$ Ca. (§ 112.) It is sometimes called calcium chloro-hypochlorite, and graphically symbolized as follows: Cl-Ca-O-Cl.

Experiment 266.—Place a little lime water in a test tube and pass through it a stream of CO_2. Notice the precipitation of $CaCO_3$ that renders the liquid turbid. Notice also that as the passage of CO_2 into the liquid continues, the latter becomes clear again, the precipitate being dissolved. Boil the clear liquid to expel some of the absorbed CO_2, and the precipitate again appears. Test the liquid at each step of the experiment with litmus paper to determine whether it gives an acid or an alkaline reaction.

293. Calcium Carbonate. — Calcium carbonate ($CaCO_3$) occurs in many forms, both crystallized and amorphous. The shells of oysters, clams and other mollusks are almost wholly calcium carbonate. It forms the greater part of egg shells and is found in bones. It is found in enormous masses forming whole mountain ranges. It is barely soluble in water but more easily soluble in water charged with carbon dioxide. When calcareous mineral waters are exposed to the air, they lose part of their carbon dioxide and, consequently, precipitate the calcium carbonate previously held in solution. Hence, the formation of stalactites, stalagmites, tufa, travertine, *etc.* All of the forms of calcium carbonate are easily acted upon by even dilute acids, the action being attended by effervescence due to the escape of the expelled carbon dioxide.

294. Calcium Sulphate. — Calcium sulphate ($CaSO_4$) is found in nature as the mineral anhydrite. The hydrated sulphate ($CaSO_4$, $2H_2O$) is gypsum, which, when in the crystalline form, is called selenite. By heating gypsum to about 120°C., it parts with its water of crystallization forming plaster of Paris. When this plaster is mixed to a paste with water, it again unites with the water and becomes hard or "sets." Hence, its use as a cement and for making casts of various objects. Calcium sulphate is sparingly soluble in water. Water containing calcium sulphate or carbonate in solution is called "hard." Alabaster is a variety of gypsum.

(a.) When soap (sodium or potassium stearate) is added to hard water, there is a metathetical reaction, resulting in the formation of an insoluble calcium or "lime soap" (calcium stearate), which rises as a scum upon the surface of the liquid. The soap can not perform its proper office until it has precipitated the calcium salt. Other agents are often used to precipitate the calcium compound and thus "soften" the water.

295. Calcium Phosphate. — There are several calcium phosphates (§ 242), the most important of which is bone-phosphate, $Ca_3P_2O_8$. It is the chief inorganic constituent of the bones of animals. It is important as a source of phosphorus, and valuable, when ground to a powder, as a fertilizer.

☞ STRONTIUM : *symbol*, Sr ; *specific gravity, 2.5 ; atomic weight, 87.? m. c. ; quantivalence, 2 and 4.*

296. Strontium. — This rare metal closely resembles calcium in appearance and properties. It has two oxides (SrO and SrO_2). It chiefly occurs in the sulphate (celestine, $SrSO_4$) and in the carbonate (strontianite, $SrCO_3$).

☞ BARIUM: *symbol*, Ba ; *specific gravity, 4 ; atomic weight, 136.8 m. c. ; quantivalence, 2 and 4.*

297. Barium. — This rare metal closely resembles calcium in appearance and properties. Its melting point appears to be higher than that of cast iron. It has two oxides (baryta, BaO; and BaO_2), occurs in nature as a sulphate (heavy spar, $BaSO_4$) and decomposes cold water.

§ 297   METALS OF THE ALKALINE EARTHS.   251

EXERCISES.

1. Write the reaction for the burning of CaO.
2. Write the reaction for the preparation of $CaCl_2$.
3. Write the reaction for preparing calcium hydroxide.
4. Why is the formula for calcium hypochlorite $CaCl_2O_2$ instead of CaClO, the formula for hypochlorous acid being HClO?
5. When a current of CO_2 is passed through an aqueous solution of BaO_2, hydroxyl and $BaCO_3$ are formed. Write the reaction.
6. How much KNO_3 and H_2SO_4 shall I need to prepare enough HNO_3 to neutralize 5 $Kg.$ of chalk? (!)
7. What is the property that chiefly distinguishes Cl and the elements most like it from K and the elements most like it?
8. What is meant by the statement that caustic soda is formed upon the water type?
9. What are the *characteristic* properties of C?
10. Write the empirical, typical and graphic symbols for common salt, caustic potash, baryta, sulphuric acid, acetic acid and marsh gas.
11. (*a.*) What is the weight of 1 *l.* of Cl? (*b.*) Of H_2S? (*c.*) Of CO?
12. Compare and contrast P and As respecting their physical and chemical properties.
13. Symbolize the sulphates, nitrates, chlorides, chlorates, acetates, bromides and bromates of Ca, Ba and Sr.
14. How much of each of Na; NH_4; Sr and K is equivalent to one atom of Ca?

CHAPTER XVII.

METALS OF THE MAGNESIUM GROUP.

☞ MAGNESIUM : *symbol,* Mg ; *specific gravity, 1.75 ; atomic weight, 24 m.c. ; quantivalence, 2.*

298. Magnesium. — Magnesium compounds are widely and abundantly distributed but the metal is not found free in nature. It is prepared in considerable quantities by fusing together magnesium chloride ($MgCl_2$) and sodium, or from the double chloride of potassium and magnesium, called carnallite, a mineral found abundantly in the Stassfurt deposits (§ 276). It has a silver white appearance, preserves its lustre in dry air and tarnishes in moist air. It is readily acted upon by most acids with the evolution of hydrogen and, as it is perfectly free from arsenic, is often used, instead of zinc, in Marsh's test (§ 246). It is found in commerce, usually in the form of ribbon. This ribbon, when ignited, burns with a brilliant light of high actinic (Ph., § 651) power. The magnesium light has been seen from a distance of twenty-eight miles at sea and has been used for photographic purposes.

Experiment 267.—Coil 15 *cm.* of Mg ribbon around a lead pencil. Change the pencil for a knitting needle or iron wire, hold the wire horizontal and ignite one end of the ribbon. The coil of Mg will burn to an imperfect coil of MgO.

299. Magnesium Oxide. — Magnesium oxide (magnesia, MgO) is formed when the metal is burned in air. It may be prepared by the ignition of the magnesium salt of any volatile acid ; *e. g.*, the carbonate, nitrate or chloride. It is used in medicine and for making infusible crucibles, as it does not melt below the temperature of the oxyhydrogen flame.

300. Magnesium Salts. — *Magnesium Chloride* ($MgCl_2$) is found in sea water, in many saline springs and as a constituent of carnallite. It is largely used in dressing cotton goods. *Magnesium sulphate* ($MgSO_4$) is found in nature as kieserite. The hydrated salt ($MgSO_4, 7H_2O$) is called *Epsom salt*, and is found in many mineral waters. It is used as a purgative and in dressing cotton goods. *Magnesium carbonate* ($MgCO_3$) occurs as native magnesite. A mixture of the carbonate and the hydrate (MgH_2O_2) prepared by adding Na_2CO_3 to a solution of $MgCl_2$ or of Epsom salt, is called *magnesia alba*.

☞ ZINC : *symbol*, Zn ; *specific gravity*, 6.9 ; *atomic weight*, 65 m.c. ; *quantivalence*, 2.

301. Sources of Zinc.—Metallic zinc is not found in nature. The carbonate (smithsonite, zinc spar, $ZnCO_3$); the silicate (calamine, Zn_2SiO_4); the sulphide (sphalerite, blende, ZnS) and the oxide (red zinc ore, zincite, ZnO) are found native in paying quantities.

302. Preparation.—The zinc ore is first roasted and thereby converted to an oxide. This oxide is then smelted with half its weight of coal and the distilled zinc vapor condensed and purified.

(*a*.) There are several processes of smelting Zn, including the English, Belgian and Silesian. In the English process, the roasted ore and coal are put into iron crucibles covered at the top and having an iron tube fitting into the bottom. The crucibles are heated in conical furnaces. The vaporized metal passes down the tube and is collected in vessels. This process is less economical than the others.

(*b*.) In the Belgian process, fire clay cylindrical retorts, 1 *m*. long and 20 *cm*. in internal diameter are used. About 50 of these retorts are set in one furnace, slanting slightly from a horizontal direction so that the metal may run out. Each retort is provided with a tapering neck and a sheet iron condenser. The smelting is completed in eleven hours, two charges being worked per day.

(*c.*) In the Silesian process, now generally adopted, fire clay mufflers, *M, M*, about 1 *m.* long, are arranged side by side on the

FIG. III.

floor of a reverberatory furnace. The vaporized Zn passes out by the bent clay tube, *A*, and is received, as it condenses, in a vessel placed in the closed recess, *O*. Metallic Zn, in the form of fine dust, mixed with ZnO, is also obtained. The mixture is called zinc dust; it is a valuable reducing agent.

(*d.*) The Zn is then remelted, cast into slabs or cakes and sent into the market under the name of *spelter*.

Experiment 268.—Mix 20 *g.* of zinc dust and 40 *g.* of powdered KNO_3. (If you cannot get the zinc dust, pulverize granulated zinc, § 21). Heat a small Hessian crucible to redness, remove it from the fire and place it in the ventilating closet or where the fumes that may be formed will be drawn into the chimney. By means of a ladle with a handle about 1 *m.* long, drop the mixed Zn and KNO_3 into the red hot crucible. . The Zn will burn with great energy at the expense of the O of the KNO_3.

Experiment 269.—Put a pinch of finely powdered blue indigo into a test tube, add half a teaspoonful of zinc dust or fine Zn filings and two teaspoonfuls of a strong solution of NaHO. Heat the mixture. The nascent H evolved changes the blue indigo (C_8H_5NO) to white indigo (C_8H_6NO).

Experiment 270.—Dip a piece of white cloth into the solution of white indigo. When it is exposed to the air, the *reduced* indigo is oxidized to the blue variety and the cloth is *permanently* colored. The color is "fast."

FIG. 112.

Experiment 271.—Dissolve 10 g. of lead acetate (sugar of lead) in 250 cu. cm. of H_2O and add a few drops of $C_2H_4O_2$. In this solution, suspend a strip of Zn. The Zn and Pb will change places, leaving a solution of zinc acetate and a metallic "lead tree." The tree will be more beautiful if the ends of the Zn be slit into branches before immersion. The weights of the dissolved Zn and the precipitated Pb will be in the ratio of their atomic weights.

303. Properties.—Zinc is a bluish white, crystalline metal. It is ductile and malleable at about 130°C. or 140°C., under which circumstances it may be drawn into wire or rolled into sheets or plates. At the ordinary temperature and at temperatures above 200°C., it is brittle. The commercial article is seldom pure, generally containing lead, iron and carbon, while traces of arsenic and antimony are often found. Zinc dust is a valuable reducing agent. Zinc is readily acted upon by a boiling solution of sodium and potassium hydrates and by most acids, with the evolution of hydrogen. (Ph., §§ 373, 374.) It melts at 410°C., and distils at about 1000°C. Pure zinc is not easily soluble in dilute sulphuric acid while impure zinc is thus soluble. (Ph., § 386.) Zinc is not much affected by air, either dry or moist. It readily precipitates most metals from solutions of their salts.

(*a.*) Brass is an alloy of Zn and Cu. German silver is an alloy of Zn, Cu and Ni.

(*b.*) Galvanized iron is simply iron coated with Zn. The term is a gross misnomer, as galvanic action is not involved in the process.

304. Zinc Compounds.— Zinc oxide (ZnO) is

found as an ore in New Jersey. Its color is due to the presence of red oxide of manganese. Zinc oxide is known in commerce as *zinc white*, and is prepared on a large scale for use as a paint. *Zinc chloride* ($ZnCl_2$) is formed by dissolving zinc in hydrochloric acid. It is used for preserving timber, as a caustic in surgery, in cleansing the surfaces of metals for soldering and, very largely, for the fraudulent purpose of weighting cotton goods. It is soluble in alcohol and very deliquescent. *Zinc sulphate* (white vitriol, $ZnSO_4$, $7H_2O$) is used in medicine, in dyeing, and in galvanic batteries.

☞ GLUCINUM: *symbol*, Gl; *specific gravity, 2.1; atomic weight, 9 m. c.; quantivalence, 2.*

305. Glucinum.—This rare metal is also known as glucinium and as beryllium (symbol, Be). Its oxide is found in the mineral beryl. By fusing its chloride with potassium or sodium, the metal is formed as a dark gray powder which acquires a metallic lustre by burnishing. The metal may be made coherent by fusing this powder under sodium chloride. It has a silver white color and melts at a lower temperature than silver does.

☞ CADMIUM; *symbol*, Cd; *specific gravity, 8.6; atomic weight, 112 m. c.; molecular weight, 112 m. c.; quantivalence, 2.*

306. Cadmium.—This rare metal occurs in nature associated with zinc ores. As it is more volatile than zinc, its vapor comes over with the first portions of the zinc distilled. It forms compounds very similar to the corresponding zinc compounds. It has a tin white color, is susceptible of a high polish and gives a crackling sound when bent, as tin does. As its vapor density is 56, we conclude that its molecule contains but a single atom.

(*a.*) The statement that the vapor density of Cd is 56, means that the vapor is 56 times as heavy as H. Consequently (§ 61) its molecule weighs 56 times as much as the H molecule or 112 m.c. But this molecular weight is the same as its atomic weight. Hence, the inference above stated.

307. The Magnesium Group.—The metals of this group decompose water only at a high temperature and glucinum, probably, not at all. They are volatile and burn with a bright flame when heated in the air. Each member of the group forms only one oxide and one sulphide.

Exercises.

1. (*a.*) In the preparation of Mg from magnesium chloride and sodium, what is the other product of the reaction? (*b.*) How may it be separated from the metal? (*c.*) What is the other product when it is prepared from carnallite?

2. How much ZnO can be obtained by oxydizing 100 $g.$ of Zn?

3. What weight of CO_2 is yielded by the burning of 1 $l.$ of CH_4?

4. If 150 *cu. cm.* of O and 400 *cu. cm.* of H are mixed and exploded, (*a.*) what volume of steam is produced? (*b.*) Which gas, and how much of it, remains in excess?

5. By a series of electric sparks, I decompose 100 *cu. cm.* of NH_3, add 90 *cu. cm.* of O and explode the mixture. Give the name and volume of each of the remaining gases.

6. Write the name and full graphic symbol for

$$\begin{array}{l} S-(SO_2)-(HO) \\ | \\ S-(SO_2)-(HO) \end{array}$$

CHAPTER XVIII.

METALS OF THE LEAD GROUP.

☞ LEAD: *symbol*, Pb ; *specific gravity, 11.37 ; atomic weight, 206.4 m. c. ; quantivalence, 2 (and 4).*

308. Source of Lead.—Lead is seldom found free in nature but its sulphide (galena, galenite, PbS) is quite abundant and is, by far, its commonest ore. The lead sulphide is generally associated with silver sulphide.

309. Preparation.—The smelting of lead from its ore is a simple process. The ore is first heated in an open reverberatory furnace, in which one part of the sulphide is oxidized yielding lead oxide (PbO) and sulphur dioxide while another part is oxidized to lead sulphate. The furnace is then closed and heated to a higher temperature when the oxide and sulphate just formed act each upon a part of the still undecomposed ore, yielding metallic lead and sulphur dioxide.

310. Properties.—Lead is a metal so soft as to be easily cut with a knife or indented with a finger nail and to leave a streak when rubbed upon paper. It has considerable malleability and little ductility. Repeated fusion renders it hard and brittle, probably by oxidation. When freshly cut, it has a bluish gray color and a bright lustre which is quickly dulled by oxidation. It melts at 334°C. and may be crystallized by slowly cooling a large quantity of the melted metal and pouring out the still liquid portion. It is very slightly acted upon by cold sulphuric or hydrochloric acid; its best solvent is nitric acid.

(*a.*) Potable waters in general and especially well waters containing ammoniacal salts, often due to decaying organic matter, act upon lead with the formation of compounds that act as cumulative poisons. In many cases, the use of lead water pipes is very dangerous for this reason. If, upon examining the inner surface of a lead pipe that has been thus used, it is found *to be bright* it may be known that dangerous soluble salts have been formed and carried away *with the water.* " A word to the wise is sufficient."

(*b.*) In the presence of air and moisture, lead is attacked by even feeble acids like acetic or carbonic acid. Hence, the use of cooking utensils that are made of lead or that contain lead even in the form of solder or as an adulteration of otherwise harmless substances (§ 388, *b.*) sometimes leads to the formation of poisonous lead compounds. When these are taken into the system, they unite with certain tissues of the body and may accumulate until the quantity is sufficient to produce poisoning (§ 315).

311. Uses.—Lead is largely used for many purposes on account of its softness, pliability, easy fusibility and its comparative freedom from chemical action with water and most of the acids.

312. Lead Oxides.—Lead suboxide (Pb_2O) is also called plumbous oxide. Lead monoxide (PbO) is also called plumbic oxide but more frequently, *litharge*. It is prepared on the large scale by highly heating melted lead in a current of air. It is used in the manufacture of glass. Lead sesquioxide (Pb_2O_3) is considered to be a compound of the monoxide and dioxide. *Red lead* or minium (Pb_3O_4) is largely used as a paint and in the manufacture of flint glass. Lead dioxide (PbO_2) or plumbic peroxide is most easily produced by treating red lead with nitric acid.

313. Lead Sulphide.—Lead sulphide (PbS) occurs native as galenite or galena and may be prepared artificially by passing hydrogen sulphide into any solution of a lead salt. The precipitate thus formed is of a deep but varying color. This color, together with the insolubility of the precipitate is of use in detecting the presence of lead.

314. Some Lead Salts.—There are two compounds of lead and chlorine; plumbic chloride ($PbCl_2$) and plumbic perchloride ($PbCl_4$). *Lead carbonate* ($PbCO_3$) is formed as a white precipitate by adding ammonium carbonate to a cold solution of lead acetate. *White lead* is a compound of varying proportions of the carbonate and hydrate. When ground with linseed oil, it forms the basis of ordinary white paint although zinc white is used for the same purpose. *Lead acetate* is a soluble salt with a sweet, astringent taste, whence its common name, *sugar of lead*. Like the other soluble lead salts it is intensely poisonous.

315. Lead Poisoning.—While metallic lead is not poisonous, all of its soluble salts are so in a very high degree. Lead acetate, given in doses of from 0.3 g. to 0.6 g. produces symptoms of acute lead poisoning which often end fatally. Small doses of the oxides and carbonates frequently repeated often produce chronic lead poisoning (§ 310, *b*). Painter's colic is a form of chronic poisoning by lead carbonate. Soluble sulphates, *e. g.*, Epsom salt, are antidotes for lead poisons.

316. Tests.—The sweet taste and poisonous character of the soluble lead salts render their detection a matter of great importance.

(*a*.) Any Pb compound when heated on charcoal in the blowpipe flame gives a bead of malleable lead. This bead is readily soluble in warm HNO_3; and this acid solution yields a precipitate with H_2SO_4.

(*b*.) Potable waters suspected of containing Pb compounds may be tested by slightly acidulating with HCl and charging with H_2S. If a black precipitate is formed, lead is probably present. The probability is sufficient to call for the services of a chemical expert. If lead salts are present in not too minute quantities, the addition of HCl will yield a white crystalline precipitate of $PbCl_2$ which is soluble in an excess of boiling H_2O. If the solution of the lead salt be tolerably strong, the addition of KI will generally yield a yellow precipitate of PbI_2, while the addition of potassium chromate (K_2CrO_4) gives a fine yellow precipitate of lead chromate or chrome yellow ($PbCrO_4$).

☞ THALLIUM: *symbol*, Tl; *specific gravity*, *11.8;* *atomic weight*, *203.6 m. c.; quantivalence, 1 and 3.*

317. Thallium.—Thallium is a very rare metal, discovered in 1861 by spectrum analysis, by which means it has been found to be widely but very sparingly distributed. It is generally prepared from the "flue dust" that accumulates between the pyrite furnace and the leaden chambers in sulphuric acid works. It has a bluish, white tint and a lead like lustre. It leaves a streak when rubbed on paper and is easily indented by a finger nail, being softer than lead. It is malleable but not ductile. It decomposes water at a red heat and is easily soluble in dilute acids. Its salts are poisonous. It melts at 294° C.

(*a.*) Tl forms two oxides, the monoxide (Tl_2O) and the trioxide or sesquioxide (Tl_2O_3). There are also two corresponding series of salts, the thallious and the thallic.

(*b.*) Tl has a peculiar position among the metals. Like Na and K, it replaces H, atom for atom ; it also presents other analogies with the metals of that group. Like gold, it forms a trichloride ($TlCl_3$). It also, as we have seen, corresponds closely to Pb. On account of this difficulty of classification it has been termed the metallic ornithorhynchus.

318. The Lead Group.—The metals of this group are soft; they have a high specific gravity; their sulphides are black and insoluble in water; their chlorides are sparingly soluble.

EXERCISES.

1. (*a.*) Write the reaction for the formation of lead oxide in the first stage of lead smelting. (*b.*) For the formation of lead sulphate in the same stage.

2. (*a.*) Express the reaction between the lead oxide and galenite in the second stage of lead smelting. (*b.*) For the reaction between lead sulphate and the ore in the same stage.

3. Write the reaction for the preparation of lead peroxide from red lead and nitric acid.

4. (*a.*) What substance may be represented by the graphic symbol

$$O=Pb\!\!\!<\!\!{{\,O\,}\atop{\,O\,}}\!\!\!>\!\!Pb\,?$$

(*b.*) What does this symbol show concerning the quantivalence of the lead atoms in the molecule?

5. (*a.*) What substance is represented by the symbol

$$O=Pb\!\!\!<\!\!{{O-Pb}\atop{O-Pb}}\!\!\!>\!\!O\,?$$

(*b.*) What does this symbol indicate concerning the quantivalence of the lead atoms?

6. What volume of CO_2 is produced by the burning of 1 *l.* of CH_4?

7. What is the volume of 1 *Kg.* of O?

8. Write the water type symbol for lead acetate.

9. What is common washing soda? Baking soda? Why is the latter better for baking than the former?

CHAPTER XIX.

METALS OF THE COPPER GROUP.

SECTION I.

COPPER.

☞ *Symbol*, Cu; *specific gravity, 8.95; atomic weight, 63.1 m. c.; quantivalence, 2.*

319. Source.—Copper was probably the first metal used by man as it is found native and thus requires no metallurgical treatment. Native copper is found in large masses, especially in the Lake Superior mines, where a single mass weighing 480 tons was discovered.

(*a.*) Among the more important of the copper ores are cuprite or red copper ore (Cu_2O); malachite ($CuCO_3 + CuH_2O_2$); azurite ($2CuCO_3 + CuH_2O_2$); chalcocite or copper glance (Cu_2S) and chalcopyrite or copper pyrites ($CuFeS_2$), the last being the most important.

320. Preparation.—The reduction of the oxides and carbonates is easily effected by smelting with carbon. The sulphides are roasted to volatilize some of the constituents and to oxidize others. The roasted ore is then fused with a silicate, whereby a slag containing most of the iron is formed and a nearly pure copper sulphide is obtained. This sulphide is then roasted; part of the copper is oxidized and combines with the remaining sulphide, yielding metallic copper and sulphur dioxide.

(a.) In the smelting process, some of the oxide dissolves in the melted metal and makes it so brittle as to be unfit for use. It is "toughened" by "poling" or stirring the melted metal with the trunk of a young tree, the surface of the metal being covered with a thin layer of coal. Reducing gases, such as CO and various hydrocarbons, are evolved in large quantities from the green wood and sufficiently reduce the oxide. If the metal is "over-poled," completely reduced and thus made brittle again, it is exposed to the air for a short time and thus brought back to the "tough pitch" once more.

321. Properties.—Copper is a reddish metal, hard, very tenacious and highly malleable and ductile. Excepting silver, it is the best known conductor of heat and electricity (Ph., § 539, b). It is not much affected by air or by most of the acids at the ordinary temperature. It melts at about 1200°C.

(a.) Cu is readily dissolved by dilute HNO_3, yielding $Cu(NO_3)_2$ and NO (§ 83). It is dissolved in hot H_2SO_4, yielding $CuSO_4$ and SO_2 (§ 145, a.).

322. Uses.—Copper is largely used for many familiar purposes. On account of its toughness, it is used in the manufacture of tubular boilers, for coating the bottoms of ships, *etc.*; on account of its conductivity, it is employed in ocean cables and for other electric uses. Brass, bronze, bell-metal and other copper alloys are of great technical importance and are, perhaps, used more than copper itself.

Experiment 272.—Hold a *bright* Cu coin obliquely in the small flame of a gas or alcohol lamp. Move it to and fro and notice the beautiful play of iridescent colors. Cool the coin in H_2O and notice its coating of red oxide. Heat the coin again, holding it in the hot, oxidizing part of the flame, just above the luminous cone and notice that it becomes coated with a black oxide. Quickly cool the coin in H_2O and notice that the black coat scales off and reveals the red coat beneath.

Experiment 273.—Place a small quantity of dry $Cu(NO_3)_2$ upon a piece of porcelain and heat it until red fumes are no longer given off. A black copper oxide will be left upon the porcelain.

323. Copper Oxides.—Copper tetrantoxide or quadrant oxide (Cu_4O) is an olive green powder that absorbs oxygen when exposed to the air. Copper suboxide, (copper hemioxide, cuprous oxide, red oxide of copper or ruby copper, Cu_2O) is found native and prepared artificially. It is used in coloring glass. Copper monoxide (cupric oxide, black oxide of copper, CuO) may be prepared by heating the metal in a current of air, or by igniting the carbonate, hydrate or nitrate. It is used in coloring glass green. Copper dioxide (cupric peroxide, CuO_2) is a yellowish brown powder that decomposes easily into CuO and O (see § 341, *a*).

Experiment 274.—Saturate a strip of filter paper with a solution of $Cu(NO_3)_2$ to within an inch of the end. Hold the strip, dry end downward, over a hot stove. The paper will ignite at the lower edge of the saturated part of the paper.

Experiment 275.—Powder some blue vitriol and heat it upon a piece of porcelain; as it loses its H_2O, the light blue powder will turn white. A drop of H_2O upon the anhydrous powder will restore the color.

324. Some Copper Salts.— *Copper nitrate* (CuN_2O_6) is prepared by treating copper with nitric acid and evaporating the solution. On crystallizing from its solution, it absorbs three molecules of water (CuN_2O_6, $3H_2O$). It is easily decomposable and, therefore, has strong oxidizing properties. *Copper sulphate* ($CuSO_4$) is formed by dissolving copper in hot sulphuric acid or the oxide in dilute sulphuric acid. It is also prepared from the ores and, as a secondary product, in silver refining. It is generally found as hydrated crystals ($CuSO_4$, $5H_2O$) known as *blue vitriol*, which is largely used in the arts. The color of blue vitriol depends upon the presence of its water of crystallization. Two native carbonates, *malachite* and *azurite*, have been mentioned. Some varieties of malachite are susceptible of a high polish and are highly prized for jewels and other ornamental articles. *Copper acetate* is called *verdigris*, although the term is sometimes used to designate the green carbonate that forms on the exposure of copper to moist air. *Paris green* is a copper arsenite. It is used in green paints and in modern potato culture.

Note.—The soluble copper salts are active poisons. Such salts are formed in copper cooking utensils that are not kept bright. Acid solutions (*e. g.*, vinegar) form poisonous compounds with brass or copper utensils even when they are kept perfectly clean. Some persons prefer to pickle cucumbers in brass or copper kettles because they take a more brilliant color. This added color is due to the formation of *poisonous verdigris*.

EXERCISES.

1. Read the following equation by unit volumes:

$$CH_4 + 2O_2 = CO_2 + 2H_2O.$$

2. What weight of Cu is necessary to prepare 1 *l.* of NO at 0°C. and 760 *mm.*?

3. The combustion of 1 *l.* of CH_4 requires what volume of O?

4. What volume of CH_4 is needed to yield 1 *cu. m.* of steam in its combustion?

5. How many *cu. cm.* of SO_2 (at 20°C and 740 *mm.*, Pb. § 494,) can be obtained by the action of Cu upon 20 *g.* of H_2SO_4?

6. What is the symbol and name of a substance the vapor density of which is 30 and the percentage composition of which is as follows: C, 40%; H, 6.67%; O, 53.33%?

7. Compare the cost of making HNO_3 from KNO_3 and from $NaNO_3$ when the cost of KNO_3 is 44 cents per *Kg.*, that of $NaNO_3$ is 33 cents per *Kg.* and that of H_2SO_4 is 11 cents per *Kg.*

8. Required the volume of gases in an eudiometer after the explosion of 50 *cu. cm.* of H with 75 *cu. cm.* of O at 150°C. and 760 *mm.*

9. Assuming Cu to be a dyad, write graphic symbols for Cu_4O, Cu_2O, CuO, CuO_2 and Cu_2Cl_2.

SECTION II.

SILVER.

☞ *Symbol,* Ag ; *specific gravity, 10.5 ; atomic weight, 107.6 m. c. ; quantivalence, 1 and 3.*

325. Source.—Silver is a widely diffused and somewhat abundant element and has been known from the earliest times. It is found native, sometimes in masses weighing several hundred pounds and often alloyed with copper, mercury and gold. It more commonly is found as a sulphide, mixed with other metallic sulphides. Its most abundant source is argentiferous galena although the carbonates have been found in richly paying quantities, especially in the Leadville (Colorado) mining region.

326. Preparation.— The processes of preparing metallic silver from its ores are numerous and widely different, depending largely, in any given case, upon the nature of the ore, the position of the mine, the price of labor, fuel, *etc.*

327. Properties.— Silver is a beautiful, brilliant white metal, harder than gold, softer than copper, exceedingly malleable and ductile and the best known conductor of heat and electricity. It melts at 1040°C. and then absorbs 22 times its volume of oxygen. When the melted silver cools quickly, the oxygen escaping from the interior of the mass breaks through the hardening crust driving out some of the molten metal and giving the phenomenon known as "spitting" of silver. The metal is unaltered in the air and resists the action of hydrochloric and cold sulphuric acid but dissolves readily in nitric acid.

(*a.*) Ag is so malleable that it may be formed into leaves so thin that 4000 measure only 1 *mm.* in thickness; so ductile that 1 *g.* of it may make 1800 *m.* of wire and so tenacious that a wire 2 *mm.* thick will sustain a weight of more than 80 *Kg.*

(*b.*) Ag unites slowly with the halogen elements and more readily with S and P. The tarnishing of Ag is generally due to the formation of a silver sulphide by the action of H_2S present in the atmosphere.

328. Uses.—Owing to its susceptibility of high polish, its permanency and other properties, silver is much used for jewelry, plate and coin. Owing to its softness, it is generally hardened with copper. American and French coin contain ten *per cent.* and English coin 7.5 *per cent.* of copper. It is used for chemical utensils as it is not acted upon by the fused hydrates of the alkali metals as glass and platinum are.

329. Oxides.—There are three oxides of silver; silver tetrantoxide or argentous oxide (Ag_4O); silver hemioxide or silver oxide (Ag_2O) and silver peroxide or dioxide (Ag_2O_2). When silver oxide (Ag_2O) is digested with ammonia, it forms a very explosive, black powder, known as *fulminating silver*. Its composition has not yet been satisfactorily determined.

Experiment 276.—Fill three test tubes one-third full of H_2O and pour into each a few drops of a strong solution of $AgNO_3$. Add 2 or 3 *cu. cm.* of a solution of NaCl to the contents of the first tube and shake it vigorously, AgCl will be precipitated as a dense, white curdy mass. Add 2 or 3 *cu. cm.* of a solution of KBr to the contents of the second tube and shake as before; a yellowish precipitate of AgBr will be thrown down. Add 1 or 2 *cu. cm.* of a solution of KI to the contents of the third tube and shake as before; yellowish, flocculent AgI will be formed.

Experiment 277.—Try to dissolve one-third of each of these precipitates separately in HNO_3. They will not thus dissolve.

Experiment 278.—Treat a second third of each precipitate with (NH_4)HO. Determine which dissolves most easily and which least easily.

Experiment 279.—Treat the last third of each precipitate with a strong solution of sodium thiosulphate (§ 158, *b*). Each of the halogen salts is quickly dissolved.

Experiment 280.—Precipitate more AgCl from a solution of $AgNO_3$ by HCl or a solution of NaCl. Filter the solution and wash the precipitate retained upon the filter thoroughly with H_2O. Open the filter, spread the curdy AgCl evenly over it and expose it to the direct rays of the sun. (Ph., § 651.) The white precipitate quickly changes to violet, the color deepening with continued exposure.

Note.—The last five experiments illustrate the principal processes of photography.

330. The Silver Haloids.

—Silver chloride (AgCl) is found native in semi-transparent masses, called *horn silver*. It may be prepared by precipitation from a solution of any silver salt by a solution of hydrochloric acid or any other chloride. It is insoluble in water and acids but easily soluble in ammonia water. Silver iodide or bromide is precipitated from a similar solution by a solution of an iodide or bromide. These compounds are much used in photography.

331. Silver Sulphide and Cyanide.

—*Silver sulphide* (Ag_2S) is an important silver ore and is formed artificially by the action of sulphur or hydrogen sulphide upon the metal. *Silver cyanide* (AgCN) is a white curdy precipitate, insoluble in dilute nitric acid but soluble in ammonia water or in solutions of the cyanides of the alkali or alkaline earth metals. It is used in electro-plating (Ph., § 399, *a*).

(*a*.) When a silver spoon is left for a time in an egg or in mustard it becomes blackened by the formation of silver sulphide. Hence, silver egg-spoons are often gilded.

332. Silver Nitrate.

— Silver nitrate ($AgNO_3$) is prepared on a large scale by dissolving silver in dilute nitric acid and evaporating to crystallization. It is found in commerce in crystals. When fused and cast into sticks, it is called *lunar caustic*. In this form, it is used in surgery, acting as a powerful cautery. Pure silver nitrate is not altered by exposure to sunlight, but when in contact with organic substances it blackens, forming insoluble compounds of great stability. It is, consequently, used in making indelible inks and hair dyes. It is also used in medicine and in photography. Like all of the other soluble silver salts, it is poisonous.

333. Other Silver Salts.—Silver sulphate (Ag_2SO_4); silver phosphate (Ag_3PO_4) and silver carbonate (Ag_2CO_3) are among the many important silver salts.

Exercises.

1. Why do silver coins become blackened when carried in the pocket with common friction matches?

2. 504 $Kg.$ of lead sulphite will yield how much Pb?

3. At a very high temperature, Ag_2O may be decomposed much as the HgO was in Exp. 56. Write the reaction in molecular symbols.

4. What action have the alkalies upon Ag?

5. If recently precipitated and moist AgCl be placed upon a sheet of Zn, a dark color will soon appear at the edge of the salt. The chloride will soon be converted into a dark gray powder of finely divided Ag. Explain.

6. The change mentioned in Exercise 5 will be much more rapid if the AgCl be moistened with HCl. Why?

7. When AgCl is fused with an alkaline hydrate, the chloride is reduced to a metal, a non-combustible gas is set free and an alkaline chloride is formed. What is the gas?

8. If a silver dime be dissolved in HNO_3, the solution will be blue. A solution of $AgNO_3$ is colorless. Whence the blue color?

9. I want $\dfrac{10}{.0896 \times 16}$ $l.$ of O. What weight of $KClO_3$ must I use?

10. (a.) How many $cu.$ $cm.$ of H may be obtained from 1 $l.$ of NH_3? (b.) Of N? (c.) How may the elementary gases be obtained from the compound? (d.) How may the eudiometer be used to free the N from the H?

11. If HCl be used instead of cream of tartar with $HNaCO_3$, what residue would remain in the biscuit

SECTION III.

MERCURY.

☞ *Symbol,* Hg ; *specific gravity, 13.6 ; atomic weight, 200 m. c. ; molecular weight, 200 m. c. ; quantivalence, 2.*

334. Source. — Mercury, or quicksilver, is found native in small quantities but chiefly as a sulphide (HgS) called cinnabar. The best known deposits of cinnabar are at Idria in Austria, Almaden in Spain, and New Almaden in California. Mercury is also brought from China and Japan.

335. Preparation. — The sulphide is generally mixed with quicklime or iron turnings and distilled. The sulphur unites with the lime or iron and the mercury vapor is condensed by being brought into contact with water.

336. Properties. — Mercury is a silver white metal, liquid at the ordinary temperature. It vaporizes slowly at ordinary temperatures, boils at about 357°C. and freezes at —39.4°C., becoming a ductile, malleable, white solid which can be cut with a knife. The liquid is scarcely affected by exposure to the air but, when heated for a long time in the air, it oxidizes. It is soluble in strong, boiling sulphuric acid but its best solvent is nitric acid.

(*a.*) The vapor density of Hg is 100. We, consequently, conclude that the molecule of this element contains but a single atom (§ 306, *a*).

337. Uses. — Mercury is largely used in the construction of thermometers, barometers and other physical and chemical apparatus, for the collection of gases that are soluble in water, for the preparation of mirrors, for the extraction of gold and silver from their ores, and for the preparation of various mercurial compounds.

Experiment 281.—Prepare an amalgam by adding bits of Na to Hg slightly warmed in an evaporating dish.

338. Amalgams.—Compounds or mixtures of the metals with mercury are called amalgams. They are generally formed by the direct union of the two metals. Many of these amalgams, or mercury alloys, are largely used in the arts. Tin amalgam is used in "silvering" mirrors; cadmium amalgam, which gradually hardens, has been used for filling teeth; zinc and tin amalgam is used for coating the rubbers of electric machines (Ph., §§ 322, 345).

339. Mercury Oxides.—Mercury forms two oxides, mercurous oxide (suboxide of mercury, gray oxide of mercury, Hg_2O) and mercuric oxide (red oxide of mercury, red precipitate, HgO). The latter is a powerful poison. It is prepared by heating mercury for a long time in air or, on the large scale, by heating an intimate mixture of mercury and mercuric nitrate. It decomposes, at a red heat, into its elementary constituents (Exp. 56).

340. Mercury Sulphide.—This compound (HgS) is largely found native as cinnabar. When prepared artificially, it is called vermillion. It is of a brilliant red color and is used as an oil and water-color paint, in lithographers' and printers' inks and in coloring sealing-wax.

341. Mercury Salts.—Mercury forms two series of salts, corresponding to the two oxides, *viz.*, the mercurous salts and the mercuric salts. The members of the two series are widely different in their properties. The mercuric compounds are more powerfully poisonous than are the mercurous.

(*a.*) Mercury is generally considered a dyad, even in the mercurous compounds. In such cases, the quantivalence is explained by assuming that the double atom $(Hg_2)''$ partly saturates itself as is shown by the graphic symbol, $\begin{array}{c} Hg-Cl \\ | \\ Hg-Cl \end{array}$. A similar explanation may be made concerning the quantivalence of Cu.

(*b.*) Mercury may be detected in almost any soluble mercurous or mercuric salt by placing a piece of clean Cu into a solution of the salt.

342. Mercurous Salts.—The most important mercurous salt is mercurous chloride (calomel, Hg_2Cl_2). It is tasteless, odorless and insoluble in water and is, even now, largely used in medicine. It is commonly prepared by sublimation from an intimate mixture of mercury and mercuric chloride.

(*a.*) Mercurous nitrate $[Hg_2(NO_3)_2]$ is formed by the action of cold, dilute HNO_3 on Hg. Mercurous sulphate (Hg_2SO_4) is formed by heating concentrated H_2SO_4 with an excess of Hg or by precipitating $Hg_2(NO_3)_2$ with H_2SO_4.

(*b.*) Hg_2Br_2 may be precipitated by adding HBr or KBr to a solution of $Hg_2(NO_3)_2$. Similarly, Hg_2I_2 may be precipitated by adding KI to a solution of $Hg_2(NO_3)_2$. It is also formed when iodine is rubbed with the right proportion of Hg, a small quantity of C_2H_6O being added. It is a green powder and gradually decomposes into HgI_2 and Hg.

Experiment 282.—Place a drop of a solution of $Hg_2(NO_3)_2$ or of corrosive sublimate upon a clean copper coin. Rub the drop over the coin and Hg will be deposited upon the Cu.

343. Mercuric Salts.—Mercuric chloride (corrosive sublimate, $HgCl_2$) is a powerful poison. It coagulates albumen, forming an insoluble compound, in consequence of which the white of eggs (§ 223) furnishes the best antidote in case of poisoning by this salt. It unites with many other organic substances to form insoluble, stable compounds and is used in preserving animal and vegetable tissues from decay. It is somewhat soluble in cold water and easily soluble in hot water. It is prepared by subliming a mixture of mercuric sulphate and sodium chloride.

(*a.*) Botanical and zoological specimens are preserved from decay and from the attacks of insects by brushing over them a solution of $HgCl_2$ in C_2H_6O.

(*b.*) Mercuric nitrate [$Hg(NO_3)_2$] is prepared by boiling Hg in HNO_3 until a portion of the liquid no longer gives a precipitate with NaCl. Mercuric sulphate ($HgSO_4$) is prepared by heating Hg with at least $1\frac{1}{2}$ times its weight of H_2SO_4. It is decomposed by heat into Hg_2SO_4, SO_2, O and Hg.

(*c.*) Hg combines directly with Br, forming $HgBr_2$ and evolving heat. When Hg is rubbed in a mortar with I and a small quantity of C_2H_6O, it forms HgI_2 and evolves heat. It may be precipitated by adding KI to a solution of $HgCl_2$. It is a scarlet powder. (See Exp. 8.)

EXERCISES.

1. An old process of preparing Hg_2Cl_2 was to sublime a mixture that gave this reaction: $HgSO_4 + Hg + 2NaCl = Na_2SO_4 + Hg_2Cl_2$. (*a.*) Write this equation in full molecular symbols. (*b.*) What weight of metallic Hg is needed thus to combine with 1 *Kg.* of NaCl?

2. Is $Hg(CN)_2$ a mercurous or a mercuric compound? What is its name?

3. Is cinnabar a mercurous or a mercuric compound?

4. Zinc nitrate and potassium carbonate react as follows:
$$Zn(NO_3)_2 + K_2CO_3 = ZnCO_3 + 2KNO_3.$$
How much $Zn(NO_3)_2$ is required to give 103.17 *g.* of $ZnCO_3$?

5. How much $ZnCO_3$ may be obtained from 156 *g.* of $Zn(NO_3)_2$?

6. How much K_2CO_3 is needed to decompose 75 *g.* of $Zn(NO_3)_2$?

7. What quantity of KNO_3 will result?

8. How much K_2CO_3 must be used to obtain 54 *g.* of $ZnCO_3$?

9. How much KNO_3 will be produced?

10. It is said that 1 *sq. m.* of leaf in sunlight will decompose 1.108 *l.* of CO_2 *per* hour. (*a.*) What weight of C will be assimilated in an hour by 1,000,000 trees, each of which has 100,000 leaves, each leaf measuring 25 *sq. cm.*? (*b.*) What will be the volume of the carbon assimilated, assuming that its specific gravity is 1.6?

CHAPTER XX.

METALS OF THE ALUMINUM AND CERIUM GROUPS.

☞ ALUMINUM: *symbol,* Al ; *specific gravity, 2.6 ; atomic weight, 27.3 m. c.; quantivalence of the double atom* (Al$_2$), *6.*

344. Source.—Aluminum (or aluminium) ranks third among the elements and first among the metals in quantity and extent of distribution. It is not found native; its oxide is found in the minerals emery and corundum, among the purer varieties of which are the ruby and the sapphire; its fluoride, in cryolite; its silicates, in the feldspars and micas, the disintegration of which, by weathering, gives rise to the several kinds of clay. It is also found in the topaz, emerald and garnet. It constitutes about one-twelfth of the earth's crust, and is contained in all fertile soils but is not taken up by any plants except a few cryptogams.

345. Preparation.—Notwithstanding the abundance of aluminum compounds, no cheap method of preparing the metal has yet been found. It is generally prepared by fusing together, in a reverberatory furnace, 100 *Kg.* of an artificial double chloride of aluminum and sodium with 35 *Kg.* of sodium, adding 40 *Kg.* of cryolite to act as a flux.

346. Properties.—Aluminum is a remarkably light and sonorous metal. It is of a bluish white color and susceptible of a bright polish. It is tenacious and very malleable and ductile. It is best worked at a temperature of from 100°C. to 150°C. It does not readily oxidize in air, is insoluble in nitric acid and is not easily soluble in sulphuric acid. Its best solvent is hydrochloric acid although it dissolves easily in boiling solutions of the alkali hydrates.

347. Uses.—The lightness, lustre, strength, unalterability in air and hydrogen sulphide, ease of working, sonorous and non-poisonous qualities of aluminum would lead to an extensive use of the metal were it not for its high price. It is used chiefly in making delicate balances, light weights, opera glasses and other instruments calling especially for lightness and moderate strength. Aluminum bronze (90 *per cent.* Cu + 10 *per cent.* Al) is very hard and malleable, yields fine castings, has the tenacity of steel, the color of gold and takes a high polish.

348. Aluminum Oxide.—Aluminum oxide (alumina, Al_2O_3) occurs native in corundum, ruby, sapphire, *etc.* Its crystals are second in hardness only to the diamond. An impure, granular variety is called emery.

349. Other Aluminum Compounds.—The most important of the aluminum compounds are the silicates, some of which have been mentioned. Common alum is a double sulphate of aluminum and potassium $[Al_2(SO_4)_3 + K_2SO_4 + 24H_2O]$. Ammonium alum, now becoming common, differs in composition by having ammonium sulphate $[(NH_4)_2SO_4]$ in place of the potassium sulphate. Cryolite is a double fluoride of aluminum and sodium (Al_2F_6 + 6NaF). A deposit 80 feet thick and 300 feet long is known on the west coast of Greenland.

☞ INDIUM: *symbol,* In; *specific gravity,* 7.4; *atomic weight,* 113.4 *m. c.*

350. Indium.—Indium is a rare metal discovered in blende by means of the spectroscope in the year 1863. It is white, non-crystalline, easily malleable and softer than lead. It dissolves slowly in hydrochloric or dilute sulphuric acid but easily in nitric acid.

☞ GALLIUM: *symbol*, Ga; *specific gravity*, 5.9; *atomic weight*, 69.8 *m. c.*

351. Gallium.—Gallium is a rare metal, discovered in blende by means of the spectroscope in the year 1875. It is bluish white, tough, may be cut with a knife and fuses at the remarkably low temperature of about 30°C. It is not easily soluble in nitric acid but dissolves readily in dilute hydrochloric acid or an alkaline hydrate solution with the evolution of hydrogen.

352. The Aluminum Group.—The metals of this group form feebly basic sesquioxides. Their sulphates form double salts with the sulphates of the alkali metals. Common alum is a familiar example of these double salts. They crystallize in regular octohedrons.

(*a.*) The apparent quantivalence of these elements may be seen in the symbols of their compounds, in which the double atom of each metal acts as a hexad. Some of these known compounds are symbolized thus:

Al_2O_3	Al_2S_3	Al_2Cl_6	$Al_2(SO_4)_3$	$Al_2(NO_3)_6$
In_2O_3	In_2S_3	In_2Cl_6	$In_2(SO_4)_3$	$In_2(NO_3)_6$
Ga_2O_3	Ga_2S_3	Ga_2Cl_6	$Ga_2(SO_4)_3$	$Ga_2(NO_3)_6$

353. The Cerium Group.—This group consists of six rare metals, the separation of which, one from the other, is very difficult. Two of them, erbium and terbium, have not yet been isolated. The metals of this group are contained, chiefly as silicates, in several rare minerals found in Scandinavia, Siberia and Greenland. Cerium is the best known. It is malleable and ductile and, when it is scraped with a knife or struck with a piece of flint, the metallic particles struck off burn with great brilliancy. Cerium burns in a flame with a light more brilliant than that of magnesium. It forms both cerous and ceric compounds. When these metals are present, they are easily distinguished by means of the spectroscope.

(*a.*) The following table exhibits the leading known properties and compounds of these metals:

Elements.	Symbol.	Atomic weight in m. criths.	Specific gravity.	Compounds.					
Cerium........	Ce	141.2	6.7	Ce_2O_3 Ce_2O_2	Ce_2S_3	$CeCl_3$	$Ce_2(SO_4)_3$ $Ce(SO_4)_2$	$Ce(NO_3)_3$	$Ce_2(CO_3)_3$
Didymium....	Di	147	6.5	Di_2O_3	Di_2S_3	$DiCl_3$	$Di_2(SO_4)_3$	$Di(NO_3)_3$	$Di_2(CO_3)_3$
Erbium........	Er	160(?)	....	Er_2O_3	......	......	......	......	......
Terbium.......	Tr	96	....	Tr_2O_3	......	......	$Tr_2(SO_4)_3$	......	......
Lanthanum...	La	139	6.1	La_2O_3	La_2S_3	$LaCl_3$	$La_2(SO_4)_3$	$La(NO_3)_3$	$La_2(CO_3)_3$
Yttrium......	Y	92.5	....	Y_2O_3	Y_2S_3	YCl_3	$Y_2(SO_4)_3$	$Y(NO_3)_3$	$Y_2(CO_3)_3$

EXERCISES.

1. (*a*) Assuming Al''', write the graphic symbol for Al_2O_3. (*b.*) Assuming Al''''. (*c.*) Assuming Al''.

2. (*a.*) How many cu. cm. of O may be obtained by the electrolysis of 10 g. of H_2O? (*b.*) How many of H?

3. Calculate the weight of air required to burn a ton of coal, having the percentage composition: C, 88.42 ; H, 5.61 ; O, etc., 5.97.

4. Write equations for the following reactions: (*a.*) Copper and nitric acid yield copper nitrate, nitric oxide and water. (*b.*) Mercury and sulphuric acid yield mercuric sulphate, sulphurous anhydride and water.

5. The symbol for water was formerly written HO and (for some years subsequently) H_2O_2. What inconsistency do you see in these symbols other than any based on atomic weights?

6. (*a.*) What would be a systematic chemical name for microcosmic salt ($NaNH_4HPO_4 + 4H_2O$)? (*b.*). What weight of H in 10 g. of this salt?

7. Write the graphic symbol for Al_2F_6, assuming the metal to be a tetrad.

CHAPTER XXI.

METALS OF THE IRON GROUP.

SECTION I.

IRON.

☞ *Symbol*, Fe ; *specific gravity, 7.8 ; atomic weight, 56 m. c.; quantivalence, 2, 4 and 6.*

354. Occurrence.—Iron, the most important of all the metals, is seldom found native. Metallic iron of meteoric origin has been found. This element is widely distributed, traces of it being found in the blood of animals, in the ashes of most plants, in spring, river and ocean waters, and, in fact, in nearly all natural substances. Its ores are numerous, abundant and comparatively pure.

(*a*.) The most important iron ores are specular iron or hematite (Fe_2O_3); limonite or brown hematite [$Fe_4O_3(HO)_6$] : magnetite or magnetic iron (Fe_3O_4) ; spathic iron ($FeCO_3$) and clay iron-stone or black-band iron-stone, which is a spathic iron containing clay or sand with other substances and generally found as nodules or bands in the coal measures.

(*b*.) The value of an iron ore often depends more upon the nature of its impurities than upon its percentage of Fe.

355. Calcination.—The hydrate, the carbonate and the "black-band" iron ores are generally prepared for smelting by roasting them. In this way the water and carbon dioxide are expelled, the ores are oxidized and rendered more porous, while any sulphides that may be present are oxidized and the sulphur driven off.

356. Preparation; Direct Process.—The native or artificial oxides, are sometimes reduced in "bloomery forges" of simple construction. The broken ore is heated with charcoal, the fire being supplied with a hot-air blast. The charcoal deoxidizes the ore, the reduced iron collects as a pasty mass called "the bloom" which separates from the fusible mass called "slag." The "bloom" needs only to be hammered to yield a good quality of wrought iron. The process is simple and time-honored but expensive on account of the quantity of fuel consumed and of iron lost in the slag.

357. Preparation; Indirect Process.—The indirect process of forming wrought or malleable iron consists of two distinct stages: *1st*, the production of cast iron from the ore; *2d*, the production of wrought iron from the cast iron.

358. Cast Iron.—This is a carbonized, fusible product of the blast furnace, which will soon be described. The preparation of cast iron involves four steps. The first is the preliminary calcination of the ore for the purposes mentioned in § 355. With some ores, this step is not necessary; in other cases, it is effected in the upper part of the blast furnace. The second step is the reduction of the oxide to the metallic state by heating it with carbon. The third step is the separation of the silicious or calcareous impurities of the ore by fusion with some other substance, called a flux, to form a fusible slag. The fourth step is the carbonizing and melting of the iron. This addition of the carbon renders the product more easily fusible. The melted iron is finally run into rough moulds and forms semi-cylindrical masses, known as pig-iron.

359. The Blast Furnace.—The blast furnace

§ 359   IRON.   281

(Fig. 113) is a shaft of fire-brick and masonry, often cased in iron plate. It is from 50 to 90 feet in height and from 14 to 18 feet in diameter at the "belly" or widest part. Alternate layers of coal, coke, flux and ore are introduced from above as the heated mass settles in the furnace and

FIG. 113.

the molten iron and slag are drawn off below. With ores that contain siliceous impurities, the flux is limestone; with ores that contain calcareous impurities, the flux is clay or of a siliceous character. The fusible silicate formed by the union of the flux and the impurities of the ore constitute the slag. A blast of hot air is forced in at the hearth, through pipes, *t*, called *tuyères* (pronounced *tweers*) and the combustion thus sustained and invigorated. The melted iron settles to the crucible or lowest part of the hearth while the melted slag floats upon its surface and overflows a dam in an almost continuous stream. When the crucible is full of molten metal, the latter is drawn off through a tapping hole which is, at other times, stopped with sand.

(*a*.) The throat of the blast furnace is closed with a cup and cone arrangement, as shown in Fig. 113. The cone, *b*, is lowered by a chain when a charge is to be introduced. When *b* is raised against the cup, *a*, the throat of the furnace is closed and the escape of the blast furnace gases into the air is prevented. These gases consist of very hot hydrocarbons with H, CO, CO_2, N, *etc*. These heated gases, some of which are combustible, are conveyed by pipes from the throat of the furnace and utilized for heating the tuyères and the boilers for steam power purposes.

(*b*.) The chemical changes that take place in the blast furnace are of great interest and have been carefully studied, but our knowledge of them is still far from complete. At the lower part, where the temperature is highest, the fuel burns to CO_2; in the widest part of the furnace, the CO_2 is reduced by the glowing C to CO ; at a point still further up, where the temperature is from 600°C. to 900°C. the CO reduces the ore to a spongy mass of metallic iron. As the spongy metal descends to the bottom part of the furnace, near the belly where the temperature is from 1000°C. to 1400°C., it takes up C, becoming thus more fusible, melts completely and runs down into the crucible below the level of the mouth of the *tuyères*. In the meantime, the fusible slag has been formed and melted. It then floats on the surface of the heavier iron in the crucible and thus protects the metal from the oxidizing action of the blast.

(*c*.) Cast iron is generally contaminated with S, Si, P, and frequently with Mn, and contains from two to six *per cent*. of C.

(*d*.) Pig iron includes *white cast iron, gray cast iron* and several intermediate varieties called *mottled cast iron*. White cast iron contains all of its C in chemical union. When it is dissolved in HCl or H_2SO_4, various hydrocarbons are formed that give a disagreeable odor to the H evolved. In gray cast iron, part of the C crystallizes out in cooling, forming graphite, which is left in the form of black scales when the iron is dissolved in an acid. White cast iron contracts on solidifying ; gray cast iron expands on solidifying and is, therefore, the better adapted for foundry use although it is less easily melted. *Spiegeleisen* is a variety of white cast iron very rich in C, and containing Mn. It is very hard and crystalline and is used in the Bessemer process of steel manufacture. When it contains 25 *per cent.* or more of Mn it becomes granular and is called *ferromanganese*.

360. Wrought Iron. — Cast iron is changed to wrought iron by a process called puddling, in which most of the carbon, silicon, sulphur and phosphorus of the cast iron is burned out. Wrought iron contains less than half of one *per cent.* of carbon, its malleability increasing and its fusibility decreasing as the quantity of carbon diminishes. It may be welded at a red heat.

(*a.*) A puddling furnace is shown in elevation in Fig. 114 and in

FIG. 114.

section in Fig. 115. The charge of pig iron and, generally, a quantity of iron scale or other iron oxide, are placed in the bed, h, separated from the fire grate by the fire bridge, b, and from the chimney by the flue bridge, d. A strong draft is furnished by the chimney and controlled by a damper at the top of the chimney, which damper may be opened or closed by the workman. After the charge has

FIG. 115.

been melted, it is vigorously stirred or puddled, and the C, S, Si and P thus removed. The iron becomes less easily fusible by the decarbonizing. The pasty mass is then carried from the furnace, the fusible slag removed and the porous Fe welded into a solid mass by hammering or squeezing.

Experiment 283.—Place about 15 $g.$ of pulverized Fe_2O_3 in the bulb of the tube, c, Fig. 116. Pass a current of dry H through the bulb tube.

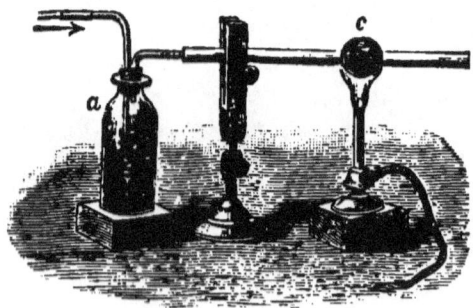

FIG. 116.

When all of the air has been driven from the apparatus, heat the oxide to redness. When it has been reduced to a black powder of metallic Fe, remove the lamp and allow the contents of the bulb to cool *in a current of* H.

$$Fe_2O_3 + 3H_2 = Fe_2 + 3H_2O.$$

This black powder may be set on fire by a lighted splinter. It oxidizes so easily, that it will take fire if emptied from the bulb tube into the air while it is still hot.

361. Properties of Iron.—Iron may be prepared in a pure state by reducing the oxide with hydrogen or carbon monoxide. In the compact state, it is ductile, malleable, tenacious and highly magnetic. It does not oxidize in dry air at ordinary temperatures. When heated in air, an oxide forms. This "scale oxide" is beaten off by hammering and may be found in considerable quantities about a blacksmith's anvil. Iron oxidizes or rusts rapidly in moist air. It is readily acted upon by dilute hydrochloric, nitric or sulphuric acid. It fuses at a white heat but softens before it melts. In this softened state it may be welded. Sand or borax is sprinkled upon the heated surfaces that are to be united and a fusible slag is thus formed with the coating film of oxide. When the two pieces of iron are then hammered together, the slag is driven out leaving clean surfaces of iron in contact. The blows of the hammer bring the metallic particles within the range of molecular attraction (Ph., § 46, *a*), cohesion binds them fast and the iron is welded.

(*a.*) Commercial iron is never pure. If P is present as an impurity, the iron is brittle when cold and is said to be "cold-short." The presence of S renders the iron brittle when hot; the iron is then said to be "red short."

362. Oxides of Iron.—Iron forms three well-known oxides; ferrous oxide (iron monoxide, FeO), ferric oxide (iron sesquioxide, Fe_2O_3) and ferroso-ferric oxide (magnetic oxide of iron, Fe_3O_4). The ferric and magnetic oxides are found native as iron ores.

(*a.*) FeO may be prepared by heating ferrous oxalate in a close vessel, or by passing H over Fe_2O_3 heated to 300°C. If exposed to the air within a few hours after its preparation, it oxidizes so rapidly as to take fire.

(*b.*) Fe_2O_3 is one of the most important iron ores. This oxide is prepared artificially for use as a paint. A fine variety is known as *jeweller's rouge*, and is used for polishing glass and metals. Another artificial variety is called *crocus*, and is also used for polishing metals.

(*c.*) Fe_3O_4 is found in large quantities as the richest of iron ores. Many specimens attract iron and are called loadstones (Ph., § 302). Scale oxide is chiefly Fe_3O_4. We may consider Fe_3O_4 as a mixture or compound of FeO and Fe_2O_3.

Experiment 284.—Cover a teaspoonful of fine iron filings with three or four times its volume of dilute H_2SO_4. When the evolution of H ceases, pour off the clear liquor, add a few drops of strong HNO_3 and boil the liquid. The yellowish-red color is due to the presence of ferric sulphate. Add NH_4HO to the solution and shake the liquids together. A red precipitate of ferric hydrate will be formed; it may be collected upon a filter.

363. Iron Hydrates.—*Ferrous hydrate* (FeH_2O_2) is obtained by treating a solution of a pure ferrous salt with potassium or sodium hydrate in absence of air. The precipitate thus formed is an unstable, white powder, which rapidly oxidizes with change of color, evolution of heat and, sometimes, incandescence when exposed to the air. *Ferric hydrate* ($Fe_2H_6O_6$) is prepared by precipitating a moderately dilute solution of a ferric salt (*e.g.*, Fe_2Cl_6) with an excess of ammonia water. When freshly prepared, it is one of the best antidotes for arsenic (§ 247).

364. Iron Sulphides.—Iron and sulphur form two well-known compounds, iron monosulphide (FeS) and iron disulphide (FeS_2). Iron monosulphide is formed by direct union of its constituents. A roll of brimstone may be made to penetrate a red hot plate of steel or wrought iron with formation of melted sulphide. It is generally prepared by gradually throwing a mixture of three parts of iron filings and two parts of sulphur into a red hot crucible. It is the cheapest source of hydrogen sulphide and, hence, very important. Iron disulphide occurs widely distributed in nature as pyrite (or iron pyrites). It is largely used in the manufacture of sulphuric acid and ferrous sulphate.

365. Iron Salts.—Iron forms two well defined series of salts. In the ferrous series, the iron atom acts as a dyad as it does in ferrous oxide. In the ferric series, the iron double atom $(Fe_2)^{VI}$ acts as a hexad as it does in ferric oxide. (See also Ex. 2, page 289.)

(*a*.) Solutions of ferrous salts readily absorb O and precipitate ferric salts unless an excess of acid is present. They, therefore, act as powerful reducing agents and are largely used as such in the laboratory and the arts.

(*b*.) The ferric salts are readily reduced to the corresponding ferrous compounds.

366. Iron Chlorides.—The halogen elements form, with iron, both ferrous and ferric compounds. These series are well typified by ferrous and ferric chlorides. *Ferrous chloride* ($FeCl_2$) is best prepared by passing a current of hydrochloric acid gas over an excess of red hot iron filings or wire. *Ferric chloride* (Fe_2Cl_6) may be prepared by passing a current of chlorine through a solution of ferrous chloride until the solution smells strongly of the gas and then displacing the excess of chlorine by passing a current of carbon dioxide through the warm liquid. This solution, when concentrated, has a dark brown color and an oily consistency.

Experiment 285.—Dip a piece of cotton cloth into a solution of nut-galls and allow it to dry; dip it into a solution of green vitriol and hang it up in a moist atmosphere. It will be *permanently* colored by the precipitation of an insoluble iron tannate.

367. Iron Sulphates, etc. — *Ferrous sulphate* (green vitriol, $FeSO_4$, $7H_2O$) is made in immense quantities by exposing pyrite (FeS_2) to the action of the atmosphere, as an incidental product in the manufacture of copper sulphate or by dissolving iron in dilute sulphuric acid. It is largely used in the arts. *Ferric sulphate* [$Fe_2(SO_4)_3$] is prepared by the action of nitric acid upon an acidulated solution of ferrous sulphate:

$$6FeSO_4 + 3H_2SO_4 + 2HNO_3 = 3Fe_2(SO_4)_3 + 2NO + 4H_2O.$$

(*a.*) Ferrous nitrate [$Fe(NO_3)_2$] is a very soluble, unstable compound. Ferric nitrate [$Fe_2(NO_3)_6$] is prepared by dissolving Fe in HNO_3. It is largely used as a mordant in dyeing and calico printing. Ferrous carbonate ($FeCO_3$) is found as an iron ore.

368. Iron Cyanides. — Iron unites with cyanogen to form ferrous and ferric cyanides. The most important iron cyanides, however, are double compounds. When crude potash (K_2CO_3) is fused with nitrogenous organic matter, such as horn, feathers, dried blood, leather clippings, *etc.*, in the presence of iron filings, the fused mass leached with water and the liquid evaporated, large yellow crystals are formed. These crystals are *potassium ferrocyanide* [$K_8(CN)_{12}Fe_2$, $3H_2O$], better known as *yellow prussiate of potash*. This compound is important as it serves as the point of departure for the preparation of nearly all the cyanogen compounds. It may also be formed by the addition of a ferrous salt to an aqueous solution of potassium cyanide. $12KCN + 2FeSO_4 = K_8(CN)_{12}Fe_2 + 2K_2SO_4$. The tendency to form this salt is so great that metallic iron is rapidly dissolved when heated in such a solution of potassium cyanide. When a current of chlorine is passed into a solution of potassium ferrocyanide, the reaction yields *potassium ferricyanide* [$K_6(CN)_{12}Fe_2$] or *red prussiate of potash*. The class of compounds known as Prussian-blues are chiefly compounds of ferrous and ferric cyanides, generally united with potassium.

Experiment 286. — Half fill each of two test glasses with a very dilute solution of $FeSO_4$ and each of two other glasses with a similar solution of $Fe_2(SO_4)_3$. Prepare a dilute solution of $K_8Cy_{12}Fe_2$ and one of $K_6Cy_{12}Fe_2$. Add a drop of $K_6Cy_{12}Fe_2$ to one of the glasses of $Fe_2(SO_4)_3$; a blue precipitate will be formed and color the liquid. In similar manner, add $K_8Cy_{12}Fe_2$ to $FeSO_4$; no color will appear. In similar manner, add $K_6Cy_{12}Fe_2$ to $FeSO_4$; the blue color will appear. In similar manner, add $K_6Cy_{12}Fe_2$ to $Fe_2(SO_4)_3$; no color will appear. In the name of $K_8Cy_{12}Fe_2$, the pupil will notice a contraction for ferrous; a similar contraction for ferric appears in the name of $K_6Cy_{12}Fe_2$. When, in this experiment, we brought two -*ous* or two -*ic* compounds together, no color was produced. When an -*ous* compound and an -*ic* compound were brought together, a blue color was formed. Potassium ferro- and ferricyanides act thus with all ferrous and ferric salts and may, consequently, be used as tests to detect the presence of these salts in any solution or to distinguish between them.

Experiment 287.—Soak a piece of cotton cloth in a solution of $Fe_2(SO_4)_3$ and then dip it into an acidulated solution of $K_8Cy_{12}Fe_2$. Prussian blue is precipitated upon the cloth which is thus colored.

EXERCISES.

1. Name the compounds symbolized as follows: $FeBr_2$; Fe_2Br_6; $K_8C_{12}N_{12}Fe_2$: $Fe_2(SO_4)_3$.
2. State two things indicated by the following graphic symbol:

$$Cl-\underset{\underset{Cl}{|}}{\overset{\overset{Cl}{|}}{Fe}}-\underset{\underset{Cl}{|}}{\overset{\overset{Cl}{|}}{Fe}}-Cl.$$

3. A certain iron oxide has a molecular weight of 232 *m. c.* and contains 27.6 *per cent.* of O. What is the symbol?
4. (*a.*) What weight of FeS will be needed to yield 1 *l.* of H_2S? (*b.*) How much air will be required to burn the H_2S?
5. What weight of marble is needed to convert a ton of soda crystals into bicarbonate of soda?
6. How many liters of air will be necessary to burn a liter each of (*a.*) marsh gas, (*b.*) olefiant gas and (*c.*) acetylene?
7. The vapor density of NH_4Cl is one-fourth of the number of microcriths in its molecular weight. (*a.*) Why is it said to be abnormal? (*b.*) Can you suggest an explanation of the variation?

Section II.

STEEL.

369. Steel.—Steel is intermediate between cast iron and wrought iron in respect to properties and chemical composition. It contains from 0.7 to 2 *per cent.* of carbon. Its most characteristic property is that of acquiring remarkable hardness by heating and quickly cooling as by plunging into water. Steel thus hardened cannot be worked with a file and is very brittle and elastic. The hardness and brittleness are lessened by tempering, which process consists in heating the steel to 220°C. — 331°C. and then cooling it quickly. The hardest temper is obtained at the lowest temperature. The workman judges the temperature by observing the tints on the surface of the metal. These colors are caused by different thicknesses of the oxide formed.

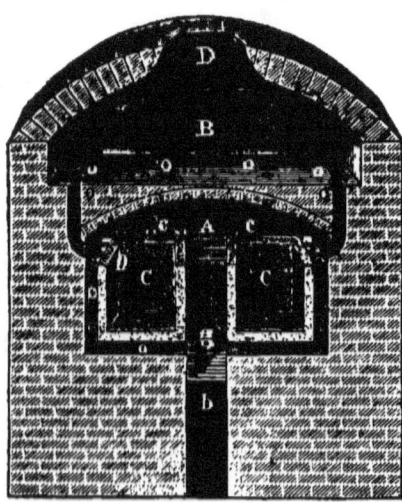

FIG. 117.

370. The Cementation Process. — A few years ago, the only method of making steel was to decarbonize cast iron in the puddling furnace and then to recarbonize the wrought iron in the cementation furnace (Fig. 117.) The furnace contains two square boxes, *c*, made of infusible fire clay, into which are put bars of wrought iron packed in soot or powdered charcoal. Six or seven tons of iron are put into each box. A fire is built on the hearth, *g*, and the boxes kept at a temperature of 1000°C. or 1200°C. for from seven to ten days. At the end of the process, it is found that the metal has become finer grained, more brittle, more fusible, that its surface has a blistered appearance, whence the name, "blister steel," and that carbon has penetrated the metal, *although the iron has not been melted or the carbon vaporized.* Several hypotheses have been advanced to account for the phenomena involved, but none of them is satisfactory.

371. The Bessemer Process.—In this process, steel is made by decarbonizing cast iron by a current of air forced through the melted metal in an egg-shaped vessel called the converter (Fig. 118.) The converter is made of iron plates lined with infusible material. The bottom is a shallow wind box, *e*, from which numerous small openings lead into the converter. The vessel is supported upon trunnions, one of which, *i*, is hollow and connected with the wind or tuyère-box. When the interior of the converter has been heated to whiteness, it is turned upon its trunnions until the line, *ac*, is horizontal. Melted cast iron is then run through the mouth into the belly, *abc*. The air blast is then turned on through *i*, the converter raised into

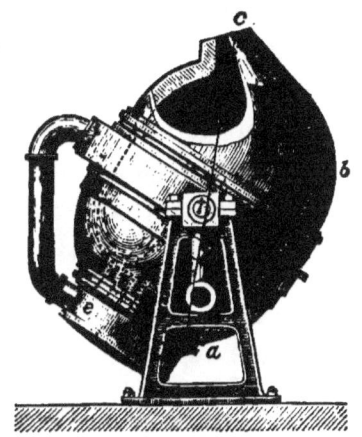

Fig. 118.

an upright position, the compressed air bubbling through the molten metal, burning out the carbon and silicon and combining with part of the iron. This combustion in the converter causes intense heat which keeps the iron melted despite its approach to the less easily fusible condition of wrought iron. During this time, the flame that rushes from the mouth of the converter is accompanied by a magnificent display of sparks due to the combustion of iron particles (Exps. 38–40). When this pyrotechnic exhibition has continued for six or eight minutes, the exact moment being indicated to the trained eye of the overseer by the appearance of the flame, the converter is turned until the melted iron leaves the tuyère openings uncovered and the air blast is stopped. The decarbonized iron is now recarbonized by the addition of a carefully determined quantity of spiegeleisen. The molten mass is poured into a ladle and thence into moulds, and the cast steel worked up under the hammer or in the rolling mill. In less than half an hour, from five to twelve tons of cast iron has been converted into steel.

(*a.*) All of the movements of the converter, ladle, cranes, *etc.*, are produced by hydraulic power and controlled by a workman at "the piano," as the assemblage of wheels and levers is called.

(*b.*) Steel might be produced by stopping the oxidation before all of the C of the cast iron had been burned out. But the difficulties arising from too nearly complete oxidation and the practical impossibility of making successive "blows" yield the same quality of steel led to the adoption of the present plan. Bessemer steel is largely used in the construction of railway tracks, bridges, *etc.*

372. The Siemens-Martin Process. — In this process, hydrocarbon gases and air are heated, mixed and burned, the flame passing over a hearth containing a charge of cast iron and wrought iron scrap mixed in definite proportions. The melted metal is run from the hearth into a ladle containing the proper amount of spiegel or ferro-manganese, after which the steel is ready for casting. The sides and top of the furnace, the exposed parts of the flues, and the hearth are made of such highly infusible material as silica brick.

373. Crucible Steel.—A very fine quality of steel is made for edge tools by fusing, in graphite crucibles, a fine quality of wrought iron with powdered charcoal. The crucibles are closely covered and heated in a coke fire. The steel is cast into ingots and worked into bars under the hammer.

374. Malleable Iron. — Intermediate between cast iron and wrought iron is an article, known in commerce as "malleable iron." Small castings are made of white cast iron for a great variety of purposes, such as for harness, wagons, agricultural implements, *etc.* These castings are packed with iron scale or oxide in "annealing boxes" and then heated to a high temperature. The carbon of the cast iron is thus removed in great part and the material changed from white, hard and brittle cast iron to black, soft and tough "malleable iron." Articles thus made are nearly as tough as they would be if made of wrought iron and much less expensive. Compare the process with the cementation process for making steel.

EXERCISES.

1. Give the names and atomic weights of the elements represented by the following symbols: Fe, Mg, Hg, Zn, Ca, C, Cl, I, P, K, N, Na, S, Ag, Br, Cu, Fl, H, Pb, O, Al, Sb, Si.

Equation	H_2	+	Cl_2	=	2HCl
Names of molecules.	Hydrogen		Chlorine	Yield	Hydrochloric acid.
Nos. " "	1		1	"	2
Weight " molecule.	2 m. c.		71 m. c.	"	36.5 m. c.
Total weights......	2 m. c. used.		71 m. c. used.	"	73 m. c. obtained.
Gaseous volumes....	2 unit volumes "		2 unit volumes "	"	4 unit volumes "
Laboratory Exp.....	500 cu. cm.		500 cu. cm.	"	1 liter.

2. According to the above or a similar schedule, write out the following equations:

(a.) $2H_2O + 2Cl_2 = 4HCl + O_2$.
(b.) $2CO + O_2 = 2CO_2$.
(c.) $CO_2 + C(solid) = 2CO$.
(d.) $2NH_3 = N_2 + 3H_2$.
(e.) $2NH_3 + 3Cl_2 = N_2 + 6HCl$.
(f.) $NH_4NO_3(solid) = N_2O + 2H_2O$.
(g.) $MnO_2 + 4HCl = MnCl_2 + Cl_2 + 2H_2O$.
(h.) $SO_2 + 2H_2O + Cl_2 = H_2SO_4 + 2HCl$.
(i.) $2MnO_2 + 2H_2SO_4 = 2MnSO_4 + 2H_2O + O_2$.

3. Why is it not practicable to obtain more than a small quantity of mixed H and O by electric sparks in an atmosphere of steam?

Section III.

MANGANESE, COBALT AND NICKEL.

☞ MANGANESE: *symbol*, Mn ; *specific gravity, 8 ; atomic weight, 54.8 m. c. ; quantivalence, 2 (4 and 6).*

375. Manganese.—The principal source of manganese is the dioxide (MnO_2) which is found in nature as the mineral pyrolusite. Among the other manganese ores are braunite (Mn_2O_3) and hausmanite (Mn_3O_4). The metal is seldom prepared but may be obtained by heating one of the oxides with carbon at an intense white heat for several hours. It is very hard and brittle, easily soluble in dilute acids, and decomposes warm water with the evolution of hydrogen. When pure, it is almost as infusible as platinum and oxidizes easily in the air. It is best kept in petroleum. It is feebly magnetic (Ph., § 310) and forms a beautiful alloy with copper.

376. Oxides.—At least five distinct manganese oxides are known:

(*a.*) Manganese monoxide (manganous oxide, MnO) is powerfully basic.

(*b.*) Red oxide of manganese (mangano-manganic oxide, Mn_3O_4) may be considered a compound of MnO and Mn_2O_3. It is analogous to magnetic iron ore.

(*c.*) Manganese sesquioxide (manganic oxide, Mn_2O_3) is isomorphous with Al_2O_3 and Fe_2O_3. The corresponding hydrate [$Mn_2O_3(HO)_2$] is found in nature as manganite.

(*d.*) Manganese dioxide (manganese peroxide, black oxide of manganese, MnO_2) is the most important manganese ore. It is used in preparing O and Cl, and in coloring glass. At a bright red heat, it yields up O and is reduced to Mn_3O_4.

(e.) Manganic anhydride (MnO_3) and manganic acid (H_2MnO_4) have not yet been isolated but several manganates (e. g., K_2MnO_4) are well known. K_2MnO_4 is isomorphous with K_2SO_4.

(f.) Manganese heptoxide (Mn_2O_7) is an anhydride, yielding permanganic acid ($H_2Mn_2O_8$) when brought into contact with H_2O.

Experiment 288.—Put a small quantity of MnO_2 into an ignition tube and add enough H_2SO_4 to wet it thoroughly. Arrange the tube as shown in Exp. 56. Heat gently, collect the gas and find out what it is.

Experiment 289.—Dissolve 0.5 g. of oxalic acid ($C_2H_2O_4$) crystals in 50 cu. cm. of H_2O; add 5 cu. cm. of H_2SO_4; warm to about 60°C. To this colorless solution, add, drop by drop, a solution of $K_2Mn_2O_8$. The $K_2Mn_2O_8$ gives up O and converts the $C_2H_2O_4$ to H_2O and CO_2 and is reduced to $MnSO_4$ and K_2SO_4, in which process, its rich color is destroyed. If an excess of the potassium permanganate be added, it will not be decolorized.

Experiment 290.—Repeat the last experiment, using $FeSO_4$ instead of $C_2H_2O_4$. The $K_2Mn_2O_8$ oxidizes the ferrous to ferric sulphate.

Note.—Knowing the reactions for these experiments and the quantity of $K_2Mn_2O_8$ used, before the decoloration ceases, the quantity of oxidizable matter ($C_2H_2O_4$ or $FeSO_4$) present is easily calculated (quantitative analysis).

Experiment 291.—Mix some $K_2Mn_2O_8$ and BaO_2 in a mortar. Transfer the mixture to a flask and moisten it with H_2SO_4. A starch and potassium iodide test paper held at the mouth of the flask will be colored blue. *Explain the discoloration.*

377. Manganese Salts.—A few years ago, the manganates and permanganates were found only in the laboratory where they were used as oxidizing agents. They are now manufactured on the large scale for use as disinfectants.

☞ COBALT: *symbol,* Co; *specific gravity,* 8.6; *atomic weight,* 58.6 m. c.

378. Cobalt.—Cobalt is not found free, except in meteoric matter. Its ores are not widely distributed. The metal may be obtained from an artificially prepared oxide by reduction with hydrogen or from a chloride by ignition. It is harder than iron and melts more easily. It is magnetic, malleable and very tough. When pure, it is silvery white.

(*a.*) Cobalt has three oxides, the monoxide (cobaltous oxide, CoO), the sesquioxide (cobaltic oxide, Co_2O_3) and an intermediate compound, cobaltous-cobaltic oxide (Co_3O_4) which corresponds to the magnetic oxide of iron. There are also two series of salts, the cobaltous and the cobaltic.

Experiment 292.—Partly fill a test tube with a concentrated solution of chloride of lime. Add a small quantity of Co_2O_3 and heat gently. A brisk effervescence takes place. Test the gas evolved with a glowing splinter. The calcium hypochlorite contained in the bleaching powder is, under the catalytic influence of the sesquioxide, decomposed. Write the reaction.

Experiment 293.—Prepare an aqueous solution of $CoCl_2$ by dissolving CoO or Co_2O_3 in HCl. Make a drawing with this nearly colorless solution. Heat the sketch to about $150°C.$; it will appear blue. Breathe upon it; the blue color will disappear.

Experiment 294.—To 2 *cu. cm.* of the pink solution of $CoCl_2$ in a test glass, add an equal quantity of sodium silicate or "water glass," well diluted so as to be thin. A blue precipitate appears.

$$CoCl_2 + Na_2SiO_3 = 2NaCl + CoSiO_3,$$
$$\text{or} \quad 2CoCl_2 + Na_4Si_5O_{12} = 4NaCl + Co_2Si_5O_{12}.$$

☞ NICKEL; *symbol*, Ni; *specific gravity, 8.9; atomic weight, 58.6 m. c.*

379. Nickel.—Nickel is almost always associated with cobalt in either terrestrial or extra-terrestrial matter. It is a lustrous, white metal, ductile, malleable, magnetic, very hard and susceptible of a high polish. It can be welded. It is largely used for plating articles of iron and steel to protect them from rusting. It is also used in coinage and for making alloys. German silver is an alloy of nickel, copper and zinc.

(*a.*) The oxides of Ni are the monoxide (nickel oxide, NiO) and the sesquioxide (nickel peroxide, Ni_2O_3). Nickel salts are derived from the monoxide. The most important salt is the nitrate.

380. The Iron Group.—The metals of this group form basic monoxides; they also form sesquioxides and corresponding series of salts. Cobalt and nickel have the same atomic weight and are seldom separated in nature.

Exercises.

1. Pyrolusite may be reduced to Mn_3O_4 by intense heat. Write the reaction.
2. Write a graphic symbol for K_2MnO_4.
3. Write two graphic symbols for $K_2Mn_2O_8$.
4. Write a graphic symbol for manganese sesquioxide, representing the metal as a dyad.
5. Write a graphic symbol for nickel sesquioxide, representing the metal as a tetrad.
6. Write a graphic symbol for $Mn''O_3$.
7. Which is the correct symbol for nickel hydrate, NiHO or NiH_2O_3? Give a reason for your answer.
8. (*a.*) Write the symbol for cobaltous hydrate. (*b.*) For cobaltic hydrate.
9. (*a.*) Write the equation representing the reaction for Exp. 289. (*b.*) For Exp. 290.
10. Write the symbol for the potassium salt of the hydrate of manganese heptoxide. What is the name of the salt?

CHAPTER XXII.

METALS OF THE CHROMIUM GROUP.

☞ CHROMIUM: *symbol*, Cr; *specific gravity*, *4.78* ; *atomic weight*, *52.4 m. c.*

381. Chromium.—Chromium is a rather rare, almost silver white metal and is not found free in nature. Its chief ore is chromite or chrome iron ore ($FeCr_2O_4$). It forms the green coloring matter of emerald, serpentine and other minerals. The fused metal is almost as hard as the diamond and melts less easily than platinum. At a white heat, it combines directly with oxygen or nitrogen, forming, with the latter, a brown chromium nitride. It is a good conductor of electricity and is magnetic. The presence of 0.5 to 0.75 *per cent.* of this metal renders steel ("chromium steel") harder than carbon alone can do. Several chromium compounds are somewhat extensively used in the arts.

(*a.*) Chromium forms three oxides; the monoxide (chromous oxide, CrO); the sesquioxide (chromic oxide, green oxide of chromium, Cr_2O_3) and the trioxide (chromic anhydride, CrO_3).

(*b.*) Chromic trioxide may be obtained by treating potassium dichromate with H_2SO_4. The red crystals thus formed may be dissolved in H_2O forming *chromic acid* (H_2CrO_4).

(*c.*) *Potassium chromate* (yellow chromate of potash, K_2CrO_4) is used in the arts, but the *potassium dichromate* (bichromate of potash, $K_2Cr_2O_7$) is, by far, the most important of the Cr compounds, as it serves as the starting point in the preparation of nearly all of the others. It crystallizes in beautiful garnet red prisms and is prepared in large quantities from $FeCr_2O_4$. *Chrome yellow* is a lead chromate ($PbCrO_4$). It is largely used as a pigment.

(*d.*) *Chrome alum* [K_2SO_4, $Cr_2(SO_4)_3$, $24H_2O$] is used in dyeing, calico printing and tanning.

Experiment 295.—Dissolve 15 g. of pulverized $K_2Cr_2O_7$ in 100 *cu.cm.* of warm H_2O. When the solution has cooled, add 15 *cu. cm.* of strong H_2SO_4, and pour it into a porcelain dish placed in cold H_2O. When the liquid is cool, slowly stir in 8 *cu. cm.* of C_2H_6O and set the whole aside for a day. At the end of that time, crystals of $K_2SO_4, Cr_2(SO_4)_3, 24H_2O$ will cover the bottom of the dish.

☞ MOLYBDENUM; *symbol,* Mo; *specific gravity, 8.6; atomic weight, 95.8 m. c.*

382. Molybdenum.—This metal is rare and has been but imperfectly studied. It is prepared by heating its trioxide or one of its chlorides to redness in a current of hydrogen. It has a silver white color, and is highly infusible. Molybdenum has four known oxides: MoO; Mo_2O_3; MoO_2; MoO_3. Molybdic acid has the composition, H_2MoO_4.

☞ TUNGSTEN: *symbol,* W; *specific gravity, 19.1 (?); atomic weight, 183.5 m. c.*

383. Tungsten.—Tungsten is a rare metal, being found in only a few minerals, the most important of which is wolfram, a tungstate of iron and manganese. It is said that the addition of tungsten to steel improves the hardness and tenacity of the latter. Tungsten forms two oxides, WO_2 and WO_3. Tungstic acid has the composition, H_2WO_4.

☞ URANIUM: *symbol,* U; *specific gravity, 18.33; atomic weight, 240 m. c.*

384. Uranium.—This is a rare metal, the chief ore of which is pitch blende, an impure uranium oxide (U_3O_8). The metal is malleable and hard and has a color resembling that of nickel. It has two well-known oxides, the dioxide (uranyl, uranous oxide, UO_2) and the trioxide (uranyl oxide, uranic oxide, UO_3). These oxides mix to form the intermediate oxides, U_2O_5 (black oxide of uranium $= UO_2 + UO_3$) and U_3O_8 (green oxide of uranium $= UO_2 + 2UO_3$). Uranium dioxide is a basic oxide; by dissolving it in strong acids, green uranous salts are formed. Uranium trioxide is an acid forming oxide. The uranic salts are yellow and most of them have a remarkable power of fluorescence, which they impart to glass (Ph., § 371, 31). Uranium yellow ($Na_2U_2O_7$) is largely used for giving the beautiful yellowish green color to glass known as "uranium glass."

Note.—Uranium was formerly classed in the iron group, its atomic weight given as 120 *m. c.* and its oxides symbolized by UO and U_2O_3. The metals of this group form acid-forming trioxides and yield very characteristic salts.

Exercises.

1. Assuming Cr to be a tetrad, write the graphic symbol for Cr_2Cl_6.
2. Write the graphic symbol for $K_2\overset{vi}{Cr}O_4$.
3. Read the following, naming each symbolized substance by its full systematic name: $FeSO_4, 7H_2O$ is pale green; $MnSO_4, 7H_2O$ is pale pink; $CoSO_4, 7H_2O$ is bright red; $NiSO_4, 7H_2O$ is bright green; and $CrSO_4, 7H_2O$ is pale blue.
4. Can you detect any difference in the apparent quantivalence of any two metals, the compounds of which are symbolized in the third Exercise?
5. Write the empirical symbol for hydrated sulphuryl oxide.

CHAPTER XXIII.

METALS OF THE TIN GROUP.

☞ TIN: *symbol*, Sn; *specific gravity, 7.29; atomic weight, 118 m. c.; quantivalence, 2 and 4.*

385. Source.—The principal tin ore is a dioxide called casserite or tin-stone. It is found in but few localities, the principal ones being Cornwall in England, Banca and Malacca in India. It has also been found in Australia, New Hampshire and California. Native tin has been found in small quantities.

386. Preparation.—Tin is prepared by pulverizing, washing and roasting the ore and then smelting it with charcoal or anthracite.

Experiment 296. — The familiar, so-called "tin-ware" is only tinned ware, iron coated with tin. Heat a piece of tinned iron over the lamp until the Sn has melted; thrust the plate into cold H_2O to harden the Sn quickly; remove the smooth surface of the metal by rubbing it first with a bit of paper moistened with dilute aqua regia, and then with paper wet with soda-lye. Notice the crystalline figures thus produced, resembling frost upon a window pane.

Experiment 297.—If you have a cake of Sn, wash one surface of it with dilute aqua regia until the crystalline forms, above mentioned, appear.

Experiment 298.—Hold a bar of Sn near the ear and bend the bar. Notice the peculiar crackling sound. Continue the bending and notice that the bar becomes heated. The phenomena noticed seem to be caused by the friction of the crystalline particles.

387. Properties.—Tin is a lustrous, soft, white metal, that melts at about 230°C. It is highly malleable, slightly tenacious, ductile at 100°C. and brittle at 200°C. It has a marked tendency to crystallize on cooling from a melted condition. It unites readily with oxygen, chlorine, sulphur and phosphorus when heated with them. It is not easily tarnished by even moist air but is easily acted upon by acids. Heated in the air, it burns to the dioxide (stannic oxide, SnO_2). It forms two series of compounds, the stannous and the stannic.

388. Uses.—Tin is largely employed in the form of foil (Pb., § 353) and as a coating for other metals; *e. g.*, copper used for bath tubs or cooking utensils, sheet iron for "tin-plate" and iron tacks and as a lining for lead water pipes. It is largely used in making numerous alloys.

(*a*.) Bronze and bell metal are alloys of Cu and Sn. Plumber's solder and pewter are alloys of Pb and Sn. Britannia metal is an alloy of Cu, Sb and Sn. The "silvering" of mirrors is an amalgam of Hg and Sn.

(*b*.) The Sn of tinned ware is sometimes adulterated with Pb which is less costly. This alloy of Pb and Sn will oxidize much more readily than Sn will. This lead oxide is easily dissolved by the $C_2H_4O_2$ of vinegar forming the dangerous poison, lead acetate, or "sugar of lead." The various acids of our common fruits unite with the lead oxide to form salts and all of the soluble lead salts are poisonous. Dr. Kedzie, President of the Michigan State Board of Health, says: "It is an astonishing fact that a large proportion of the tinned wares in the market is unfit to use because of the large quantity of lead with which the tin is alloyed." As these compounds are cumulative poisons, he adds: "A person may not be poisoned by one or two small doses but even if a very minute dose is taken for a long time, the person may be broken in health or even lose his life." As a test for this Pb adulteration, he recommends that a drop of HNO_3 be placed on the tinned surface and rubbed over a space as large as a dime, that the metal be warmed until dry and that two drops of a solution of KI be placed on the spot. "If the tin contains lead, a bright yellow iodide of lead will be formed on the spot."

389. Tin Compounds.—Tin forms two oxides, the monoxide (stannous oxide, SnO) and the dioxide (stannic oxide, SnO_2). The former is basic; the latter is both a basic and an acid forming oxide. Their compounds are designated as stannous and stannic salts. Stannic acid (H_2SnO_3) is a white solid. Stannous chloride (Sn_2Cl_4) is prepared by dissolving tin in warm hydrochloric acid. Tin tetrachloride (stannic chloride, $SnCl_4$) may be prepared by passing chlorine over tin-foil or fused tin in a retort. If a quick stream of chlorine be forced through melted tin, heat and light are evolved. Stannic chloride is a colorless liquid, which, when treated with one-third its weight of water, forms a crystalline mass called " butter of tin."

☞ TITANIUM : *symbol*, Ti ; *atomic weight, 48 m. c.*

390. Titanium.—This is a rare metal, not found in the metallic state. It has the remarkable power of combining directly with free nitrogen at high temperatures, forming three distinct nitrides, Ti_5N_2, Ti_3N_4, Ti_2N_2. Titanium dioxide (TiO_2) is trimorphous.

☞ ZIRCONIUM: *symbol*, Zr ; *specific gravity, 4.15 ; atomic weight, 90 m. c.*

391. Zirconium.—This rare metal has been obtained in the form of an iron gray powder and in a crystallized state. The crystalline variety can be ignited only at the temperature of the oxyhydrogen flame or in chlorine at a red heat. It has only one known oxide (zirconia, ZrO_2), which is white and infusible.

☞ THORIUM: *symbol*, Th ; *specific gravity, 7.7 ; atomic weight, 231.5 m. c.*

392. Thorium.—This rare metal is a constituent of thorite and a few other rare minerals. It has been prepared as a gray powder that takes an iron gray lustre when burnished. It takes fire when heated in the air. Its oxide (ThO_2) is sometimes called thoria.

Note.—The metals of this group are closely connected with the non-metal, silicon, in that they form dioxides corresponding to SiO_2 and present other chemical analogies. Ti and Zr occupy a position intermediate, in many respects, between carbon and silicon on one hand and the metals on the other.

EXERCISES.

1. Define normal, acid, basic and double salts. Illustrate
2. A molecule of a certain oxide contains one atom of Sn and has a weight of 150 m. c. What is its symbol?
3. Write the symbol for triferric tetroxide.
4. A number of salts having the general symbol M'HSO$_3$ were called by their discoverer, "hydrosulphites." What is their proper systematic name?
5. Show how far each of the following compounds agrees with the definitions of acid, base and salt:

(a.) Chlorides of H, K, Al, P and S.
(b.) Oxides of H, K and C.
(c.) Hydrates of K, Na, SO$_2$ and Ca.

6. How many liters of marsh gas will weigh as much as 25 l. of ethene?
7. A certain compound has a molecular weight of 60 m. c. Its centesimal composition is as follows: 40 of C; 53.4 of O and 6.6 of H. What is the compound?
8. Indicate the quantivalence of each of the following radicals: S, O, Cl, HO, NH$_4$, PO, SO$_2$.
9. Write the graphic symbol for phosphoryl trichloride.

CHAPTER XXIV.

METALS OF THE GOLD GROUP.

 GOLD: *symbol*, Au; *specific gravity*, 19.265; *atomic weight*, 196.2 m.c.; *quantivalence*, 1 and 3.

393. Occurrence.—Gold is widely distributed in nature but in only a few places is it found in quantities sufficient to repay the cost of obtaining it. It is generally found in the native state alloyed with silver. Native gold is found in the quartz veins that intersect metamorphic rocks and in the alluvial deposits, called placers, formed by the disintegration of gold bearing rocks.

(*a.*) The richest deposits of Au are in California, Colorado, Nevada and Australia. Native Au is found in crystals, nuggets, grains and scales. While the particles are sometimes so small as to be invisible in even " paying " quartz, a single nugget, weighing 184 pounds and valued at £8376, 10*s.* 6*d.*, was found in Australia. Gold compounds are also found in nature. Two mines in Nevada produced in 1877, $15,597,263 in Au and $17,061,587 in Ag.

394. Preparation.—In quartz mining, the ore is first pulverized. The gold is then extracted from the powdered mineral by means of mercury. The gold amalgam thus formed is subjected to distillation. In "placer digging," the lighter constituents of the alluvial deposit are washed away, the heavier gold remaining in the "washpan" or "cradle." In "hydraulic mining," immense streams of water are directed, under great pressure, against the surface of the auriferous deposit. In this way, great quantities of sand, clay and gravel are disintegrated and hurried forward in a turbid torrent, from which the heavy gold particles settle into interstices previously prepared in the tunnel, through which the muddy mass is caused to flow. The amount of labor and capital expended in California upon canals, aqueducts, shafts and tunnels for hydraulic mining is very great.

Experiment 299.—Add a few drops of a strong solution of $AuCl_3$ to a liter of H_2O. Into this dilute solution, drop one or two pieces of P, the size of a mustard-seed, and place the whole in the sunlight. In the course of a few hours, the water will have a distinct purplish tint. This will deepen in color until finally, if the solution has the proper strength, a beautiful ruby-red liquid will be obtained. The color of this liquid is due to finely divided *metallic gold.*

395. Properties.—Gold is a brilliant, beautiful, orange-yellow metal. It is the most malleable and ductile of the metals. It may be beaten into leaves not more than 0.0001 *mm.* thick ; 1 *g.* of it may be drawn into 3240 *m.* of wire. It is softer than silver, nearly as soft as lead. It fuses at about 1100°C., and volatilizes at very high temperatures. It is not attacked by oxygen or water at any temperature. It does not dissolve in any simple acid except selenic but dissolves readily in aqua regia or in any other acid liquid that evolves chlorine.

(*a.*) One ounce of Au leaf may be made to cover 189 *sq. ft.*, while 280,000 leaves placed one upon another measure only one inch in thickness. One grain of Au will gild two miles of fine Ag wire, the deposit of Au being about 0.000002 *mm.* thick. Ordinary gold leaf transmits green light. Au may be precipitated in so fine a state that it remains suspended in the liquid, causing it to appear ruby-red by reflected light or blue by transmitted light. The red color of ruby glass is due to the presence of Au in a finely divided state. Au is sometimes called the "king of metals."

396. Uses.—Gold is used for coinage, jewels, gilding

and other purposes, for which it is well adapted by its beautiful color and lustre, its unalterability and comparative rarity. Pure gold is so soft that coins and jewels made of it would soon wear out. It is, therefore, hardened by alloying with copper. American and French gold coins contain one-tenth copper; British gold coins, one-twelfth.

(*a.*) The purity of Au in jewels is estimated in carats, pure Au being "24 carats fine." An alloy containing $\frac{2}{3}$ gold is "16 carats fine."

(*b.*) The compounds of Au are of little chemical interest. There are two oxides, the monoxide (aurous oxide, Au_2O) and the trioxide (auric oxide, gold sesquioxide (Au_2O_3). There are two chlorides, AuCl and $AuCl_3$. Aurous cyanide (AuCN) dissolved in a solution of KCN is used in electro-gilding (Ph., § 399, *a*).

☞ PLATINUM : *symbol*, Pt ; *specific gravity*, 21.5 ; *atomic weight*, 196.7 m. c.

397. Occurrence, etc.—Platinum is found only in the native state, but very seldom pure. The so called "platinum ore" is an alloy of the metals of this group, with iron, copper, *etc.* It is found in the Ural mountains, in Brazil, Borneo, California and other places. The preparation of pure platinum is a matter of great difficulty. For fusing the metal on the large scale, a crucible made of two pieces of lime is used with a compound blowpipe (Fig. 119). The upper part of the blowpipe is made of copper; the lower part, of platinum. Coal gas is generally used instead of hydrogen. The lime of the crucible successfully resists the high temperature produced and absorbs the slags formed during the operation.

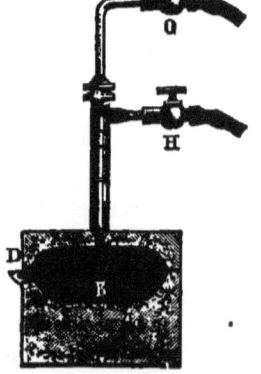

FIG. 119.

§ 397   PLATINUM.   309

Experiment 300.—Boil 0.5 *g*. of Pt in small fragments in a teaspoonful of *aqua regia* as long as the metal seems to be acted upon. Pour the liquid into an evaporating dish, add *aqua regia* to the remaining Pt and proceed as before, continuing thus until all of the Pt has been dissolved. Evaporate the solution to dryness upon the water bath. Dissolve this residue ($PtCl_4$) in H_2O.

Experiment 301.—Heat a few drops of the solution of $PtCl_4$ in a test-tube. Notice the odor of the gas evolved. Hold a strip of moistened litmus at the mouth of the test tube. It will be bleached.

$$2PtCl_4 = Pt_2 + 4Cl_2.$$

Experiment 302.—Pour a teaspoonful of a solution of NH_4Cl into a test tube, acidulate it with HCl, and to it add a drop of the solution of the $PtCl_4$ just prepared. A yellow, insoluble powder ($2NH_4Cl,PtCl_4$) will soon be precipitated. Repeat the experiment, taking enough of the solutions to make half a teaspoonful of the yellow precipitate, being careful that at last there shall be a slight excess of free NH_4Cl rather than of $PtCl_4$ in the overlying liquid. Allow the precipitate to settle, separate it from the clear liquor by decantation and partly dry it at a gentle heat. When the precipitate has acquired the consistence of slightly moistened earth, transfer it to a cup-shaped piece of Pt foil, and heat it to redness in the gas flame, until fumes of NH_4Cl are no longer driven off. A gray, loosely-coherent, sponge-like mass of metallic platinum will remain in the cup ; it is *platinum sponge*.

Experiment 303.—Repeat Exp. 30, using either illuminating gas or H.

Experiment 304.—Fill a spirit lamp with a mixture of C_2H_6O and $(C_2H_5)_2O$. Suspend a spiral of Pt wire over the wick (Fig. 120) and light the lamp. When the wire is red hot, blow out the flame. The mixed vapors rising from the wick are oxidized by the heated Pt; the spiral is thus kept brightly incandescent. This is Davy's glow lamp. The experiment may be varied by suspending the spiral in a loosely covered test glass containing $(C_2H_5)_2O$, as shown in Fig. 121, or by heating a bit of Pt foil in a Bunsen flame and blowing out the flame. The foil will glow and may reignite the gas if held near enough to the burner.

FIG. 120.

FIG. 121.

398. Properties.—Platinum is a heavy, soft metal of tin-white color. It is infusible at the highest temperature of the blast furnace but yields before the oxyhydrogen flame. Its melting point has been estimated at 2000°C. It is very malleable and so ductile that it may be drawn into a wire less than 0.001 *mm.* in diameter. Like gold, it has little affinity for the other elements. It is not oxidized by oxygen, water, nitric or sulphuric acid at any temperature. It dissolves in *aqua regia* more slowly than gold does. It also dissolves in chlorine water. Like iron, it may be welded at a white heat.

(*a.*) Red hot Pt absorbs 3.8 volumes of H, which it gives off when heated in a vacuum, the surface of the Pt becoming then covered with bubbles. Similarly, H is absorbed by Pt, at the negative electrode in the electrolysis of H_2O (Exp. 12), the occluded H being given off when the current is reversed so as to make the Pt the positive electrode.

(*b.*) O is not absorbed by Pt but it is condensed on a clean surface of the metal. Thus, mixtures of O or air with H, CO, C_2H_4, C_2H_6O or $(C_2H_5)_2O$ vapor, and other easily inflammable gases or vapors may be made to combine, sometimes slowly, sometimes quickly, sometimes with explosion (Exps. 30 and 52).

(*c.*) The preparation of platinum sponge has been illustrated in Exps. 300 and 302. Owing to its large surface, compared with its volume, it is able to condense large quantities of O.

(*d.*) Platinum-black is a form of metallic Pt, even more finely divided than platinum-sponge. It is a soft, dull, black powder. It can absorb more than 800 times its volume of O. When boiled in H_2O and dried in a vacuum over H_2SO_4, it absorbs O from the air so rapidly that the mass becomes red hot. If upon the powder, when cooled after such absorption of O, some C_2H_6O or $(C_2H_5)_2O$ be dropped, the oxidation of the liquids will heat the metal red hot.

(*e.*) Pt unites readily with other metals forming alloys which are generally more easily fusible than the element.

399. Uses. — On account of its infusibility and its chemical inertness, platinum is invaluable to the chemist. In the laboratory, it is used for crucibles, evaporating dishes, stills, tubes, spatulas, forceps, wire, blowpipe tips, *etc.* In sulphuric acid manufacture, large platinum stills and siphons (§ 152, *c*) are used for concentrating the acid. As its rate of expansion is nearly equal to that of glass (Ph., § 485, *a*), it is used in the manufacture of eudiometers, Geissler tubes, incandescent electric lamps, *etc.*

(*a.*) On account of Pt forming easily fusible alloys, care should be had not to heat Pt utensils with an easily fusible metal, *e. g.*, Pb, Bi, Sn or Sb, or any easily reducible compound of a metal. They should not be used for fusion with nitre, the alkalies, or alkaline cyanides. They should not be heated in contact with P or As nor brought into direct contact with burning charcoal.

(*b.*) "Without Pt, it would be impossible, in many cases, to make the analysis of a mineral. The mineral must be dissolved. Vessels of glass and all non-metallic substances are destroyed by the means we use for that purpose. Crucibles of Au and Ag would melt at high temperatures. But Pt is cheaper than Au, harder and more durable than Ag, infusible at all temperatures of our furnaces and is left intact by acids and alkaline carbonates. Pt unites all the valuable properties of Au and of porcelain, resisting the action of heat and of almost all chemical agents. Without Pt, the composition of most minerals would have yet remained unknown."—*Liebig.*

☞ PALLADIUM : *symbol*, Pd ; *specific gravity*, *11.4* ; *atomic weight*, *106.2 m. c.*

400. Palladium.—This metal is contained in most platinum "ores," and is found native. Is has a color resembling that of platinum. Its melting point is about that of wrought iron, the lowest of any of the metals of this group. It possesses the power of absorbing hydrogen in a greater degree than any other metal (§ 24, *d*). It has not been largely employed in the arts although its silver-white color and unalterability in the air have led to its use in preparing the graduated surfaces of astronomical instruments. It does not tarnish on exposure to hydrogen sulphide and has been, therefore, used for coating silver articles and by dentists as a substitute for gold.

☞ RHODIUM : *symbol*, Rh ; *specific gravity, 12.1 ; atomic weight, 104.1 m. c.*

401. Rhodium.—This metal is found in platinum "ore." It has the color and lustre of aluminum. It is melted with greater difficulty than platinum. It is almost insoluble in acids, but is more easily acted upon by chlorine than any other of the platinum metals.

☞ IRIDIUM ; *symbol*, Ir ; *specific gravity, 22.38 ; atomic weight, 192.7 m. c.*

402. Iridium.—This metal also is found in platinum "ore." It has a white lustre, resembling that of polished steel. It is very brittle when cold but slightly malleable at a white heat. Pure, massive iridium is not attacked by aqua regia. An alloy of one part of iridium and nine parts of platinum is extremely hard, as elastic as steel, more difficultly fusible than platinum, unalterable in the air and susceptible of a beautiful polish. This alloy was adopted by the International Commission at Paris in 1872 for the standard metric measures. Iridium is the most difficultly fusible of the platinum metals except ruthenium and osmium. It has been used for the negative electrodes in electric lamps.

☞ RUTHENIUM : *symbol*, Ru ; *specific gravity, 12.26 ; atomic weight, 103.5 m. c.*

403. Ruthenium.—This metal is found in platinum and other ores. It combines with oxygen more readily than any of the other platinum metals except osmium. It is hard and brittle, and, next to osmium, the most difficultly fusible metal of this group. It is only slightly acted upon by *aqua regia*. It combines with chlorine at a white heat.

☞ OSMIUM: *symbol*, Os; *specific gravity*, 22.477; *atomic weight*, 198.6 *m. c.*

404. Osmium.—This metal is found in platinum "ore," from the other constituents of which it is easily separated, as it unites directly with oxygen to form a very volatile compound, OsO_4. Osmium crystals have a bluish white color and are harder than glass. Osmium is the heaviest known substance and has not yet been fused. It is not used in the arts but its alloy with iridium (osmiridium) is used for tipping gold pens as it is not attacked by acids, and for the bearings of the mariner's compass as it does not oxidize and is non-magnetic.

Note.—Gold, silver, platinum, palladium, rhodium and iridium are sometimes called "the noble metals."

EXERCISES.

1. What takes place when Na is thrown into H_2O?
2. Describe an experiment showing the difference between a mixture and a compound.
3. State the effect of heat upon MnO_2, $KClO_3$, NH_4Cl, NH_4NO_3, P and S respectively.
4. You are given Zn, H_2SO_4, KHO and H_2O and required to prepare H from them by two distinct processes. Describe the processes and write the reaction for each.
5. I have two cylindrical jars of H, one of which I hold mouth upward, the other mouth downward. At the end of 30 seconds, I plunge a lighted taper into each jar. Tell what you would expect to take place in each case.
6. What are the products of the combustion of H_2S in the air?
7. How can you make H_2SO_4 from S, H_2O and HNO_3?
8. What elements can be obtained from HCl, NH_3 and H_2O? How would you obtain them in each case?
9. (*a.*) When H is burned in air, what is the product? (*b.*) When burned in Cl?
10. An electric spark is produced in a mixture of 120 *cu. cm.* of H and 60 *cu. cm.* of O. How would you conduct the experiment so as to show the gaseous condensation?

314   OSMIUM.   § 404

11. You are required to prepare O from Cl and H_2O. How would you do it?

12. You are given some Hg, a glass flask, a lamp, some glass tubing and required to make pure O. How will you do it under ordinary barometric conditions?

13. When HNO_3 is poured on Cu, how does the action differ from a simple solution?

14. You are given ammonium carbonate and nitric acid and required to prepare laughing gas from the materials. How will you do it?

15. What is the fineness of British gold coin in carats?

16. When a positive monad radical replaces an atom of H in NH_3, the compound ammonia is called an amine. See § 96, a. Write the typical symbol for di-ethylamine; for potassamine.

17. When a negative (or acid) monad radical replaces an atom of H in NH_3, the compound ammonia is called an amide. Write the symbol for di-iodamide. The symbol for acetyl is given on p. 183. Write the symbol for acetamide.

18. Write the symbols for potassium sulphite; hydrogen potassium sulphite; calcium sulphite and hydrogen calcium sulphite.

19. Write the name and full graphic symbol for

$$\mathrm{S} \begin{cases} -(SO_2)-(HO) \\ -(SO_2)-(HO) \end{cases}$$

20. Which of the graphic symbols called for in Ex. 5, p. 227, is preferable? Why? See § 164, a.

21. Write the graphic symbol for phosphorus tetriodide (P_2I_4) indicating trivalent P.

22. Write the graphic symbol for pyrophosphoric chloride, $Cl_4P_2O_3$.

23. (a.) Write the graphic symbol for H_3PO_4. (b.) Does this symbol indicate a dibasic or a tribasic acid?

24. Explain the fact that when new flannel is first washed in an alkaline soap, it becomes yellow.

25. What weight of O is needed to burn 9 g. of CS_2?

26. How would you distinguish between Pt and Ag? Between Pt and Sn? Between Ag and Sn?

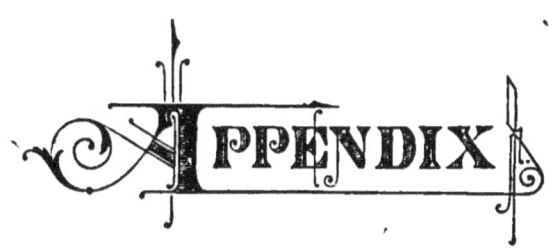

APPENDIX

1. Table of the Elements,—An alphabetical list of the elements with their symbols and atomic weights is given below. In the body of the work some of the atomic weights were given in approximate numbers, for greater ease in memorizing and computation. In the table below, the atomic weights are given according to the most accurate determinations yet made. The less important elements are printed in *italic*.

Name.	Symbol.	Microcriths.
Aluminum	Al	27.3
Antimony (*stibium*)	Sb	122
Arsenic	As	74.9
Barium	Ba	136.8
Beryllium	Be	
(See *Glucinum*.)		
Bismuth	Bi	.210
Boron	B	11
Bromine	Br	79.75
Cadmium	Cd	111.6
Cæsium	Cs	132.5
Calcium	Ca	39.9
Carbon	C	11.97
Cerium	Ce	141.2
Chlorine	Cl	35.37
Chromium	Cr	52.4
Cobalt	Co	58.6
Columbium	Cb	94
Copper (*cuprum*)	Cu	63.1
Davyum	Da	153
Decipium	De	157
Didymium	Di	147
Erbium	Er	169
Fluorine	F	19.1
Gallium	Ga	69.8
Glucinium		
(See *Glucinum*.)		
Glucinum	Gl	92
Gold (*aurum*)	Au	196.2
Hydrogen	H	1
Indium	In	113.4
Iodine	I	126.53
Iridium	Ir	192.7
Iron	Fe	55.9
Lanthanum	La	139
Lead (*plumbum*)	Pb	206.4
Lithium	Li	7.01
Magnesium	Mg	23.98
Manganese	Mn	54.8
Mercury (*hydrargyrum*)	Hg	199.8
Molybdenum	Mo	95.8
Nickel	Ni	58.6
Niobium (See *Columbium*).	Nb	
Nitrogen	N	14.01
Norwegium	No	72
Osmium	Os	198.6
Oxygen	O	15.96
Palladium	Pd	106.2
Phosphorus	P	30.96
Platinum	Pt	196.7
Potassium (*kalium*)	K	39.04
Rhodium	Rh	104.1
Rubidium	Rb	85.2
Ruthenium	Ru	103.5
Selenium	Se	79
Silicium (See *Silicon*.)	Si	

Name.	Symbol.	Microcriths.	Name.	Symbol.	Microcriths.
Silicon	Si	.28	Thorium	Th.	231.5
Silver (*argentum*)	Ag	107.66	Tin (*stannum*)	Sn.	117.8
Sodium (*natrium*)	Na.	22.29	Titanium	Ti	..48.15
Strontium	Sr	..87.2	Tungsten (*wolframium*)	W.	183.5
Sulphur	S	...31.98	Uranium	Ur.	240
Tantalum	Ta	182	Vanadium	V..	51.2
Tellurium	Te	128	Yttrium	Yt.	..92.5
Terbium	Tr.	.99	Zinc	Zn.	..64.9
Thallium	Tl.	203.6	Zirconium	Zr.	.90

2. Metric Measures.—For a fuller consideration of the international or metric measures, the pupil is referred to Avery's Natural Philosophy, §§ 24–30 and 35–36. Chemists of all countries use these units, almost exclusively. The decimeter rule (Fig. 122) is shown as being divided into ten centimeters, each of which is divided into ten millimeters. The cubic decimeter measures a volume called a liter (pronounced *leeter*). The cubic centimeter (*cu. cm.*) is 0.001 of a liter (*l*). The weight of one *cu. cm.* of water at the freezing temperature is a gram (*g*). These three units, the liter, the cubic centimeter and the gram are the ones of most frequent occurrence in chemical works. The actual weights and measures should be habitually used in every school laboratory.

100 millimeters = 10 centimeters = 1 decimeters = 3.937 inches.

1 inch = 2.540 *cm.* | 1 cu. in. = 16.386 *cu.cm.* | 1 grain = 0.0648 *g.*
1 foot = 3.049 *dm.* | 1 liquid qt. = 0.946 *l.* | 1oz. Troy = 31.1035*g.*
1 yard = 0.9144*m.* | 1 fl'd oz. = 29.562 *cu.cm.* | 1lb. Av. = 0.4535*Kg.*

3. Thermometers.—Chemists use the centigrade thermometer almost exclusively. One or more centigrade thermometers (chemical), having the scale marked on the glass tube, and having no frame like that of the ordinary house thermometer, should be in every school laboratory. In this book temperatures are always given in centigrade degrees. To change centigrade readings to Fahrenheit readings, multiply the number of centigrade degrees by ⅘ and add 32. To change Fahrenheit readings to centigrade readings, subtract 32 from the number of Fahrenheit degrees and multiply the remainder by ⅝. (See Ph., §§ 480, 481.)

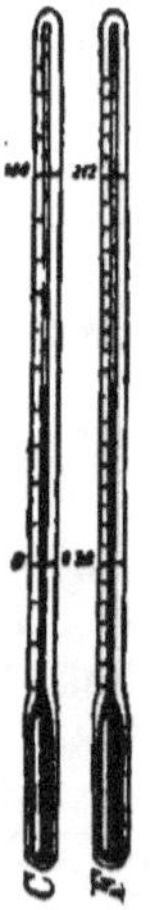

The best thermometers are straight glass tubes, of uniform diameter, with cylindrical instead of spherical bulbs; such instruments can be passed tightly through a cork, and are free from many liabilities to error to which thermometers with paper or metal scales are

FIG. 122.

FIG. 123

always exposed. A cheaper kind of thermometer, having a paper scale enclosed in a glass envelope, will answer for most experiments.

4. Glass Working. — Much of the chemist's apparatus is made of glass which softens and becomes plastic when heated. Skillful workers in wood or metal may be found in almost any town, but glass working will generally devolve upon the teacher and pupil. It is, therefore, discussed at some length in this place.

(*a.*) *Glass Tubing.*—Glass tubes bent into various shapes are constantly needed. The pupil should acquire dexterity in preparing these for himself. Glass tubing is of two qualities, hard and soft. The former softens with difficulty and is desirable only for ignition or combustion tubes. (Fig. 18.) But little of it will be needed. It is generally better to buy the ignition tubes required. Soft glass tubing will be needed in larger quantities. In purchasing, it is recommended that the greater part be of a single size. Fig. 124 shows desirable sizes and the proper thickness of the glass for each size. By using, habitually, one given size of tubing, the various articles made therefrom are more easily interchangeable than they would otherwise be.

FIG. 124.

(*b.*) *Cutting and Bending Tubes.*—Glass tubing and rods must generally be cut the desired length. For this purpose, lay the tube or rod upon the table and make a scratch at the required distance from one end with a three-cornered file. Hold the tubing in both hands, as shown in Fig. 125, with the scratch away from you and the two thumbs opposite the mark. With a sharp jerk, push out the thumbs and pull back the fingers. The glass will snap squarely off at the desired place. The best flame for bending ordinary tubes is that of a fish-tail gas burner, but that of a spirit lamp will do. Be sure that the tube is dry; do not breathe into it before heating it. Bring the part of the tube where the bend is desired into the hot air above the flame; when it is thoroughly warm, bring it into the flame itself. Heat about an inch of the tube, holding it with both hands and turning it constantly that it may be heated uniformly on all sides. The tube should be held between the thumb and first two fingers of each hand, the hands being below the tube, palms upward and the lamp between the hands. The desired yielding condition of the glass will be detected by feel-

FIG. 125.

ing better than by seeing, *i. e.*, the fingers will detect the yielding of the glass before the eye notices any change of color or form.

FIG. 126.

When the glass yields easily, remove it from the flame and gently bend the ends from you. If the concave side of the glass be too hot, it will "buckle;" if the convex side be too hot, the curve will be flattened and its channel contracted. Practice, and practice only, will enable you to bend a tube neatly. When a tube or rod is to be bent or drawn near its end, a temporary handle may be attached to it by softening the end of the tube or rod, and pressing against the soft glass a fragment of glass tube, which will adhere strongly to the softened end. This handle may subsequently be removed by a slight blow or by the aid of a file. If a considerable bend is to be made, so that the angle between the arms will be very small or nothing, as in a siphon, the curvature can not be well produced at one place in the tube, but should be made by heating, progressively, several *cm.* of the tube, and bending continuously from one end of the heated portion to the other (Fig. 127). The several parts of such a bent tube should all lie in the same plane so that the finished tube may lie flat on a level surface. It is difficult to bend tubing large enough for U-tubes (Fig. 14). They would better be bought. When the end of a tube or rod is to be heated, it is best to begin heating the glass about 2 *cm.* from the end, as cracks start easily from an edge. Smooth the sharp edges at the ends of the tube by heating them to redness. Anneal the bent tube by withdrawing it very gradually from the flame so as not to let it cool suddenly. Never lay a hot tube on the bench but put it on some poor conductor of heat until it is cool. Gradual heating and gradual cooling are alike necessary. Glass tubing may be advantageously united by rubber or caoutchouc tubing when the substance to be conducted will not corrode the latter, or when the temperature employed is not too high. Short pieces of rubber tubing are much used

FIG. 127.

as connectors to make flexible joints in apparatus. Gas delivery tubes, *etc.* (Fig. 6), are generally made in several pieces joined with caoutchouc connectors, which, by their flexibility, add much to the durability of the apparatus. Long glass tubes bent several times and connecting heavier pieces of apparatus are almost sure to break, even with careful use. The internal diameter of the connector should be a little less than the external diameter of the glass tubing. The connection may be made more easily by wetting the glass.

(*c.*) *Drawing Tubes.*—In order to draw a glass tube down to a finer bore, thoroughly soften it on all sides uniformly for 1 or 2 *cm.* of its length and then, taking the glass from the flame, pull the parts asunder by a cautious movement of the hands. The length and fineness of the drawn out tube will depend upon the length of tube heated and the rapidity of motion of the hands. If the drawn out part of the tube is to have thicker walls in proportion to its bore

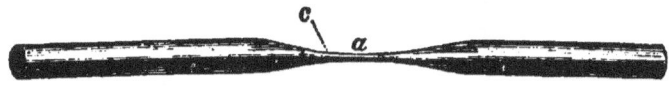

FIG. 128.

than the original tube, keep the heated portion soft for two or three minutes before drawing out the tube, pressing the parts slightly together the while. By this process the glass will be thickened at the hot ring. By cutting the neck at *a*, with a file, jets are formed such as are needed for Exps. 21, 26, *etc.*

(*d.*) *Closing Tubes.*—Take a piece of tubing long enough to make two closed tubes of the desired length. Heat a narrow ring at the middle of the tube and draw it out slightly. Direct the point of the flame upon the point *c* (Fig. 128) which is to become the bottom of one tube, draw out the heated part and melt it off. Each half of the original tube is now closed at one end but they are of different forms. (Fig. 129.) You can not close both ends satisfactorily at the same time. A superfluous knob of glass generally remains upon the end. If small, it may be removed by heating the whole end of the tube, and blowing moderately into the open end. The knob being hotter than any other part, yields to the pressure from within and disappears. If the knob is large, it may be drawn off by sticking to it a fragment of tube, and then softening the glass above the junction. The same process may be applied to

FIG. 129.

the too pointed end of the right hand half of the original tube, or to any bit of tube that is too short to make two closed tubes. When the closed end of a tube is too thin, it may be strengthened by keeping the whole end at a red heat for two or three minutes, turning the tube constantly between the fingers. In all of these processes, keep the tube in constant rotation that it may be heated on all sides alike. It will be difficult for the pupil satisfactorily to work tubing large enough for test tubes (Fig. 7). They would better be bought. They come in nests of assorted sizes.

(*e.*) *Blowing Bulbs.*—This is a more delicate operation than any yet described. It requires considerable practice to secure even moderate success. If the bulb is to be large compared with the size of the tube carrying it, the glass must be thickened before the bulb can be blown. If the bulb is to be at the middle of a piece of tubing, the tube is to be heated red hot at that place, removed from the flame, and the ends gently pressed toward each other. If the glass "wrinkles" in thickening, as it may do if too highly heated, a good bulb cannot be blown there. If the bulb is to be at the end of the tube, the end is closed and the glass then thickened by holding the closed end in the flame, keeping it in constant rotation. When the glass is so soft that it bends from its own weight, the end of the tube is placed between the lips, the other end, if open, is closed with the finger, and air is steadily pressed into the tube by the mouth rather than by the lungs, the tube being kept in rotation. This must be done quickly but cautiously, the eye being kept upon the heated part. Practice will soon enable you to determine when to stop the pressure. If the bulb thus obtained be not large enough, it may be reheated and again expanded, provided the glass be thick enough. The pressure must not be too strong or sudden and never applied while the glass is in the flame. It is better, as a general thing, to buy funnel tubes (Fig. 6) and bulb tubes (Fig. 16) than to make them.

(*f.*) *Welding Glass Tubes.*—The well fitted ends of two pieces of glass tubing may be joined by heating them to redness and pressing them together while in a plastic condition. Practice is necessary to good results, but the skill should be acquired as funnel tubes and other pieces of apparatus often need mending. If necessary, the end of one tube may be enlarged by rapidly turning the glass in the flame until it is highly heated, and then, while it is still in the flame, flaring it outward with an iron rod. Hold the ends together and heat them well with a pointed flame, until they are united all around. Force air in at one end to swell out the joint a little, heat it again until the swelling sinks in, blow it out again, and repeat the process until the joint is smooth and the pieces well fused into each other. Without this repeated heating and blowing out, the joint is likely to crack open when cooled.

(*g.*) *Piercing Tubes.*—A hole may be made in the side of a tube or other thin glass apparatus by directing a pointed blowpipe flame upon the glass until a spot is red hot, closing the other end, if open, with the finger and blowing *forcibly* into the open end. The glass is blown out at the heated spot. The edge may be strengthened by laying on a thread of glass around it, and fusing the thread to the tube in the blowpipe flame.

(*h.*) *Glass Cutting and Cracking, etc.*—For cutting glass plates, a glazier's diamond is desirable but efficient and cheap " glass-cutters," made of hardened steel have been put upon the market within a few years. For shaping broken flasks, retorts and other pieces of thin glassware, cracking is more satisfactory. A scratch is made with a file, preferably at the edge of the glass. Apply a pointed piece of glowing charcoal, a fine pointed flame or a heated glass or metal rod to this scratch. The sudden expansion by heat will generally produce a crack. If the heat does not make one, touch the hot spot with a wet stick. A crack thus started may be led in any desired direction by keeping the heated rod or fine flame moving slowly a few *mm.* in front of it as it advances.

A flask or retort neck may sometimes be cracked round by tying a string soaked in alcohol or turpentine round the place, setting fire to the string and keeping the flask turning. When the string has burnt out, invert the flask and plunge it into water up to the heated circle. It will generally crack as desired.

The lower ends of glass funnels, and the ends of gas delivery tubes that enter the generating bottle or flask should be ground off obliquely on a wet grindstone, or shaped thus with a file wet with a solution of camphor in turpentine, to facilitate the dropping of liquids from such extremities. With a little care and patience, a hole may be drilled through glass by using a file kept wet with the solution mentioned. Such a hole may easily be enlarged or given any desired shape with a file thus wet.

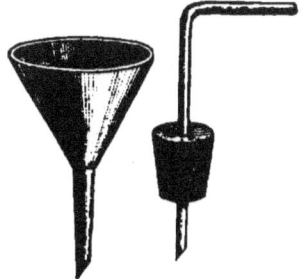

FIG. 130.

The lips of bottles may be ground flat by rubbing them on a flat surface sprinkled with emery powder kept wet. The bottle should be grasped by the neck and rubbed around with a gyratory motion, pains being taken to prevent a rocking motion whereby first one side of the lip shall be ground and then another, thus leaving the bottle in as bad a condition at the end of the work as at the beginning. The work may be finished by rubbing with fine emery powder on a piece of plate or window glass, until all parts of the ground surface lie in the same plane. See Frick's *Physical Technics* [17].

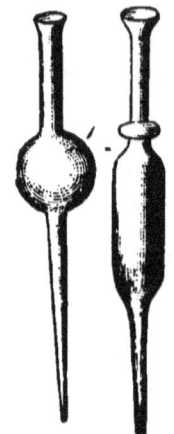

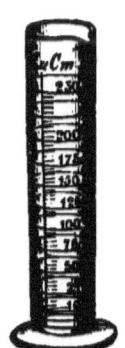

FIG. 131.   FIG. 132.   FIG. 133.

5. Pipettes and Graduates.—Tubes drawn out to a small opening at one end and used to remove a small quantity of a liquid from a vessel without disturbing the bulk of its contents, are called pipettes. They often carry a bulb or cylindrical enlargement, as appears in the forms shown in Fig. 131. The manner of using them is shown in Fig. 132. They are often graduated. A cylindrical measuring glass, graduated to cubic centimeters (Fig. 133) is almost indispensable in the laboratory.

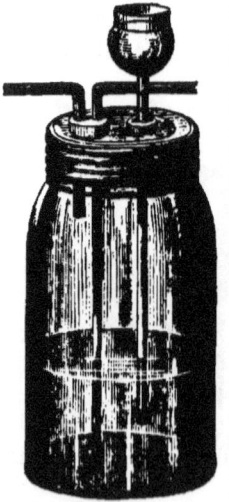

FIG. 134.

6. Woulffe Bottles.—A very convenient substitute for Woulffe bottles may be made by perforating the glass cover of a fruit jar according to directions given in App. 4, *h*. The holes carry cork or caoutchouc stoppers through which the several tubes pass, as shown in Fig. 134.

7. Thin Bottomed Glassware.—Glass vessels are largely used for heating liquids in the laboratory. All such vessels have uniformly thin bottoms that they may not be broken by unequal expansion when heated. If moisture from the atmosphere or other source accumulates on the outer surface, it should be carefully wiped off before or during the heating.

Retorts are often used. Those that have tubulures (Fig. 37, *s*) are preferable to those that have not (Fig. 43).

Florence Flasks are now much used instead of retorts as they cost much less. They may be bought in any size desired and with the bottom rounded or flattened. (See Figs. 13, 32, 37*r*, 50, *etc.*) Heated retorts and flasks should not be placed on the table as the sudden cooling may break them. They may better be placed on rings covered with listing or made of straw or other poor conductor of heat, as shown in Figs. 43 and 71.

Beakers are thin, flat-bottomed glasses with slightly flaring rims, as shown in Figs. 9, 58, *etc.* They are conveniently used for heating liquids when it is desirable to reach every part of the vessel as with a stirring rod. They are generally sold in nests of different sizes. Beakers of more than a liter's capacity are too fragile to be desirable.

Test Tubes are thin glass cylinders, closed at one end and having lips slightly flared. The mouth should be of such a size that it may be closed by the ball of the thumb. The tube may be held in the flame with the fingers, with wooden nippers, as in Fig. 2, or by a band of folded paper around the upper end. A test tube rack, somewhat similar to the one shown in Fig. 135, should be made or bought, to hold the tubes upright when in use and to hold them inverted when not in use.

Test tubes may be held in an inverted position, as at the pneumatic trough or water pan, by weighting them with lead rings cut with a saw from lead pipe. The ring should be of such a size that it will easily slip over the tube but not over the lip of the tube. Test tubes may be easily cleaned with little cylindrical brushes made of bristles held between twisted wires. They cost but a few cents each. The chief danger in cleaning a test tube is that the bottom may be broken out. The brush should, therefore, have a tuft of bristles at its end. When the upper end of a tube is held in the fingers during the heating, the tube should be rolled or turned in the flame so that all sides may be equally heated.

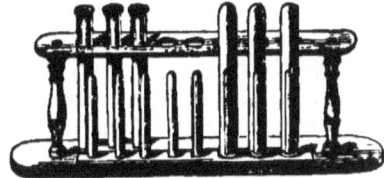

FIG. 135.

8. Filtering.

Funnels that have an angle of exactly 60° should be chosen. The circular piece of filter paper should be folded first on its diameter, then again at right-angles to the first fold and then opened out so as to leave three folds on one side and one on the other, as shown in Fig. 136. It is then to be placed in a funnel, the funnel placed in proper position and the liquid to be filtered carefully poured upon the paper. If the first filtration does not clear the liquid, the filtrate should be poured back upon the same filter for refiltration. Another way of folding the filter paper is to make the first fold as above. Then a fold equal to a quarter of the semicircle is made upon each side of the paper. Each of these smaller folds is then folded back upon itself. The sheet is then opened, as shown in Fig. 137, and thus placed in the funnel.

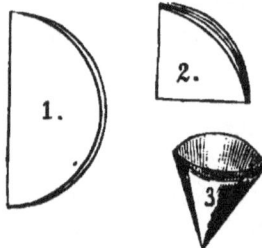

FIG. 136.

Rapid filtration may be secured by making a ribbed filter as follows: Fold the paper as before on two diameters at right-angles to each other.

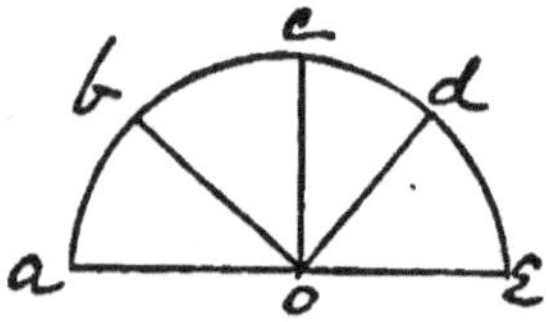

FIG. 137.

FIG. 138.

Open at the last fold and spread out the paper, *ace*, which will have a crease, *co*. Bring the corners *a* and *e* to the point *c* and make the creased lines, *bo* and *do*, so that the paper shall be creased in the same way at *bo*, *co* and *do*. Open the paper as shown in Fig. 138, and fold the corner *a* upon *b*, creasing the paper in the opposite direction. Make similar creases midway between *b* and *c*, between *c* and *d*, and between *d* and *e*. The last four folds leave creases opposite in direction to those made at *bo*, *co* and *do*. On opening the paper and putting it into the funnel, it will stand out from the glass, touching it only at several of the edges of the folds.

Filters may be folded at leisure moments and kept ready for use.

For coarse and rapid filtering, the neck of the funnel may be plugged with tow or cotton. For filtering solutions that would destroy the texture of the filter paper, a plug of asbestos or of gun cotton is placed in the neck of the funnel.

The funnel may be supported in any convenient way. Sometimes it may be placed in the neck of the bottle (Fig. 79), care being had that it does not fit air tight. It may often be supported from the retort stand or other independent support. When convenient, the

APPENDIX. 325

lower end of the funnel should touch the side of the vessel that receives the filtrate so that the latter shall fall quietly rather than in splashing drops. The end of the funnel neck should be ground off obliquely, as stated in App. 4, *h*.

When a precipitate has been collected upon a filter, it may be washed by filling the filter two or three times with distilled water and allowing it to run through. A washing bottle (Fig. 139) is of great convenience, the stream of water being driven out at *c* by air from the lungs forced in at *a*. The stream of water is directed so as to wash the precipitate from the sides of the filter toward its apex. The jet may be carried by a piece of flexible tubing attached to *c*, so that it may be turned in any direction without moving the bottle. When a precipitate is very heavy, it may be washed by shaking it up with successive quantities of water in a test tube, and pouring off the water when the precipitate has settled down. A wet glass rod held against the lip of the test tube greatly assists in pouring off the liquid without disturbing the precipitate.

FIG. 139.

9. Corks, etc.—It is not always easy to obtain corks of good quality and considerable size. Many experiments have failed through defects in corks used. Use bottles with small mouths when you can. Choose corks cut across the grain rather than those cut with the grain, as the latter often provide continuous channels for the escape of gases. Select those that are as fine grained as you can get. They will generally need to be softened before use. This may be done by rolling on the floor with the foot, on the table with a board or with a cork squeezer made for that purpose. Corks may be made less porous by holding them, for a few minutes, under the surface of melted paraffine wax.

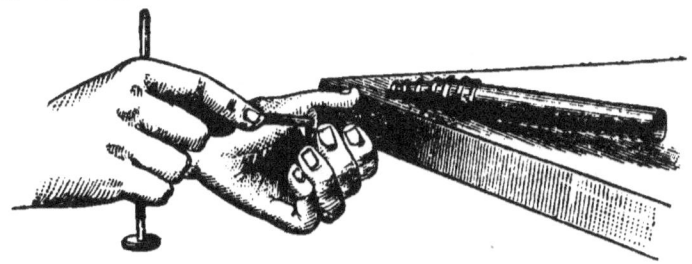

FIG. 140.

In boring holes through corks, a small knife blade or rat-tail file may be used, but a set of brass cylinders, made for the purpose, is more convenient. Such a set of cork borers and the way of using them are shown in Fig. 140. Use a borer with a diameter a little less than that of the glass tubing to be used. When the borer becomes dull, grind or file the outer bevelled edge and, with a sharp knife blade, pare off the rough metal on the inside of the edge.

Caoutchouc stoppers are more durable than cork and much to be preferred. They may be bored as above described. If they harden, they may be softened by being kept for a time in a closed flask containing a few drops of turpentine. If the glass tube enters the bored stopper with much difficulty, wet the outside of the tube with turpentine.

In passing glass tubes through stoppers of cork or caoutchouc, see that the end of the tube is smooth (see App. 4, *b*), hold the tube as near as possible to the stopper and force it in with a slow, steady, rotary, onward motion. Do not hold a funnel tube by the funnel, or a bent tube at the bend if you can avoid doing so. If the glass tube enters the bored cork with much difficulty, smear the outside of the tube with soap and water. Test all joints made, in the manner described in § 21.

The sticking of glass stoppers is a frequent source of trouble in the laboratory. Many methods of loosening them have been suggested. When one fails another must be tried. Under such circumstances, patience and persistence are necessary. It is hardly ever necessary to break the bottle. Generally, the stopper may be started by tapping it lightly on opposite sides alternately with a block of soft wood. The expansion of the bottle neck by heat will often loosen the stopper. The heat may be applied by friction with the fingers or a piece of tape, by a flame or by hot water. If the application of heat be continued too long, the stopper will expand as well as the neck, and the trial end in failure. As a last resort, fit two pieces of soft wood between the lip of the bottle and the lower side of the projecting part of the stopper. Tie them firmly in place and soak in water for several hours. If the wood does not swell enough to start the stopper, pour hot water over the wooden pieces, and the trouble will generally be at an end.

When you pour a liquid from a bottle, as into a test tube, hold the bottle in the right hand with the label toward the palm. Remove the stopper with the little finger or with the third and fourth fingers of the left hand, the thumb and forefinger of which may hold the test tube. Remove the liquid drop that adheres to the lip of the bottle by touching it with the stopper, replace the stopper and return the bottle to its proper place. It is seldom necessary to place either stopper or bottle on the table. In a little while you will acquire the habit of doing these things in this way and thus avoid much annoyance.

10. Stands, Supports, Baths, etc. — Flasks, *etc.*, are often supported over the lamp by a retort stand, as shown in Figs. 37 and 38. This stand has a heavy base and several movable iron rings of graduated sizes secured to the vertical rod by binding screws. Glass vessels thus supported are well protected from the direct flame of the lamp by a piece of wire gauze, as shown in Fig. 37. Occasionally, a very gradual and even heating is desired. Under such circumstances, the wire gauze may be replaced by a sand bath, which consists of a shallow pan, beaten out of sheet iron and filled with sand, as shown in Fig. 42. Sometimes, it is desirable to heat a vessel moderately, keeping it continuously below a certain temperature. This may be accomplished by placing the vessel in another vessel partly filled with water and heating the water, as shown in Fig. 89. Copper cups with tops made of concentric rings that may be adapted to the size of the vessel are offered for sale. A good enough water bath may be made of an old tinned fruit can. Care should be had that the water of the bath is not allowed to boil away. Fig. 141 shows various clamps and fittings for a retort stand, by means of which tubes, flasks, retorts, *etc.*, are easily held in any desired position. See Fig. 37. Many convenient supports may be made with corks and glass rods stuck on inverted funnels. A convenient support for a small vessel may be made in the form of an equilateral triangle by twisting together three pieces of soft iron wire at the corners, as shown in Fig. 142. Each of the wires may be run through the stem of an ordinary clay pipe. The support may be placed upon the ring of a retort stand or held by a cork into which the twisted wires at one corner have been thrust. A convenient support for test tubes, *etc.*, may be made by binding the middle part of a copper

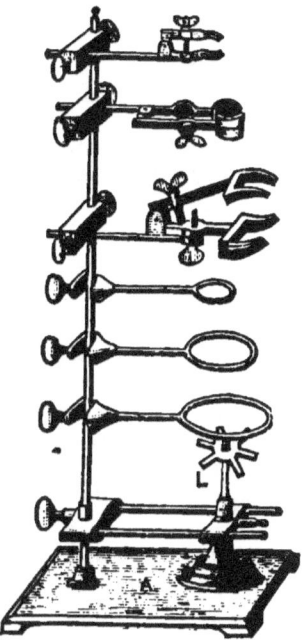

FIG. 141.

FIG. 142.

wire, 1 or 2 *mm.* in diameter, about a stout cork. The free ends of the easily flexible wire may be wound spirally around the test tube. The cork serves as a handle; if perforated, it may be placed upon the rod of the retort stand. The wire may be bent so as to place the tube in any desired position.

11. Mortars.—A mortar is a vessel, *m*, in which solid substances may be powdered with a pestle, *i*. They are made of iron, porcelain, agate, *etc.* Porcelain mortars' of the best quality are made of "Wedgewood;" they are unglazed, should not be suddenly heated and may be cleaned by rubbing with sand wet with nitric or sulphuric acid or caustic potash or soda, according to the nature of the substance

FIG. 143.

to be removed. Agate mortars are very small and expensive. In many cases, a stout bowl will answer as a mortar, while a pestle may be made of *hard* wood. Many substances may be powdered on a hard surface by the use of a rolling pin, like that used by a pastry cook, or by rolling a stout bottle over them. If a solid is to be broken by blows preparatory to powdering, an iron mortar and pestle are desirable. The pestle may be worked

FIG. 144.

through a hole in a pasteboard cover, which will prevent fragments of the solid from flying out of the mortar. Often, it is better to wrap the solid in a paper or cloth and then to break it with blows of a hammer. In using a mortar for pulverizing, it is better to put only a small quantity of the substance into the mortar at once, sifting it frequently and returning the coarser particles to the mortar for further trituration. The sifting may be done by rubbing the powder lightly with the finger upon a piece of muslin tightly stretched over the mouth of a beaker (Fig. 144).

12. The Pneumatic Trough.—For collecting gases over water, the pneumatic trough, in some form, is indispensable. A convenient trough is shown in Fig. 6 and described in § 20. The pan, *f*, may be of earthenware, while a flower pot saucer will answer for *e*. Two flat blocks of any material heavier than water may be used, instead of the saucer, for the support of the inverted gas receiver, *g*. With this apparatus, the receiver must be filled outside of the trough. The mouth being closed with the hand, a flat piece of wood, glass or card board, the bottle may be quickly inverted and placed in position so that its mouth is closed by the water in f. If any air gets into g during this operation, the work must be done again. While one bottle is filling with gas, another is to be made ready. When filled with gas, the first bottle may be removed from the trough by slipping a shallow plate or saucer beneath its mouth and removing plate and bottle together. Enough water will be retained in the plate to seal the mouth of the bottle. If the lip of the bottle has been ground flat, as recommended in App. 4, h, a piece of window glass will answer instead of the plate. As successive bottles are filled, the trough may become inconveniently full of water some of which may be dipped out or removed with a rubber tube siphon (Ph., § 298).

Any bucket or tub with a hanging shelf having holes bored in it, will make an efficient pneumatic trough.

When it can be secured, a pneumatic trough similar to that shown in Fig. 145, is desirable. It may be made of boards carefully joined and painted, but is preferably lined with sheet lead. It should be sunk in a table and provided with a water cock and drain pipe. Gas receivers are easily filled with water in the well, mn, and placed upon the shelf, b, which is to be below the water level.

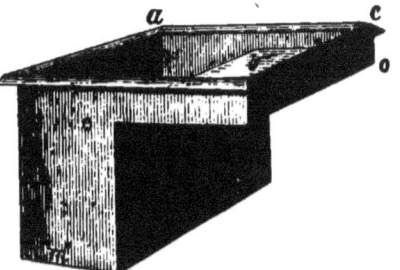

Fig. 145.

The dimensions of mn are to be determined by the size of the largest vessels that are to be sunk in it and the size of b by the size and number of gas receivers that are likely to be in use at any one time. Grooves may be provided in the shelf, b, running parallel to the side, ac. These grooves allow the rubber delivery tube to pass under the edge of the receivers without compression. In lifting large receivers from the well of a small trough, the water level may be brought below the shelf, b. Under such circumstances, more water may be introduced from a pail or by the water-cock, or a jug of water previously placed within convenient reach, may be placed in the well and subsequently removed when the filling of the receiver with gas raises the level of the water too high.

Porcelain pneumatic troughs for use with mercury (Exp. 6) may be bought for a little money, of any dealer in chemical wares, but one may be made of a block of hard wood. Its principal dimension should be horizontal, the bottom being rounded so that it will conform to the outline of a test tube or cylinder placed in it. Its depth should be a little more than the diameter of the test tube or cylinder used.

In collecting gases over water, two difficulties must be guarded against. First, if from any cause, the tension of the gas within the apparatus becomes less than the atmospheric pressure, water from the pneumatic trough may be forced back through the delivery tube into the generating flask. Cold water being thus suddenly admitted to a hot flask, the latter is broken and sometimes a more serious explosion takes place. This danger is especially present in thus collecting a gas somewhat soluble in water. See Exp. 65 and § 79. In stopping the evolution of a gas, remove the delivery tube from the trough, and remove the adhering water drops before removing the lamp. Whenever the delivery of a gas begins to slacken, watch the delivery tube; if water begins to "suck back" toward the flask, quickly remove the delivery tube from the water, or, still better, break the caoutchouc connection recommended in App. 4, b (as shown at c, Fig. 6,) or loosen the stopper of the generating flask. When a liquid is used in the flask, this danger of "sucking back" may be avoided by the use of a safety tube, as shown at s, Fig. 34. In case a partial vacuum should be formed in the flask, b, atmospheric pressure would force down the liquid in the lower part of the tube, s, and thus admit air instead of raising the liquid in c, to the greater height necessary to allow it to enter b. The funnel tubes shown in Figs. 32 and 62 act, similarly, as safety tubes.

The second difficulty to be guarded against is the production of too great a pressure within the apparatus by allowing any part of the delivery tube to dip too far beneath the surface of the water in the trough. Owing to the high specific gravity of the liquid used, this difficulty is especially present in the collection of gases over mercury. The pressure thus produced may develop leaks in the apparatus or, in certain cases (Fig. 32), force the liquid of a flask out through the funnel or safety tube.

13. Gas Holders.—It is often convenient to have a supply of oxygen, hydrogen and other gases on hand. Gas holders (often improperly called gasometers) are convenient for storing such gases for use. One form of easy construction is shown in Fig. 146. It consists of an outer vessel, a, open at the top, and an inner vessel, b, open at the bottom. Both may well be made of galvanized iron; a may be a barrel, cask or earthen crock. The upper end of b is hammered into saucer shape so that its highest point shall be at the middle. At this highest point is inserted a gas cock, having its free end smooth and slightly tapering, for the reception of rubber tubing. Three hooks or eyes are attached to the edge of the upper end of b, from which extend cords that are knotted together at the lower end of the supporting cord, c. The cord, c, may pass over pulleys in a frame, as shown in the figure, or over pulleys supported from the ceiling, the frame being omitted. Fill a with water. Open the stop cock, remove the weights from c and allow b to sink into a. Be sure that there is enough water in a to cover the highest point of b. Connect the stop cock, by rubber tubing, with the gas generator, but not until all air has been expelled from the tubing. Open the stop cock and place weights at the free end of c. By making these weights heavier than b the pressure in the generating apparatus may be reduced as far as desired. As gas is delivered, b will rise. The apparatus is shown on a larger scale at G, Fig. 93.

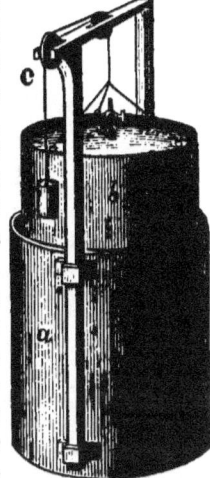

FIG. 146.

When the generation of gas has ceased, or when b is full, close the stop cock, remove the tubing and leave suspended from c only enough weights to counterbalance b. For most schools, a 6 or 8 gallon crock (preferably tall and narrow) will be large enough for the outer vessel. The stop cock may be had of any plumber or gas fitter; any tinsmith can make the vessel, b,

When gas is wanted from the holder, as in Exp. 49, connect the gas cock of b with the apparatus to be used, open the cock, remove weights from c and, if necessary to produce the desired pressure, place them upon b. It is customary to paint the oxygen holder red and the hydrogen holder black, for purposes of ready distinction.

A convenient form of gas holder, which may be made of metal and of any desired size is shown in Fig. 147. The open cistern, s, which is better made cylindrical, is connected with the closed cistern, g, by two tubes provided with stop cocks. One of these, t, passes nearly to the bottom of g, while the other just enters the top of g without projecting into it. A third tube, also provided with a stop cock, passes from the top of g and carries a piece of rubber tubing. The oblique tube, i, at the bottom of g, may be closed with a cork or screw plug. The apparatus may be placed over a tub or in a shallow pan provided with a drain pipe. To fill this holder, close i, open all three stop cocks and pour water into s. As water enters g, air escapes through the rubber tube. When g is filled with water, close the stop cocks, remove the plug from i and insert the delivery tube of the gas generator. As gas enters *g*, water escapes at *i*. When *g* is filled with gas, remove the tube from *i* and insert the plug. When desired, *s* may be used as a pneumatic trough by partly filling it with water, inverting a receiver filled with water over the upper end of *n*, and opening the stop-cocks of *n* and *t*. Water enters *g* by *t* and gas rises through *n* into *s* and the inverted receiver. When desired, the cock of *n* may be left closed and the other two opened. Water from *s* will then force gas out through the rubber tube.

A convenient gas holder may be made from a large glass bottle or a jug by passing two glass tubes through the cork, providing one with a piece of rubber tubing and the other with a stop or pinch cock (App. 20) all as shown in Fig. 148. The bottle being filled with water, the gas generator is connected with the stop-cock which is

FIG. 147.

then quickly opened. As the gas enters *g* through *a*, water escapes through the siphon, *c*. The pressure on the generator at starting, may be relieved by sucking at *c* to start the action of the siphon. Gas is delivered from *g* through *a*, by connecting *c* with a supply of water elevated on a shelf (siphon delivery, if desired) or with any other supply of water under moderate pressure. Any one of these three forms of gas holders, when filled with water, may be used as an aspirator (Exp. 57).

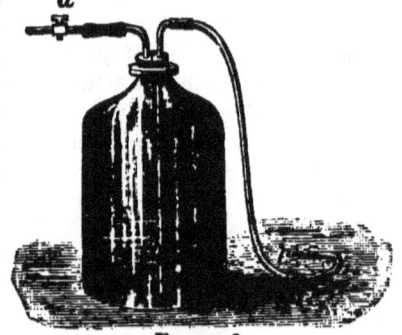

FIG. 148.

When a gas is to be kept for only a short time, a caoutchouc gas bag is a convenient substitute for a gas holder. It is easily portable and has other advantages. One may be bought for two or three dollars.

14. Drying Gases. — Several ways of freeing gases from aqueous vapor are illustrated in Exps. 28, 31, 57, 61 and 88. When sulphuric acid is used, the method given in Exp. 31 is preferable to that given in Exp. 88. See Figs. 45 and 64. Drying tubes of various other forms may be had of dealers in chemical glassware. In using a drying tube, care should be taken that there are no straight passages through which the gas can find quick and easy passage. A loose plug of cotton wool is generally placed at each end of the drying tube to keep the solid drying agent in place. If quicklime be used, allowance must be made for its expansion when acted upon by moisture. The choice of drying agent must often be determined by the chemical relations of the gas to be dried. Thus, sulphuric acid or calcium chloride could not be successfully employed in Exp. 61, nor quicklime in Exp. 146. Phosphoric anhydride is sometimes used for drying gases.

15. Lamps.—In laboratories, where illuminating gas is provided, the most convenient form of lamp for heating purposes is the Bunsen burner, represented in Figs. 16, 18, *etc.* It gives a very hot and smokeless flame. A fair substitute for a Bunsen burner may be made by inverting a wide necked glass funnel over any ordinary gas burner, supporting it in any convenient way so that air may have free passage between the sides of the burner and the glass as shown in Fig. 149. The funnel is to be put into position before the gas is lighted. The gas supply is to be controlled so as to produce a smokeless flame.

FIG. 149.

When a very small flame is used with the Bunsen burner, the flame may drop down into the tube. This may be prevented by laying a small piece of wire gauze over the top of the tube and pressing its edges down against the sides of the tube, before lighting the gas. A long flame for heating tubing may be secured by slipping the attachment represented in Fig. 150 over the tube of the Bunsen burner.

FIG. 150.

A Bunsen burner may be obtained of any dealer in chemical supplies. Write for a catalogue of chemical apparatus to Bullock and Crenshaw, Philadelphia.

When gas is not provided, the alcohol lamp, represented in Figs. 3, 60, *etc.*, is generally used. Under similar circumstances, the Vapor Bunsen Burner, represented in Fig. 151, will be found very efficient. It is provided with additional burners for evaporating and blowpipe urposes, burns gasoline, and serves as a retort stand. Gasoline is much cheaper than alcohol. The lamp may be obtained of James S. Kellogg, Cleveland, O.

The Berzelius or argand lamp burns alcohol, and is convenient for many purposes where much heat is necessary, *e. g.*, the preparation of oxygen in considerable quantity. It may be had of Queen & Co., Philadelphia, or any other dealer in apparatus.

FIG. 152.

FIG. 151.

FIG. 153.

16. Fletcher Burners.—Special heating apparatus is now

FIG. 154.

FIG. 155.

made in great variety. Of the many forms offered to the public, none seem more desirable than those designed by Thomas Fletcher of Warrington, England, and supplied in this country by the Buffalo (N. Y.) Dental Manufacturing Co. This paragraph is devoted to this apparatus. The "Low Temperature Burner" is shown in Fig. 152. It gives a wide range of temperature and dispenses with drying closets, sand and water baths. It burns gas and is furnished with or without the blast pipe, *C*. (See App. 17.) Fig. 153 represents the "Evaporating Burner," which is very convenient for heating flasks, as in § 79, *a*, and for many other purposes. By the addition of a perforated cylinder carrying strong wire netting to the "Evaporating Burner," we produce a "Hot Air Bath," convenient for many laboratory purposes. It is shown in Fig. 154. The "Solid Flame Burner" is shown at one-fourth actual size in Fig. 155. It will boil 2 l. of water in six or seven minutes, and may be used for melting zinc in an iron ladle, as directed in § 21.

Other pieces of the "Fletcher" apparatus will be mentioned.

17. Blowers and Blowpipes. — For working tubes of considerable size, a blower and blast lamp are necessary. The blower

FIG. 156.   FIG. 157.

may easily be made. Fig. 156 shows it in perspective, and Fig. 157 in section. The sides of the bellows, m, and of the reservoir, n, are

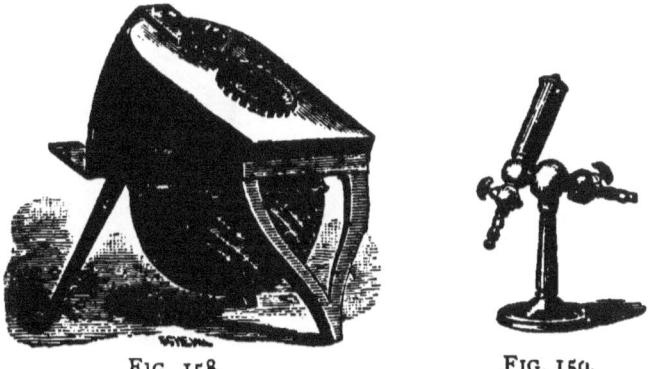

FIG. 158.   FIG. 159.

made of leather nailed to the boards at top and bottom. The arrangement of valves is evident from Fig. 157. A spring keeps a constant pressure on the air in n. Air is delivered through the tube, t, and conducted to the blast lamp by flexible tubing. The length, ab, may be about 60 *cm*. A more desirable form, made by the Buffalo (N. Y.) Dental Manufacturing Co., is shown in Fig. 158. A Bunsen blast lamp is shown in Fig. 159. Gas enters by the tube at the right. The other tube is connected with the blower. It may be had of James W. Queen & Co., Philadelphia. The temperature may be increased by placing the glass to be heated before a piece of charcoal upon which the flame plays. Fig. 160 shows a "Hot Blast Blowpipe" furnished by the Buffalo Dental Manufacturing Co. The upright jet may be used for light or for a moderate heat for bending tubing, *etc.* It is arranged so that it may be bent down to ignite the blowpipe jet at *c*, as shown by the dotted lines. The air pipe is coiled around the gas pipe and both are heated by a small Bunsen burner beneath. This blowpipe gives a pointed flame that will melt a fine platinum wire.

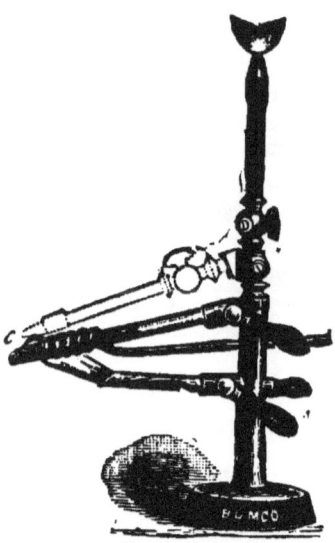

FIG. 160.

When gas can not be had, alcohol, naphtha or oil may be used with the mouth or blast blowpipe for many purposes. A large wick is essential which, with its holder, should be cut obliquely, so that the flame may be directed downward when necessary. The lamp should be of such a form that the work may be held close to the wick. A desirable lamp for such purposes, furnished by the Buffalo Dental Manufacturing Co., is shown in Fig. 161. The wick holder may be adjusted at any angle desired by turning it in its collar. The cut is half the size of the actual lamp. Any such lamp may be used with a common mouth blowpipe,

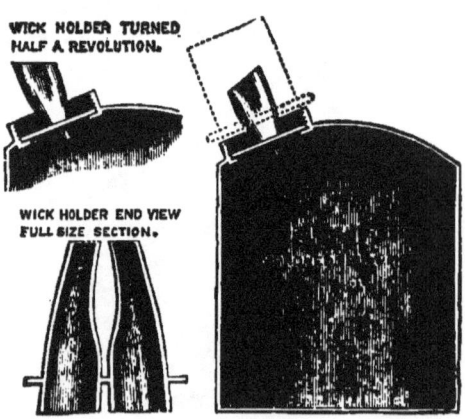

FIG. 161.

such as is shown in Fig. 162, or with the blast from the blower. An attachment, similar to that shown in Fig. 150, may be added to the Bunsen burner for blowpipe purposes. A blowpipe, sufficient for many purposes, may be made from glass tubing.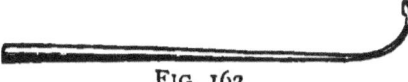

FIG. 162.

Blowpipes may be bought in a great variety of forms. In using the mouth blowpipe, air should be forced through it by the action of the cheeks rather than by the action of the lungs. A little practice will enable teacher or pupil thus to maintain a *continuous current* of air from the nozzle, breathing naturally in the meantime. See the Tinner's Soldering Lamp, App. 18.

18. Soldering.—The teacher or pupil will often find it very convenient to be able to solder together two pieces of metal. A bit of soft solder, the size of a hazlenut, may be had gratis of any good natured tinsmith or plumber. Cut this into bits the size of a grain of wheat. Dissolve a teaspoonful of zinc chloride in water and bottle it. It may be labelled "soldering fluid." Having bought or made an alcohol lamp (Ph., App. B), you are ready for work. For example, suppose you are to solder a bit of wire to a piece of tinned ware. If the wire be rusty, scrape or file it clean at the place of joining. By pincers or in any convenient way hold the wire and tin together. Put a few drops of "soldering fluid" on the joint, hold the tin in the flame so that the wire shall be on the upper side, place a bit of solder on the joint and hold in position until the solder melts. Remove from the flame holding the tin and wire together until the solder has cooled. The work is done. The mouth or blast blowpipe, previously mentioned, will be a convenient substitute, in many cases, for the alcohol lamp. Where gas can not be had, the "tinner's soldering lamp" is convenient. It may also be used in working glass. At the base of a perforated sheet iron cylinder, M, is a metal alcohol lamp. The cylinder supports a strong metal cup, C, beaten into shape. The opening by which the alcohol is introduced into this cup may be closed by a cork, which will then act as a safety valve. A bent tube passes from the upper part of the cup and terminates in a nozzle of 1 *mm.* aperture, midway between the wick of the lamp, a, and the bottom of the cup, C. The flame of a vaporizes part of the alcohol in C. This vapor escapes under pressure at the nozzle, where it ignites, forming a pointed, horizontal and very hot flame, which protrudes through the opening in front. The bent tube may pass through a slit in the back side of the cylinder. If you have a "soldering

Fig. 163.

iron," you can do a wider range of work, as many pieces of work cannot be held in the lamp flame. Fig. 163 shows a convenient form of heater for such soldering irons. It burns gas.

19. Deflagration Spoon.—A deflagrating spoon for burning phosphorus, sulphur, *etc.*, in oxygen may be bought for a few cents of any apparatus dealer. One may be made by soldering the bowl of any ordinary metal spoon or any other metal cup to a long wire handle and bending the wire upward at a right angle near the cup. A cup may be hollowed in the side of a piece of chalk or lime and then fastened to a wire handle. If a metal cup be used for combustions in oxygen, it is well to line it with some infusible material like clay, powdered chalk, lime or plaster of Paris. A coated cork capsule, smaller than the one mentioned in Exp. 58, may be provided with a wire handle and used as a deflagrating spoon. In any case, the upper part of the wire handle should be straight so that it may be thrust through the cover of the jar.

20. Cocks.—Whenever flexible tubing is used, pinch cocks furnish cheap substitutes for stop cocks. Fig. 164 shows one form; other forms may be found represented in catalogues of dealers in chemical wares. When the gas is to flow, the pinch cock is placed so that the tubing passes through the open space, o; when the supply is to be cut off, the tubing is compressed between the arms at c.

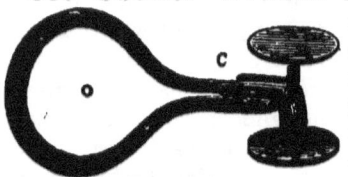

Fig. 164.

A stop cock may be made as follows: Provide two glass tubes, one of which slides easily into the other. Close one end of the smaller tube (App. 4, d,) and with a rat-tail file wet with a solution of camphor in turpentine, make a hole in the side 2 or 3 cm. from the closed end. Connect the tubes by a piece of rubber tubing that snugly fits the smaller tube. When the smaller tube is pushed into the larger one until the hole in the side is visible (Fig. 165) the cock is open; when the smaller tube is drawn back (Fig. 166), the hole is closed by the rubber tubing and the cock is closed.

FIG. 165.

FIG. 166.

A very simple valve for controlling the flow of fluids may be made by placing a glass ball in a piece of *soft* rubber tubing. The ball should be larger than the opening in the tubing. By pinching the rubber at the side of the ball, a little channel is made through which the liquid or gas may pass.

21. Evaporating Dishes, Crucibles and Furnaces.—Evaporating dishes may be had made of porcelain and pro-

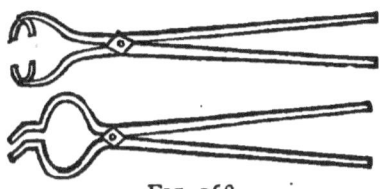

FIG. 167.   FIG. 168.

vided with a projecting lip and glazed on both sides or only on the inside. The latter are the cheaper but the former are the more desirable. Sizes from 8 to 15 *cm.* in diameter are best adapted to the needs of most classes. They should be supported upon wire gauze, the sand or water bath and never exposed to the naked flame. For granulating zinc (§ 21) or fusing salt (§ 99), Hessian crucibles are cheap and largely used. They will endure a very high temperature but should be heated somewhat gradually. They may be heated in a coal or coke fire in any ordinary stove. Heated crucibles may be handled conveniently with crucible tongs, two common

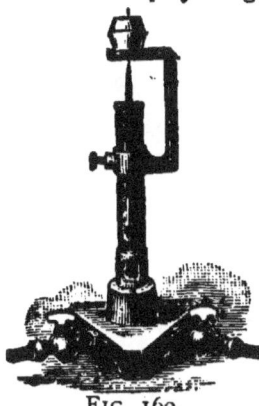

FIG. 169.

forms of which are represented in Fig. 168. They may be had of Bullock & Crenshaw, Philadelphia. Small clay crucibles and capsules are very valuable pieces of apparatus. With the Fletcher "Blowpipe Furnace" and the clay crucible shown in Fig. 169, several grams of cast iron may be melted in a very few minutes. For melting iron, brass, copper, *etc.*, up to quantities of five or six pounds, the "Injector Gas Furnace," shown in Fig. 170, and a plumbago crucible,

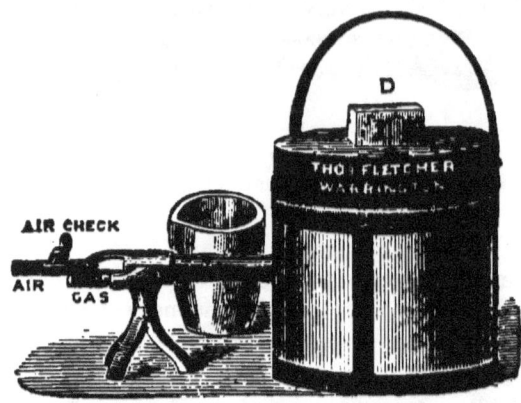

FIG. 170.

are convenient and efficient. The plumbago crucible must be heated slowly the first time it is used. Smaller quantities (about 1 *Kg.*) of such metals may be melted in a plumbago crucible, by the Fletcher

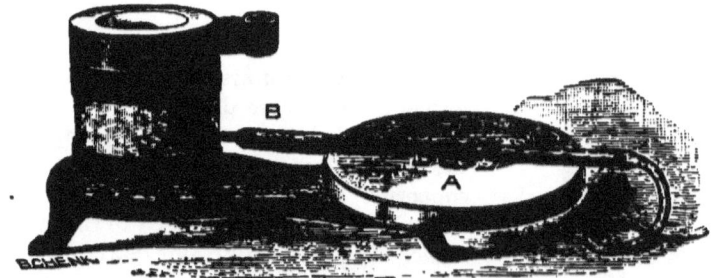

FIG. 171.

"Crucible Furnace for Petroleum," shown in Fig. 171. These three Fletcher Furnaces require the aid of the "Blower," shown in Fig. 156 or 158.

22. Metal Retorts.—Oxygen may be prepared by carefully heating the materials in a Florence flask or glass retort, but for this and other processes, where high temperatures are used, as in the preparation of illuminating and marsh gases, an iron or copper retort is very desirable. Such retorts may be had in a variety of forms, made of iron, sheet iron or copper, of dealers in chemical or philosophical apparatus, at prices ranging from $1 upwards. The author has made a very cheap and wholly efficient retort as follows : Cut a thread on each end of a piece of inch or $\frac{3}{4}$-inch gas pipe, a, 6 or 8 inches long. Screw an iron cap, k, over one end. For the other end, provide an iron "reducer," t, carrying a piece of $\frac{3}{8}$-inch gas pipe, e, about 15 or 18 inches long.

FIG. 172.

The materials being placed in the capped tube, the reducer with its pipe is screwed on the open end of the tube. The closed retort may then be thrust into the coals of any ordinary stove. A piece of glass tubing may be sealed, with plaster of Paris, into the end of the small iron tube. This affords a good means for connecting the retort with rubber tubing and protects the latter from burning. If desirable, the inner surface of k may be smeared with wet plaster of Paris before screwing it upon a. If, at the end of the experiment, t is not easily removed from a, a few blows will generally start it. The parts of this retort may be had of any gas or steam fitter.

FIG. 173.

A sheet iron retort may be made by any tinner as follows: the conical piece, ia, has a horizontal flange turned around its lower edge at a. The circular bottom piece has its edge turned over this flange, as shown in the sectional figure, and hammered down. The joint on the sloping side, ia, is lapped and hammered, as is generally done in making stove pipe. The mouth at i is made slightly flaring by hammering, to admit a cork carrying a glass delivery tube. The joints may be sealed by washing them *on the inside* with a thin paste of plaster of Paris. The cork may be protected from over heating by providing a cup, cc, which may be filled with water or a wet cloth.

A good retort may be made by luting on the cover of a small iron kettle and connecting a delivery tube with its nose.

23. Ventilating Chamber, etc.—A chamber, 50 cm. by 75 cm. or larger, with glass sides and provided with a ventilating flue *that has a good draft*, is important for experiments with chlorine, hydrogen sulphide, etc. The ventilating flue may, in some cases, be advantageously connected with the chimney. It may be built against the chimney and provided with two or three narrow slits through the brick work from top to bottom of the closet. At least one side of the chamber should be made so that it may be opened, but when shut, it should fit closely. Openings that may be closed, should be made in the bottom of the chamber for the admission of air so that a current may be obtained. A lamp burning in the chamber will aid in keeping up the current and carrying off the offensive gases.

24. Test Papers, etc.—Litmus paper, both blue and red, should be kept on hand for the detection of acids and alkalies. Litmus is a blue coloring matter prepared from certain lichens and found in commerce in small cubical masses somewhat soluble in water. White, unsized paper is stained with an infusion of 30 $g.$ of litmus in 250 $cu. cm.$ of boiling water. Such a paper is reddened by an acid (Exps. 41, 106, *etc.*). The blue litmus paper may be faintly reddened by immersion in vinegar or any other dilute acid. This reddened paper is colored blue by the action of an alkali (Exp. 64).

A purple liquid may be prepared by steeping red cabbage leaves in water and filtering. Such a cabbage solution will be colored red by an acid, or green by an alkali. Prepare such a solution. To a part of it, add a few drops of sulphuric acid; it will become red. To another part, add a few drops of a solution of potassium hydrate: it will become green. With constant stirring, cautiously pour the red liquid into the green. At first, the red color will disappear and the compound appear green, but, by continued addition of the red liquid, a point will be reached when the compound will be blue instead of green. The acid and alkali are then mutually neutralized. Compare Exp. 78.

A ruby red tincture of cochineal may be prepared by digesting 3 $g.$ of cochineal in a mixture of 50 $cu. cm.$ of alcohol and 200 $cu. cm.$ of water at the ordinary temperature for several days. Acids will change the color of such a tincture to orange; alkalies will change it to violet carmine.

Turmeric paper, prepared by staining unsized paper with a tincture (alcoholic solution) of turmeric root (curcuma), is sometimes used as a test for alkalies which turn it from yellow to brown (Exp 64). See also Exps. 99 and 100.

INDEX

☞ FIGURES REFER TO PARAGRAPHS, UNLESS OTHERWISE SPECIFIED. ☚

A

Acetic acid, 215.
Acetyl, 215 *a*.
" hydrate, 215, *a*.
" hydride, 215, *a*.
Acetylene, 219.
Acid, Acetic, 215.
" Anhydrosulphuric, Ex. 6, p. 136.
" Arsenic, *etc.*, 249.
" Basicity of an, 164.
" Binary, 163, *b*.
" Boracic, 173.
" Boric, 173.
" Bromic, *etc.*, 116.
" Carbonic, 198.
" Chamber, 152, *c*.
" Chlorhydric, 104.
" Chloric, *etc.*, 112.
" Chromic, 381, *b*.
" Cyanhydric, 205.
" Definition of, 163.
" Disulphuric, 156.
" Fluorhydric, 122.
" Fuming sulphuric, 156.
" Glacial phosphoric, 242, *e*.
" Haloid, 123, *b*.
" Hydrochloric, 104.
" Hydrocyanic, 205.
" Hydrofluoric, 122.
" hydrogen, 166, *b*.
" Hydrosulphuric, 137.
" Hyponitrous, 82.
" Iodic, *etc.*, 118.
" Manganic, 376, *e*.
" Metaphosphoric, *see* Phosphoric.
" Molybdic, 382.
" Muriatic, 104.
" Nitric, 73.

Acid, Nitro-hydrochloric, 114.
" Nitro-muriatic, 114.
" Nitrous, 86.
" Nordhausen, 156.
" Oxalic, Exp. 289.
" oxides, 165.
" Permanganic, 376, *f*.
" Phosphoric, *etc.*, 242.
" Prussic, 205.
" Pyroboric, 173, *b*.
" Pyroligneous, 215.
" Pyrophosphoric, 242.
" salts, 170.
" Silicic, Exp. 217.
" Stannic, 389.
" Sulphuric, *etc.*, 149, 151, 157, 158.
" Ternary, 163, *c*.
" Thionic, 158.
" Tungstic, 383.
Acidity of bases, 166, *b*.
Acids, Nomenclature of, 163.
Affinity, Chemical, 8, 9.
Agate, 232, *a*.
Air, 45-49.
" slaked lime, 290, *c*.
Alabaster, 294.
Albumen, 223.
Alcohol, 210.
Aldehyde, 215, *a*.
Alkali, 167, *b*.
" The volatile, 168.
Allotropism, 39.
Alloys, 322; 303, *a*.
Alum, 349.
Alumina, 348.
Aluminium, *see* Aluminum.
Aluminum, 344.
" bronze, 347.

Figures refer to Paragraphs, unless otherwise specified.

Aluminum, group, 352.
" oxide, 348.
" sulphate, 349.
Amalgam, 338.
Amethyst, 232, *a*.
Amide, Ex. 17, p. 314.
Amine, 96, *a*; Ex. 16, p. 314.
Ammonia, 66, 168.
" type, 96.
Ammonium, 168, 286.
" chloride, 287.
" nitrate, 288.
Amorphous, Note, p. 113.
Ampère's law, 61.
Analysis defined, 18.
" of water, 14.
" Quantitative, Note, p. 296.
Anhydride, 165.
Anhydrite, 294.
Anhydrosulphuric acid, Ex. 6, p. 136.
Animal charcoal, 186.
Anthracite, 181.
Antimoniuretted hydrogen, 253, *a*.
Antimony, 251.
" chlorides, 253, *d*.
" glance, 251.
" hydride, 253, *a*.
" oxides, 253, *b*.
" sulphides, 253, *c*.
Antozone, 38, *a*.
Aqua fortis, 73.
" regia, 114.
Argentum, *etc., see* Silver.
Arrow root, 228.
Arsenic, 243.
" acid, 249.
" hydride, 245.
" oxides, 247, 248.
" sulphides, 250.
" White, 247.
Arseniuret, Note, p. 217.
Arseniuretted hydrogen, 253, *a*.
Arsine, 245.
Aspirator, App. 13.
Atom defined, 5.
Atomic attraction, 8, 9.
" symbols, 56, 93.
" volume, 175, *a*; 240. *e*.
" weight, 64.
Atomicity, 65; 92, *d*; 174.

Attraction, Forms of, 8.
Auric, *see* Gold.
Aurous, *see* Gold.
Avogadro's law, 61.
Azurite, 319, *a*.

B

Barley sugar, 226, *c*.
Barite, 131, *b*.
Barium, 297.
Baryta, 297.
Base defined, 166.
Bases, Acidity of, 166, *b*.
Basic ammonia, 168.
" hydrogen, 164.
" oxides, 166, *a*.
" salts, 170.
Basicity of acids, 164.
Bauxite,
Beakers, App. 7.
Beet sugar, 226, *b*.
Bell metal, 322, 388.
Benzol, 221, *c*.
Beryllium, 305.
Bessemer steel, 371.
Bicarbonate of sodium, 269.
" of potassium, 279.
Bichromate of potassium, 381, *c*.
Binary acids, 123, *b*.
" compounds, 59.
Bismuth, 254.
Bisulphide of carbon, 201.
Bisulphate of sodium, 267, *c*.
Bituminous coal, 181.
Bivalent, 92, *a*.
Black ash, 268, *a*.
Black-band iron stone, 354, *a*.
Black lead, 179.
Black oxide of manganese, 376, *d*.
Blast furnace, 359.
Bleaching powder, 292, *b*.
Blende, 131, *a*; 301.
Blister steel, 370.
Bloom, 356.
Blower, App. 17.
Blowpipes, App. 17.
Blowpipe, The compound, 41.
Blue vitriol, 324.
Bohemian glass, 234, *a*.
Bone-black, 186.

Figures refer to Paragraphs, unless otherwise specified.

Bone phosphate, 295.
Boracic acid, 173.
Borax, 172, 271.
Boric acid, 173.
Boron, 172.
Bottle glass, 234, c.
Brass, 303, a ; 322.
Braunite, 375.
Bread making, 229.
Brimstone, 132, d.
Britannia metal, 388, a.
Bromine, 115.
Bronze. 322, 347, 388.
Brown sugar, 226.
Bulbs, Blowing, App. 4, e.
Bunsen burner, App. 15.
Butter of antimony, 253, d.
" of tin, 389.

C

Cadmium, 306.
Cæsium, 285.
Cairngorm-stone, 232, a.
Calamine, 301.
Calcareous waters, 293.
Calcic, *see* Calcium.
Calcite, 289.
Calcium, 289.
" carbonate, 293.
" chloride, 291.
" chloro-hypochlorite, 292, b.
" hydrate, 292,
" hypochlorite, 292, b.
" light, Exp. 49 ; 290.
" oxides, 290.
" phosphate, 295.
" stearate, 294, a.
" sulphate, 294.
Calomel, 342.
Calx, Note, p. 246.
Cane sugar, 226.
Caoutchouc stoppers, App. 8.
Caramel, 226, c.
Carbon, 177.
" disulphide, 201.
" dioxide, 196.
" group, p. 155.
" monoxide, 193.
" oxides, 192.
Carbonic acid, 198.

Carbonic anhydride, 196.
Carbonyl, 194, b.
Carburet, Note, p. 164.
Carnallite, 276.
Carnelian, 232, a.
Casein, 223.
Casserite, 385.
Cast iron, 358.
Catalysis, 31.
Caustic lime, 292.
" lunar, 332.
" potash, 280.
" soda, 270.
Celestine, 296.
Cellulose, 230.
Cementation steel, 370.
Centesimal computations, 130.
Ceric, *see* Cerium.
Cerium, 353.
Cerous, *see* Cerium.
Chalcedony, 232, a.
Chalcocite, 131, a ; 319, a.
Chalcopyrite, 319, a.
Chalk, 289.
Chamber acid, 152, c.
Charcoal, 184-191.
Chemical action, 11.
" affinity, 8.
" changes, 10.
" equations, 127.
Chemism, 8.
Chemistry defined, 13.
Chili nitre or saltpeter, 271, b.
Chlorate of potash, 281.
" of potassium, 281.
Chlorohydric acid, 104.
Chloride of antimony, 253, d.
" of ethylene, Exp. 209.
" of hydrogen, 104.
" of lime, 292, b.
" of methyl, 209.
" of nitrogen, 113.
Chlorine, 98.
" acids, 112.
" Diatomic, 174.
" group, 123.
" oxides, 111.
Chloroform, 209.
Chrome alum, 381, d.
" iron ore, 381.

Figures refer to Paragraphs, unless otherwise specified.

Chrome, yellow, 316, b; 381, c.
Chromic acid, 381, b
Chromite, 381.
Chromium, 381.
" steel, 381.
Cinnabar, 334, 340.
Clay, 233, 344.
" iron-stone, 354, a.
Coal, 181, 184, 186.
" gas, 221.
" tar, 221, c.
Cobalt, 378.
Cocks, App. 20.
Coin, 328, 379; 396.
Coke, 182.
Collection of gases, 21 ; Exps. 15, 185.
Colloid, Exp. 218.
Colored glass, 234, h.
Columbium, 260.
Combining weight of compounds, 63.
" " of elements, 64, a.
Combustion, 33.
Combustible, 43.
Composition of elementary molecules, 65.
Computations, 128–130.
Compound blowpipe, 41.
" radicals, 97.
Compounds, 6, 12.
Concentrated lye, 270.
Constitutional symbols, 95.
Cooking soda, 269.
Copper, 319.
" acetate, 215, c ; 324.
" arsenite, 324.
" carbonate, 324.
" glance, 319, a.
" nitrate, 324.
" oxides, 323.
" pyrites, 319, a.
" Ruby, 323.
" sulphate, 324.
Coral, 289.
Corks, App. 9.
Corrosive sublimate, 343.
Corundum, 348.
Cream of lime, 292.
Crith defined, 24.
Crocus, 362, b.
Crown glass, 234, b.

Crucibles, App. 21.
Crucible steel, 373.
Cryolite, 120, 349.
Crystal, 234, d.
Crystals, Classes of, Note, p. 113.
Crystallization, 268, b.
" water of, 268, c.
Crystalloid, Exp. 218.
Cupric, *see* Copper.
Cuprite, 319, a.
Cuprous, *see* Copper.
Cyanhydric acid, 205.
Cyanogen, 204.

D

Davy's glow lamp, Exp. 304.
Davyum, App. 1.
Decipium, App. 1.
Definite proportions, Law of, 90.
Deflagrating spoon, App. 19.
Deliquescence, 280, a.
Dextrin, 228.
Dextrose, 227.
Dialyser, Exp. 218.
Dialysis, Exp. 218.
Diamond, 178.
Di——, *see* bi——.
Dicarbonate, *see* Bicarbonate.
Dichromate, *see* Bichromate.
Didymium, 353.
Dimorphous, Note, p. 113.
Disulphate, see Bisulphate.
Disulphide of carbon, 201.
Double salts, 170.
Drummond light, Exp. 49, 290.
Drying gases, Exps. 61, 88 ; App. 14.
Dutch leaf, Exp. 74.
" liquid, Exp. 209.
Dyad, 92, a.

E

Efflorescence, 268, c.
Egg shells, 293.
Element defined, 6.
Elements, Molecular composition of, 65.
" Nomenclature of, 58.
" Electro-negative, 166.
" Electro-positive, 163.
" Table of, App. 1.
Emerald, 344, 381.
Emery, 348.

Figures refer to Paragraphs, unless otherwise specified.

Empirical symbols, 94.
Epsom salt, 300.
Equations, Chemical, 127.
Equivalence, 92, *d*.
Erbium, 353.
Etched glass. 234, *f*.
Etching, 77, Exps. 126–8.
Ethene, 217.
Ether, 213.
Ethine, 219.
Ethyl, 211.
" hydrate, 211.
" oxide, 213.
Ethylene, 217.
" chloride, Exp. 209.
Eudiometer, 42.
Evaporating dishes, App. 21.

F

Factors, 126.
Feldspar, 233, 344.
Fermentation, 210, Exp. 187.
Ferric, *see* Iron.
Ferrous, *see* Iron.
Fibrin, 223.
Filtering, App. 8.
Flasks, App. 7.
Flint, 232, *a*.
" glass, 234, *d*.
Florence flasks, App. 7.
Flowers of sulphur, 132, *d*.
Flue dust, 317.
Fluorhydric acid, 122.
Fluorine, 120.
Fluor spar, 120.
Flux, 359.
Formulas, Molecular, Note, p. 54.
Fruit sugar, 227.
Fulminating silver, 329.
Fuming sulphuric acid, 156.
Funnels, App. 8.
Funnel tubes, App. 4, *e*.
Furnaces, App. 16 and 21.
Fusible metals, 256.

G

Galena, 131, *a*; 308, 313.
Galenite, 308, 313.
Gallium, 351.
Galvanized iron, 303, *b*.

Garnet, 344.
Gas carbon, 183.
" holders, App. 13.
" Illuminating, 221.
Gases, Collection of, 21, Exps. 15, 185.
" Drying, Exps. 61, 88 ; App. 14.
Gay-Lussac's law, 176.
" tower, 152, *c*.
Gelatin, 224.
German silver, 303, *a*; 379.
Glacial phosphoric acid, 242, *e*.
Glass, 234.
" stoppers, App. 9.
" Ruby, 395, *a*.
" tubing, App. 4, *a*.
" Uranium, 384.
" working, App. 4.
Glauber's salt, 267, *b*.
Glucinum, 305.
Glucose, 227.
Glow lamp, Davy's, Exp. 304.
Glover tower, 152, *c*.
Glue, 224.
Gold, 393.
Graduates, App. 5.
Grape sugar, 227.
Graphic symbols, 95.
Graphite, 179.
Gravimetric computations, 128.
Green vitriol, 367.
Gray antimony, 251.
" oxide of mercury, 339.
Gun cotton, 230, *b*.
Gypsum, 131, *b*; 294.

H

Hæmatite, 354, *a*.
Halogen group, 123.
Haloids, 123, *b*.
Hard coal, 181.
" soap, 270 ; 278, *b*.
" water, 294.
Hartshorn, 66.
Hausmanite, 375.
Heavy spar, 131, *b*; 297.
Hematite, 354, *a*.
Hemioxide, 323, 329.
Heptad, 92, *a*.
Hexad, 92, *a*.
Hexivalent, 92, *a*.

Figures refer to Paragraphs, unless otherwise specified.

Homologous series, 220.
Horn silver, 330.
Hydrargillite,
Hydrates, 167.
Hydraulic main, 221, *e.*
Hydrocarbons, 206.
Hydrochloric acid, 104.
" " type, 96.
Hydrocyanic acid, 205.
Hydrofluoric acid, 122.
Hydrogen, 15, 19.
" Acid, 166, *b.*
" antimonide, 253, *a.*
" arsenide, 245.
" Basic, 164.
" carbide, 207.
" chloride, 104.
" Collection of, 22.
" Combustion of, 40.
" Diatomic, 174.
" dicarbide, 217.
" dioxide, 44.
" oxides, 44.
" peroxide, 44.
" persulphide, Note, p. 122.
" phosphide, 240.
" pistol, Note, p. 40.
" potassium carbonate, 279.
" preparation of, 21.
" properties of, 24, 25.
" purification of, 26.
" salts, 170, *c*, Note, p. 144.
" silicide, 231, *d.*
" sodium carbonate, 269.
" sodium sulphate, 267, *c.*
" sulphate, 151.
" sulphide, 137.
" Tests of, 28.
" tones, Exp. 29.
" type, 96.
" Uses of, 27.
Hydrosulphites, Ex. 4, p. 305.
Hydroxides, 167.
Hydroxyl, 44.
Hyponitrous acid, 82.
Hyposulphites, 157 ; 158, *b.*

I

Illuminating gas, 221.
Indigo, Exps. 269 and 270.

Indium, 350.
Inorganic substances, 7.
International measures, App. 2.
Inulin, 228.
Inverted sugar, 227.
Iodide of nitrogen, 119.
Iodine, 117.
Iridium, 402.
Iron, 354.
" carbonate, 367, *a.*
" Cast, 358.
" chloride, 366.
" cyanide, 368.
" Galvanized, 303, *b.*
" group, 380.
" hydrates, 363.
" Malleable, 374.
" nitrate, 367, *a.*
" ores, 354, *a.*
" oxides, 362.
" Pig, 358.
" pyrites, 132, *c* : 364.
" salts, 365.
" spathic, 354, *a.*
" specular, 354, *a.*
" sulphate, 367.
" sulphide, 364.
" Wrought, 360.
Isinglass, 224.
Isomerism, 216.
Isomorphism, Note, p. 113.

J

Jasper, 232, *a.*
Jeweller's rouge, 362, *b.*

K

Kieserite, 300.
King of metals, 395, *a.*

L

Lactose, 226, *d.*
Lagoon, 173, *d.*
Lamp-black, 185.
Lamps, App. 15 and 16.
Lanthanum, 353.
Laughing gas, 79.
Law, Ampere's or Avogadro's, 61.
" Gay-Lussac's, 176.
" of definite proportions, 90.

Figures refer to Paragraphs, unless otherwise specified.

Law of multiple proportions, 91.
Lead, 308.
" acetate, 215, c; 314.
" Black, 179.
" carbonate, 314.
" chloride, 314; 316, b.
" chromate, 316, b.
" group, 318.
" iodide, 316, b.
" oxides, 312.
" pencils, 179.
" poisoning, 315.
" Red, 312.
" Sugar of, 314.
" sulphide, 313.
" Tests for, 316.
" tree, Exp. 271.
" White, 314.
Leblanc, 268.
Levulose, 227.
Lichtenberg's metal, 256.
Liebig condenser, Exp. 202.
Lignite, 181.
Lime, 290.
" Air slaked, 290, c.
" Caustic, 292.
" Chloride of, 292, b.
" Cream of, 292.
" light, 290.
" Milk of, 292.
" Slaked, 292.
" soap, 292, a; 294, a.
" stone, 289, 293.
" water, 292.
Limestone, 289, 293.
Limonite, 354, a.
Litharge, 312.
Lithium, 283.
Litmus paper, App. 24.
Loadstone, 362, c.
Lunar caustic, 332.
Lye, 270, 278.

M

Matter defined, 1.
" Divisions of, 2.
Mass defined, 3.
Magnesia, 299.
" alba, 300.
Magnesite, 300.

Magnesium, 298.
" carbonate, 300.
" chloride, 300.
" group, 307.
" oxide, 299.
" sulphate, 300.
Magnetite, 354, a.
Malachite, 319, a; 324.
Malleable iron, 374.
Maltose, 226, d.
Manganese, 375.
" salts, 377.
" oxides, 376.
Manganic acid, 376, e.
" anhydride, 376, e.
Manganite, 376, c.
Maple sugar, 226, b.
Marble, 289.
Marsh gas, 207.
" type, 96.
Marsh's test, 246.
Mercury, 334.
" bromides, 342, b; 343, c.
" chlorides, 342, 343.
" iodides, 342, b; 343, c.
" nitrates, 342, a; 343, b.
" oxides, 339.
" salts, 342, 343.
" sulphates, 342, a; 343, b.
" sulphide, 340.
Metaboric acid, 173, a.
Metallic oxides, 166, a.
Metalloids, see Non-metals.
Metals, 261.
Metamerism, 216.
Meta-phosphoric acid, 242; 242, e.
Metathesis, 18.
Methane, 207.
Methyl, 208.
" chloride, 209.
" hydride, 207.
Metric measures, App. 2.
Mica, 233, 344.
Microcosmic salt, Ex. 6, p. 278.
Microcrith, 62.
Milk of lime, 292.
Milk sugar, 226, d.
Minium, 312.
Mineral coal, 181.
Mirrors, 338.

Figures refer to Paragraphs, unless otherwise specified.

Mispickel, 243.
Mixed gases, Note, p. 39.
Mixtures, 12.
Molasses, 226.
Molecular composition, 65.
" formulas, Note, p. 54.
" symbols, 57, 94-96; 261, c.
" volume, 175.
" weight, 63.
Molecule defined, 4.
" Size of, 4, a
Molybdenum, 382.
Monad, 92, a.
Mortar, 292, a; App. 11.
Multiple proportions, Law of, 91.
Muriatic acid, 104.
Muscovado sugar, 226.

N

Nascent state, 114, b.
Natural groups, 123, 162, 257, 318, 352.
Nessler reagent, Exp. 70.
Neutral salts, 170.
Newton's metal, 256.
Nickel, 379.
Niobium, 260.
Nitre, 282.
" Chili, 271, b.
Nitric acid, 73.
" anhydride, 89.
Nitrocellulose, 230, b.
Nitrogen, 50.
" chloride, 113.
" group, 257; 261, a.
" hydride, 66.
" iodide, 119.
" oxides, 79-91.
Nitro-hydrochloric acid, 114.
Nitro-muriatic acid, 114.
Nitrosyl, 83.
Nitrous anhydride, 86.
Nitryl, 87.
Noble metals, Note, p. 313.
Non-metals, 261.
Nomenclature, 58-60.
Nordhausen acid, 156.
Normal salts, 170.
Norwegium, App. 1.

O

Occlusion of gases, 24, b, d.

Oil of the Dutch Chemists, Exp. 209.
" vitriol, 151.
Olefiant gas, 217.
Onyx, 232, a.
Opal, 232, a.
Organic chemistry, 222.
" substances, 7, 222.
Ornithorhyncus, The metallic, 317, b.
Orpiment, 250.
Orthoboric acid, 173.
Osmiridium, 404.
Osmium, 404.
Ossein, 224.
Oxalic acid, Exp. 289.
Oxides, 33.
Oxygen, 16, 29.
" Linking, 163, c.
" Preparation of, 30.
" Properties of, 32, 33.
" Relation to animal life, 35.
" salts, 171.
" Saturating, 163, c.
" Tests for, 36.
" Uses of, 34.
Oxyhydrogen flame, 41.
Oyster shells, 293.
Ozone, 37.

P

Painter's colic, 315.
Palladium, 400.
Paraffin, 138, e.
Parchment, Vegetable, Exp. 216.
Paris green, 324.
Paste, 234, d.
Pearlash, 278.
Peat, 181.
Pentad, 92, a.
Percentage computations, 130.
Permanganic acid, 376, f.
Pewter, 388, a.
Philosopher's candle, Exp. 26.
Phosgene gas, 194, b.
Phosphine, 240.
Phosphoric sun, Exp. 37.
Phosphorus, 235.
" acids, 242.
" hydride, 240.
" oxides, 241, Exp. 58.
" Red, 238.

Figures refer to Paragraphs, unless otherwise specified.

Phosphoryl, 242, *d.*
Phosphurets, Note, p. 205.
Phosphuretted hydrogen, 240.
Photography, Note, p. 269.
Physical changes, 10.
Pig iron, 358.
Pinch cocks, App. 20.
Pipettes, App. 5.
Plaster of Paris, 294.
Plate glass, 234, *b.*
Platinum, 397.
" black, 398, *d.*
" sponge, 398, *c.*
Plumbago, 179.
Plumbic, *see* Lead,
Plumbous, *see* Lead.
Pneumatic trough, App. 12.
Polymerism, 216.
Potash, 278.
Potassium, 272.
" bicarbonate, 279.
" carbonate, 278.
" chlorate, 281.
" chloride, 276.
" chromate, 381, *c.*
" cyanide, 277.
" dichromate, 381, *c.*
" ferricyanide, 368.
" ferrocyanide, 368.
" hydrate, 280.
" nitrate, 282.
" oxides, 275.
" tartrate, 273, *a.*
Precipitated silica, Exp. 217.
Precipitate, Red, 339.
Products, 126.
Proportions, Law of definite, 90.
" Law of multiple, 91.
Prussian blue, 368.
Prussic acid, 205.
Puddling furnace, 360, *a.*
Pyroboric acid, 173, *b.*
Pyroligneous acid, 215.
Pyrophosphoric acid, 242.
Pyrite, 131, *a* ; 364.
Pyroxylin, 230, *b.*

Q

Quadrantoxide, 323.
Quadrivalent, 92, *a.*

Quantitative analysis, Note, p. 296.
Quantivalence, 92 ; 341, *a.*
Quartz, 232.
Quicklime, 290.
Quicksilver, 334.
Quinquivalent, 92, *a.*

R

Radicals, 97.
Rational symbols, 94, 216, *b.*
Reactions, 124, 125.
Reagents, 124.
Realgar, 250.
Red lead, 312.
" oxide of manganese, 376, *b.*
" oxide of mercury, 339.
" phosphorus, 238.
" precipitate, 339.
" prussiate of potash, 368.
Reduction of oxides, Exp. 31.
Red zinc ore, 301, 304.
Regent diamond, 178, *a.*
Retorts, App. 7 and 22.
Retort stands, App. 10.
Rhodium, 401.
Rochelle salt, 269, *a.*
Rock crystal, 232.
" salt, 266.
Rose quartz, 232, *a.*
Rose's metal, 256.
Rouge, Jeweller's, 362, *b.*
Rubidium, 284.
Ruby, 348.
" copper, 323.
" glass, 395, *a.*
Ruthenium, 403.

S

Sago, 228.
Sal-ammoniac, 287.
Saleratus, 279.
Salsoda, 268.
Salt, 266.
" Epsom, 300.
" Glauber, 267, *b.*
" of tartar, 278.
" Rochelle, 269, *a.*
Saltpetre, 282.
" South American, 271, *b.*
Salts classified, 170.

352 INDEX.

Figures refer to Paragraphs, unless otherwise specified.

Salts defined, 169.
" Nomenclature of, 60.
" Sulphur, 171.
Sand, 232, *a*.
" bath, 74, *a*; App. 10.
Sapphire, 348.
Scale oxide, 362, *c*.
Scrubber, 221, *h*.
Selenite, 294.
Selenium, 160.
Septivalent, 92, *a*.
Serpentine, 381.
Sesqui— 143, *a*.
Sexivalent, 92, *a*.
Shells, 293.
Siemens-Martin steel, 372.
Silica, 232.
Silicic acid, Exp. 217.
" anhydride, 232.
Silicon, 231.
Silver, 325.
" bromide, 330.
" carbonate, 333.
" chloride, 330.
" cyanide, 331.
" Fulminating, 329.
" German, 303, *a*.
" haloids, 330.
" Horn, 330.
" iodide, 330.
" nitrate, 332.
" oxides, 329.
" phosphate, 333.
" sulphate, 333.
" sulphide, 331.
Simple radicals, 97.
Slag, 359.
Slaked lime, 290, *c*; 292.
Smithsonite, 301.
Soap, Hard, 270; 278, *b*.
" Lime, 292, *a*.
" Soft, 278, *b*; 280.
Soda, 269.
" ash, 268, *a*.
" Caustic, 270.
" Cooking, 269.
" crystals, 268, *b*.
" Washing, 268, *b*.
" water, 199.
Sodium, 262.

Sodium biborate, 271.
" bicarbonate, 269.
" bisulphate, 267, *c*.
" carbonate, 268.
" chloride, 266.
" hydrate, 270.
" nitrate, 271.
" oxides, 265.
" pyroborate, 271.
" sulphate, 267.
Soft coal, 181.
" soap, 278, *b*; 280.
" water, 294.
Solder, 388, *a*.
Soldering, App. 18.
Soluble glass, 234.
Solution, 9, *a*.
Soot, 185.
South American nitre or saltpeter, 271, *b*.
Spathic iron, 354, *a*.
Specular iron, 354, *a*.
Spelter, 302, *d*.
Sphalerite, 301.
Spiegeleisen, 359, *d*.
Stalactite, 293.
Stalagmite, 293.
Stannic, *see* Tin.
Stannous, *see* Tin.
Starch, 228.
" sugar, 227.
" test for iodine, Note, p. 99.
Stassfurt, 276, 298.
Steel, 369-373.
Stibine, 253.
Stibnite, 251.
Stoichiometry, Note, p. 108.
Stop-cocks, App. 20.
Strass, 234, *d*.
Strontianite, 296.
Strontium, 296.
Suboxide of mercury, 339.
" of copper, 323.
Sucrose, 226.
Suffioni, 173.
Sugar, 225-227.
" of lead, 314.
Sulphur, 131.
" acids, 149, 151, 157.
" group, 162.
" Linking, 171.

INDEX. 353

Figures refer to Paragraphs, unless otherwise specified.

Sulphur oxides, 143, 150, 157.
" salts. 171.
" Saturating, 171.
Sulphuret, Note, p. 115.
Sulphuretted hydrogen, 137.
Sulphuric acid, 151.
" ether, 213.
Supporters of combustion, 43.
Symbols, 56, 57, 93–96, 261, *c*.
Synthesis defined, 18.
" of water, 17.

T

Table salt, 266.
Tantalum, 259.
Tapioca, 228.
Tar, Coal, 221, *c*.
Tartar, Salt of, 278.
Tellurium, 161.
Terbium, 353.
Ternary compounds, Nomenclature of, 60.
Test papers, App. 24.
" tubes, App. 4, *d*; App. 7.
Tetrad, 92, *a*.
Tetrantoxide, 323, 329.
Tetravalent, *see* Quadrivalent.
Thallium, 317.
Thermometers, App. 3.
Thionic acids, 158.
Thoria, 392.
Thorium, 392.
Tin, 385.
" Adulterations of, 388, *b*.
" compounds, 389.
" oxide, 389.
" stone, 385.
" ware, Exp. 296.
Titanium, 390.
Toluol, 221, *c*.
Topaz, 344.
Toughened glass, 234, *g*.
Travertine, 293.
Triad, 92, *a*.
Trimorphous, Note, p. 113.
Trivalent, 92, *a*.
Tubing, App. 4, *a*.
Tufa, 293.
Tungsten, 383.
Tungstic acid, 383.
Turpentine, Exp. 93.

Tuyeres, 359.
Types, 96.
Typical symbols, 96.

U

Unit volume, 175.
Univalent, 92, *a*.
Uranium, 384.
Uranyl, 384.
U-tubes, App. 4, *b*.

V

Valence, 92, *d*.
Vanadium, 258.
Vegetable parchment, Exp. 216.
Ventilating chamber, App. 23.
Ventilation, 194, 199.
Verdigris, 215, *c*; 324.
Vermillion, 340.
Vinegar, 215.
Vital air, 35.
Vitriol, Blue, 324.
" Green, 367.
" Oil of, 151.
" White, 304.
Volatile alkali, 168.
Volumetric combination, Law of, 176.
" computations, 129.

W

Wash bottle, App. 8.
Washing soda, 268, *b*.
Water, Analysis of, 14.
" bath, App. 10.
" composition of, 14, 17, 40,
" glass, 234.
" Hard and soft, 294.
" of crystallization, 268, *c*.
" synthesis of, 17.
" type, 96.
White arsenic, 247.
" lead, 314.
" vitriol, 304.
Window-glass, 234, *b*.
Wood's metal, 256.
Woulffe bottle, Note, p. 23; App. 6.

Y

Yellow chromate of potash, 381, *c*.

Figures refer to Paragraphs, unless otherwise specified.

Yellow prussiate of potash, 368.
Yttrium, 353.

Z

Zinc, 301.
" carbonate, 301.
" chloride, 304.
" dust, 302, c.
" ore, 301.

Zinc oxide, 304.
" silicate, 301.
" spar, 301.
" sulphate, 304.
" sulphide, 301.
" white, 304.

Zincite, 301.
Zirconia, 391.
Zirconium, 391.

NEW AND VALUBLE TEXT-BOOKS.

AVERY'S
ELEMENTS OF NATURAL PHILOSOPHY.

It is the most elegantly illustrated text-book on Natural Philosophy that has been published for Schools.

1st. It is well known that thoroughly good text-books on the Natural Sciences are the most difficult to obtain. This book was prepared by Prof. AVERY two or three years since, and has been used in his own and other classes in the High Schools of Cleveland. His work has thus had the practical test of the class-room, and from the hints thus obtained he has carefully re-written the work.

2d. Its great accuracy and usability in the class-room. Many text-books on this subject are full of matter useless to the learner.

3d. The experiments are admirably adapted to this purpose, showing (as does every page of the book) the hand of the live and practical teacher. These experiments are fully illustrated, especial attention being given to simple and home-made apparatus.

4th. The chapter on Electricity has met with the warmest expressions of approval from prominent teachers.

5th. The large number of problems, exercises, and review questions will be found very valuable in the actual work of the class-room.

A Teacher's Hand-Book, containing Solutions of Problems, Practical Suggestions for teaching Natural Philosophy, etc., has been prepared by Prof. AVERY to accompany his Natural Philosophy. It is of great value to all who teach this science.

We have now in press

"AVERY'S CHEMISTRY,"

which is being prepared with such care that it will be a text-book in all respects fitted to accompany his " Natural Philosophy."

Avery's Natural Philosophy has been adopted in over two hundred cities and large institutions.

JUST THE BOOK THAT IS NEEDED!

THE ELEMENTS OF BOOK-KEEPING,

EMBRACING

SINGLE AND DOUBLE ENTRY,

WITH A GREAT VARIETY OF EXAMPLES FOR PRACTICE.

WITH KEY AND BLANKS.

By JOSEPH H. PALMER, A. M.,

Author of a Treatise on Double-Entry Book-keeping, and for 20 years First Tutor of Mathematics in the College of the City of New York.

A really good elementary and higher work on Book-keeping; one which begins with single accounts, and, step by step, finally embraces single and double entry, and supplies material from the every-day business affairs of life for interesting and useful "**practice in Book-keeping,**" has long been needed.

Most works on this subject have been prepared by persons of limited experience, both as teachers and as business men; and are therefore wanting in matter and adaptation. Such books are full of wearisome forms and unclassified matter without references. This work contains brief sets, apt illustrations, and concisely stated principles, numbered consecutively for convenient references, and followed by a variety of examples for "**practice in Book-keeping.**"

This work has been in the public schools of New York, Brooklyn, and other cities but a few months, and already the teachers unite in saying that the learners—girls as well as boys—see the uses and abuses of money, catch the business spirit of the exercises, develop a fitness for business affairs, become interested in and enthusiastic over our "**practice in Book-keeping.**" The faculties of the dullest learners become aroused, thoroughly stirred up, and the pupils incited to better habits.

PROFESSOR OLNEY'S
NEW
MATHEMATICAL SERIES.

The success of Prof. Olney's series has been most wonderful.

With all their admitted excellencies, both the Author and Publishers have felt that it was possible to retain their many attractive features and yet adapt the books more perfectly to the special school-room wants.

To accomplish this most desirable end, Professor Olney has been accumulating very valuable suggestions. He has also, for several years, had associated with him in the preparation of this new series, some of the best practical teachers in the country.

The design is to present to the educational public the best and most teachable series of Mathematics ever published. The work is now so far advanced that the Publishers are able to make the above pleasing announcement, which they feel will be of great interest to all who are engaged in teaching.

THE NEW SERIES EMBRACES:

I.
Olney's First Lessons in Arithmetic. JUST PUBLISHED.

II.
Olney's Practical Arithmetic.

This book has been published but a short time, but it has already had *the most wonderful success.*

They are models of beauty and cheapness.

For schools of a high grade, Professor Olney has prepared—

III.
The Science of Arithmetic.

IV.
The First Principles of Algebra.

AN INTRODUCTION TO THE AUTHOR'S COMPLETE AND UNIVERSITY ALGEBRAS.

V.
Olney's Complete Algebra. NEW EDITION, IN LARGE TYPE.

This book is now entirely re-electrotyped in *larger and more attractive type.* The explanatory matter is greatly lessened. The attractive features of this book, which have made it *the most popular Algebra ever published in this country,* are all retained.

NEW AND VALUALE TEXT-BOOKS.

HILL'S
ELEMENTS OF RHETORIC AND COMPOSITION.

Teachers of Rhetoric in our schools and academies will, we think, be gratified to learn that their demand for a fresh and practical work on Rhetoric has been met by Professor HILL. His "Science of Rhetoric," designed only for advanced classes in colleges, is regarded as the most comprehensive and philosophical text-book on the subject. The Elements has been prepared with special reference to the wants of less advanced students.

1st. **It is Complete.** *Beginning with the selection of a theme, this book conducts the learner through every process of composition,* including the accumulation of material, its arrangement, the choice of words, the construction of sentences, the variation of expression, the use of figures, the formation of paragraphs, the preparation of manuscript, and the criticism of the completed composition. Special forms of composition, such as Letters, Orations, and Poems, are specifically discussed.

2d. **It is Clear and Simple in Style.** As the book is designed for learners, no pains have been spared to make *every fact and principle perfectly intelligible.* Every statement is illustrated by a brief and appropriate example.

3d. **It is Philosophical in Method.** The Author's familiarity with the whole subject, acquired as a teacher, and evinced in his "Science of Rhetoric," has enabled him to write in a truly philosophical spirit, without rendering his book abstruse.

4th. **The Topical Arrangement** adapts the book to the most approved methods of recitation.

5th. **It contains Numerous and Original Exercises.** Every principle of invention, style, and punctuation is practically applied in a series of carefully-prepared exercises.

6th. **Correct and Effective Composition** is the chief aim of the book. The mere learning of rules and definitions will never make good writers.

Prof. W. T. GRIER says in the *National Baptist,* in speaking of Prof. Hill, the newly-elected President of Lewisburg University, and his book "The Elements of Rhetoric and Composition":

"*Within two months from the date of its publication in New York it was reprinted in London. Think of a London firm coming to our own loved Lewisburg to find the man to make the proper Text book for the English people!*"

COLTON'S NEW SERIES OF GEOGRAPHIES.

The Simplest, most Practical, and Cheapest Series yet published.

The whole subject for Common School Use embraced in **Two Books.** *With three full sets of Maps, entirely separate.* 1st. *The Study Maps*, containing all that the scholar should learn. 2d. *The Railroad Maps*, full and complete, showing all the great routes of travel. 3d. *The Reference Maps*, as full and accurate as in any $20 reference atlas, and marvels of beauty.

Colton's New Introductory Geography. (103 pages.)

In Two Parts. Part First, containing Preliminary Development Lessons, is designed to impart to the pupil the simple, elementary ideas necessary to a clear comprehension of the more formal and concise statements of the text. Part Second contains Recitation Lessons, elegantly illustrated with 18 entirely new Maps, drawn expressly for this book. This book contains the best and clearest Maps which have ever been issued in an introductory Geography, and is in every respect an admirable book for the beginner.

The language used is clear and simple, and can easily be understood by any child old enough to begin the study of Geography.

Colton's Common School Geography. (134 pages.)

Elegantly illustrated by numerous Engravings and 38 Maps, drawn expressly for this book. The general principles of Physical Geography are embraced in this book. It contains two large *Railroad Maps* constructed on an entirely original plan, which renders all the great routes of travel perfectly distinct. Also, fifteen full and *complete Commercial and Reference Maps* of the United States in sections.

Colton's New Series of Geographies, embracing *two large Railroad* and *fifteen complete Reference Maps*, is by far the *best* Series of Geographies ever offered to the American public. They are perfectly adapted to the *wants* of the *school-room*. They present in the most attractive and intelligible form what every intelligent child should learn.

The *Maps* have been constructed with the single idea of meeting the exact requirements of the class-room, and removing all *unnecessary difficulty* in their use by the scholar.

The series is rendered very attractive by the *two large double-paged Railroad Maps*, constructed on an entirely original plan, on which *all the great routes of travel* are rendered perfectly distinct by heavy black lines, and the name of each railroad distinctly engraved on the map. These *Railroad Maps* are valuable, both for purposes of study and reference.

The series of Reference Maps is fully worth the entire price of the book, and obviates the necessity of any other maps of our own country for family and reference use.

LOSSING'S
HISTORIES OF THE UNITED STATES.

Lossing's Primary History of the United States.
   238 pages............................. ....
      For the youngest scholars, and illustrated with numerous engravings. By BENSON J. LOSSING, LL.D.

Lossing's Outline History of the United States.
   400 pages............ ....

In *elegance of appearance* and *copious illustrations,* both by pictures and maps, the OUTLINE HISTORY surpasses any book of the kind yet published.

   1. The work is marked by *uncommon clearness of statement*, and the most important facts in our history are presented in few words and small space, and in the attractive form of an easy-flowing narrative.

   2. The narrative is divided into *Six Distinct Periods,* namely: *Discoveries, Settlements, Colonies, The Revolution, The Nation,* and *The Civil War and its Consequences.*

   3. The work is *arranged in Short Sentences,* so that the substance of each may be easily comprehended.

   4. The *Most Important Events* are indicated in the text by *heavy-faced letter.* All *proper names are printed in italic letter.*

   5. *Full Questions* are framed for every verse.

   6. *A Pronouncing Vocabulary* is furnished in foot-notes wherever required.

   7. *A Brief Synopsis* of topics is given at the close of *each section.*

   8. *An Outline History* of *important events* is given at the close of *every chapter.*

   9. The work is *Profusely Illustrated* by maps, charts and plans explanatory of the text, and by carefully-drawn pictures of objects and events.

   10. The *Colonial Seals* are believed to be the *only strictly accurate ones published,* and have been engraved especially for this book.

   11. A few pages devoted to *Biographical Notes, Facts to be specially remembered,* and a *Topical Review* constitute a valuable feature of the work.

www.ingramcontent.com/pod-product-compliance
Lightning Source LLC
Chambersburg PA
CBHW020309240426
43673CB00039B/749